OXFORD CONSTITUTIONAL THEORY

*Series Editors:*
*Martin Loughlin, John P. McCormick, and Neil Walker*

# Constitutionalism

# OXFORD CONSTITUTIONAL THEORY

*Series Editors:*

*Martin Loughlin, John P. McCormick, and Neil Walker*

*Oxford Constitutional Theory* has rapidly established itself as the primary point of reference for theoretical reflections on the growing interest in constitutions and constitutional law in domestic, regional, and global contexts. The majority of the works published in the series are monographs that advance new understandings of their subject. But the series aims to provide a forum for further innovation in the field by also including well-conceived edited collections that bring a variety of perspectives and disciplinary approaches to bear on specific themes in constitutional thought and by publishing English translations of leading monographs in constitutional theory that have originally been written in languages other than English.

## ALSO AVAILABLE IN THE SERIES

**Europe's Functional Constitution**
**A Theory of Constitutionalism Beyond the State**
Turkuler Isiksel

**Post Sovereign Constitution Making Learning and Legitimacy**
Andrew Arato

**Popular Sovereignty in Early Modern Constitutional Thought**
Daniel Lee

**The Cultural Defense of Nations A Liberal Theory of Majority Rights**
Liav Orgad

**The Cosmopolitan Constitution**
Alexander Somek

**The Structure of Pluralism**
Victor M. Muniz-Fraticelli

**Constitutional Courts and Deliberative Democracy**
Conrado Hübner Mendes

**Fault Lines of Globalization Legal Order and the Politics of A-Legality**
Hans Lindahl

**The Cosmopolitan State**
H Patrick Glenn

**After Public Law**
Edited by Cormac Mac Amhlaigh, Claudio Michelon, and Neil Walker

**The Three Branches A Comparative Model of Separation of Powers**
Christoph Möllers

**The Global Model of Constitutional Rights**
Kai Möller

**The Twilight of Constitutionalism?**
Edited by Petra Dobner and Martin Loughlin

**Beyond Constitutionalism The Pluralist Structure of Postnational Law**
Nico Krisch

**Constituting Economic and Social Rights**
Katharine G. Young

**Constitutional Referendums The Theory and Practice of Republican Deliberation**
Stephen Tierney

**Constitutional Fragments Societal Constitutionalism and Globalization**
Gunther Teubner

# Constitutionalism

## Past, Present, and Future

Dieter Grimm

*Professor of Law, Humboldt University of Berlin*
*Former Justice of the Federal Constitutional Court of Germany*
*Former Director of the Wissenschaftskolleg zu Berlin Institute*
*for Advanced Study*

OXFORD
UNIVERSITY PRESS

# OXFORD

UNIVERSITY PRESS

Great Clarendon Street, Oxford, OX2 6DP,
United Kingdom

Oxford University Press is a department of the University of Oxford.
It furthers the University's objective of excellence in research, scholarship,
and education by publishing worldwide. Oxford is a registered trade mark of
Oxford University Press in the UK and in certain other countries

First Edition published in 2016

Published in the United States of America by Oxford University Press
198 Madison Avenue, New York, NY 10016, United States of America

British Library Cataloguing in Publication Data
Data available

ISBN 978-0-19-876612-4

# *Preface*

The modern constitution is rightly regarded as one of the great civilizing achievements of our time. Two hundred years after its emergence at the periphery of the Western world it has become the generally accepted pattern for establishing and legitimizing political rule. Virtually all states in the world have now a constitution. But from the beginning the constitution was an endangered achievement. The vast majority of constitutions that were enacted with much hope for a better future sooner or later failed. Most countries have had more than one constitution. The United States is a rare exception. Its constitution, which had been preceded by a number of constitutions in the former colonies, was not only the first one, it is also the oldest one still in force.

Constitutions are an endangered species in yet another way. Once the modern constitution had been invented and become an object of yearning for many peoples, it became possible to use the model for purposes other than those originally combined with it. There were and are many constitutions which have been enacted not to limit government in the interest of equal freedom of the citizens, but to camouflage the authoritarian or even totalitarian character of the state. Among the constitutions currently in force, the number of those that are not taken seriously or are disregarded as soon as their provisions enter into conflict with interests of the ruling class or the elected majority is not small.

It is true that safeguards like constitutional review, which also was an American exception for about 150 years, are now the norm and have greatly enhanced the relevance of constitutional law. But even constitutional courts do not always and everywhere guarantee compliance with constitutional law. Today, a number of constitutional courts find themselves under political pressure, and some were, from the very beginning, so organized or their judges so appointed that those in power had nothing to fear from them.

The modern constitution is finally endangered because the circumstances under which it emerged have changed considerably. The object of constitutionalization was public power, and public power was until recently identical with state power. The state, in turn, could be clearly distinguished from civil society. Today we are facing an erosion of these preconditions of modern constitutionalism. Internally, the borderline between private and public is being blurred. Private actors share public power without being submitted to the requirements of the constitution. Externally, the identity of public power and state power is dissolved. There are now institutions that exercise public power on the international level with direct effect in the states. Whether or not they can be constitutionalized remains an open question.

The essays contained in this book deal with these questions. They explore the history of modern constitutionalism, the characteristics that must exist if the constitution may be called an achievement, the appropriate way to understand and apply constitutional law under changed circumstances, the remaining role for national constitutions in times of internationalization and globalization as well as the possibility of supra-national constitutionalism.

Many of these essays have influenced the German and European discussion on constitutionalism, but only a few of them were available in English. Therefore, I am extremely grateful for the opportunity to be able to present my work on constitutional-ism in the form of some selected articles, old and new, to an English speaking audience in a series that has rapidly gained primary importance and attention in the field of constitutional theory.

Martin Loughlin from the London School of Economics was the driving force behind the project. I relied on his advice as to the selection of articles; his final editing gave me confidence that the text will not estrange the native speakers. Dev Josephs translated the articles written in German with great ability and accuracy. A grant from the Volkswagen-Stiftung made the translation possible. To all I am deeply indebted.

The function of the constitution as an anticipatory self-restraint of a society in view of future temptations is often symbolized by Odysseus tied to the mast of his ship in order not to yield to the songs of the sirens while passing their island. This is why an old mosaic image of this scene bedecks the cover of the book.

*Dieter Grimm (Berlin)*
DECEMBER 2015

# Contents

# PART I

# INTRODUCTION

# ❧ 1 ❧

# The Origins and Transformation of the Concept of the Constitution

## I. ORIGINS

### 1. The Development of the Legal Concept of Constitution

Every political unit is constituted, but not every one of them has a constitution. The term 'constitution' covers both conditions, but the two are not the same.[1] The term has two different meanings. Constitution in the first sense of the word refers to the nature of a country with reference to its political conditions. Constitution in the second sense refers to a law that concerns itself with the establishment and exercise of political rule. Consequently, the first definition refers to an empirical or descriptive constitution and the second a normative and prescriptive concept. Used empirically, constitution reflects the political conditions that in fact prevail in a specific region at a given time. In the normative sense, constitution establishes the rules by which political rule should be exercised under law.

Whereas constitutions in the empirical sense have always existed, the constitution in the normative sense is a relatively modern phenomenon. It emerged towards the end of the eighteenth century in the course of the American and French Revolutions and has propagated throughout the world over the last 200 years. This does not mean that before the emergence of the normative constitution legal rules relating to political rule and binding on the holders of the ruling function did not exist. But not every such form of rule can claim to have a constitution within the sense that emerged as a consequence of the late eighteenth-century revolutions and which have since characterized the term. Rather, a distinction must be drawn between *legalization* and *constitutionalization*. The constitution represents a specific type of legalization of political rule that is linked to historical conditions which did not always exist and which could also disappear over the course of history.[2]

---

[1] For the history of the term 'constitution', see Heinz Mohnhaupt and Dieter Grimm, *Verfassung: Zur Geschichte des Begriffs von der Antike bis zur Gegenwart* (Berlin: Duncker & Humblot, 2nd edn, 2002).

[2] See further, Ch. 2 of this volume; Dieter Grimm, *Deutsche Verfassungsgeschichte 1776-1866* (Frankfurt am Main: Suhrkamp, 3rd edn, 1995), p. 10 et seq.

Constitutionalism: Past, Present, and Future. First Edition. Dieter Grimm. © Dieter Grimm 2016. Published 2016 by Oxford University Press.

For a long time, an object for a law specializing in setting norms for political rule was lacking. Until society had become functionally differentiated, it had no system specializing in the exercise of political rule to the exclusion of other systems.[3] Rather, tasks of rulership were distributed among numerous mutually independent bearers in terms of their object, function, and physical location. Closed political units could not be formed under these circumstances. Authority to rule related primarily to persons and not territories. The holders of such authority did not exercise it as an independent function, but rather as an annex to a specific status as head of a family, landowner, or member of a social class or corporation. Under these circumstances, what is today distinguished as private and public was still intermingled, and this did not permit any autonomous public law.[4]

That does not mean that the authority to rule was not subject to legal constraints. On the contrary, it was subject to a tight web of legal ties that were valid largely from tradition and often based on divine will. Consequently, they not only took precedence over codified law but could not be amended by it either. However, these rules did not represent a constitution in the sense of a law specifically relating to the establishment and exercise of political rule. Just as ruling authority was a dependent annex of other legal positions, legal norms referring to rule were part of the general law. The numerous studies devoted to the 'constitution' in the ancient and medieval worlds do not lose their validity on that account.[5] But they should not be confused with the normative text that seeks to regulate rule and is enacted by a political decision: this was an innovative product of the revolutions of the late eighteenth century.

An object capable of being subject to a constitution did not take form until the religious schism destroyed the basis of the medieval order and, in the course of the religious civil wars of the sixteenth and seventeenth centuries, a new form of political rule emerged on the European continent. This was based on the conviction that civil war could only be resolved by a superior force that possessed both the authority to create a new order independent of disputed religious truth and the power to restore peace on this basis. Guided by this conviction, and starting in France, rulers began to unite the dispersed powers and condensed them into a comprehensive public power relating to a territory. This power included the right to make laws without any limitation imposed through a higher-ranking, divinely derived law. What was once a legal commandment retreated to the moral sphere, where it lacked the force of legal obligation.

---

[3] Cf. Niklas Luhmann, *Theory of Society* (Stanford: Stanford University Press, 1997); Niklas Luhmann, *Die Politik der Gesellschaft* (Frankfurt am Main: Suhrkamp, 2000), p. 69 et seq.; Niklas Luhmann, Metamorphosen des Staates' in his *Gesellschaftsstruktur und Semantik*, vol. IV (Frankfurt am Main: Suhrkamp, 1995), p. 101 et seq.

[4] On the order of the Middle Ages, see: Otto Brunner, *Land and Lordship. Structures of Governance in Medieval Austria* (Philadelphia: University of Pennsylvania Press, 1992); further, Helmut Quaritsch, *Staat und Souveränität* (Frankfurt am Main: Athenaeum, 1970), p. 107, esp. pp. 184, 196 et seq; Walter Ullmann, *Principles of Government and Politics in the Middle Ages* (London: Methuen, 3rd edn, 1974).

[5] Cf. Fritz Kern, *Recht und Verfassung im Mittelalter* (Tübingen: Wissenschaftliche Buchgesellschaft, 1952).

New terminology soon emerged to describe this new phenomenon: that of the state as the political unit, and of sovereignty for its plenary power.[6] The primary significance of this new phenomenon was not its outward but its inward independence, which found expression in the right of the ruler to make law for all others without being subject to legal constraints.[7] Naturally, the emergence of the state and sovereignty was not an event but a process that commenced at different times in the various regions of continental Europe, proceeded in different forms and at different speeds, and produced differing results, without anywhere coming to an end. Rather, intermediary powers persisted and which contested the ruler's sole possession of public power. In particular, the absolute state allowed the feudal system to continue to exist, and thus the landowner-peasant relationship was largely left unchanged.

Regardless, the modern state with its extensive military powers, its own civil service, and its own revenues independent of the consent of the estates emerged as a structure that could become the object of a uniform regulation. If this era did not bring forth a constitution in the modern sense, this was because the state had emerged as an absolute princely state for the reasons described above. The bearer of all powers was the monarch, who claimed these powers on the basis of his own right and who saw himself subject to no legal limitation in its exercise. Although an object capable of being subject to a constitution was no longer lacking, there was no need for a constitution: absolute rule is characterized by the absence of legal constraints.

However, there was in this regard also a gap between the idea and the reality. The princely power that emerged soon awakened a need for legal constraints. In the favourable event that the ruler was absent or weak, this frequently manifested itself in so-called forms of government, bodies of law intended to secure the rights of the estates against the princely power. Although these forms of government were only seldom able to prevail against state-building forces,[8] their function was gradually adopted by so-called fundamental laws, treaties, or electoral capitulation.[9] Generally established by way of contract, the ruler could not unilaterally cancel them. To this extent, they took precedent over the law set by the prince. However, these too must not be mistaken for constitutions. They left the prince's traditional authority to rule untouched and compelled him solely to waive certain exercises of rule in favour of the contractual

---

[6] See the entry on Staat und Souveränität' by Hans Boldt, Werner Conze, Görg Haverkate, Diethelm Klippel, and Reinhart Koselleck, in Otto Brunner, Werner Conze, Reinhart Koselleck (eds), *Geschichtliche Grundbegriffe*, vol. VI (Stuttgart: Klett-Cotta, 1990), pp. 1–154.

[7] Cf. Quaritsch (n. 4), pp. 39, 333.

[8] Fritz Hartung, *Staatsbildende Kräfte der Neuzeit* (Berlin: Duncker & Humblot, 1961).

[9] Cf. Gerhard Oestreich, 'Vom Herrschaftsvertrag zur Verfassungsurkunde' in Rudolf Vierhaus (ed.), *Herrschaftsverträge, Wahlkapitulationen, Fundamentalgesetze* (Göttingen: Vandenhoek and Ruprecht, 1977), p. 45; Heinz Mohnhaupt, 'Die Lehre von der "Lex fundamentalis" und die Hausgesetzgebung europäischer Dynastien' in Johannes Kunisch (ed.), *Der dynastische Fürstenstaat* (Berlin: Duncker & Humblot, 1982), p. 3; John W. Gough, *Fundamental Law in English Constitutional History* (Oxford: Clarendon Press, 2nd edn, 1961).

parties. The *hierachicalization* of legal norms does not by itself produce a *constitutionalization*.

Accordingly, the modern, normative constitution does not owe its emergence to an organic development of these older approaches. Rather, it was the revolutionary disruptions of 1776 and 1789 that helped to bring about a new solution to the permanent problem of legally constraining political rule, a solution that remains valid to this day. The break from the mother country in America and the overthrow of the absolute monarchy in France created a vacuum of legitimate rule that had to be filled. Naturally, revolutionary disruptions alone cannot adequately explain why a constitution was considered necessary for this purpose. The upheavals could simply have resulted in the replacement of the overthrown rulers by others, as had occurred in the countless violent eruptions that preceded these revolutions. Even if the conditions under which a new person or dynasty was appointed to rule had been formulated at this time, the upheaval would still not necessarily have led to constitutionalism.

This is affirmed by the case of England. The English revolution of the seventeenth century did not bring forth the constitution in the modern sense—even though a breach with traditional rulers occurred. In the English revolution, the nobility and the bourgeois classes united against the Stuart dynasty when it attempted to expand its rule according to the continental model without being able to rely on the reasons that justified this expansion on the continent. Thus, the Glorious Revolution did not seek to change, but rather to preserve the existing order. Accordingly, this did not result in a change in the system of rule, but merely a change in the dynasty, and the normative document that accompanied this transition, the Bill of Rights of 1689, was a contract between Parliament and the new monarch that affirmed the old rights.[10] For just one brief moment after Cromwell had abolished the monarchy, a constitution in the modern sense was imposed in 1653,[11] but it became obsolete through the restoration of the old regime after his death.

### 2. The Conditions for the Emergence of Constitutionalism

The emergence of the constitution as a lasting achievement of the great revolutions of the eighteenth century is due, above all, to two circumstances. The first is that the discontent of American and French revolutionaries was not limited to the person of the ruler, but encompassed the system of rule. Admittedly, the two countries differed greatly as to the degree.[12] Unlike the French, the English monarchy, to which the colonies were subject, had not become absolute. On the

---

[10] See further Ch. 3 of this volume.

[11] 'Instrument of Government' in Samuel R. Gardiner (ed.), *The Constitutional Documents of the Puritan Revolution, 1625-1660* (Oxford: Oxford University Press, 1968), p. 405.

[12] Cf. Jürgen Habermas, 'Natural Law and Revolution' in his *Theory and Practice* (Boston: Beacon Press, 1963); Dieter Grimm, 'Europäisches Naturrecht und amerikanische Revolution' (1970) 3 *Ius commune* 120.

contrary, the importance of Parliament had steadily grown. Additionally, class barriers had become permeable, and the feudal and guild bonds of the economy had largely fallen away. At that time, England was considered the freest nation in the world, and even remnants of the older order had not found their way to the American colonies. Under these circumstances, the colonists were concerned not with better laws but with better security of their rights, which Parliament had withheld from them without their consent. It was this refusal of the mother country that drove them to issue a Declaration of Independence.

By contrast, France had an especially strong absolutism. Furthermore, the physiocratically guided attempts at modernizing the economic system had failed. The more the feudal system lost its internal justification, the more vociferously it was defended against dissolution tendencies and criticism. In addition to the traditional bourgeoisie of guild-affiliated tradesmen, promoted by the needs of the absolute monarchy a new bourgeoisie based on higher education and economic power had emerged. This was unable to find a place in the prevailing legal and social order commensurate with its societal importance and economic strength since the traditional legal order prevented it from fully developing its economic potential. Thus, the French Revolution, unlike the American, did not seek merely to change political conditions; it primarily aimed to eliminate the estates-based, feudal social order, which had been unattainable under the old regime.

These revolutionary forces were also able to invoke ideas of a just order that virtually demanded to be transformed into positive law. These ideas, which had already formed before the revolutions, became templates for action. After the schism had undermined the transcendent legitimation of political rule, theories of natural law had emerged to take the place of divine revelation.[13] To determine how the rule of persons over other persons could be justified, the social philosophy of that era imagined a state of nature in which everyone was by definition equal and free. Under this prerequisite, rule could only be established through an agreement of all. Whatever form this agreement took, it was thus certain that the legitimation principle of political rule was the consent on the part of the ruled and the only question remaining concerned the form of rule that would be acceptable to rational beings.

The social-contract theorists saw the reason for the willingness to exchange freedom and equality for the state in the fundamental uncertainty of freedom in a state of nature. The establishment of an organized compulsory force was thus viewed as an imperative of reason. Naturally, the question then arose as to the extent to which each individual must surrender his natural rights in order to enjoy the security guaranteed by the state. Under the influence of the religious civil wars, the answer originally was that the state could only guarantee

---

[13] Cf. Otto von Gierke, *Johannes Althusius und die Entwicklung der naturrechtlichen Staatstheorien: zugleich ein Beitrag zur Geschichte der Rechtssystematik* (Aalen: Scientia-Verlag, 5th edn, 1958); Wolfgang Kersting, *Die politische Philosophie des Gesellschaftsvertrages* (Darmstadt: Wissenschaftliche Buchgesellschaft, 1994); Diethelm Klippel, *Politische Freiheit und Freiheitsrechte im deutschen Naturrecht des 18. Jahrhunderts* (Paderborn: Schöningh, 1976).

life, limb, and property when all natural rights were first ceded to it. But in this form social-contract theory did not lead in a constitutional direction, even though it assumed the consent of all those subject to rule. Rather, in its original formulation it served to justify absolute rule, which is irreconcilable with constitutionalism.

Following the resolution of the religious civil wars, however, the plausibility of this position declined and was gradually displaced by the idea that the enjoyment of security did not necessitate the surrender of all natural rights to the state on the part of the individual. Rather, it was deemed sufficient to cede the right to assert one's own legal claims by force to the state while other natural rights could remain with the individual as natural and inalienable rights without thereby risking social peace. Soon, even releasing the individual from the bonds of state care, the feudal and guild order, and church oversight of virtue and making him self-reliant became seen as a necessity. For some, this followed from the nature of humanity, which could only fulfil its destiny as a rational and moral being through freedom. For others, freedom was the prerequisite for a just reconciliation of interests between individuals and for material prosperity, which depended on the free development of all forces and encouragement of competition.

This formalized the problem of justice. The state no longer derived its *raison d'être* from the assertion of a general welfare of which it had knowledge and with which it was entrusted, which all subjects had to obey and from which no one could claim freedom. Rather, freedom itself became a condition of the general welfare. The just social order derived from the free activities of individuals, and the state was reduced to the task of securing the prerequisite for realizing the general welfare, namely, individual freedom. This task could not be resolved by society through its own efforts because the equal freedom of all precluded any individual right to rule; it required the maintenance of the monopoly of force established by the absolute state. But provision now had to be made to ensure that it could not be utilized for any purposes other than those of securing and coordinating freedom.

Provided with this content, the social-contract doctrine no longer supported the absolute, princely state and the estate-based feudal social order which the monarchs had never fundamentally called into question, but acquired a trajectory opposed to both. The existing conditions appeared unnatural in the light of social and philosophical teachings. Those who wished to overcome them could feel justified, by claiming the authority of a higher law over the applicable law. Resistance to the monarchy was based precisely on this justification, after the claim to 'good old law' in America and the call for reform of the estate-based, feudal, and dirigiste law in France had been in vain. It was precisely this appeal to natural law, which challenged the legitimacy of the positive law and abrogated obedience to it, that constituted the step from resistance to revolution that was to bring forth a new order.

Although the substance of later constitutions which expressed this new ideal of order were to a great extent shaped in the post-absolutist theories of social contract, the social contract could not be equated with the constitution. The social contract was merely an imaginary construct that defined the conditions for legitimate rule and thus enabled a critique of political orders that did not conform to it. It claimed to constitute the standard for formulating just law, but was not positive law itself. It was only the revolutionary situation that provided the opportunity to implement the ideas of social philosophy in positive law. The main reason this occurred may be found in three characteristics of these ideas.

The first characteristic was the fundamental premise of social-contract theories that under the conditions of a state of nature, in which all persons were by definition equally free, rule could only originate through a contract of all individuals with each other. In philosophy not more than a regulative idea from which the requirements of a just social order could be derived and the legitimacy of concrete orders could be tested, this premise itself became now the legitimating principle of political rule. In this connection, the Americans had little difficulty in seeing this principle already realized in their founding history in the form of the covenants of the first settlers, on which they now built,[14] whereas the French adopted only the consequence of social-contract theory: the necessity for rule to be legitimized by subjects without having to forge a real contract.

In both cases the result was the same. The transcendentally or traditionally derived principle of monarchical sovereignty—realized in its pure form in France and attributed to the 'King in Parliament' in absolutism-resistant England—gave way to a rationally justified democratic principle, though admittedly with different emphases. In France, the country of origin of the state and sovereignty, this was understood as a type of popular sovereignty. In America, where the concept of sovereignty had remained as alien as in the mother country, it was interpreted more as self-government in the context of the colonial experience. However, these differing perceptions in no way changed the fact that rule under democratic principles could no longer be regarded as original but only as derived right, conferred on office-holders by the people and exercised on their behalf.

But even rule instituted by the people does not necessarily lead to a constitution; it arises only under the additional prerequisite that the mandate to rule is not bestowed unconditionally or irrevocably. This is so because otherwise the democratic principle would be exhausted in the first bestowal of the mandate justifying a new form of absolute rule which differed from the old only in that it derives from the grace of the people rather than the grace of God. In this case, establishment of democratic rule requires a constitutional act but does not create a constitution.[15] Such a concept is neither reconcilable with the natural law theory of innate and inalienable human rights nor with an understanding of the mandate

---

[14] Cf. Alfred H. Kelly and Winfred A. Harbison, *The American Constitution: Its Origins and Development* (New York: Norton, 4th edn, 1963), chs. 1–2; Willi Paul Adams, *The First American Constitutions: Republican Ideology and the Making of the State Constitutions in the Revolutionary Era* (Lanham: Madison House, 2001); Donald S. Lutz, *The Origins of American Constitutionalism* (Baton Rouge: Louisiana State University Press, 1988), p. 13 et seq.

[15] See further Ch. 2 of this volume.

relationship as finite, revocable, and based on responsibility to the principals. This was foreign to the revolutionaries who understood that sovereignty of the people required an organization that created and maintained this relationship.

The second characteristic flowed from the Enlightenment idea that equal freedom of all individuals was the highest principle of the social order and that the state derived its *raison d'être* solely from its protection. To ensure this protection against domestic malcontents and foreign invaders, the monopoly of force had to be conceded to it, which did not achieve its final form following the overthrow of all intermediate powers standing between the individual and the state until the revolution.[16] In the same breath however, it was necessary to ensure that the state exercised its power only in the interests of maintaining freedom and equality and abandoned all controlling ambitions beyond this purpose. It was no longer called upon to shape a social order on the basis of a material ideal of justice, but had to restrict itself to preserving an independent order that was assumed to be just.

Consequently, the various social tasks were decoupled from political control and entrusted to social self-control by means of individual freedom. State and society parted ways, and a clear distinction between the public and the private became discernable. The exercise of public power in society became an intervention requiring justification. This too demanded rules that restricted the state to its residual tasks and distinguished between societal and state responsibilities as well as organizing the apparatus of the state so as to make abuse of state power unlikely. Finally, the divided spheres of the state and society needed to be reconnected in such a way as to prevent the state from distancing itself from the needs and interests of the people and giving precedence to its own institutional needs or the interests of office-holders.

The third characteristic lay in a change in the notion of public welfare. After the reconstruction of the social order on the fundamental principle of equal individual freedom, welfare was to result from social self-regulation without any act on the part of the state. This did not make the idea of the general welfare obsolete as a basis for socialization and justification of political rule. However, it lost its character as a fixed, substantial quantity. Multiple opinions as to the question of what best serves the general welfare could co-exist, so that any choice based on an absolute truth was no longer permissible. To this extent, the general welfare was pluralized. The unavoidable question as to what is to be considered as the general welfare then needed to be decided in a process of political opinion and will formation. To this extent, the general welfare was proceduralized. It became transformed into the results of a social process whose orderly unfolding was guaranteed by the state.

It was this ongoing need to determine what constituted the general welfare that also required regulation.[17] In this process, two needs emerged. The first

---

[16] See Dieter Grimm, 'The State Monopoly of Force' in Wilhelm Heitmeyer and John Hagan (eds), *International Handbook of Violence Research* (Dordrecht: Kluwer, 2003), p. 1043.

[17] See Dieter Grimm, 'Gemeinwohl in der Rechtsprechung des Bundesverfassungsgerichts' in Herfried Münkler and Karsten Fischer (eds), *Gemeinwohl und Gemeinsinn*, vol. III (Berlin: De Gruyter, 2002), p. 125.

derived from the proceduralization of the general welfare, and the second from pluralization. Procedurally, the opinion- and will-forming process from which it originates had to be organized. Participatory rights and definitional competence had to be formally established. With respect to pluralization, a demarcation was necessary. As pluralization was a consequence of the transition from truth to freedom, freedom and all its prerequisites had to be excluded from pluralization. This required material definitions that served as indispensible premises for determining the general welfare.

### 3. Realization of the Constitutional Programme

The task was such that it found its appropriate solution in law. The solution had to originate in a social consensus. But the consensus quickly becomes history and thus is transitory. Only law could make the consensus permanent and binding. The fundamental question then becomes: how is the acting generation able to acquire the legitimacy to bind future generations?[18] The answer lies in the possibility of changing the law. Law also provides a suitable answer to the regulatory problems that the programme of the social-contract theory creates. It achieves its greatest effectiveness in regulatory measures of a demarcating and organizing nature.

But first it was necessary to overcome the problem that ever since law was made positive it was seen as a product of state decision-making and had to bind the state, even in its power of law-making. This problem was resolved by building on the idea of a hierarchy of legal norms which was well known in the Middle Ages and had been preserved in the 'leges fundamentales' and contracts of rule.[19] This became transformed into a novel division of the legal order into two parts. One part was the traditional ordinary law that emanated from the state and was binding on the individual. The other was the new law, which issued from the sovereign and was binding on the state. This latter was subsequently termed the constitution, and the term gained its modern meaning with this innovation.

This construction could succeed only if both parts of the legal order were not only separate but organized hierarchically. Constitutional law had to take precedence over legislation and its acts of application, so that law could be applied to law and thus increase its potentialities.[20] This priority is essential to the concept

---

[18] See particularly Thomas Jefferson, *The Writings of Thomas Jefferson*, vol. V, 1895 (Whitefisch: Kessinger Publishing, reprint 2009); see also Stephen Holmes, 'Precommitment and the Paradox of Democracy' in Jon Elster and Rune Slagstad (eds), *Constitutionalism and Democracy* (Cambridge: Cambridge University Press, 1988), p. 195.

[19] On *lex aeterna, lex naturae, lex humana*, see Thomas Aquinas, *Summa theologica II-II*, qu. 57–79; for the leges fundamentales see n. 9.

[20] Cf. Niklas Luhmann, *Rechtssoziologie*, vol. II (Reinbek bei Hamburg: Rowohlt, 1972), p. 213; Niklas Luhmann, *Das Recht der Gesellschaft* (Frankfurt am Main: Suhrkamp, 1993), p. 470.

of the constitution.[21] It is distinctive of the constitution, and the constitution cannot fulfil its role where recognition of this priority is lacking. This lack of priority is also what distinguishes the British 'constitution' from those constitutions that emerged from the American and French Revolutions: all provisions of the unwritten English constitution are with reservation of parliamentary sovereignty.

The supremacy of the constitution was enacted at its birth both in America and France. Sieyès, who provided the theoretical basis for transforming the Estates General, instituted for the first time in 300 years, into a National Assembly, discovered the distinction between 'pouvoir constituant' and 'pouvoir constitué' that remains valid today.[22] The former rested with the nation as the holder of all public power. The latter comprised the institutions created by the people through the enacting of a constitution. These acted on behalf of the people under conditions laid down by the people in the constitution and could thus not change it of their own accord if the entire structure were not to collapse. They could only act on the basis and within the framework of the constitution and their acts could only be legally binding when enacted in conformity with the constitution.

Thus, the new aspect of the constitution was neither the theoretical draft of an overall plan of legitimate rule nor the hierarchic legal order. Both these features had existed previously. Rather, the new aspect was the merging of these two lines of development. The theoretically drafted plan was endowed with legal validity, and placed above all acts of the state as a 'supreme law' formulated by the people. By this method, rule was transformed into a matter of mandate and since the constitution was a consequence of mandatory rule, the constituent power of the people was an indispensable part of it.[23] Persons were authorized to rule only on the basis of the constitution and could only demand obedience to their acts of rule when they observed the parameters of their legally defined mandate and exercised their authority in conformity with the law. It was this construction that permitted the constitutional state to be spoken of as a 'government of laws and not of men'.[24]

This limitation of the state to its reduced aims as well as the guarantee of individual freedom and the autonomy of the various social functions which resulted was achieved by fundamental rights. In both France and Virginia—the first American colony to adopt a constitution—these rights were enacted before the provisions governing the organization of the state, while the Constitution of the United States of 1787 initially treated a Bill of Rights as dispensable,

---

[21] Cf. Rainer Wahl, 'Der Vorrang der Verfassung' (1981) 20 *Der Staat* 485.

[22] Emmanuel Sieyès, 'What is the Third Estate' in his *Political Writings* (Indianapolis: Hackett, 2003), p. 92; James Madison, *The Federalist* No. 49 (1788); cf. Egon Zweig, *Die Lehre vom 'Pouvoir constituant'* (Tübingen: Mohr, 1909); Pasquale Pasquino, *Sieyès et l'invention de la constitution en France* (Paris: Jacob, 1998).

[23] See Ernst-Wolfgang Böckenförde, 'Die verfassunggebende Gewalt des Volkes' in his *Staat, Verfassung, Demokratie* (Frankfurt am Main: Suhrkamp, 1991), p. 96.

[24] *Marbury v. Madison*, 5 U. S. (1 Cranch) 137 (1803).

before adding them in the form of amendments. The French formulation of fundamental rights derived mainly from the philosophy of the Enlightenment, which since the mid-eighteenth century had developed an increasingly detailed catalogue of human rights. The Americans, by contrast, were guided by English catalogues of rights, to which they added nothing of substance. But because of their experiences with Parliament they placed these not only above the executive but also above the legislative branch, elevating them from the level of fundamental rights to that of constitutional rights and thus to basic rights within the meaning of constitutional law.[25]

Since the American Revolution exhausted itself in the political objectives of achieving independence from the mother country and establishing self-government, the existing social order was left largely unchanged. Fundamental rights could therefore be concentrated on deterring state infringements on freedom and they were realized in their negative function. By contrast, the French Revolution aimed not only at changing the political system but also the social system. This comprised the entire legal order, which was of a feudalistic, dirigiste, and canonical nature. Here, fundamental rights were assigned the role of guiding the grand act of replacing an entire legal system. This was the declared reason for the early adoption of the *Déclaration des Droits de l'Homme et du Citoyen* on 26 August 1789. Under these circumstances, fundamental rights could not functionally be limited to that of state prohibitions. They set out binding objectives for state action and could not revert to their negative function until the transformation of the legal order to the principles of freedom and equality had been achieved.[26]

In both countries, the state was organized in such a way that state and society, which were separated under the premise that society was capable of controlling itself, were rejoined by a representative body elected by the people which had the right to make law and the right to raise and appropriate taxes. The state executive was bound by the law enacted by Parliament and a relatively strict separation of powers guarded against the abuse of power. In both countries, the separation of powers became virtually a defining characteristic of the constitution, so that the catalogues of fundamental rights could assert that a land without separation of powers did not have a constitution. But although establishing this basic pattern, America and France went different ways, particularly in the choice between presidential and parliamentary democracy and between a federal and centralized state organization.

---

[25] See Gerald Stourzh, *Wege zur Grundrechtsdemokratie* (Vienna: Böhlau, 1989), in particular pp. 1, 37, 75, 155; Gerald Stourzh, 'Staatsformenlehre und Fundamentalgesetze in England und Nordamerika im 17. Jahrhundert' in Rudolf Vierhaus (ed.), *Herrschaftsverträge, Wahlkapitulationen, Fundamentalgesetze* (Göttingen: Vandenhoek and Ruprecht, 1977).

[26] Cf. Dieter Grimm, 'Grundrechte und Privatrecht in der bürgerlichen Sozialordnung' in his *Recht und Staat der bürgerlichen Gesellschaft* (Frankfurt am Main: Suhrkamp, 1987), p. 192. For the legal content of the French Declaration see Patrick Wachsmann, 'Déclaration ou constitution de droits' in Michel Troper and Lucien Jaume (eds), *1789 et l'invention de la constitution* (Paris: LGDJ, 1994), p. 44.

Well-conceived though it may have been, constitutional law remained in a precarious condition. It not only structured the highest power but also required this power to attain its legitimacy by submitting itself to legal rules. Constitutional law thus differed from statute law in one important respect: whereas the latter was supported by the organized sanctioning power of the state, so that violations could be met with compulsion, the former lacked such protection because it acted on the highest power itself. The addressee and guarantor of regulation are identical. In the event of a conflict, there is no superior power that can assert the constitutional requirements. Therein lies the unique weakness of the highest law.

During the emergent phase of constitutionalism, only America found an answer to this weakness. France had lived under an absolute monarchy for 300 years without any bodies representing the estates; they therefore saw sufficient security in an elected representative body. The American colonists, by contrast, had no such faith in a popular representative body. Due to their experiences with the excesses of the British Parliament and some abuse of power by their own legislative assemblies, particularly during the revolutionary phase, they were aware that the constitution was imperilled not only by the executive, but also by the legislative branch. Consequently, they provided that the judicial system should oversee compliance with the constitutional institutions of federalism, the separation of powers, and the fundamental rights. Consequently, the birth of the constitutional state went along with constitutional review,[27] though for more than 100 years this remained unique to the United States.

The difference between the older legal bonds of political rule and the modern constitution in the form in which it emerged towards the end of the eighteenth century can now be more precisely described.[28] While the older bonds always assumed legitimate rule and limited themselves to the ways in which it was exercised, the modern constitution not only modifies but also constitutes rule.[29] It produces legitimate state power, and only then organizes it in accordance with its purpose. Whereas the older bonds always related solely to individual modalities of an exercise of rule assumed to be all-inclusive, the modern constitution acted in a comprehensive and not an isolated manner. It permitted neither extra-constitutional bearers of ruling authority nor extraconstitutional modalities of exercise. Where the old legal bonds only applied between

---

[27] This was masterminded by Alexander Hamilton, *The Federalist* No. 78 (1788). It is unsettled whether the possibility of constitutional review was installed in the constitution itself or whether it was a creation of the U. S. Supreme Court in the judgment of *Marbury v. Madison*, 5 U. S. (1 Cranch), 137; cf. David P. Currie, *The Constitution and the Supreme Court* vol. I (Chicago: University of Chicago Press, 1985), p. 66.

[28] Cf. Grimm (n. 2), p. 34; Charles H. McIlwain, *Constitutionalism Ancient and Modern* (Ithaca, NY: 3rd edn, 1966).

[29] This counts independently of whether Isensee is correct in his opinion that the state inevitably preceeds before the constitution: Josef Isensee, 'Staat und Verfassung' in Josef Isensee and Paul Kirchhof (eds), *Handbuch des Staatsrechts I* (Heidelberg: C.F. Müller, 2nd edn, 1995), § 13. See also Christoph Möllers, *Staat als Argument* (München: Beck, 2000), p. 256.

contractual parties, modern constitutions pertained to the entire people. Their effect was universal and not particular.

### 4. The Constitution as an Evolutionary Achievement

Due to these unique characteristics, the constitution has rightly been called an evolutionary achievement.[30] It restored the legal bonds on political rule that had been lost with the collapse of the medieval order under the altered conditions of the modern state, the attendant positive nature of law, and the transition to the functional differentiation of society. By means of the constitution, political rule was structured according to a new legitimating principle of popular sovereignty and made compatible with the need of a functionally differentiated society for autonomy and harmony.[31] By such means, the constitution simultaneously made it possible to distinguish legitimate from illegitimate claims to rule and acts of rule. In fulfilling this function, it might fail or lose its acceptance. But the character of an achievement became apparent in the fact that its function in this case could only be assumed by another constitution, and it cannot be maintained independent of the constitution.[32]

The new instrument of the constitution reflected its originating conditions. In accordance with constitutionalism's aim of legally codifying political rule, it took up the form that political rule had taken on at the time of its emergence. That was the state as it emerged in reaction to the decay of the medieval order first in France and later in other European countries. Under these circumstances, the state emerged as the nation state. In this form, it existed before the constitution emerged. The nation state was thus assumed in the constitution.[33] The consequence of this was that, although fuelled by principles that claimed universal applicability, the idea of the constitution was realized as a particular instrument. From the start, the constitutions of nation states varied the constitutional programme.

Consequently, right from the beginning the constitution was as universal as it was limited. It was universal in the sense that it asserted that public power could only be exercised on the basis and within the framework of its provisions. It was limited in the sense that the public power subject to its provisions was limited to a specific territory which was demarcated from other territories by borders. Every constitution applied only within the territory of the state it

[30] Cf. Niklas Luhmann, 'Verfassung als evolutionäre Errungenschaft' (1990) 9 *Rechtshistorisches Journal* 176; Peter Häberle describes it as a 'cultural achievement' in his *Verfassungslehre als Kulturwissenschaft* (Berlin: Duncker & Humblot, 1998), p. 28.

[31] Cf. Niklas Luhmann, 'Politische Verfassungen im Kontext des Gesellschaftssystems' (1972) 12 *Der Staat* 6, 165, 168.

[32] Cf. Luhmann, Politische Verfassungen, ibid., p. 168.

[33] Cf. Ernst-Wolfgang Böckenförde, 'Geschichtliche Entwicklung und Bedeutungswandel der Verfassung' in his *Staat, Verfassung, Demokratie* (Frankfurt am Main: Suhrkamp, 1991), p. 9; Luhmann, *Das Recht der Gesellschaft* (n. 20), p. 478.

constituted, while other rules with the same claim to exclusivity applied in the neighbouring states. The difference between the internal and external marked by state boundaries was the prerequisite for a uniform and universal state power and thus for its constitutionalization. But at the same time, this meant that the effectiveness of the constitution depended on the difference between the internal and external remaining clear and the state border effectively shielded the territory against foreign acts of rule.

As a law referring specifically to the state, the constitution could only make good on its claim to complete legalization of political rule if this was identical with state power. It was thus not without reason that enactment of the constitution in France was preceded by the dissolution of all intermediary powers and the transfer of ruling functions to the state. The melange of public and private elements in older social formations and their remnants in absolutism, which was an obstacle to the constitution, were thus eliminated. On the one hand, society was stripped of all ruling authority and this was the prerequisite for empowering it to control itself by means of the market. On the other hand, the authority to rule was completely deprivatized, but needed to be legally constrained precisely on account of its concentration in the state. On that account, in a constitutional state the principle of freedom applies fundamentally for society, and that of constraint applies for the state.[34] This is not merely a conceivable variant of the constitutional state, but its constituting feature. The constitutional state would be unseated if the state enjoyed the freedom of private individuals or if by the same token private individuals could exercise the state's means of rule.

The altered conditions of legal constraint also affected the nature and degree of legalization. As a component of positive law, legal constraint could neither be an external constraint nor be considered invariant. External constraint was not possible because no pre-political or apolitical source or law existed in the state any longer. Constitutional law was no exception. In this respect, constitutional constraint on politics is always a self-constraint.[35] One must not be misled by the circumstance that the constitution, unlike statute law, was based on the sovereign itself, the people (in America), or the nation (in France). Although the constitution is the wellspring of legitimate state power, the sovereign cannot effect this without being provisionally organized politically or being represented by appropriate bodies.[36]

This point does not affect the fundamental difference between constituent power and constituted power. Rather, this is a difference within the political system. As the first constitutions show, the difference can be structured so that decisions respecting constitutional law can be made both by other institutions and by other processes than decisions respecting legislation. The United States Constitution and the French revolutionary constitutions went especially far in

---

[34] Cf. Carl Schmitt, *Verfassungslehre* (München: Duncker & Humblot, 1928), p. 126.

[35] Cf. Luhmann, *Die Politik der Gesellschaft* (n. 3), p. 358; Böckenförde (n. 23), p. 90.

[36] Böckenförde (n. 23), p. 96.

this respect.[37] But even where institutions and processes for decisions respecting the constitution are largely identical (as in Germany), the distinction retains its significance. It ensures that the institutions are active in different capacities that may not be conflated, thus stabilizing the primacy of the constitution.

For the same reasons, constitutional law cannot be invariant law. Just as it comes into being through a political decision, it can be modified again by the same type of decision. Even prohibitions of change enshrined in constitutional law, which create a further gradient within constitutional law, are effective only as long as the constitution containing such a prohibition remains in force and is not annulled by contrary resolutions. But this does not harm the legalization function because with the aid of the constitution decisions regarding the premises of political decisions are separated from the political decisions themselves. The primacy of the constitution does not preclude its amendment, but that the constitutional premises are ignored in political decisions as long as they are not amended.

Additionally, the legal constraint of politics by the constitution cannot be a total constraint.[38] Since all law within the state is politically created, total legalization would be equivalent to a negation of politics. Politics would be reduced to executing the constitution, and thus ultimately become administration. Yet the constitution should not make politics superfluous, but should channel and rationalize it. Consequently, it can never be more than a framework for political action. It defines the constraints under which political decisions can command binding force, but determines neither the input into constitutional channels nor the results of constitutional processes. But it remains a comprehensive regulation to the extent that it does not permit any extraconstitutional powers nor any extraconstitutional procedures. The result can only claim to be binding when the constitutionally legitimated actors act within the constitutionally established bounds.

The constitution fulfils its function as 'the fundamental legal order of the state'[39] by removing those principles of social coexistence that rest on a broad consensus across all opponents from the ongoing political debate. They serve this debate as a standard and a boundary, while procedural rules are established for the sphere ceded to debate. By providing and symbolizing a stock of commonalities in this manner with which adherents to differing convictions and holders of diverging interests are in agreement, the constitution describes the identity of the political system and contributes to the integration of society.[40]

[37] Cf. Title VII of the French constitution of 3 September 1791 and Art. V of the American Constitution, with the consequence that the American Constitution was revised seldom and the French one was replaced by a new constitution at the first moment of a need for change.

[38] Cf. Dieter Grimm, 'Politik und Recht' in Eckart Klein, *Grundrechte, soziale Ordnung und Verfassungsgerichtsbarkeit, Festschrift für Ernst Benda* (Heidelberg: C.F. Müller, 1995), p. 96; also Dieter Grimm, *Die Verfassung und die Politik* (München: Beck, 2001), p. 21.

[39] See Werner Kägi, *Die Verfassung als rechtliche Grundordnung des Staates* (Zürich: Polygraph Verlag, 1945).

[40] Cf. Hans Vorländer, *Verfassung und Konsens* (Berlin: Duncker & Humblot, 1981); Hans Vorländer (ed.), *Integration durch Verfassung* (Wiesbaden: Westdeutscher Verlag, 2002).

This is particularly significant for those societies in which the integrating power of other community-building institutions tends to decline due to the constitutionally guaranteed individual freedom.

In formal legal terms, the constitution performs its function by erecting greater hurdles for changes to the principles and ground rules than it does for ongoing political decisions. This decouples the alteration of the principles and processes for ongoing political decisions from these decisions themselves. This separation creates differing discourses and time horizons for both, which has numerous advantages. The political debate becomes civilized because the controversies can be waged against the background of a fundamental consensus on which the opponents are in agreement. This promotes the waiver of violence in politics. The minority need not fear for their lives and can continue to pursue their own ends. At the same time, ongoing politics is relieved of having constantly to find principles and choose procedures, which would overtax it in view of the constant pressure of reaching decisions on complex matters. The content of the constitution is no longer the object, but the premise of political decisions.

Finally, the constitution organizes the political process in a chronological sense. The principles that ensure identity have the chance of remaining valid over a longer term. Greater confidence may be placed in their stability than in ongoing political decisions. Short-term adaptations to changing situations and needs are thereby facilitated. They find support in principles with long-term validity, which diminishes disillusionment. In this way, the constitution ensures continuity in change. These advantages of constitutionalism all flow from the differentiation of levels between the principles for political decisions and the decisions themselves. The constitution is a *fundamental* order for precisely this reason. To be sure, there are no binding standards for this delineation. But if constitutions are formulated in such a way as to level this difference, their function is threatened.[41]

Besides, the constitution shares those limitations to which the medium of law is generally subject. As the fundamental legal order of the state, it is not a description but the epitome of norms that the political system must uphold. It does not depict social reality but makes demands of it. The constitution thus distances itself from reality and from this it gains the ability to serve as a standard for behaviour and assessment in politics. Thus it cannot be resolved in a one-time decision as to the nature and form of the political unit or in a continuing process. Rather, as a norm it becomes independent of the decision to which it owes its political validity and provides support for the process that it assumes as a prerequisite.[42]

---

[41] Cf. Dieter Grimm, 'Wie man eine Verfassung verderben kann' in his *Die Verfassung und die Politik* (n. 38), p. 126.

[42] For the decisionistic version see Schmitt (n. 34), p. 20, for the procedural see Rudolf Smend, *Verfassung und Verfassungsrecht* (München: Duncker & Humblot, 1928), p. 78. For the normativity of the constitution see especially Konrad Hesse, *Die normative Kraft der Verfassung* (Tübingen: Mohr, 1959).

On the other hand, the constitution as the epitome of legal norms is not self-executing. It cannot guarantee its own realization. Whether and to what extent the constitution succeeds in making good on its normative ambition over time depends largely on extra-legal actions. The place where these are to be looked for is the empirical constitution. This is not replaced by the normative constitution. Nor do the two stand in parallel and remain unrelated; rather, they interact. The legal constitution is influenced by the empirical one not only at the moment of its enactment but also during its application, and the legal constitution in turn acts upon the empirical constitution. Whenever the political process leaves the constitutionally stipulated track, the empirical constitution usually emerges from behind the legal one as the cause of the failure. This is what Lassalle meant when termed the social power relationships the true constitution.[43]

Where it succeeds, on the other hand, the political process runs according to the rules of the legal constitution. This is not to say that the social power relationships that influence the empirical constitution are eliminated or neutralized. Every normative constitution is confronted with all types of power relationships. Constitutions that grant social subsystems like the economy, the media, etc. autonomy through the medium of individual freedom even permit the formation of powerful societal actors. The legal constitution, however, prevents social power from directly being implemented in applicable law or other collectively binding decisions. Rather, social power must submit to a process in which certain rules apply that were formulated under the premise that they produce results that are generally acceptable. The original constitutions in France and the United States provide examples for both success and failure.

## II. DEVELOPMENT OF THE CONSTITUTION

### 1. The Spread of Constitutionalism

As this reconstruction with regards to the originating nations of constitutionalism shows, the modern constitution was not a random product of history. This is not to say that its emergence was inevitable, but that it could not have emerged under any arbitrary conditions. It was linked to a concatenation of different prerequisites that did not exist in all times and places. Just as they were not always present in the past, there is no guarantee that they will be preserved in future. In the course of social change, they too can alter or disappear. What effect this would have on the constitution depends on whether these prerequisites are determinative for its emergence only, or also for its continued existence. The end of the constitution would be heralded only if conditions key to its existence

---

[43] Ferdinand Lassalle, *Über Verfassungswesen* (Berlin: G. Jansen, 1862), which highlights the problem of constitutional law and constitutional reality.

cease to obtain. If despite this it survives, it would only be as an obsolete form without its original meaning, or as a term for something different.

For the time being, however, the constitution is a success story. Even though the prerequisites that nurtured its breakthrough in America and France in the last quarter of the eighteenth century did not exist everywhere, it provoked uproar in the rest of Europe and gave rise to widespread constitution movements. The constitution was the great issue of the nineteenth century. Such high expectations were attached to it that innumerable people were prepared to risk their careers, their property, their freedom, and even their lives for it. The nineteenth century can be described as the century of constitutional struggle. Revolutions determine its periodization. Multiple waves of revolution churned through numerous European countries at the same time, and only a few countries, above all Britain, remained entirely unmarked by constitutional struggles. When the long nineteenth century ended with the First World War, constitutionalism had prevailed virtually throughout Europe and in many parts of the world subject to European influence.[44]

The twentieth century, which began with such constitutional promise, brought grave setbacks over its course through the rise of dictatorships of various descriptions. But at the end of the century, the constitutional state was more unchallenged than ever. Fascist dictatorships, military dictatorships, and finally the apartheid regime and socialist party dictatorships fell almost without exception, often through military defeats, sometimes through revolutions, in many cases through implosions. Even though the struggle was not being fought explicitly for the constitution, as was the case in the nineteenth century, new or renewed constitutions were the invariable outcome.[45] The setbacks and experiences with ineffective or marginally effective constitutions also heightened awareness of the need to have its own means of assertion. This led to constitutional jurisdiction being propagated universally in the second half of the twentieth century, after its modest beginnings following the First World War.[46]

This generalized overview shows that the constitution, after coming into being as the product of two successful revolutions, no longer depends on revolution in each case of emulation. The German constitutional development in the nineteenth century confirms this view. Although several constitutions in individual German states were preceded by revolutions, none of these were successful in the sense of resulting in a break with the existing rule. Constitutions only came into being when the traditional ruler, for whatever motive, agreed

---

[44] For an overview for Europe, see Dieter Grimm, 'Die verfassungsrechtlichen Grundlagen der Privatrechtsgesetzgebung' in Helmut Coing (ed.), *Handbuch der Quellen und Literatur der neueren europäischen Privatrechtsgeschichte*, vol. III/1 (München: Beck, 1982), pp. 17–173.

[45] Cf. Douglas Greenberg (ed.), *Constitutionalism and Democracy: Transitions in the Contemporary World* (New York: Oxford University Press, 1993); Peter Häberle, *Rechtsvergleichung im Kraftfeld des Verfassungsstaates* (Berlin: Duncker & Humblot, 1992).

[46] Cf. Neal Tate and Torbjörn Vallinder (eds), *The Global Expansion of Judicial Power* (New York: New York University Press, 1995).

to restrictions on his power.[47] The first pan-German constitution, the Imperial Constitution of 1871, lacks all revolutionary background. It was the result of the agreement by treaty of sovereign princes to found a new state which had to be given a form.

Nonetheless, major discontinuities remain the most frequent reason for creating constitutions.[48] In many cases, though, it is not triumphant revolution but catastrophic collapse that impels constitution. This is also true for the German constitutions of the twentieth century; the Weimar Constitution, the Basic Law, and the constitution of the German Democratic Republic (GDR). After the collapse of the Socialist Unity Party of Germany (SED) regime, the GDR set out on the path towards creating a constitution before such efforts were rendered moot by the resolution to reunify under the umbrella of the Basic Law. Constitutional renewals without such breaks, such as in Switzerland in 2000, are exceptions. Here, the attempt did not succeed until the revolutionary-sounding-term 'new creation' was abandoned and replaced with the term 'revision' ('*Nachführung*'), which implied continuity.[49]

Once the constitution had been invented and developed its popularity, it also became possible to copy the form without having to adopt the meaning. Form and function became separable. France itself provided the first example under Napoleon. Although considering repeal of the constitution to be awkward, he was not prepared to bind himself to it. Many of the constitutions that subsequently followed the American and French prototypes were pseudo- or semi-constitutions. The German constitutions granted by rulers in the nineteenth century fell short of the constitutional project as it had taken shape in the American and French Revolutions.[50] The same applies for many constitutions in today's world. The label 'success story', however, is still justified, because even those who would prefer to rule without constraint wrap themselves in at least the appearance of constitutionality so as to exploit the gain in legitimacy that a constitution promises.

The existence of pseudo- or semi-constitutions gives rise to terminological difficulties. What deserves to be called a 'constitution', and what does not? There is no generally valid answer to this question, which can only be answered by looking at what one wishes to learn. If the aim is to compare constitutions so as to identify differences and form classifications, or to study constitutional history, national or comparative, it is not helpful to prematurely narrow the object

---

[47] Cf. Grimm (n. 2), pp. 43, 142.

[48] Bruce Ackerman, *The Future of Liberal Revolution* (New Haven: Yale University Press, 1992). See particularly the term 'constitutional moments', which also established itself in Germany. In Ackerman, 'The Rise of World Constitutionalism' (1997) 83 *Virginia Law Review* 775, the terms 'new beginning scenario' in contrast to 'federalism scenario' are mentioned. Cf. also Ulrich K. Preuß, *Revolution, Fortschritt und Verfassung: zu einem neuen Verfassungsverständnis* (Frankfurt am Main: Fischer-Taschenbuch-Verlag, extended new edition, 1994).

[49] Cf., for the history of the revision attempts, René Rhinow, *Die Bundesverfassung 2000: eine Einführung* (Basel: Helbing und Lichtenhahn, 2000), p. 1.

[50] Cf. Grimm (n. 2), p. 110; Ernst-Wolfgang Böckenförde, 'Der deutsche Typ der konstitutionellen Monarchie im 19. Jahrhundert' in his *Recht, Staat, Freiheit* (Frankfurt am Main: Suhrkamp, 1991), p. 273.

of study. If, on the other hand, the aim is to study the outlook for success of constitutionalism in the various regions of the globe and its chances of survival in the twenty-first century, including its capability of being transferred to supra-national units, it is worthwhile adhering to a *demanding concept of constitution*,[51] as is delineated in the history of the development of modern constitutionalism, so as not to prematurely take the name for the substance.

In view of how the content of a constitution can vary, the functional concept deserves to be emphasized above the material concept. The following internally interrelated features derive from the arguments of the first part:

1. The constitution must lay claim to being normatively valid. Constitutional texts without a willingness to make them legally binding do not meet this criterion.
2. The legal constraint must relate to the establishment and exercise of political rule. It is not sufficient to constrain subordinate instances while the highest remain free.
3. The legal constraint must be comprehensive in the sense that extraconstitutional forces cannot exercise rule, nor can binding decisions issue from extra-constitutional processes.
4. The constitutional constraints must act to the benefit of all persons subject to rule, and not only privileged groups.
5. The constitution must form the basis for the legitimation of political rule. A basis of legitimacy existing outside the constitution is not permissible.
6. The legitimacy to rule must derive from the people subject to rule. Legitimation through truth instead of consensus undermines the constitution.
7. The constitution must have priority over the exercises of ruling power. A constitution at the disposition of the ordinary legislature is not sufficient.

The following discusses the question as to whether constitutions which claim to meet these criteria remain able to fulfil this claim in view of altered conditions for realization. The alterations referred to here are large-scale tendencies that affect constitutionalism itself, and not just individual constitutions or individual constitutional norms. Among these are first the transition from the liberal state to the welfare state, which impinges above all on the limiting function of the constitution. These also include the emergence of new actors, instruments, and processes not taken into account by the original constitutions, which blur the boundary between public and private that is constitutive for the constitution. Finally, there is the process of internationalization and globalization, whose corollary is denationalization, which also obliterates the constitutionally fundamental boundary between internal and external.

---

[51] Cf. Brun-Otto Bryde, *Verfassungsentwicklung: Stabilität und Dynamik im Verfassungsrecht der Bundesrepublik Deutschland* (Baden-Baden: Nomos, 1982), p. 33.

## 2. The Constitution in the Welfare State

The term 'welfare state' stands for a number of complexes that differ according to time and place whose common denominator is that they represent a response to the deficits of liberalism that are generally characterized as failures of the market. This affects the constitution insofar as it was the expectations placed on the market that created the need for limitation of the state which was then satisfied by the constitution. By contrast, the social problems that arise as a consequence of market failure could not be resolved by limiting the state. On the contrary, the re-materialization of the question of justice demanded state activism. If the aim of a just social order was to be upheld, the state could no longer restrict itself to the guarantee function defined in the constitution; it needed once more to actively create an order.

The responses to this were varied. In part, liberalism petrified dogmatically. In opposition to the intention, limitation of the state through fundamental rights were not viewed as means for achieving prosperity and justice but were elevated to an end in themselves, and the liberal understanding of freedom including its constitutional equivalent: the purely state-deterrent function of fundamental rights was defended without consideration of social consequences. The French July Monarchy provides the best example for this attitude: it was able to prevail because the political participation rights had been limited to a small circle of extremely wealthy individuals in the constitution of 1830. The revolution of 1848, which in Germany was still mainly a revolution in favour of establishing a constitutional state and making protection of fundamental rights effective,[52] thus bore primarily social characteristics in France.

The opposing reaction consisted of the radical rejection of liberalism that manifested itself in the socialist and fascist states in the latter half of the twentieth century. As much as these two directions differed in their substance, they differed hardly at all with respect to their consequences for constitutionalism. Both legitimated political rule not through consensus, but through 'truth'. Individual freedom could not stand before it. Instead, an elite that claimed the knowledge of truth as their own derived from this the right to assert it using the power of the state without consideration of differing convictions. The basis for the constitution as a means of legitimation and limitation of power was thus eliminated and the mechanisms that served to fulfil these functions became nuisances.

Still, the great majority of these states also had constitutions. Fascist states usually allowed the old constitutions to stand, but they suspended important parts or replaced them with other provisions. In socialist states, new constitutions were usually created which in their form resembled those of constitutional nations but these could not fulfil the key functions of constitutionalism.[53]

---

[52] Cf. Dieter Grimm, 'Grundrechtliche Freiheit 1848 und heute' in his *Die Verfassung und die Politik* (n. 41), p. 91.

[53] Cf. Giuseppe de Vergottini, *Diritto costituzionale comparato* (Padova: CEDAM, 2nd edn, 1987), pp. 576, 791. In particular for Germany cf. Heinrich Herrfahrdt, *Die Verfassungsgesetze des nationalsozialistischen Staates dem Text der Weimarer Verfassung gegenübergestellt* (Marburg: Elwert, 1935); Ernst Rudolf Huber,

Since law was not autonomous but had only an instrumental role in view of the legitimation deriving from truth, these constitutions did not limit the ruling power. Insofar as they contained passages limiting rule, these were not accorded priority. Where they adopted the model of separation of powers, this was subverted by unity parties with authority to act on the state apparatus. In this way, the claim to truth resulted in a form of neoabsolutism that was much more radical than the monarchical absolutism of the sixteenth to nineteenth centuries.

The third type of response was to open the constitution to social issues. Before it came to this, however, extensive social legislation had developed below the constitution, which, particularly in Germany, climaxed with the introduction of social security insurance.[54] Although this represented a break with the liberal social model, which was determinative of the emergence of constitutionalism, no obstacles arose from the constitution. This was due not only to the lack of a catalogue of fundamental rights in the Imperial Constitution of 1871. The concept of fundamental rights prevailing in the German Empire would not have permitted recourse to fundamental rights because they had been deemed not applicable to the legislature.[55] Also, there would have been no institution available that could have kept the legislature within the bounds of the fundamental rights. Thus, characteristically, social legislation became a constitutional problem only in the United States: the nation that had from the beginning secured the primacy of the constitution institutionally as well as through judicial review.[56]

Before a solution by means of constitutional interpretation was arrived at there, the idea of the social state had already been adopted in constitutional provisions in Europe.[57] In the Weimar Constitution of 1919, the new legitimation principle of popular sovereignty was joined with an equally new social provision. Although the Weimar National Assembly retained the catalogue of classical rights of freedom and equality that had taken shape in the revolutions, it added to this a considerable number of fundamental social rights and subordinated economic freedom to the principle of social justice. However, as constitutional theory continued to deny that fundamental rights applied to the legislature,[58] their significance was reduced to requiring that the administration

*Verfassungsrecht des Großdeutschen Reichs* (Hamburg: Hanseatische Verlags-Anstalt, 1939); Uwe Bachnick, *Die Verfassungsreformvorstellungen im nationalsozialistischen Deutschen Reich und ihre Verwirklichung* (Berlin: Duncker & Humblot, 1995).

[54] Cf. Michael Stolleis, 'Die Entstehung des Interventionsstaates und das öffentliche Recht' in his *Konstitution und Intervention* (Frankfurt am Main: Suhrkamp, 2001), p. 253.

[55] Cf. Dieter Grimm, 'Die Entwicklung der Grundrechtstheorie in der deutschen Staatsrechtslehre des 19. Jahrhunderts' in his *Recht und Staat* (n. 26), p. 333.

[56] Cf. Currie (n. 27), pp. 136, 208; Cass Sunstein, 'Constitutionalism after the New Deal' (1987) 101 *Harvard Law Review* 421.

[57] Cf. Dieter Grimm, 'Die sozialgeschichtliche und verfassungsrechtliche Entwicklung zum Sozialstaat' in his *Recht und Staat* (n. 26), p. 153.

[58] Cf. Christoph Gusy, 'Die Grundrechte in der Weimarer Republik' (1993) *Zeitschrift für neuere Rechtsgeschichte* 163.

have a legal basis for infringing on fundamental rights. Under these circumstances, fundamental social rights, which were all designed to be mediated by law, entirely lost their normative force. They were regarded as nothing more than points in a political programme.

The Basic Law removed the basis for this interpretation in Art. 1(3), but rather than enumerating social and economic rights, it professed a general avowal of the social state. However, for the German Federal Constitutional Court this serves as the foundation for a socially enriched understanding of the liberal fundamental rights.[59] Building on the assumption that equal individual freedom is the goal of fundamental rights and limitation of the state is merely a means, this has today culminated in the concept of the protective duty that the state has with respect to all dangers to freedoms guaranteed by fundamental rights that cannot be assigned to the state itself but which obtain as a consequence of the acts of private parties or social developments. These protective duties derived from the classical fundamental rights, just like their equivalents in the form of post-liberal fundamental rights or state objectives, are an attempt to adapt the constitution to problems that were not yet identifiable at the time it was enacted or were created by the constitution itself.[60]

The importance of this adaptation of the constitution to altered conditions becomes particularly clear when one considers that today, at least in economically developed nations, the social question of the nineteenth century no longer represents the greatest challenge for constitutionalism. Rather, a demand for security has emerged which is determined in particular by the dangers entailed in scientific and technical progress and its commercial exploitation. It is in this area that the duty to protect is most often applied.[61] A general protection against risk is expected from the state that goes far beyond the traditional state task of protection against imminent threats, which was generally acknowledged also under liberalism. The state responds to this by placing greater priority on prevention, which remains related to recognized legally protected interests but is divorced from impending violation. It focuses instead on recognizing and sealing off sources of danger before a concrete danger can emerge.[62]

This adaptation of the constitution to the altered realization conditions of individual freedom is not without cost to its normative power. It pays a price in both its limiting effect and its degree of certainty. Obligations to protect fundamental rights demand that the state act in the interests of freedom. By definition, this action focuses on threats to freedom that originate from society

[59] Cf. Ernst-Wolfgang Böckenförde, 'Grundrechtstheorie und Grundrechtsinterpretation' in his *Staat, Verfassung, Demokratie* (n. 23), p. 115; Konrad Hesse, 'Bedeutung der Grundrechte' in Ernst Benda et al (eds), *Handbuch des Verfassungsrechts der Bundesrepublik Deutschland* (Berlin: De Gruyter, 2nd edn, 1994), p. 139.

[60] Cf. Ch. 8 of this volume; Johannes Dietlein, *Die Lehre von den grundrechtlichen Schutzpflichten* (Berlin: Duncker & Humblot, 1992).

[61] Cf. Rudolf Steinberg, *Der ökologische Verfassungsstaat* (Frankfurt am Main: Suhrkamp, 1998); Georg Hermes, *Das Grundrecht auf Schutz von Leben und Gesundheit* (Heidelberg: C.F. Müller, 1987).

[62] Cf. Erhard Denninger, 'Der Präventionsstaat' (1988) 21 *Kritische Justiz* 1.

rather than the state itself. As a result protective duties in favour of specific fundamental rights are generally fulfilled by limiting other fundamental rights. This results in a considerable increase in the number of encroachments on fundamental rights and, since their root lies in conflicts of fundamental rights of equal priority, the only solution is to balance these in the light of specific circumstances, which is always associated with a loss of certainty.

The duty to protect fundamental rights does not only lower the limits for legislative action. It also raises them insofar as the legislature may no longer remain passive vis-à-vis certain problems. However, that does not obviate the question as to whether the increased state activity itself can once again be regulated by constitutional law. The answer to this was an expansion of the reservation of statutory powers, through the extension of the concept of intervention that controls the reservation of statutory powers as well as also extending it to all significant decisions in the non-intervention area. The central role of laws enacted by parliament for the functioning of the constitutional system is expressed here. Democracy and the rule of law depend on it. The effect of the reservation of statutory powers is that the state's action programme emerges from a democratic process of opinion and will formation. The principle of administrative legality subordinates the state's executive branch to democratically formulated will and renders the behaviour of the state predictable for the citizens. Finally, it enables the courts to test the legality of state actions and correct illegal acts.

However, the welfare-related tasks of the state are much less amendable to control than its regulatory tasks. Though this does not apply for quantifiable social benefits that are linked to specifiable prerequisites, it certainly does for active state tasks. The reason is that unlike preservation or restoration of order, these tasks are of a prospective nature. They do not only affect individual perpetrators but generate a large pool of affected individuals and do not only depend on the availability of resources but on numerous factors over which the state has limited or no influence. The laws that regulate these activities must therefore often restrict themselves to setting a goal for state administration and otherwise enumerating aspects that should be considered or must be ignored in pursuing these goals.[63]

The weakness of legal control is particularly apparent in preventative state activity. As the possible sources of harm are much more numerous, varied, and obscure than the actual harm, the prevention state develops a great demand for information. Unlike the prosecution of an actual deed or prevention of a manifest danger, this can no longer be limited according to the deed or the event causing harm. The only factor that can be specified is what risks are considered so great as to justify state observation and gathering of information even when these affect persons who offer no grounds for this on a large scale. In this sphere, the activity of the state expands in time as well as physical scope and is

---

[63]   See Niklas Luhmann, *Zweckbegriff und Systemrationalität* (Frankfurt am Main: Suhrkamp, 1973), p. 257.

decoupled from reasonable grounds for suspicion. Legal control of this diverse activity is virtually impossible. Legal regulation gets a chance only with regards to the use of revealed information.

One should not be deceived by energetic legislative activity on the part of the parliament. Not only are most bills drafted by the executive branch, but the enacted texts often have only a weak controlling force on the administration. Although the constitutional principle of legality of state action still applies, the binding content of laws is lean. The graceful structure of the rule of law thereby becomes fragile.[64] To the extent that legal control of the administration falls away, the administration is forced to control itself. Where it controls itself without being constrained by statute, the courts cannot review whether the administration has adhered to the law. Although the fundamental rights have also responded to this gap by requiring that the loss of material binding forces be compensated by procedural structuring, it would be mistaken to expect procedural law to serve as a fully fledged replacement for material law.[65]

## 3. The Constitution in the Cooperative Party State

The legally binding character of the constitution concerns the power of the state. Private persons are not the objects, but rather the beneficiaries of its provisions. To this extent, the constitution is based on the delineation between the state and the private sphere. Actors or forms of action that do not conform to this division pose problems for the constitution. This first became apparent with political parties.[66] Unlike organs of the state, these were not created by the constitution; they are free social associations, which nevertheless aim to gain influence within the state. Although not anticipated when the constitution was conceived, parties emerged as a necessary consequence of fundamental constitutional decisions, particularly the pluralization of the common good rooted in the freedom of the individual and the equal participation in the formation of the will of the state through the election of representative bodies. Consequently, political parties are not illegitimate, even where they are not recognized in the constitution.

Though parties have little need of constitutional recognition, their existence has a considerable impact on the constitution. To be sure, the constitution predates parties. However, its institutions, bodies, and processes have changed with

---

[64] Cf. Helge Rossen-Stadtfeld, *Vollzug und Verhandlung* (Tübingen: Mohr Siebeck, 1999); Horst Dreier, *Hierarchische Verwaltung im demokratischen Staat* (Tübingen: Mohr, 1991); Rainer Pitschas, *Verwaltungsverantwortung und Verwaltungsverfahren* (München: Beck, 1990); Dieter Grimm (ed.), *Wachsende Staatsaufgaben – sinkende Steuerungsfähigkeit des Rechts* (Baden-Baden: Nomos, 1990).

[65] Cf. Karl-Heinz Ladeur, *Negative Freiheitsrechte und gesellschaftliche Selbstorganisation* (Tübingen: Mohr Siebeck, 2000); Karl-Heinz Ladeur, *Postmoderne Rechtstheorie: Selbstreferenz – Selbstorganisation – Prozeduralisierung* (Berlin: Duncker & Humblot, 2nd edn, 1995); Oliver Lepsius, *Steuerungsdiskussion, Systemtheorie und Parlamentarismuskritik* (Tübingen: Mohr Siebeck, 1999); Helmut Willke, *Ironie des Staates* (Frankfurt am Main: Suhrkamp, 1992).

[66] Cf. Dieter Grimm, 'Die politischen Parteien', in *Benda* (n. 59), p. 599.

the emergence of parties, without this always becoming apparent in the letter of the constitution. The reason is that their activities are not limited to preparing for elections in the social sphere. Rather, they also dominate political operations after the election. This does not mean that they displace the constitutionally mandated state bodies and processes, but certainly the membership of such bodies is appointed by the parties and the content of the processes determined by them. In formal terms, the political process operates within the constitutionally mandated boundaries, but in material terms it is transferred to the preceding party operations.

This has often been analysed in connection with the evolution of parliamentarism.[67] The election today concerns less persons than parties on which the individual deputies depend more and more. In a parliament structured along political-party lines, deliberation, and decision, which in the original idea belonged together, become separated. Parties establish their positions internally prior to plenary debate. The latter is no longer conducted with the intent to convince or persuade, but only to present the various party positions to the public. That is why it can be conducted by few speakers before empty benches. It has no influence on the decision. Although under the constitution the representatives are free, they are in fact compelled to toe the party line. Only the opposition maintains an interest in serious oversight of the government.

The principle of separation of powers as the central constitutional mechanism for preventing the abuse of power is also affected. Since democratic legitimation demands that all holders of public power be subject to election, but the election takes place between parties and the elected bodies are legitimately composed of party representatives, it is ultimately always the parties that select the individuals to fill state or state-controlled positions. As the input structure for the apparatus of the state, they are 'upstream' of its internal organization, and thus qualify it. In all cases, political parties are visible behind the separated powers. But this cannot be regarded simply as misconduct, even though it contradicts the original intention. Rather, precisely because of their democratically indispensable mediating function, parties cannot be firmly attributed to either side of the system boundary between the state and society. To a certain extent they escape the constitution constructed to reflect just this distinction.

One must not conclude from this that the constitution has failed in the face of political parties. However, in many respects it can assert its claim to comprehensively regulate the exercise of public power only indirectly or to a lesser extent. Although the free mandate guarantee does not prevent party discipline, it secures those representatives who do not wish to obey it a temporarily unassailable position, thus creating the prerequisites for party-internal plurality and discussion. Nor can the formation of political will within parties be entirely disconnected from the processes provided in the constitution. As their result must pass through parliamentary processes if they are to become generally binding,

---

[67] Cf. Carl Schmitt, *Die geistesgeschichtliche Lage des heutigen Parlamentarismus* (München: Duncker & Humblot, 1923).

intra-party consultation must also relate to this process. Internal party discussions cannot be conducted without regard to criticism from the opposition or reaction from the public. Since these must be anticipated, opponents and the public are in a sense virtually present. Minority rights subsequently adopted in the constitution compensate at least in part for the majority's lack of willingness to exercise oversight.

As the constitution cannot prevent breaches in the system of separated powers on the level of persons, the line of defence shifts to the functional level. There, constitutional means can be used to at least establish parameters to help ensure that, despite the dominance of parties in the choice of persons, the functionaries chosen in this process may not behave in a manner which places their party loyalties above the objective logic of the respective remits. The constitution achieves this primarily through the protection of a party-neutral civil service, the binding legal obligations on the administration, and the independence of the judiciary. These make party-political coercion of the holders of public office and utilization of the chain of directive authority for party purposes illegal.[68] In this way, the constitution endows those who wish to act appropriately in their role and resist any pressure with a strong legal position. The preservation of distance from political parties does not then depend on a particular moral effort of individuals; it is institutionally guaranteed by the system.

The boundary between the state and private spheres, which is constitutive for constitutionalism, is further undermined by the fact that the state is increasingly dependent on the cooperation of private entities to meet its welfare-related tasks.[69] Shaping social order and securing the future are largely beyond the specific government methods of command and compulsion. In some cases, the use of imperative means is de facto impossible because the objects of regulation are not subject to decree. Research results, economic growth, or shifts in mentalities cannot simply be mandated. In some cases this is legally impermissible because basic rights secure the decision-making freedom of social actors. The constitution would not sanction investment requirements, obligations to employ individuals or compulsory consumption. In some cases, this may be possible and permissible but not opportune, because the state lacks the information needed for formulating effective imperative programmes or because the costs of implementing imperative law are too high.

In these areas the state has long since gone over to applying indirect means of motivation, incentives and deterrents (usually financial in nature) that are intended to prompt actors to voluntarily comply with those requirements of general welfare identified by the state. In doing so, the state abandons the position of rule granted to it in the interests of the general welfare, and puts itself

---

[68] Cf. Dieter Grimm, 'Politische Parteien' in *Benda* (n. 66), p. 636; Dieter Grimm, 'Nach der Spendenaffäre: Die Aussichten, den Parteienstaat rechtlich einzugrenzen' in his *Die Verfassung und die Politik* (n. 38), p. 158; Luhmann, *Die Politik der Gesellschaft* (n. 3), p. 253; Luhmann, *Das Recht der Gesellschaft* (n. 20), p. 468, emphasizing that the decisive line of separation of powers runs between politics on the one hand and administration and judiciary on the other.

[69] Cf. Dieter Grimm, 'Verbände' in *Benda* (n. 66), p. 657.

on the same level as private actors. To this extent, it makes the realization of public ends dependent on private acquiescence. This grants private actors a veto power with respect to the state, which significantly increases their chances of asserting their own interests over those of the general welfare. Generally, this veto power is not expressed through refusal, but through a willingness to cooperate which of course the state must repay through concessions of its own in the guidance programme.

The state has responded to the new situation by creating negotiating systems in which public and private interests can be reconciled. In this situation, the process of state decision-making with respect to the needs of the general welfare is sometimes followed by negotiations with private parties causing the general problem on the extent to which the objective can be attained without requiring an excess of money or consensus-building. But sometimes the state also limits itself to defining a problem that requires a solution in the interests of the general welfare but then leaves the solution to a negotiation process. This leads either to agreements between state and private actors about the content of a statute or to the state waiving regulation in return for private promises of good behaviour.[70] The law then functions solely as a threat to increase the willingness to make concessions. The advantage for the private side is less stringent requirements, whereas the state receives information relevant for guidance or saves the implementation costs.

Although agreements of this type remain informal in nature, they can only achieve the desired effect when both sides feel bound by them. Particularly on account of this bond, this approach can no longer be understood in categories of influence, but only in categories of participation. However, this undermines key rationality standards that the constitution implemented in the interests of legitimacy of rule.[71] For one thing, private actors now exist that are no longer limited to general citizen status as voters, participants in public discourse, and representatives of their own interests, but participate directly in the state decision-making process without being subject to the democratic legitimation and responsibility matrix that applies for every holder of public power. For another, the decision-making instances and processes defined in the constitution are debased to the extent that the state detours into negotiation systems.

The central legislative instance, the parliament, is most affected. It is not involved in the negotiations. On the state side, these are always conducted by the executive branch. If the negotiations result in draft legislation, only a parliamentary resolution can enact it as valid law; however, the parliament is in a ratification situation similar to the ratification of an international treaty. It can only either accept or reject the negotiation result; it cannot modify this. Unlike international treaties, however, parliament's scope for action is limited in fact, but not in law. This restriction does not appear any less imperative, however,

---

[70] Cf. Arthur Benz, *Kooperative Verwaltung* (Baden-Baden: Nomos, 1994).

[71] Cf. Ernst-Wolfgang Böckenförde, 'Die politische Funktion wirtschaftlich-sozialer Verbände und Interessenträger in der sozial-staatlichen Demokratie' in his *Staat, Verfassung, Demokratie* (n. 59), p. 406.

because every attempted modification would put the overall result at risk. If a waiver of regulation is negotiated, parliament plays no role at all. It is true that a waiver of regulation by the government cannot prevent the parliament from taking legislative action on its own initiative but if it succeeds the majority would have to disavow the government that it supports, and this is highly unlikely.

The marginalization of parliament also means the loss of all those advantages that the parliamentary stage of the legislative process confers. Above all, this means public debate, in which the necessity, ends and means of a proposal, is justified and subjected to criticism, and which enables the public to adopt a position and influence the process. This is particularly important for those groups whose opinions are not solicited in the preparatory phase. By contrast, if negotiations result in draft legislation that must undergo a parliamentary process, parliamentary debate can certainly take place, but it lacks the force needed to link the social with the state discourse. Because the negotiating result is fixed, debate no longer provides a forum that permits the public to serve effective notice on neglected interests or to assert other opinions.

These weaknesses persist in the content of the law or its informal substrate, the voluntary commitment of private actors. It will generally not attain the level of acceptance that engenders legitimacy. After all, negotiations are not conducted with all affected parties, but only those with veto powers. Their interests, which have their basis not only in their strength as accumulated in the pre-state phase, but in the procedure provided by the state, are more likely to be taken into consideration. This rewards those social power positions which constitutional regulation wanted to neutralize with respect to law-giving. In reality, privileges emerge where the constitution mandates strict equality. To the same extent, the importance of elections declines, because they are no longer the only means of distributing political weights in the law-making process. Ultimately, judicial protection also fails if the object of judicial review and the standard for administrative review are lacking.

In spite of the democratic and due-process attrition which the constitution suffers through the practice of negotiation, summarily prohibiting it would probably have little impact, as it has structural causes that are largely immune to constitutional prohibitions. On the other hand, it creates broad gaps in the constitutional rationality of legislative action. These are due less to a lack of willingness to adhere to a constitution than to growing structural obstacles for the implementation of a more demanding constitutional model. Even if the negotiating arrangements were constitutionalized,[72] this would in no way eliminate their unique character, which is above all their informality. Rather, one

---

[72] For suggestions, see Winfried Brohm, 'Rechtsgrundsätze für normersetzende Absprachen' (1992) *Die Öffentliche Verwaltung* 1025; Matthias Herdegen and Martin Morlok, 'Informalisierung und Entparlamentarisierung politischer Entscheidungen als Gefährdung der Verfassung?' in (2003) 62 *Veröffentlichungen der Vereinigung der Deutschen Staatsrechtslehrer* 7 and 37.

must get used to the fact that the constitution can fulfil its normative intent to only a limited extent, without the prospect of any compensation for the losses.

### 4. *Constitutionalization Beyond the State*

The constitution emerged as the constitution of a state. Its purpose was to juridify public power, which at the time of its emergence and long after was synonymous with state power. Although every state was surrounded by other states, the borders between the states acquired their significance as the boundaries of state power. The border could change, usually as a result of wars, and this changed the area to which state power applied. In the extreme case of annexation, a new state power replaced the old. None of this in any way altered the fact that only one state power existed in the territory of any state and this state power did not need to share its ruling authority with anyone. Above this level, the relations between states were regulated by international law. But there was no supranational public power able to assert this against the states.

The identity of public and state power was the prerequisite that enabled the constitution to fulfil its claim to comprehensively juridify political rule. In this sense, the boundary between the interior and exterior is constitutive for the constitution.[73] This boundary has not disappeared; it retains its traditional significance in relationships between states: state power is limited to the territory of the state and cannot be extended to the territory of another state without the latter's consent. But political organizations have emerged on the level above the states which, although they owe their existence to international treaties, are not restricted in their actions to the inter-state sphere. They act on the internal affairs of the states and in some cases exercise public power with claims to direct validity within the states although they cannot be seen as a union of different states to form a super-state, which would shift, but not relativize, the boundary between the interior and the exterior.

The most advanced example of this is the European Union. Member states have assigned to it a number of sovereign rights, including rights to enact legislation, which are exercised by the Union in its own legal system, apply directly in the member states, and take precedence over national law. Although EU law cannot be enacted without the approval of member states, which in this process are subject to the requirements of their own national constitutions, the integrity of national constitutions is preserved only for so long as the principle of unanimity applies whose scope has, however, been continuously circumscribed. By contrast, the Union possesses no means of compulsion and must depend on member states for enforcing community law and its applying acts. To date, the transfer of sovereign rights has not extended to the monopoly of power. Although the Union can define objectives insofar as its regulatory competence

---

[73] For the importance of national borders, see Udo Di Fabio, *Der Verfassungsstaat in der Weltgesellschaft* (Tübingen: Mohr Siebeck, 2001), p. 51.

permits this, the actual exercise and the modalities to be observed remain the responsibility of the member states.[74]

To date, no organization similar to the European Union exists in any other region, nor on an international scale. But the World Trade Organization (WTO) also contributes to a relativization of the boundary between the interior and exterior. It has no legislative competence of its own, being only a forum for treaty negotiations of the member states, and to that extent it does not exceed the framework of international law. But owing to the conflict resolution mechanism created in 1995, which employs court-like methods, the law created by treaty is becoming autonomous.[75] Other globally active organizations, such as the World Bank and the International Monetary Fund, lack such authority and they derive their effectiveness primarily from the fact that they can make financial assistance contingent on conditions, which countries theoretically but not practically could refuse.[76]

Meanwhile, the institutions founded by states are confronted with a variety of globally active private actors, primarily enterprises but also non-governmental organizations, which, due to their global sphere of action, can largely follow their own systemic logic without having to observe the standards and obligations that apply within states. Nevertheless actors in the global sector of the economy cannot dispense with legal regulations. They are dependent on transnational law, which, logically, no national law-giver can provide. In the absence of a global legislator, these actors have taken the formation of law into their own hands. Global markets are creating legal regulations independently of the political sphere. In this way, forms of law formation are emerging outside of nation states and the international organizations they have established and which states and organizations can no longer influence.[77]

These developments are not directed specifically against the constitution. For example, the German Basic Law contains an opening clause in Art. 24, making the border of the state permeable to foreign public powers. For the European Union, this was supplemented in 1990 by Art. 23 (1). Still, this is not without effects on the constitution as a whole.[78] For one thing, in spite of its claim to

---

[74] See Joseph H. H. Weiler, *The Constitution of Europe* (Cambridge: Cambridge University Press, 1999), p 188 et seq; for the interaction of the European Court of Justice and national courts see Anne-Marie Slaughter, Alec Stone Sweet, and J. H. H. Weiler (eds), *The European Court and National Courts: Doctrine and Jurisprudence* (Oxford: Oxford University Press, 1998).

[75] See Armin v. Bogdandy, 'Verfassungsrechtliche Dimensionen der Welthandelsorganisation' (2001) 34 *Kritische Justiz* 264, 425; Markus Krajewski, *Verfassungsperspektiven und Legitimation des Rechts der Welthandelsorganisation* (Berlin: Duncker & Humblot, 2001).

[76] Cf. Jerzy Kranz, *Entre l'influence et l'intervention: Certains aspects juridiques de l'assistance financière multilatérale* (Frankfurt am Main: Lang, 1994); Ibrahim Shihata, *The World Bank in a Changing World*, 2 vols (Dordrecht: Nijhoff, 1991, 1995).

[77] Cf. Gunther Teubner, *Global Law Without a State* (Aldershot: Dartmouth, 1997); Yves Dezalay and Bryant G. Garth, *Dealing in Virtue: International Commercial Arbitration and the Construction of a Transnational Legal Order* (Chicago: University of Chicago Press, 1998); Boaventura de Sousa Santos, *Toward a New Common Sense* (New York: Routledge, 1995).

[78] See Udo Di Fabio, *Das Recht offener Staaten: Grundlinien einer Staats- und Rechtstheorie* (Tübingen: Mohr Siebeck, 1998); Di Fabio, *Verfassungsstaat* (n. 73); Rainer Wahl, 'Internationalisierung des Staates' in Joachim

comprehensive applicability, it only partly regulates public power within its area of application, namely only insofar as this is state power. For another, not all law that is valid within the territory of a state derives from the national source of law regulated in the constitution. Not only do independent possessors of sovereignty rights compete in one and the same territory, but the law applicable there is also pluralized, making the constitution unable to unify the legal order derived from disparate sources.

However, the constitution can come under pressure even where no external law is superimposed on it. This is particularly apparent in countries that are dependent on the aid of the World Bank or the International Monetary Fund for their stability. Although intervention in the political affairs of the countries is forbidden, reforms to the legal and justice systems are not considered political. Rather, the granting of loans is to a great extent made contingent on legal and even constitutional changes in the affected countries.[79] By themselves, these conditions may be justified. Still, one should not be under any illusion that, to the extent that these countries feel compelled to comply with these conditions, their own constitutional requirements for political decision-making are displaced, assuming that a constitution worthy of the name already exists. Economic strength is thus purchased at the expense of a constitutional weakening. Even the constitutions of stable industrial nations cannot always fully withstand the pressure of globalization.

This begs the question as to how the achievements of constitutionalism can be preserved in the face of this development. On the national level, the possibilities appear slight. A provision such as Art. 23 (1) of the German Basic Law formulates conditions for participation in the further integration of Europe. These essentially stipulate that the fundamental constitutional principles of the German Constitution must be ensured on the European level. Additionally, national constitutions can take precautions to ensure that the constitutional requirements for law-making applicable domestically are observed in determining the national negotiating position in the supranational law-making process. This is important because supranational law-making is usually governmental law-making, and as such not covered by the mechanisms for securing democracy in that area within national constitutions. The Basic Law contains such precautions with respect to the European Union in Art. 23 (2)–(7) with respect to the active participation of the *Länder* and in Art. 45 with respect to the active participation of parliament.

---

Bohnert (ed.), *Verfassung – Philosophie – Kirche. Festschrift für Alexander Hollerbach* (Berlin: Duncker & Humblot, 2001), p. 193; Volkmar Gessner and Ali Cem Budak (eds), *Emerging Legal Certainty: Empirical Studies on the Globalisation of Law* (Aldershot: Ashgate, 1998).

[79] See Kranz, *Intervention* (n. 76), p. 218; Shihata, *World Bank*, above n. 76; Ibrahim Shihata, *The World Bank Legal Papers* (The Hague: Nijhoff, 2000); Anne Orford, 'Locating the International: Military and Monetary Interventions After the Cold War' (1997) 38 *Harvard International Law Journal* 443; Paul Mosley, Jane Harrigan, and John Toye, *Aid and Power: The World Bank and Policy Based Lending* (London: Routledge, 2nd edn, 1995); Jonathan Cahn, 'Challenging the New Imperial Authority' (1993) 6 *Harvard Human Rights Journal* 159.

Naturally, that does not entirely compensate. Consequently, the real question is whether the achievement of constitutionalism can be raised to the supranational level.[80] There is a reason why the question was not posed earlier. As late as 1973, Luhmann was able to claim that a radical change in the constitutional order, comparable to the establishment of the constitutional state in the late eighteenth century, had never again taken place.[81] Since then, such a change has occurred in which public power and state power are diverging and public power is now being exercised also by non-state organizations. In response, ever more areas are being made accessible to the concept of constitutionalization. The constitutionalization of the European Union has been a subject of discussion for some time. But the term has now also been extended to a broad range of international organizations, particularly the World Trade Organization. Even the constitutionalization of international law as such has recently been discussed.[82]

As the foregoing historical review shows, constitutionalization is a specific form for the legalization of political rule. It was predicated on the concentration of all ruling authority in the state and was characterized by a particular standard of juridification. The need for juridification emerges wherever rule occurs. Whether it can be satisfied in the form of a constitution depends on whether the prerequisites exist and the standard aspired to can be achieved. Consequently, the material question is whether the constitution as a form of juridification that relates to the state is so closely associated with the latter as to be inseparable from it, or whether it can be applied to non-state political units that exercise public power.

If we first apply this question to the European Union, it is obvious that, without possessing the qualities of a state, it has acquired a large number of sovereign rights that it exercises through a variety of organs with direct validity in the member states. These are not restricted to a single political field. In addition to the economic goal of a common market, competencies in numerous other areas have also been added. The legal systems of the member states are so tightly integrated with that of the Community that they can no longer be

[80] See Ulrich Haltern, 'Internationales Verfassungsrecht' (2003) *Archiv des öffentlichen Rechts* 128; David Held, *Democracy and the Global Order* (Cambridge: Polity Press, 1995); Stefan Gosepath and Jean-Christophe Merle, *Weltrepublik* (München: Beck, 2002).

[81] Luhmann, Politische Verfassungen (n. 31), p. 4.

[82] For the constitutionalization of the EU, see Weiler, *Constitution* (n. 74), p. 10; Armin v. Bogdandy (ed.), *Europäisches Verfassungsrecht: theoretische und dogmatische Grundzüge* (Berlin: Springer, 2003). For the European Convention on Human Rights, see Christian Walter, 'Die EMRK als Konstitutionalisierungsprozeß' (1999) 59 *ZaöRV* 961. For the WTO at an early stage, see Ernst-Ulrich Petersmann, *Constitutional Functions and Constitutional Problems of International Economic Law* (Fribourg: Fribourg University Press, 1991); further Stefan Langer, *Grundlagen einer internationalen Wirtschaftsverfassung* (München: Beck, 1995). For the United Nations, see Bardo Faßbender, 'The United Nations Charter as Constitution of the International Community' (1998) 36 *Columbia Journal of Transnational Law* 529. For international law, see Jochen A. Frowein, 'Konstitutionalisierung des Völkerrechts' (2000) 39 *Berichte der Deutschen Gesellschaft für Völkerrecht* 427; generally Rainer Wahl, 'Konstitutionalisierung – Leitbegriff oder Allerweltsbegriff?', in *Der Wandel des Staates vor den Herausforderungen der Gegenwart. FS für Winfried Brohm* (München: Beck, 2002), p. 191.

adequately described without consideration of Community law. The same is true for the political system. Any attempt to describe national politics omitting the European level must fail to do the subject justice. The European Union is thus no less an entity capable of a constitution than the federal level of a federative state.

However, a juridification of the public authority ceded to it has never been lacking. The European Communities were created by a single legal act, the conclusion of the Treaties of Rome by the six founding states. But the treaties provided for more than the founding of the Community. They also defined the Community's ends, assigned it authority, created the bodies to exercise this, delineated these, organized their staffing and appointments, mandated procedures, regulated the relationship between the Community and the member states as well as its citizens. This enumeration alone illustrates how the treaties assume functions in the European Union which in a nation state are performed by the constitution. They are frequently termed the 'constitution' of the European Union.[83]

Yet, the legal basis for the Community differs from traditional state constitutions in that to this day it remains an international treaty. Consequently, the public power that the European Union exercises does not derive from the people but from member states. Just as member states founded the European Union through negotiation of the treaty and subsequent ratification in each member state, these also reserve the right to change the fundamental order. It is not an expression of the people's constituent power and is not the responsibility of any body of the European Union that represents it. As far as its legal basis is concerned, the European Union, unlike a state, is heteronomously determined, and not self-determined. According to the criteria enumerated here for constitutions in the higher sense as opposed to mere juridification, only the democratic component is lacking for a constitution in the full meaning of the word.[84]

Naturally, there is nothing to prevent member states from surrendering their rule over the basic legal order of the European Union through a final treaty that places the Union on a democratic footing and thus grants it self-determination over its basic legal order.[85] Even if the member states retain a voice in future changes, they could no longer exercise this from the outside by negotiating a treaty, but only internally as an organ of the European Union. The treaties would thus become a constitution in the full sense of the word without

---

[83] Cf. Anne Peters, *Elemente einer Theorie der Verfassung Europas* (Berlin: Duncker & Humblot, 2001).

[84] See further Dieter Grimm, 'Does Europe Need a Constitution?' (1995) 1 *European Law Journal* 278; Larry Siedentop, *Democracy in Europe* (London: Penguin Press, 2000); Marcel Kaufmann, *Europäische Integration und Demokratieprinzip* (Baden-Baden: Nomos, 1997); Joseph Weiler, Ulrich Haltern, Franz Mayer, 'European Democracy and Its Critique' (1995) 18 (3) *West European Politics* 4.

[85] Cf. Neil MacCormick, *Questioning Sovereignty: Law, State, and Practical Reason* (Oxford: Oxford University Press, 1999); Ingolf Pernice, 'Multilevel Constitutionalism and the Treaty of Amsterdam' (1999) 36 *Common Market Law Review* 427; Paul Craig, 'Constitutions, Constitutionalism, and the European Union' (2001) 7 *European Law Journal* 125; However, desirability should be distinguished from capability: see Grimm, Europe (n. 84).

requiring any amendment to their wording. However, this would tacitly transform the European Union into a (federal) state, as between external determination and self-determination with respect to the fundamental legal order runs the fine difference between a federation of states and a federal state.

However, a constitutionalized European Union would be as little proof against a relativization of its borders as nation states.[86] The constitutional question thus continues on the global level. On this level, a process of juridification has commenced that is leaving a lasting impression on international law. The main areas of application, though unrelated, are economic relations and human rights. However, when observed closely, this does not mean that internal constitutionalization will be followed by an external one.[87] When one considers the difference between juridification and hierarchalization, on the one hand, and constitutionalization on the other, it becomes apparent that the basic prerequisite for constitutionalization on the international level is lacking: to date there is no constitutional object on the global level. Rather, the emerging international order with its plurality of unconnected centres of rule and sources of law is reminiscent of pre-state conditions. Their bundling and democratic legitimation are a long way off. The standard embodied in the concept of the constitution here cannot be realized even approximately. That is no reason to denigrate the progress made in juridification. But the world-wide propagation of the constitution cannot conceal the fact that the incipient 'post-state era' also means that the constitution has passed its zenith.

[86] Walter (n. 82).      [87] See Di Fabio (n. 73), p. 68.

# PART II

# ORIGINS

# Conditions for the Emergence and Effectiveness of Modern Constitutionalism

## I. THE CONSTITUTION AS A NOVELTY

### 1. Aim of the Study

The emergence of the modern constitution in North America and France at the end of the eighteenth century is relatively well researched and documented. However, a satisfactory explanation as to why the constitution could emerge at that time and soon become the predominant topic of the era is still lacking. Such a radical and momentous new development naturally indicates the occurrence of certain conditions which did not previously exist and which could since have disappeared. Thus, it is not possible either to understand the constitution historically or to forecast its development without reconstructing these conditions. The question as to the future of the constitution is anything but superfluous. The global propagation of the constitution and its growing enforceability by means of constitutional courts must not distract us from the peculiar weakness and dissipation of meaning that it evidences in the face of the problems of the modern welfare state. The aim of this chapter is to offer an explanation of the past that is relevant to the present and the future; the emphasis is on the historical side, and the problems of the present are only addressed in outline at the end.

### 2. Tradition and Innovation

The fact that the constitution is a novel development is not self-evident in view of the much older use of the term and its continuing application to older epochs. Consequently, it is first necessary to identify those elements that make its development a novel occurrence. In this undertaking, the genesis of the phenomena that gave rise to the modern constitution can serve as initial clues. Both the constitutions of the North American states since 1776 and the American federal constitution of 1787 with its Bill of Rights of 1791 as well as the French constitution of 1791 with its integrated Declaration of the Rights of Man and Citizens of 1789 were products of revolutions that overthrew the old order and replaced it with a new one. Such events, of course, are not rare in history. But

Constitutionalism: Past, Present, and Future. First Edition. Dieter Grimm. © Dieter Grimm 2016. Published 2016 by Oxford University Press.

these two differed from previous overthrows in that their proponents were not merely concerned with a change in rulers, but had previously conceived of a structure of conditions of legitimate rule and realized this structure in the form of legally binding norms. Individuals were appointed to rule only on the basis of these normative conditions, and were authorized to exercise their rule on this basis alone.

However, the novel element did not consist in the theoretical construction of the conditions of legitimate rule nor in the legal binding of the power of rule in itself.[1] The legitimization of rule had always formed a core problem of social philosophy. Since the fading of the religious template for legitimization as a consequence of the Protestant schism, new answers were needed, and they were found in the doctrine of the social contract. Political rule was deemed legitimate when it could be considered as being based on a contract. Although legal validity was often claimed for the legitimization conditions developed in social-contract theory, this validity was not legal in nature. It received neither broad acceptance of rulers nor an implementation in positive law. Rather, the natural law derived from the social contract remained either a critical or an affirmative theory with respect to positive public law.

Evidently, the non-binding nature of natural law does not imply the existence of unrestricted rule. Jean Bodin's theory of sovereignty, which stated that the ruler had the right to determine law for all without himself being bound by law, legitimated the right of the ruler to dispose over the social order following the collapse of the medieval order, but did not provide a complete description of reality. On the contrary, the incipient concentration of territorial power in the hands of monarchs gave rise to a need for legal restriction. Indeed, a series of regulatory structures emerged in the mid-seventeenth century under the favourable circumstance of an absent or weak ruler, which limited the exercise of public power in favour of the endangered rights of the estates.[2] However, such attempts to normatively limit the rise of the modern sovereign state, which originated not from subjective despotism but the objective pressure of problems, were mostly failures. Few of the 'forms of government' enjoyed validity for very long.

Yet even the absolute monarch who was able to throw off the co-government of the estates and secure his own power base in the form of the army and civil administrators, did not enjoy legally unfettered power. Even where he succeeded in fending off the attempts at comprehensive regulation, which was the objective of the estates-based form of government, he was confronted by a series of 'fundamental laws' or 'contractual obligations' that bound the ruler through

[1] See Hasso Hofmann, 'Zur Idee des Staatsgrundgesetzes' in his *Recht – Politik – Verfassung. Studien zur Geschichte der politischen Philosophie* (Frankfurt am Main: Metzner, 1986), p. 261; Werner Näf, 'Der Durchbruch des Verfassungsgedankens im 18. Jahrhundert' (1953) 11 *Schweizer Beiträge zur Allgemeinen Geschichte* 108.

[2] See Gerhard Oestreich, 'Vom Herrschaftsvertrag zur Verfassungsurkunde. Die "Regierungsformen" des 17. Jahrhunderts als konstitutionelle Instrumente' in Rudolf Vierhaus (ed.), *Herrschaftsverträge, Wahlkapitulationen, Fundamentalgesetze* (Göttingen: Vandenhoek & Ruprecht, 1977), p. 45.

positive law and which he could not unilaterally alter. Usually established in writing and often enforceable through the courts, these fulfilled all the conditions for a higher-ranking law and were certainly understood as frameworks for the power of the ruler, including the exercise of legislative power.[3] On examination of their origin, most of them were contractual in nature. This origin indicates that the process was driven by social power groups that had at their disposal services vital for the continued existence of monarchical rule. They therefore possessed the capacity to demand that the ruler relinquish individual prerogatives as part of a quid pro quo and to have this secured in a legally binding manner. But since these were contractually based they always presumed the power of rule as a prerequisite instead of establishing it. Rather, they only regulated individual aspects to the benefit of individual privileged subjects.

The novel element of modern constitutions, by contrast, lies in the combination of both lines. They endowed the theoretically derived model with legal validity. The constitution differs from natural law through the validity of positive law. It diverges from the older legal bonds of state power through an expansion of its function and validity in three respects:

1. While governmental contracts and fundamental laws always assumed legitimate state power and only imposed regulation on isolated aspects of its exercise, the modern constitution brought forth legitimate state power in the first place. Its effect was thus not to modify, but to *constitute* rule.

2. Where the older forms of legally binding rules only related to individual aspects of the accumulated power, the modern constitution aspired to regulate rule in its entirety. Its action was thus not selective but *comprehensive*.

3. Finally, while the older forms of legal bonding were contractual in their origin and thus only applied between the parties to that contract, the modern bonds of constitutional law benefited all persons subject to rule. Their action was thus not particular but *universal*.

### 3. Ancient and Modern Concepts of Constitution

The revolutionary significance of the modern constitution often remained unrecognized on account of the linkage with existing traditions and the use of commonly used terms. Even before the revolutions, the term 'constitution' (or the equivalent term in the respective language) was in use. However, at that time this had a different meaning.[4] The term 'constitutio' was originally

---

[3] Cf. Vierhaus (n. 2) ; Heinz Mohnhaupt, 'Die Lehre von der "Lex fundamentalis" und die Hausgesetzgebung europäischer Dynastien' in Johannes Kunisch (ed.), *Der dynastische Fürstenstaat: zur Bedeutung von Sukzessionsordnungen für die Entstehung des frühmodernen Staates* (Berlin: Duncker & Humblot, 1982), p. 3; John W. Gough, *Fundamental Law in English Constitutional History* (Oxford: Clarendon Press, 1955).

[4] See Ch. 4 of this volume; further Ernst-Wolfgang Böckenförde, 'Geschichtliche Entwicklung und Bedeutungswandel der Verfassung' in *Festschrift für Rudolf Gmür* (Bielefeld: Gieseking, 1983), p. 7; Charles H. McIlwain, *Constitutionalism, ancient and modern* (Ithaca, NY: Cornell University Press, 1966); Charles H. McIlwain, 'Some Illustrations of the Influence of Unchanged Names for Changing Institutions' in Paul Sayre

used to denote a family of laws that did not necessarily have to relate to the exercise of rule, while 'constitution' generally meant the condition or situation of a state—initially broadly, as it was shaped by historical development, natural features, and legal order; later more narrowly focused on the status accorded it by conventions, fundamental laws, and governmental contracts. Even in this narrower focus, the constitution remained a condition determined by law. It did not designate the legal form itself. Consequently, every state was in a certain 'constitution', and where no constitution could be identified, no state existed. The older concept of constitution was thus an *empirical concept*.

By contrast, the modern constitution prescribed how state power *should be* established and exercised in the form of a systematic and exhaustive claim embodied in a legal document. In this way, the constitution became synonymous with the law that regulated the establishment and exercise of state power. It no longer designated the situation of a state as formed by its laws, but the law that formed the situation. 'Constitution' thus emerged as a *normative concept*. Certainly not all countries had a constitution in this new sense. Rather, the existence of a constitutional document that provided for basic rights and popular representation became a distinguishing feature of the categorization of the world of nations, and the question as to whether only the constitutional state in this sense could claim legitimacy was a dominant theme throughout the nineteenth century.

The older empirical concept of the constitution was correspondingly displaced by the increasing prevalence of the modern normative concept of the constitution. Admittedly, the disappearance of the older concept of constitution did not mean that the factual conditions of rule and its normative regulation disappeared as well. Consequently, it was later picked up by the new empirical science of sociology.[5] In addition, one can observe that the older, ontological constitutional concept was rediscovered by the opponents of the liberal content originally associated with the normative constitution, or emerges at moments of crisis for the normative constitution in the form of the so-called material or social constitution and serves as an explanation of the enforcement deficits or failures of normative constitutions.[6]

(ed.), *Interpretations of Modern Legal Philosophies. Essays in Honor of Roscoe Pound* (New York: Oxford University Press, 1947).

[5] Cf. in explicit divergence from the legal science the definition by Max Weber, *Wirtschaft und Gesellschaft* (Tübingen: Mohr, 5th edn., 1972), pp. 27, 194.

[6] See e.g. Friedrich Engels, 'Die Lage Englands', Marx Engels Werke vol. 1 (Berlin: Dietz, 1970), p. 572; Lorenz von Stein, 'Zur preußischen Verfassungsfrage' [1852] (Darmstadt: Wissenschaftliche Buchgesellschaft, 1961); Ferdinand Lassalle, 'Über Verfassungswesen' (1862) in Eduard Bernstein, *Gesammelte Reden und Schriften*, vol. 2 (Berlin: Cassirer, 1967); Carl Schmitt, *Verfassungslehre* (Munich: Duncker & Humblot, 1928); Carl Schmitt, *Der Hüter der Verfassung* (1931) (Berlin: Duncker & Humblot, 2nd edn, 1969); Ernst R. Huber, *Wesen und Inhalt der politischen Verfassung* (Hamburg: Hanseatische Verlagsanstalt, 1935); Gustav A. Walz, *Der Begriff der Verfassung* (Berlin: Duncker & Humblot, 1942).

## II. PREREQUISITES FOR THE EMERGENCE OF
## THE CONSTITUTION

### 1. *Explanatory Model*

#### a) Preconditions

Characteristic of the modern constitution is its claim to comprehensively and uniformly regulate political rule in terms of its formation and means of execution in
a law superior to all other legal norms. Even though the desire for limited political
rule expressed therein is in no way new, it could only be satisfied in the form of a
constitution under certain modern conditions. As a systematic determination of
the conditions of legitimate rule, the constitution depended on the political order
being subject to human decision-making. This only became the case in modern
history when faith in the divine establishment and formation of secular rule was
shaken, as in the course of the Protestant schism. The loss of a transcendental
basis for consensus forced the new formation of rule on a secular basis,[7] which
did not prevent the search for guiding principles with supra-temporal validity, but
required their deliberate transformation into political reality. Thus, no constitution in the modern sense was possible without the previous positivization of law.

In its function as a comprehensive and uniform regulation of the establishment and exercise of rule, the constitution was also dependent on the existence
of an object that permitted such a concentrated normative intervention. This
too did not emerge until the collapse of the medieval order. The polyarchic system of prerogatives exercised as outgrowths of property ownership and objectively and functionally distributed among numerous autonomous holders of
equivalent status, which did not recognize a differentiation between the state
and society and public and private spheres, was not yet capable of constitutionalism in the modern sense.[8] Rather, it was the emergence of a public power in
the singular, distinguishable from society, that furnished the possible starting
point for a set of rules relating specifically to the establishment and exercise
of rule and regulating them systematically and comprehensively. Consequently,
the modern constitution was not possible before the amalgamation of the scattered sovereign rights and their concentration in the form of comprehensive
state power, as was fuelled by the religious civil wars.

#### b) Actors

While it was the monarchical state that gradually emerged in the course of the
religious civil wars of the sixteenth and seventeenth centuries that created a
key prerequisite for the modern constitution, this state itself could not possibly

---

[7] See Ernst-Wolfgang Böckenförde, 'Die Entstehung des Staates als Vorgang der Säkularisation' in his *Staat, Gesellschaft, Freiheit* (Frankfurt am Main: Suhrkamp, 1976), p. 42.

[8] On the medieval situation, see Otto Brunner, *Land und Herrschaft* (Darmstadt: Wissenschaftliche Buchgesellschaft, 6th edn, 1970), p. 111. For the consistent and comprehensive state powers as a precondition for the modern constitution, see Helmut Quaritsch, *Staat und Souveränität* (Frankfurt am Main: Athenäum, 1970), p. 184.

be interested in the constitutionalization of public power. With constitutions in the sense described here, the monarch would have had to disavow his *raison d'être* as an autonomously legitimate ruler independent of consensus and be content with a role as an organ of a state conceived of as independent of him. For the same reason, ascribing constitutional character to the self-restrictions of rule as adopted under the influence of the Enlightenment in the drafts of the codification of Austrian and Prussian private law in the last third of the eighteenth century, which in some cases acquired the force of law, also appears problematic.[9] Although they shared the function of limitation of power with the later constitutions, they lacked three characteristics of modern constitutions: they did not constitute legitimate rule; they did not even refer to the so-called 'inner constitutional law', that is, the sovereign rights and the relationship between the state and the nation, but only the relationship between state power and the rights of individuals;[10] and they did not bind the ruler from a position of higher law. Rather, they were on the level of ordinary law and, in a system in which the monarch was the exclusive legislator, could be altered by the latter at any time.[11] Leopold II of Austria who as Grand Duke of Tuscany wanted to issue a formal constitution on his own initiative, remained a solitary phenomenon in the contemporary princely world.[12] He did not revisit these plans in his short reign on the Hapsburg throne following the death of Joseph II in 1790.

Nor can an interest in a constitution in the modern sense be assumed on the part of the privileged estates of the clergy and nobility. They did indeed have an interest in restricting monarchic power and participating in political decisions. But this desire challenged neither the monarch's inherent right of rule nor did it aim at including the entire population. This is most clearly expressed in the discussion that developed in connection with the convention of the Estates General in France from 1787 onwards.[13] The higher estates sought to return to the pre-absolutist forms of estate-monarchic dualism, and not project forward towards a representation of the whole nation in which they would be absorbed or at least mediated, as would be the consequence of a modern constitution. Thus, as estates, the clergy and nobility were not on the side of the modern constitution, which of course neither precludes the support of individual members,

---

[9] See Hermann Conrad, *Rechtsstaatliche Bestrebungen im Absolutismus Preußens und Österreichs am Ende des 18. Jahrhunderts* (Köln: Westdeutscher Verlag, 1961) and Hermann Conrad, *Das Allgemeine Landrecht von 1794 als Grundgesetz des friderizianischen Staates* (Berlin: de Gruyter, 1965).

[10] Cf. Günter Birtsch, 'Zum konstitutionellen Charakter des preußischen Allgemeinen Landrechts von 1794' in Kurt Kluxen and Wolfgang Mommsen (eds), *Politische Ideologien und nationalstaatliche Ordnung: Studien zur Geschichte des 19. und 20. Jahrhunderts, Festschrift für Theodor Schieder* (München: Oldenbourg, 1968), p. 98, at 100.

[11] See Martin Kriele, *Einführung in die Staatslehre: die geschichtlichen Legitimitätsgrundlagen des demokratischen Verfassungsstaates* (Reinbek bei Hamburg: Rowohlt, 1975), p. 116.

[12] Cf. Joachim Zimmermann, *Das Verfassungsprojekt des Großherzogs Peter Leopold von Toskana* (Heidelberg: Winter, 1901); Adam Wandruszka, *Leopold II.*, vol. 1 (Wien: Herold-Verlag, 1963), p. 368.

[13] Cf. Eberhard Schmitt, *Repräsentation und Revolution* (München: Beck, 1969), pp. 89, 147.

nor the willingness of individual princes to place their authority to rule on a constitutional basis.

The third estate thus remains as the social bearer of the constitutional idea. But here also distinctions must be made. The third estate was united only in its exclusion from the privileges of the higher estates; otherwise it did not represent a homogeneous group[14] and thus possessed differing affinities to the constitution. In some cases an objective interest in fundamental systemic change was lacking, in others the subjective consciousness necessary to realize and benefit from systemic change. The former was largely true for the traditional feudal bourgeoisie. Its highest elements did not seek to abolish but to share in the privileges, and often enough attained this through ennoblement. But even the great majority of the broad class of urban tradesmen and merchants were not pressing for change; it derived its security from the estate-based structure and the guilds-based organization of trade, and regarded freedom and equality as threats rather than as progress. The latter case applied primarily to the peasantry, which may be assumed to have had an interest in the elimination of feudal burdens but not the degree of independence, education, and leisure that would have allowed it to implement this interest in a concept of altered structures of rule and represent it in an organized manner. This was all the more true for those classes below the estates, which constantly lived on the edge of starvation and lacked all prospect for improving their situation. Support for changes, once articulated, could be found among them, as among the peasants, but they rarely took the initiative.

Thus, only that part of the bourgeoisie which was created by the economic and administrative needs of the absolute state itself, and which is generally lumped together under the term educated or propertied bourgeoisie, remains. It was attributed to the third estate, but it essentially broke the bounds of estate-attribution and planted the seed of dissolution in the old order. The objective prerequisite for its role as standard-bearer in the emergence of the constitution lay in the increasing importance of the services it performed in preserving and developing the society, with the concurrent decline in importance of the social functions performed by clergy and nobility. Subjectively, the awareness of its own importance, based on ownership and education, and the perception of the growing discrepancy between social standing and legal/political position were the key factors.

Multiple indications of this change in consciousness from the mid-eighteenth century on may be observed. Initially culturally oriented, it was made manifest in literary salons, reading clubs, periodicals, concerts, exhibitions, and artistic works free of court and church services. With such aids, the new bourgeoisie satisfied its need for self-affirmation, identity, and meaning.

---

[14] Cf. for instance Georges Lefebvre, *La révolution française* (Paris: Presses universitaires de France, 3rd edn, 1963), p. 52; in general Régine Pernoud, *Histoire de la Bourgeoisie en France*, 2 vols. (Paris: Ed. du Seuil, 1960/62). For Germany cf. e.g. Reinhart Koselleck, *Preußen zwischen Reform und Revolution* (Stuttgart: Klett, 2nd edn, 1975), p. 87.

This gave rise to forums which challenged the state's monopoly of the public sphere and, for the first time, constituted public opinion as an actively reasoning part of society.[15] However, reasoning soon shifted from the seemingly interest-free realm of art and philosophy to social conditions and produced a rapidly growing body of literature in which the intellectual paternalism and the feudal and corporative bonds were subjected to a philosophically and economically justified criticism.[16] The criticism ultimately resulted in demands for autonomy for cultural and economic processes, which meant no less than a decoupling of these social functions from political control and their release into individual decision-making.

In exploring the question of the emergence of the constitution, it is enlightening to note that the postulate of autonomy was not initially associated with the call for a change in the conditions of rule. On the contrary, given the resistance of the privileged estates towards all reform demands that threatened their prior rights and economic basis, it was the absolute monarch who was expected to implement the reforms. This was equally true for the physiocrats, the encyclopaedists, the Voltairians, and the Kantians. However, the social reforms demanded could not leave the monarch's position entirely untouched, as autonomy of social subsystems and individual decision-making freedom also meant waiver of the state's entitlement to universal guidance.

Social philosophy arrived at this understanding in the second half of the eighteenth century, when it infused the social contract, with which initially unrestricted state power had been justified, with new content.[17] This now no longer called for the cession of all natural rights of individuals to the state to enable it to effectively guarantee the elementary prerequisites of peaceful coexistence, namely security of life and limb, as previously under the impression of the religious civil wars. Rather, the consolidated situation of the actualized absolute state, which suppressed the religious civil wars and restored social peace, made it possible to transfer the natural rights of individuals into the state and entrust the state with their protection, so that only the right to assert one's own rights by force remained to be ceded. In this context natural rights, which in the early stages of contract theory were only generally designated as freedom

---

[15] Cf. Jürgen Habermas, *Strukturwandel der Öffentlichkeit* (Neuwied: Luchterhand, 1962), p. 38; Dieter Grimm, 'Kulturauftrag des Staates' in his *Recht und Staat der bürgerlichen Gesellschaft* (Frankfurt am Main: Suhrkamp, 1987), p. 104; Dieter Grimm, 'Soziale Voraussetzungen und verfassungsrechtliche Gewährleistungen der Meinungsfreiheit' in his *Recht und Staat*, p. 232; Lucian Hölscher, 'Öffentlichkeit' in *Geschichtliche Grundbegriffe* (annotation 3), vol. IV (Stuttgart: Klett-Cotta, 1978), p. 413, esp. at p. 430.

[16] See Reinhart Koselleck, *Kritik und Krise* (Frankfurt am Main: Suhrkamp, 3rd edn, 1973); Ira O. Wade, *The Structure and Form of the French Enlightenment*, 2 vols. (Princeton: Princeton University Press, 1977); Paul Hazard, *La pensée européenne au XVIIIe siècle de Montesquieu à Lessing*, 2 vols. (Paris: Boivin, 2nd edn, 1963); Georges Weulersee, *Le mouvement physiocratique en France*, 2 vols. (Paris: Mouton, reprint 1968); Fritz Valjavec, *Die Entstehung der politischen Strömungen in Deutschland* (Kronberg: Athenäum, 1978); Diethelm Klippel, *Politische Freiheit und Freiheitsrechte im deutschen Naturrecht des 18. Jahrhunderts* (Paderborn: Schöningh, 1976).

[17] Cf. Klippel (n. 16), p. 186; J. W. Gough, *The Social Contract: a Critical Study of its Development* (Oxford: Clarendon Press, 2nd edn, 1957).

and property or life and limb, were developed into ever more detailed catalogues and, as the means of securing freedom, were linked with concepts for the division of power.

The content of the later constitution was thus largely anticipated in the new social-contract theory. Still, this failed to make the step to the modern constitution. Rather, the social contract was associated with the older concept of constitution even where it aimed at restriction of the state and division of power in the interest of individual freedom, or even, as in the case of Rousseau, took on a radical democratic character.[18] The contract remained a conceptual measure for the rational organization of states. It was the defining factor determining the constitution, but was not to be equated with the constitution itself.

## c) Revolutionary Break

The step from the theoretically founded interest in social reforms to the promulgation of the modern constitution was triggered only by the conflict between the bourgeoisie, economically strong, aware of its strength, and supported by the sub-bourgeois classes, and the French state, neither willing to nor capable of reform. The pre-existing right of rule of the French king had been exempted from bourgeois demands for reform as long as the prospect existed of achieving the ends in view with him. It was not until the evolutionary path appeared to be permanently blocked, through a resolution of the third estate of the Estates General to constitute itself as a National Assembly and take control of France's destiny itself, that the revolutionary break occurred. This resolution did not initially affect the monarchy itself, but it did affect its basis for legitimacy and this did not pass unnoticed by contemporary observers.[19]

Although the resolution that marked the revolutionary break did not mention a constitution, it acquired enormous significance for the emergence of the constitution. The destruction of monarchic sovereignty and the proclamation of popular sovereignty left a vacuum—not a power vacuum, since the royal government remained in power, with committees of the National Assembly installed on a par with or above it, but a vacuum of legitimacy of its exercise. The revolutionary act of the National Assembly had stripped the monarch and his administration of their legitimacy. The National Assembly, self-appointed rather than elected by the people and formed from the estates of the *ancien régime*, could only exercise state power in a makeshift and interim manner. The people, to whom it was now attributed, were of themselves unable to act, but rather had to be rendered able to form will and unity by means of procedures and representatives. The revolutionary break with traditional state power, and emergence of popular sovereignty as a new legitimization principle of political

---

[18] Cf. Ch. 4 of this volume.

[19] Cf. Jules Madival (ed.), *Archives parlementaires de 1787 à 1860*, vol. 8 (Paris: Dupont, 1875), p. 127; Schmitt (n. 13), pp. 131, 261, 277.

rule that was not realizable without representative bodies, almost inevitably resulted in a constituting act.

This necessary constituting *act*, however, should not be mistaken for the constitution itself. Authorized state power, the only possible form under the principle of popular sovereignty, always requires a legitimating legal principle by means of which the mandate is assigned; it necessarily takes precedence over the assigned power and the legal rules emanating from it. However, this legal principle need not necessarily condense into a modern constitutional law. Rather, the people can also unconditionally and irrevocably bestow the authorization to rule. The older social contract doctrine had proved this logically. In this case, the consequence is absolute rule, though admittedly by transferred and not from inherent right. Unlimited right of rule concentrated in a single individual, however, neither requires nor is it amenable to constitutional regulation. Public law is then limited to determining the omnipotence of the ruler and regulation of succession. Thus, if the commissioning character of rule does not by itself lead to the modern constitution, it can only be a specific form of bestowing this commission. This requires an examination of the bourgeois conceptions of the state.

### d) Separation of State and Society

The bourgeois social model was based on the premise that society possesses self-regulatory mechanisms that, if allowed to operate unhindered, would automatically lead to prosperity and justice.[20] The prerequisite for their effectiveness was the autonomy of the social subsystems, which allowed them to develop according to their own criteria of rationality free from political direction. Equal individual freedom for all served as the medium for this autonomy. It promised a considerable increase in prosperity, as it released the talent and industry of the individual from the fetters of the old social order, left to each the wages of their work, and in this way spurred society's will to perform. Furthermore, because social bonds in this system of equal freedom were only conceivable as voluntarily assumed, that is contractually negotiated commitments, it also promised a fairer reconciliation of interests than was possible under central political control. Under these circumstances, the common good was no longer a materially defined quantity determined in advance, but resulted automatically from the interaction of individual decisions. It was formalized and proceduralized.

This system did not render the state superfluous because equal individual freedom, on which the function of the social order depended, required both organization and protection; on the other hand, society, dissolved into dissociated individuals and stripped of all authority to rule, lacked the collective ability to act and to organize and protect freedom itself. Rather, it had to reconstruct this ability to act outside of itself—in the form of the state.[21] However, in light of society's ability to regulate itself, the state lost its former range of powers. As

---

[20] For more details, see Dieter Grimm, 'Bürgerlichkeit im Recht' in his *Recht und Staat* (n. 15), p. 11.

[21] Cf. Niklas Luhmann, 'Politische Verfassungen im Kontext des Gesellschaftssystems' (1973) 12 *Der Staat* 5.

the common good was no longer the product of planned state action, but rather was viewed as the automatically occurring consequence of individual freedom, it lost its role as the central controlling instance for all social subsystems. On the contrary, these were decoupled from political influence and became autonomous, while the only role of politics was to protect the prerequisites for self-control, that is, freedom and equality, from interference. This led to a reversal of the principle of distribution that was valid until that point: private interests took precedence over public, society over the state; the latter was limited in principle, the former fundamentally free. The separation of state and society has become the common term for this model.[22]

This separation should not be understood as disaffiliation but as a reorientation of relationships. Bourgeois society was faced with a problem of construction. On the one hand, it had to provide the state with the monopoly of the legitimate use of force which the absolute monarch had sought but never attained, and thus once again increase the power of the state. On the other, society had to prevent the state from using this force against social autonomy and deploying it to advance its own ambitions of control. The modern constitution provided the answer to the compatibility problems between social and political order.[23] Its resolution capacity derives from the fact that all matters requiring regulation following the fundamental material decision in favour of social self-control by means of individual decisions were of a formal nature. One aim was to limit the state in the interests of social autonomy and individual freedom. The other was that the state, excluded from society, had to be reconnected with it such that it could not resile from the social interests it served in the process of performing its guarantee function.

At this point, it is important to recognize that the nature of this task was such that it could be satisfactorily resolved in law and specifically, as it concerned the regulation of state power, in constitutional law.[24] For the law develops its specific rationality best when it has to solve formal problems. Whereas material tasks can be ordered and initiated by legal norms, fulfilment is always secondary to the simple application of law. This only occurs with the realization of normative imperatives. However, it depends on a series of factors, such as money, acceptance, staffing, etc., over which law has extremely limited disposition. By contrast, the problem of the limitation and organization of state power can in principle be resolved only through the promulgation of corresponding norms. To be sure, these must also be realized. But the realization of formal norms is identical with the application of law. Resources are irrelevant in this respect: there is no scarcity of omission, and violations can generally be dealt with in the legal system itself, namely through the annulment of illegal acts. It is thus only a slight exaggeration to say that, under the conditions of the

---

[22] Cf. Ernst-Wolfgang Böckenförde (ed.), *Staat und Gesellschaft* (Darmstadt: Wissenschaftliche Buchgesellschaft, 1976); Ernst-Wolfgang Böckenförde, *Die verfassungstheoretische Unterscheidung von Staat und Gesellschaft als Bedingung der individuellen Freiheit* (Opladen: Westdeutscher Verlag, 1973).

[23] Cf. Luhmann (n. 21), p. 6.     [24] For more details, see Grimm (n. 20).

bourgeois social model, law did not just contribute to the solution of the problem, but was *itself* the solution.

In terms of specifics, the boundaries and limits of the state were established in the form of fundamental rights, and the mediation between state and society in the form of the division of power. Fundamental rights excluded those areas from the state's authority to rule, previously conceived of as comprehensive, in which the private and not the public interest was primary. They thus marked the boundary between the state and society. Therefore, from the perspective of the state, these represented restrictions on action, while from the viewpoint of society they were seen as defensive rights. Naturally, the freedoms guaranteed by fundamental rights could not be unbounded, as this would protect exercises of freedom that themselves threatened freedom and therefore the foundations of the system. Consequently, the freedom of the individual had to be limitable in the interests of the freedom of all others. As a result, the state also retained action capabilities in the area of freedoms. In view of the fundamental decision in favour of individual freedom, however, these actions represented interventions and the objective of the entire organization of the state was the restraint of the dangers inherent in state intervention.

Accordingly, the state itself was not competent to judge when it was authorized to infringe on freedoms in order to protect them. Rather, society itself, through its elected representatives, determined what restraints on freedom each individual had to tolerate in the interests of equal freedom. The law served as the means for this, and in this way could appear as the 'expression of the general will'. The state received its action programme through laws enacted through parliamentary procedure. It could only intervene in the sphere protected by the fundamental rights on the basis of an authorization in law. Courts petitioned by affected individuals could determine whether the state's action was covered by a legal programme and put the illegally acting state in its place. In this system, the classical model of division of power, which aimed to prevent the abuse of public power by dividing it among different mutually independent and mutually monitoring poles of authority, emerged spontaneously.

## e) Interim Summary

The foregoing analysis brings the conditions for the emergence of the modern constitution (though not necessarily for its subsequent spread) into sharper focus:

The general conditions were:

- First, the emergence of an object capable of being regulated by a constitution, in the form of modern state power; and
- Secondly, the decidability of problems of order or, in other words, the transition to positive law.

Following early attempts, both conditions emerged in the course of the Protestant schism and characterize, to a more or less advanced extent, the modern sovereign state.

The specific conditions were:

- First, a population group formed on account of progressive functional differentiation as a standard-bearer that had an interest in changes in the structure of rule and possessed the strength necessary for asserting this interest;
- Secondly, a guiding concept of order, according to which society could create prosperity and justice by means of its own efforts through the medium of free, individual decisions, so that the state could relinquish its central controlling role and restrict itself to a guarantee function for the pre-established and independent order as assigned to it by society—in short, the separation of state and society.
- Thirdly, a revolutionary break with the previous conception of state power and the resulting necessity to reconstitute legitimate state power and make it compatible with the newly autonomous society.

To the extent that these conditions obtain for the modern bourgeoisie, the bourgeois social model and the bourgeois revolution, one can describe the constitution as a bourgeois phenomenon.

## 2. *Test Cases*

### a) France and America

In explaining the emergence of the modern constitution, the French case has been used as a model. Naturally, the purpose of this is not to cast doubt on the American priority in the establishment of a constitution. When the French National Assembly set about drafting a constitution, they could already refer to the American examples. However, the French decision was not merely an imitation of the American process. The French Revolution did not primarily aim to establish the constitutional state following the American pattern. Rather, its aim was to change the social order. However, this aim required a reconstitution of political rule, and only when this point was reached did France embark independently on its own path to modern constitutionalism.

That may be seen very clearly in the decisive stages of the revolution. The *cahiers de doléances*, which were prepared to inform and instruct the representatives of the various estates and districts following the king's decision to reconvene the Estates General, contain numerous constitutional demands, but no demands for a constitution in the modern sense.[25] The awareness within the National Assembly that the matter at hand concerned a new foundation of rule was equally lacking. Rather, in their pursuit of the ends of 'national restoration' and 'regeneration of France',[26] representatives vacillated between a restoration of the traditional powers by way of a contract with the monarch and a new foundation for state power by means of legislation. It was not until the king had

---

[25] Cf. G. V. Taylor, 'Les cahiers de 1789' (1973) 28 *Annales* 1495.

[26] Declaration of 17 June 1789, Archives parlementaires, vol. 8, p. 127.

rejected the fundamental reform resolutions of 4 August 1789, which abolished the differences and privileges of the estates and the feudal system, that the representatives understood that the primary ends of social reform could only be asserted in opposition to traditional state power. This determined once and for all that the task was not the modification of rule; it was the foundation of rule and the ultimate result was a constitution in the modern sense.

America's path to the modern constitution, by contrast, was easier and more direct, as it received the necessary ingredients from Europe, yet had left the European obstacles on the continent behind.[27] Accordingly, France represents the more complicated, yet historically more powerful case, in that though the American events generated much interest in Europe, they were not seen to have great relevance to the European situation. Rather, it was the French Revolution which raised the constitution as a political issue in other states on the continent. For these reasons, the explanatory model must first demonstrate its validity using the French example. Certainly, it will soon become apparent that this also encompasses the American case.

## b) England

First, however, the model explains why England remained without a formal constitution even though it was the most economically advanced and politically and economically liberal nation in the old world. England had succeeded in transitioning its society to bourgeois conditions without a revolutionary break with traditional rule. The most important reasons for this are to be found in the early decline of the feudal system which, in contrast to the continent, made the barriers between the nobility and the bourgeoisie permeable and thus facilitated both the ennoblement of deserving bourgeois and entrepreneurial activity of nobles, and the circumstance that the effect of the reformation was not to strengthen monarchic power but enhance the role of Parliament, whose support Henry VIII sought for his schism with Rome. In this way, England's nobility and bourgeoisie had more interests in common than on the continent, and possessed in Parliament a politically effective representation of interests, while at the same time suppressing assemblies of the estates and the establishment of absolute state power that was underway in the progressive continental states of that era.

Although England was not entirely uninfluenced by absolutism, the claims of absoluteness which the Stuarts asserted in the seventeenth century without the support of the legitimating circumstance of religious civil wars aroused the joint resistance of the nobility and bourgeoisie. The overthrow of Charles I in 1649 and Cromwell's elimination of the monarchy was the only revolutionary situation in England. The fact that in this phase England received a written constitution in the modern sense, the 'Instrument of Government',[28] affirms

---

[27] Cf. Dieter Grimm, 'Europäisches Naturrecht und amerikanische Revolution' (1970) III *Ius commune* 120.

[28] Text in S. R. Gardiner (ed.), *The Constitutional Documents of the Puritan Revolution 1628-1660* (Oxford: Clarendon Press, 1968), p. 405; in addition Gerald Stourzh, *Fundamental Laws and Individual Rights in the*

the relationship between revolutionary breaks and the modern constitution postulated here. In spite of the similarity in language, this document must not be confused with the contemporary 'forms of government' of the continent, which lacked the character of constituting rule. The short lifespan of this first constitution is due to the fact that Cromwell's new order quickly collapsed following his death, which increased the willingness of Parliament to restore the monarchy. The constitution that emerged out of the break with the traditional ruler and the necessity of re-establishing rule on a new basis became obsolete with the curing of the break.

The bloodless Glorious Revolution of 1688 permanently cemented the monarchic tradition, and at the same time secured the political primacy of Parliament. The leading classes of society were thus enabled to shape the social order legally according to their own concepts and needs. Consequently, economic freedom prevailed in England long before Adam Smith provided the theoretical foundation. But particularly due to the gradual liberalization, the problem of maintaining the compatibility of social subsystems with the political system, which was solved on the continent by the constitution, emerged in England as well. In this respect also, England could build on existing institutions and Parliament could grow into the mediator function, while on the continent, where absolute state power had become the norm, such a mediating agency had to be invented in the first place.

## c) America

England's North American colonies surpassed the mother country in several respects. In contrast to Europe, they never knew the feudal system and the class barriers of the estates and were not restricted in their development even by scarce resources. The social order that emerged through evolution in England and was the goal of revolution in France was the American reality from the beginning, even though based on a slave economy. Aside from this problem, which also plagued the French Revolution, the theoretical premises for the bourgeois social model were actualized nowhere as nearly as here. Consequently, America did not need a constitution to assert the bourgeois social order.

Still, America took the lead over Europe in the constitutionalization of rule. The reason for this may be found in the revolutionary break with traditional rule. This break cannot be attributed to a bourgeoisie in the continental European sense as a standard-bearer, as the term cannot be applied directly to the estate-less American society. In a non-estate sense, however, all of America at that time can be regarded as bourgeois.[29] This assumption is corroborated by the circumstance that the white inhabitants were not only politically free,

*18th Century Constitution* (Claremont/Calif.: Claremont Institute for the Study of Statesmanship and Political Philosophy, 1984).

[29] Cf, for an overview Heide Gerstenberger, *Zur politischen Ökonomie der Bürgerlichen Gesellschaft. Die historischen Bedingungen ihrer Konstitution in den USA* (Frankfurt am Main: Athenäum Fischer, 1973), p. 24.

but the great majority of them were also economically independent and they derived their independence from economic activity and not from official functions or land rents. This is not to say that the society was egalitarian. But class boundaries were significantly more permeable than the estate boundaries in Europe. In the course of the eighteenth century, this bourgeoisie not only gained considerably in economic strength, but also developed a strong political consciousness, which was nourished by the high level of self-administration that English colonial government permitted.

Admittedly, the colonists did not cause the revolutionary break in order to establish a social order based on freedom, as is the case for the French Revolution. Still, the reference point was the same. In America, the objective was to defend the already existing freedom-based social order against state encroachments. The special taxes imposed on Americans to pay for the Seven Years War, which was expensive for Britain but profitable for the colonies, was viewed as such an encroachment. These taxes were imposed by Parliament, which did not include any American representatives. However, under the prevailing theory of representation, the colonists were considered represented. This fiction could be maintained as long as Parliament did not distinguish between British and American subjects. It broke down once representatives began to discriminate against Americans. Thus, on the matter of taxation, the British Parliament behaved towards the colonies an a quasi-absolutist manner, and drove them, once the appeal to valid English law had proved fruitless, to their revolutionary break with the mother country—which, like the French Revolution later, was justified on the basis of natural law.[30]

America thus found itself facing the same situation that had remained an episode in England, but was to prove determinative in France: the vacuum of legitimate state power and the necessity of constituting legitimate power anew. This reconstitution occurred without deeper awareness of the epochal new development in the form of the modern constitution. This is understandable when one considers that a tradition of comprehensive, fundamental structures of order set down in writing already existed in the colonies.[31] In terms of their content, they did not vary appreciably from the norms of English common law. However, the new beginning and the founding character of colonization had promoted the enumeration and documentation of rights. Still, it would not be correct to see modern constitutions prefigured in the contracts of settlement and colonial charters, as these lacked any relevance to the highest state power. Situated below the English state order and valid only within its framework, these documents represented structures of order with merely regional or local scope.

In the vacuum situation of the revolutionary break, however, recourse to these basic charters in order to constitute a new state appeared natural. Some

---

[30] Jürgen Habermas, 'Naturrecht und Revolution' in his *Theorie und Praxis* (Neuwied: Luchterhand, 1963), p. 52; Grimm (n. 27), p. 120.

[31] See Stourzh (n. 28).

colonies elevated them unaltered to the status of a constitution, although most used the old documents as a basis for drafting a new constitution.[32] In accordance with social-contract theory, which appeared to have been realized in the founding of the colonies, rule was uniformly understood as a mandate by the people, and the constitution, in a naive and literal understanding of social-contract theory, was interpreted as the fundamental contract between all persons with all others which established the mandate and defined the terms of its exercise. Admittedly, the same degree of concentration of the object of regulation, that is, state power, as achieved by the absolute monarchies of the European continent could not be expected. The absence of the historical burdens of the continent meant that the colonies, like the mother country, also lacked their product, the rationally organized state supported by its army and administration.[33] Yet, they had in no way preserved the polyarchic system of the Middle Ages, but were capable of a unified formation and assertion of will, and thus capable of sustaining a constitution.

Given their origin, the American constitutions did not diverge appreciably from the English legal situation with respect to content. Functionally, however, they went beyond the English legal situation in one important aspect. English constitutional law was based on the principle of parliamentary sovereignty. Under these circumstances, the legal significance of the 'rights of Englishmen', considered fundamental, was necessarily reduced to placing limits on the executive. Parliament, as the representative of the rights-holders, was regarded as the bulwark of fundamental rights, but could dispose of them at will in the exercise of its function. The American colonies had experienced Parliament as a threat to, rather than a guardian of, fundamental rights. Consequently, they placed these rights above the legislative branch, thus constituting them as constitutional rights, and so taking an important step towards the constitution in the modern sense.[34]

## d) Sweden

Although the American constitutions fit seamlessly into the explanatory model, it must ultimately prove its soundness in those constitutions that emerged, in part before the American and French Revolutions and in part subsequent to these, without the prerequisite of an ascendant bourgeoisie asserting a liberal social model during a break with the traditional state power. The Swedish 'Instrument

---

[32] Cf. Francis N. Thorpe (ed.), *The Federal and State Constitutions, Colonial Charters and other Organic Laws of the States, Territories, and Colonies* (Buffalo, NY: W.S. Hein, 1909); Willi P. Adams, *Republikanische Verfassung und bürgerliche Freiheit. Die Verfassungen und politischen Ideen der amerikanischen Revolution* (Darmstadt: Luchterhand, 1973).

[33] Cf. Dieter Grimm, 'The Modern State: Continental Traditions' in Franz-Xaver Kaufmann et al. (eds), *Guidance, Control and Evaluation in the Public Sector* (Berlin: de Gruyter, 1986), p. 89.

[34] Cf. Gerald Stourzh, 'The Declarations of Rights, Popular Sovereignty and the Supremacy of Constitution: Divergencies between the American and the French Revolutions' in C. Fohlen/M.J. Godechot (eds), *La Révolution américaine et l'Europe* (Paris: CNRS, 1979), p. 347.

of Government' of 1772 is widely considered a 'constitution before the constitution'. This instrument was not the first of its kind. Rather, Sweden was able to look back on a long tradition of such instruments of government dating back to 1634.[35] Thus, chronologically the first instrument of government coincides with the regulatory structures that originated from the estates, also often referred to as instruments of government, which emerged in the mid-seventeenth century and were mentioned previously. But the instrument in question is comparable to these others materially as well. Enacted by the estates on the occasion of the regency for the minor heir to the throne following the death of Gustav Adolf, it reinforced the rights of the estates with respect to monarchic power and reorganized the structure of the administration.

In Sweden's varied history, which never overcame the dualism of monarchy and estates but rather swung back and forth between the primacy of the estates and the king, every subsequent change in the balance of power resulted in the alteration of the existing instrument of government of the promulgation of a new one. The Instrument of Government of 1772 also marked a phase in this contest, one in which the monarch largely succeeded in circumscribing the rights of the estates and attempted to permanently seal this victory in writing. The Instrument of Government of 1772 thus does not represent an early form of the modern constitution suitable for challenging the explanatory model, but rather a late form of the tradition of estates-based government that had elsewhere died out. Like these, the Instrument of Government shares with the modern constitutions the aim of comprehensively regulating state power. However, it lacks both the constitutive element and the universal character. Rather, it operates within the traditional framework of the dualistic state.

### e) Germany and other Countries

Following the French Revolution, constitutions spread throughout Europe. Even before the enactment of the first French constitution, Poland received a constitution on 3 May 1791. Based on the current French model, the constitution then spread with the French armies across Italy, Switzerland, Holland, Germany, and Spain.[36] The end of the Napoleonic hegemony over Europe also meant the end of these constitutions, but not of the constitutional movement. Rather, the constitution in the modern sense remained the dominant issue of domestic politics in Europe, and in many countries in Europe, specifically in a series of individual German states, constitutions heavily influenced by the French *Charte constitutionelle* of 1814 were enacted without pressure from abroad. For the great majority of these constitutions, particularly the German

---

[35] E. Hildebrandt (ed.), *Sveriges Regeringsformer 1634-1809* (1891); Michael Roberts, 'On Aristocratic Constitutionalism in Swedish History' in his *Essays in Swedish History* (London: Weidenfeld and Nicholson, 1967), p. 14: Oestreich (n. 2), p. 53; Nils Herlitz, *Grundzüge der schwedischen Verfassungsgeschichte* (Rostock: Hinstorff, 1939), p. 185.

[36] Cf. Dieter Grimm, 'Die verfassungsrechtlichen Grundlagen der Privatrechtsgesetzgebung' in H. Coing (ed.), *Handbuch der Quellen und Literatur der neueren europäischen Privatrechtsgeschichte*, vol. III/1 (München: Beck, 1982), p. 39.

ones, the conditions that have been set forth here as constitutive for the modern constitution were not entirely attained. Rather, at the time the constitutions were enacted an assertive bourgeoisie was generally lacking and thus also the type of revolutionary break that gave rise to the first modern constitutions in America and France.

To determine whether this invalidates the explanatory model, one must first examine what exactly it explains. The explanation relates to the *emergence* of the modern constitution. This was linked to the conditions described herein. Its *spread* was not. Once invented, it could also be applied to other conditions or used for other purposes. One factor in this process was the growing demand of peoples lacking either the occasion or the strength for a bourgeois revolution for constitutional attainments, and the corresponding possibility for regents to additionally legitimate their rule using constitutional forms; a further influence was the necessity to once again mediate between the state and society in the context of increasing functional differentiation, which was also occurring in the non-bourgeois states or was even politically accelerated for reasons of competition. However, it must be noted that to the same extent the conditions for emergence were lacking, these constitutions too could only be a weaker form of the modern constitutional type that emerged in America and France. This could be pushed to the extent of largely meaningless constitutions, so that they no longer served their original purpose of legitimizing and restricting political rule, but only gave the formal appearance of these benefits, as in Napoleonic France.

The Polish constitution of 1791, which might raise doubts about the soundness of the explanatory model on account of its chronological priority in Europe, also proves on closer inspection to be a truncated imitation of the new invention.[37] It originated in efforts at a governmental reform that was triggered by the first partitioning of Poland in 1772. The partitioning had made Poland, in which the primacy of the estates under a monarchy had been largely preserved, and even the *liberum veto* retained, painfully aware of its backwardness and set out to limit the role of nobility and strengthen the monarchical government. The intended aim was similar to that held under the absolute monarchies under the influence of the Enlightenment, but from the opposite position. After the emergence of the American constitutions and the efforts to draft a French constitution, whose section on fundamental rights was finalized in 1789, it was easy to transpose the Polish plans into a constitutional form, particularly as many Polish reformers had fought in the American Revolutionary War and were in communication with French revolutionaries. Unburdened, by absolutism, the country was also open to ideas about division of power. By contrast, the constitution leaves no doubt that the function of constituting rule on the basis of bourgeois freedom was in no way considered.

---

[37] Cf. Georg-Christoph von Unruh, 'Die polnische Konstitution vom 3. Mai 1791 im Rahmen der Verfassungsentwicklung der europäischen Staaten' (1974) 13 *Der Staat* 185.

When one ignores the constitutions promulgated in Europe between 1796 and 1810, as almost none of them was an autonomous creation but enacted under French pressure and thus meaningless in this context, this review must conclude with a look at Germany, where autonomous constitutions emerged following the end of the Napoleonic era. Their common characteristic is that they were voluntarily granted by the monarchs in the interest of dynastic preservation.[38] Their legal validity thus derived from the will of the ruler. As a consequence, the latter's right to rule preceded the constitution and was not founded on it. The German constitutions thus lacked the constitutive element that is characteristic of modern constitutions. These constitutions related solely to the exercise of rule and therefore were similar to the older legal bounds of rule.

They resembled modern constitutions, however, in the way in which they regulated the exercise of power. Unlike the older contractual bonds, they set out to comprehensively regulate the exercise of rule. Consequently, the presumption of competence continued to apply to the monarch on the basis of his pre-constitutional right of rule, insofar as the constitution did not explicitly provide for the participation of other bodies in the decision-making process. However, each monarchical act could be examined to ascertain its conformity with the constitution. Furthermore, constitutions no longer related to the relationship between the monarch and the estates, as the older forms of government did, but were universal. They regulated the relationship between the monarch and the people. They were based on the concept of a separation of state and society, even though this was realized much less thoroughly than in the bourgeois nations due to the lack of a bourgeois revolution and the persistence of estate-based, corporative structures. There existed, however, fundamental rights that justified an autonomy that, while limited, possessed scope for expansion and that were only subject to state intervention with the consent of society in the form of acts of parliament.[39]

Even though the monarch had granted the constitution voluntarily, he was no longer able to shake off these bonds at will. Constitutional changes now needed a legislative process and thus required the consent of the parliaments as their prerequisite. Once granted, therefore, the constitution liberated itself from the will of the monarch and became an external limit on his powers. In practice, the aim of comprehensive regulation, the universality of constitutional norms, and a bond that was not unilaterally dissoluble moderated the lack of the constitutive element and rendered the German constitutions of the nineteenth century similar to the modern constitutional type. However, its evolutionary convergence with this type was obstructed, so that in Germany as

---

[38] Cf. the characterization in Ernst-Wolfgang Böckenförde, 'Der deutsche Typ der konstitutionellen Monarchie' in his *Staat, Gesellschaft, Freiheit* (Frankfurt am Main: Suhrkamp, 1976), p. 112.

[39] Cf. Wolfgang von Rimscha, *Die Grundrechte im süddeutschen Konstitutionalismus* (Köln: Heymann, 1973); Rainer Wahl, 'Rechtliche Wirkungen und Funktionen der Grundrechte im deutschen Konstitutionalismus' (1979) 18 *Der Staat* 321; Dieter Grimm, 'Grundrechte und Privatrecht in der bürgerlichen Sozialordnung' in his *Recht und Staat* (n. 15), p. 192.

well the revolutionary break with traditional rule was ultimately required in order to finally, and with much delay, assert the modern constitution entirely.

## III. ON THE CURRENT CONDITION OF THE CONSTITUTION

### 1. *Continued Need*

The conditions under which the modern constitution was able to emerge more than two centuries ago have since changed. This forces the question as to whether the constitution can be maintained when severed from its originating conditions and under altered prerequisites. Admittedly, the outward signs would indicate the demand, because the constitution has spread across the globe and is to be found not only in those political systems with a tradition of bourgeois liberalism. However, this circumstance initially testifies only to the continuing attraction of, and possibly the lack of alternatives to, the idea of the constitution as a solution to the problem of legitimation and limitation of political power. This also endows it with a certain usefulness for rulers themselves, for whom the constitution promises greater security and acceptance of their rule. By contrast, the current global propagation of the constitution says nothing about its effectiveness today.

In one respect, however, the special situation out of which the constitution originally emerged has become the rule. It is no longer accepted that a ruler is legitimated by reasons that are pre-existing, transcendental, or inherent in the exercise of power. The vacuum left after the revolution against a consensus-independent ruler, which formed the reason for the necessity of reconstitution of rule, has thus become permanent, although in a latent way. The authority to rule depends on authorization and consent. Under these circumstances, however, legal rules that define how state power is to be created and exercised are required if the rule is to have any pretensions to legitimacy. This is not implemented in all political systems with the aim of limiting power. Still, the constitution's most dependable pillar is the need for the derivation and organization of rule.

Independently of that, however, one can observe developments that weaken the regulative power of constitutional law with respect to state power, thus calling into question its ability to solve problems in the present. This refers neither to the widespread pseudo-constitutionalism nor the lack of means of asserting constitutional requirements through legal proceedings that prevails in many places. Both have existed from the very beginning. Rather, at issue are structural limitations of the legal control of the political process, which in this form are new. They originate in an altered problem constellation that distinguishes highly complex industrial societies from preindustrial bourgeois societies. These problems have transformed both the function and the nature of the state. With regards to the originating conditions of the modern constitution, these impact the social model that underlies constitutional law and the object of constitutional regulation.

## 2. *Materialization of State Tasks*

The bourgeois model of society failed to fulfil the promises associated with it. Certainly, it unleashed the economy, thus contributing to an unimagined increase in prosperity. However, the reconciliation of interests that was also anticipated never took place. Developed under preindustrial conditions, the bourgeois social model renounced its claim of extending its benefits to the entire society following the Industrial Revolution. On the contrary, it left in its wake a class division that was every bit as abhorrent as the previous system of estates. This undercut the premise of society's ability to control itself. If the goal of equal freedom was to be preserved, the means had to be changed. Social justice could no longer be expected as the natural consequence of the free play of social forces, but rather once again had to be effected politically. This led to a materialization of the justice problem. Consequently, the state also had to move out of the role of simply the guarantor of a presupposed order assumed to be just, and once more actively shape this order with an eye to specific material objectives.

This has consequences for the constitution, as it is not designed to resolve material problems, nor can it be adapted to this task without difficulty. Thus, the regulative power of the constitution declines in proportion to the scope of the transformation from a liberal order-oriented state to the modern welfare state. The reduced congruence between the social problems and the constitutional response is initially associated with the fact that the new type of state is characterized not by individual interventions in the sphere of freedom reserved in principle to individual choice, but by planning, guiding, and establishing services of all kinds for society. However, that vitiates the constitutional law, which aims to tame state encroachment, to a corresponding extent. As modern state activities do not represent encroachments in a legal sense, they do not need a legal basis. Where no legal basis exists, the principle of the lawfulness of administrative action also does not apply. As the administration operates in a legal vacuum, judicial oversight of administrative acts also declines. The most important manifestations of the rule of law and democracy are thus rendered partially inoperative.

This danger has not gone unnoticed and judges and scholars have attempted to remedy democratic and constitutional deficits by extending the concept of encroachment and of the necessity for a basis of action in law. However, it has become apparent that, for two reasons, this is only possible to a limited extent. First, unlike formal issues, material problems cannot be resolved on the legal level. Although law can mandate a solution, the realization of the normative requirement depends largely on extra-legal factors, and the realization of the constitution, for which scarcity problems did not exist as long as it only imposed barriers, becomes contingent on what is possible. Secondly, unlike the state's guarantor functions, the structuring functions escape comprehensive legal regulation. In the fulfilment of its guarantor function, the state acted retroactively and selectively. State activities of this type are relatively easy to determine on a normative level. The norm defines what is to be considered a disturbance of order and determines the actions the state may employ to restore order. By contrast, material state activity operates on a prospective and comprehensive basis. This activity proves to be so complex that it cannot be anticipated completely and therefore not entirely determined by law. Whenever the realization of prospective objectives is concerned, the requirements of constitutional law can be fulfilled to only a limited extent due to structural reasons.

### 3. Diffusion of State Power

The modern constitution was based on the difference between state and society. Society was stripped of all means of political power and set free, while the state was equipped with the monopoly of power and then restricted. It is this difference that enabled the rational binding of state power by law. Although it regulated the relationship between state *and* society, the latter held the entitled position as a matter of principle and the former the obligated position. But this differentiation is also disappearing in the face of new state tasks, and with it the regulatory potential of the constitution. This is true in two respects.

For one thing, the extension of suffrage was inevitably associated with the emergence of political parties, for which no provision was made in the original constitutions. Even today, many constitutions take no notice of them, yet they are the determinative forces of political life. Where they are subjected to constitutional norms, however, these reveal a curious regulatory weakness. The reason for this is that the parties cannot be localized within the dualistic system of state and society. They operate as mediating instances between the people and the organs of the state, and by virtue of their function necessarily pierce the boundary between state and society that lies at the heart of the constitution. These are the organizations that staff the state's organs in the name of the people and determine their programme of action. As a consequence, it becomes clear on examination that political parties can be seen behind all state institutions. They have already completed their task before the separation of powers has the chance to become operative. As a result, independent state organs do not check and balance each other, as provided for under the constitution; rather, the political parties cooperate with themselves in different roles.

Secondly, the altered form of state activity blurs the system boundary between state and society. No longer merely the guarantor of an underlying order, the modern state today assumes the global control of social development. However, this expansion of its mission has not been accompanied by an enhancement of its powers. In particular, the economic system, protected by basic rights, remains in the private domain. As a consequence, the state cannot rely on its specific means of command and coercion but has only indirect methods at its disposal for performing its new tasks. To that extent, the state becomes dependent on the willingness of private actors to follow its lead. This places private actors in a negotiating position, and what seems to be a formal state decision is, in material terms, the result of negotiation processes in which public and private power are involved in a mixture not easily dissolved. In this way, privileged social groups participate in the fulfilment of state functions, thus pushing the system further along on the path back to the older order of scattered and independent centres of rule. The binding force of the constitution declines to the same extent, as it no longer includes the entire creation of collectively binding decisions and not all participants in the decision-making process. In spite of its aspiration, the constitution is relegated to the function of a partial order, acquiring characteristics of the older localized and sectional bond of rule.[40] It is to be anticipated that this process will refocus interest in the material constitution as awareness of it grows.

[40] The considerations that substantiate this conclusion are presented in Dieter Grimm, 'Die sozialgeschichtliche und verfassungsrechtliche Entwicklung zum Sozialstaat' in his *Recht und Staat* (n. 15), p. 138.

## ⚬ 3 ⚬

# Basic Rights in the Formative
# Era of Modern Society

### I. BASIC RIGHTS AS A MODERN PHENOMENON

*1. Definition of Basic Rights*

Basic rights are a product of the bourgeois revolutions of the late eighteenth century and are a part of the programme of the modern constitutional state that emerged from these revolutions. This has not yet been sufficiently recognized in historical scholarship. Rather, one often finds a tendency to regard every legally guaranteed freedom as a basic right. Using this definition, it is possible to trace basic rights far into the past, so that they merely enter into a new developmental stage with modern constitutionalism. It is not that they become legally valid, but rather their validity acquires greater scope.[1] This is correct in that basic rights represent a historical form of legal guarantee of freedom and as such are part of a long tradition. However, it must not be forgotten that basic rights represent a specific form of legal guarantee of freedom which broke with their predecessors in important respects and derived its continuing attractiveness from just this rupture. Thus, to comprehend the unique nature of basic rights, the best course is to examine the catalogues of basic rights in modern constitutions which institutionalize the changes brought about by revolution to identify how they differ from the older forms of legal guarantees of freedom.

The most succinct formulation of these differences may be found in the Virginia Bill of Rights of 16 August 1776, which begins by asserting 'that all men are by nature equally free'.[2] In doing so, it departs from earlier legal guarantees

---

[1] Cf. e.g. the contributions by W. Schulze, 'Der bäuerliche Widerstand und die "Rechte der Menschheit"' in G. Birtsch (ed.), *Grund- und Freiheitsrechte im Wandel von Gesellschaft und Geschichte* (Göttingen: Vandenhoeck & Ruprecht, 1981), esp. p. 56; B. Sutter, 'Der Schutz der Persönlichkeit in mittelalterlichen Rechten. Zur historischen Genese der modernen Grund- und Freiheitsrechte' in G. Birtsch (ed.), *Grund- und Freiheitsrechte von der ständischen zur spätbürgerlichen Gesellschaft* (Göttingen: Vandenhoeck & Ruprecht, 1987), p. 17. A clear distinction between literal postulation and legal validity of basic rights is also missing in the standard reference by G. Oestreich, *Geschichte der Menschenrechte und Grundfreiheiten im Umriß* (Berlin: Duncker & Humblot, 1968, 2nd edn, 1978).

[2] Text reprinted in F. Hartung, *Die Entwicklung der Menschen- und Bürgerrechte von 1776 bis zur Gegenwart* (Göttingen: Musterschmidt, 4th edn, 1972), p. 40.

Constitutionalism: Past, Present, and Future. First Edition. Dieter Grimm. © Dieter Grimm 2016. Published 2016 by Oxford University Press.

of freedom in three fundamental ways and creates new conditions, namely with regards to the rights holders, the grounds for validity, and the resulting rank as well as the content of the guarantee of rights. Thus, all people hold rights to the freedoms to be guaranteed by basic rights. The French *Déclaration des droits de l'homme et du citoyen* of 26 August 1793 emphasizes this in its very title. The individual provisions of both documents repeatedly utilize the formulations *no man, all men, any men, any person,* and *nul homme, chaque homme, tout homme.* By contrast, the older legal freedoms were not linked to the quality of personhood, but to a specific social status or corporate membership and only in exceptional cases did they benefit individuals—and even then not all persons, but rather only privileged individuals.[3] Freedoms were mediated by estate or granted as a privilege. They were thus particular, whereas the basic rights are always accorded to the individual, and are thus *universally* valid through their connection to personhood.

The Bill of Rights also declares the reason why rights to liberty are universal: people hold them *naturally.* Correspondingly, Art. 1 of the *Déclaration* states that people are *born* free and with equal rights. This asserts nothing less than the non-disposability of rights to liberty. According to the Bill of Rights, people hold these as 'inherent rights of which ... they cannot by any compact deprive or divest their posterity'. According to the clear determination of Art. 2 of the *Déclaration,* the state's *raison d'être* is solely to protect them: 'The aim of all political association is the preservation of the natural and imprescriptible rights of man.' By contrast, older guarantees of freedom were either justified through tradition or granted by or agreed upon with the ruler, and thus always by positive law. This means that they could be altered, albeit mostly, only by mutual consent. However, natural rights were also transferred into positive law by the bills of rights. But this constituted merely a recognition, and not a creation of these rights; their inclusion in the constitution, to which state power owes its existence and authority, was intended specifically so as to accord them a higher status. That is why basic rights are not merely laws that are difficult to change, but rather are unalterable and thus *higher* law.

As the object of its protections, the Bill of Rights cites equal freedom, with no further qualification. Article 4 of the French *Déclaration* describes what is meant with the words: 'Liberty consists in the freedom to do everything which injures no one else.' Freedom thus does not exist for a particular purpose or depend on a specific function. Rather, it is an end in itself, and as such an authorization to any arbitrary use. By its very nature, freedom understood in this way permits no other restrictions 'except those which assure to the other members of the society the enjoyment of the same rights'. By

---

[3] Regarding the characterization of those older legal freedoms, see O. Brunner, 'Freiheitsrechte in der altständischen Gesellschaft' in H. Büttner (ed.), *Festschrift Th. Mayer* (Lindau and Konstanz: Thorbecke, 1954), p. 293; K. v. Raumer, 'Absoluter Staat, korporative Libertät, persönliche Freiheit' in H. H. Hoffmann (ed.), *Die Entstehung des modernen souveränen Staats* (Cologne: Kiepenheuer & Witsch, 1967), p. 173.

contrast, the older social orders, based on a pre-existing, materially defined general welfare, first imposed bonds and obligations on members of society. Freedoms, on the other hand, existed only in the form of privileges or prerequisites for the fulfilment of social functions. Consequently, their exercise was both guided and restricted by this function. For the same reason, the older legal guarantees of freedom could only have individual freedoms as their object; they could even comfortably coexist with a system of general absence of freedom. As opposed to this, basic rights make a systemic decision in favour of *freedom in and of itself.* Through the elimination of a previously established, materially defined ideal of virtue, its general welfare consists of enabling individual self-determination.

It is true that the declarations of rights formulate the fundamental choice of freedom in the form of individual guarantees; however, this does not alter the fact that these do not concern particular freedoms, but rather historical specifications of the principle of general freedom. They negate the older binding obligations or state practices that were felt by the framers of the declarations to be particularly oppressive. In spite of the many differences in detail, it is possible to identify four groups of basic rights that consistently recur. The first group secures the freedom of one's person and private sphere. This includes such aspects as personal freedom with the abolition of any relationship of private rule, freedom from arbitrary imprisonment and punishment, and protection of the private sphere. The second group relates to the sphere of communication and secures freedom of conscience, freedom of opinion, and freedom of the press, as well as freedom of association and assembly. The third group relates to economic life and guarantees the free use of property, and contractual and occupational freedom. Finally, the fourth group focuses on equality, whereby the substance of these rights is a reaction to feudal society and is understood not as social equality, but as equality before the law, or more precisely: equality in freedom.

When one considers the areas of application and the properties of basic rights, which until this point had never been specified at all, or at least not compiled, then it becomes clear how radically they broke with tradition and constituted a new order. With their reference to individual freedom, they attacked a model of order that was based on a materially defined ideal of virtue. They therefore did not grant individuals or social groups self-determination, but rather imposed obligations on them and allowed them only those rights derived according to function. Through the linkage of legal status with natural personhood and the equality in law this implies, they undermined feudal society, which was built on status and estate or membership of a corporation and was thus characterized by legal inequality and privilege. With their focus on individual self-determination and the broadly guaranteed autonomy of social subsystems from political control, they militated against the absolute monarchical state, which had claimed for itself the superior understanding of the general welfare and had derived comprehensive directive authority over individual lives and social development.

## 2. Bourgeois character of Basic Rights

In view of the universal applicability that differentiates basic rights from older forms of legal guarantees of freedom, it is of course necessary to examine to what extent they are intended as an expression of bourgeois ideals and interests. The chronological coincidence with the transition from feudal to bourgeois society and the rise of the basic rights does not answer causation, but only affirms the appropriateness of the question. One may only speak of a specifically bourgeois achievement if it is possible to identify an inherent relationship between the bourgeoisie, individual freedom, and the guarantee of basic rights. The circumstance that the bourgeoisie itself represented an estate and was embedded in feudal society might cast doubt on this matter. However, this cannot be allowed to apply unmodified for the era in question. Over time, a stratum of large merchants and long-distance traders; manufacturing enterprises and banks on the one hand, and civil servants in administration and education; writers and scholars on the other, emerged primarily from the traditional bourgeoisie, promoted by the economic and administrative needs of the modern absolutist state; although they were accounted in the existing feudal society as belonging to the third estate, they were distinct from the historic core of that estate, the urban tradesmen and merchants, and their consciousness and interests were quite divergent.[4]

It was this new middle stratum, having a more rational than traditional character on account of its function, that felt increasingly inhibited in the realization of its potential by a social order based on estate boundaries, feudal and corporative bonds, and state paternalism and thus commenced a process of critical reflection. The emphasis of this reflection was sometimes on philosophical and theoretical aspects, and sometimes more economic and practical, based on the premise that either humanity cannot achieve its destiny of moral perfection in dependency but only in freedom, or that a system that permits free personal development for each individual enhances the performance capacity of society as a whole. Always, however, these lines of thought led to a social order in which freedom in the sense of individual self-determination was the guiding principle. Consequently, from the very beginning, this class, unlike the leadership of the older third estate, was in no way motivated in expanding its privileges, nor in reversing the hierarchy of privileges in its favour. Rather, the entire third estate was understood as the 'general estate' on account of its numerical superiority and the increased importance of the social services it performed, which meant nothing less than the total levelling of hierarchy of estates.[5] Its demands could thus be formulated universally: the aim was equal freedom for all.

---

[4] See J. Kocka, 'Bürgertum und Bürgerlichkeit als Problem der deutschen Geschichte vom späten 18. bis zum frühen 20. Jahrhundert' in his *Bürger und Bürgerlichkeit im 19. Jahrhundert* (Göttingen: Vandenhoeck & Ruprecht, 1987), p. 21; R. Vierhaus (ed.), *Bürger und Bürgerlichkeit im Zeitalter der Aufklärung* (Heidelberg: Schneider, 1981); R. Pernoud, *Histoire de la bourgeoisie en France* (2 vols.) (Paris: Éditions du Seuil, 1960–62); J. Raynor, *The Middle Class* (London: Longman, 1969).

[5] See E. J. Sieyès, *Qu'est-ce que le Tiers-État?* [Paris, 1789] R. Zapperi (ed.) (Geneva: Droz, 1970).

Understood in this way, freedom necessarily entailed a restructuring of the system of rule. Such diverse social sectors as economy, science and scholarship, religion, art, education, family, and more had to emancipate themselves through the agency of the freedom to take individual decisions and each pursue its own criteria of rationality. Creation of social cohesion and the establishment of a fair reconciliation of interests were then transferred to the market mechanism, which was to fulfil this task more reliably and sensitively than was possible under central political guidance. This did not make the state dispensable, as society, stripped of all ruling authority and means of compulsion and fragmented into unaffiliated individuals empowered to pursue any arbitrary behaviour, was unable to create the prerequisite for achieving its objective—equal freedom for all—through its own power. To achieve this end, it required an instance outside of itself equipped with legal means of compulsion—in other words, the state. Under the conditions of society's capacity for self-determination, however, the state surrendered its central directive authority and was forced to content itself with an assistance function for bourgeois society. Its tasks were reduced to fending off dangers to society's liberty and to restore the system of freedoms in the event that a disturbance occurred.

In the late eighteenth century, there could not possibly be any general interest in such a system, even though it was formulated in universal terms and thus promised to bestow its benefits on all. For the monarch, this meant being demoted to an organ of a state independent of him and serving an autonomous society. This system cost the higher estates their privileges. The nobility was not only deprived of its economic basis but was rendered entirely without a purpose and was forced to seek a bourgeois livelihood in the competitive system. The church lost its state support and the monopoly on truth. Clergy became a private profession. The old-bourgeois classes, protected by the guild system and commercial and trade monopolies, saw more risks than opportunities in an economy based on competition. The lower classes lacked the material means to actually exploit the legal freedoms of the new system. Thus, the main beneficiaries of the nascent system were the new bourgeoisie, who also emerged as the most important proponents of this idea and, insofar as they were sufficiently provided with land, the farmers. However, as the latter lacked a corresponding consciousness, one can justifiably speak of a bourgeois social model, which of course did not preclude members of other estates from supporting it as well due to better understanding or in the hope of gain.

Overall, the bourgeois social model had to reckon with opposition, particularly from the monarchs, the church, and the privileged estates. From this, its proponents concluded that it was not enough to simply realize the new conceptual order, which would have required ordinary law and not basic rights. Rather, they sought to bestow it with greater validity so as to secure it against relapses into external control. In this respect the state, as holder of the monopoly of force and thus the means to undermine social self-control and falsify its system objectives, represented a particular danger. Should it fall into the wrong hands or should its officials develop their own organization-specific interests, welfare, and justice could not be achieved. For this reason, the state was to be prevented from intervening in the social sphere and restricted to its function of guaranteeing equal freedom. That itself was in turn a legal task. However, as the state was entrusted with both legislation and law enforcement, this task could only be accomplished by dividing the legal order into one part which resided with the state and obligated the citizens, and one which originated with the citizens as the source of public power and thus took priority over the portion allotted to the state, and to which the state was bound when it exercised its legislative and law enforcement tasks. This is precisely the function fulfilled by the basic rights.[6]

On account of this genetic relationship between emancipation of the bourgeoisie, re-establishment of the social system on the principle of freedom, and the securing of freedom through basic rights, these basic rights can indeed be regarded as an expression of bourgeois values and interests. Consequently, it is also possible to measure the realization of bourgeois society in various countries using the time and extent of their assertion. Basic rights thus serve as an indicator for the realization of the bourgeois social model. This will be explored more fully in the following section, and the relationship between basic rights and civil society that have hitherto been described extremely abstractly will be better illustrated in this discussion. There is no uniform pattern for the realization of bourgeois society and the role which the basic rights play in them. It is precisely the differences revealed in the course of a comparative examination, however, that makes it possible to pose the question as to the function of the basic rights in asserting and securing the bourgeois social model once more with greater precision. At the same time, the interplay between basic rights and bourgeois society also necessarily poses the question as to whether this is limited to the genesis of basic rights or has shaped their function permanently. The present role and future importance of basic rights depend on the answer to this question.

## II. CASE STUDIES

### 1. England

The origins of the history of modern basic rights are often sought in England. This would appear to confirm the thesis laid out here regarding the relationship between the emergence of basic rights and the formation of civil society. And in fact, England is the country in which feudalism began to decay earlier than in any other. Thus, by the beginning of the Renaissance, personal unfreedom was already unknown in England and only remnants of special rights of estates remained.[7] Without the feudal restrictions on employment and commerce, the

---

[6] See Ch. 2 of this volume.

[7] Cf. R. Hilton, *The Decline of Serfdom in Medieval England* (London: Macmillan, 1969); H. M. Cam, 'The Decline and Fall of English Feudalism' (1940) 25 (99) *History*, 216–33 at 216; H. Perkin, *The Origins of Modern English Society* (London: Routledge & Paul, 1969).

boundary between the nobility and the bourgeoisie quickly declined in meaning. It became virtually the rule for second sons of the nobility to pursue a bourgeois profession, while the economically successful members of the bourgeoisie could eventually reckon with ennoblement. This created a broad area of coinciding interests, among which freedom from royal intervention was paramount. The political locale for asserting these interests was parliament, which unlike the estates of the of the continental territories did not suffer an interruption in tradition during the early Renaissance, but instead gained in strength during the Reformation and increasingly evolved away from its roots and into a modern representation of the assertive social forces in opposition to the monarchical executive.

In England, before any other country, this process found its legal expression in the formulation of freedom rights that were derived not from estate or corporation membership but related to the individual, and which were not simply privileges to the benefit of specific individuals or groups but accrued to all Englishmen. In part, these freedom rights derived from a universalization of older privileges of the estates, as a comparison of the Magna Carta with Coke's commentary from the early seventeenth century illustrates: the rights holders of the estates enumerated in the former, earls, barons, freemen, and merchants, are summarily replaced with 'man'.[8] In part, these rights had been added through court decisions on the basis of individual disputes. This form of emergence precluded a systematically developed catalogue of concrete formulations of the general principle of freedom. Altogether, however, the individual rights originating in different periods represent a relatively far-reaching protection of personal, communication-related, and economic liberty, so that instead of islands of freedom within a system of general lack of liberty, one can speak of a liberty-oriented system, even though Elizabethan economic legislation and its oversight by the Star Chamber in no way deserved to be called liberal.

Yet as early as the dawn of the seventeenth century, during the Elizabethan period, one may observe how rights of liberty acquired growing importance, which expressed itself in the fact that they were increasingly described as 'fundamental'—at a time when, on the continent, the concept of *leges fundamentals* or *lois fondamentales* was reserved for the highest principles of state or princely law.[9] Thus, within the context of the time these rights stand out from the mass of legal norms and lay claim to a greater degree of dignity compared to these.

---

[8] Text of the Magna Carta reproduced in C. Stephenson and F. G. Marcham (eds), *Sources of English Constitutional History*, vol. 1 (New York: Harper & Row, 1972), p. 115 et seq.; E. Coke, *The Second Part of the Institutes of the Laws of England* (London, 1642). Further, M. Ashley, *Magna Carta in the Seventeenth Century* (Charlottesville: University Press of Virginia, 1965); A. Pallister, *Magna Carta* (Oxford: Clarendon Press, 1971).

[9] J. W. Gough, *Fundamental Law in English Constitutional History* (Oxford: Clarendon Press, 1955); G. Stourzh, 'Staatsformenlehre und Fundamentgesetze in England und Nordamerika im 17. und 18. Jahrhundert' in R. Vierhaus (ed.), *Herrschaftsverträge, Wahlkapitulationen, Fundamentalgesetze* (Göttingen: Vandenhoeck & Ruprecht, 1977), p. 294; G. Stourzh, 'Grundrechte zwischen Common Law und Verfassung' in Birtsch (1981) (n. 1), p. 59; R. Pound, *The Development of Constitutional Guarantees of Liberty* (New Haven: Yale University Press, 1957); H. Mohnhaupt, 'Verfassung I' in O. Brunner et al. (eds), *Geschichtliche Grundbegriffe*, vol. 6 (Stuttgart: Klett-Cotta, 1990), p. 846 et seq.

When examined closely, however, the emphasis proved to fall on a legal priority. Basic rights found their locus in common law, which developed out of case law. They were thus a part of ordinary law and could be changed at any time through statute law. It is true that sporadic attempts to subordinate statute law to common law occured, at least when the former violated 'common right and reason', as in the opinion formulated by Coke in the case of Dr Bonham.[10] However, a general rule that common law, with the rights of liberty it embodied, held a higher status than statue law or even the entire power of the state, and was not subject to them, was no part of the English legal tradition.

Attempts to subject parliament to the rights of liberty were a reaction to the experience with the Long Parliament, which followed the phase of parliament-free rule. The Levellers responded to the excesses of the Long Parliament with a demand for a 'law paramount', which reflected the insight that parliaments, no less than governments, could rob a people of its freedom. The various constitutional proposals between 1640 and 1660, referred to as 'agreements of the people', testify to this.[11] However, the proposals of the Levellers and Officers met with strong resistance. In a response to the second 'agreement' of 1648, the opponents focused their ire primarily on the limitation of the rights of parliament, 'for the Power of Parliament here in England is without question *Supreme, Absolute, Unlimited*, extending to things of religion as well as to civil things'.[12] In the Glorious Revolution, which following Cromwell's republican experiment and the Stuarts' renewed claim to absolutism, formed the bridge to the pre-revolutionary conditions, this position prevailed over that of the Levellers. Parliament successfully fended off French-style monarchic absolutism without itself having to accept restrictions on its own power. In terms of public law, the result of the revolution was to finally cement the sovereignty of parliament, which the newly anointed monarch expressly affirmed.

However, the struggle against the absolutist efforts of the Stuarts also brought forth solemn affirmations of rights of liberty in special legal documents, firstly in the Petition of Right of 1628, then in the Bill of Rights of 1689, which affirmed the results of the revolution.[13] The question is whether this endowed the existing elements of freedom and universality with the attributes of basic rights, namely priority and inviolability, that were still lacking. The genesis and the text of these documents provide reasons for doubt. The threats to liberty that

---

[10] [1610] 8 Co Rep. 114 at 118.

[11] See S. R. Gardiner (ed.), *The Constitutional Documents of the Puritan Revolution* (Oxford: Clarendon Press, 3rd edn, 1968); D. M. Wolfe (ed.), *Leveller Manifestoes of the Puritan Revolution* (New York: Humanities, 1967); A. L. Morton (ed.), *Freedom in Arms. A Selection of Leveller Writings* (London: Lawrence and Wishart, 1975); W. W. Wittwer, *Grundrechte bei den Levellers und der New Model Army* (Düsseldorf: Henn, 1972); P. Wende, '"Liberty" und "Property" in der politischen Theorie der Levellers' [1974] 1 *Zeitschrift für Historische Forschung* 147–231; H.-C. Schröder, 'Die Grundrechtsproblematik in der englischen und der amerikanischen Revolution' in Birtsch (1981) (n. 1), p. 75; G. Stourzh, *Fundamental Laws and Individual Rights in the 18th Century Constitution* (Claremont: Claremont, 1984).

[12] Quotation in Schröder (n. 11), p. 85.

[13] Text reproduced in Stephenson and Marcham (n. 8), p. 450 et seq. and ibid., vol. 2, p. 599 et seq.

had led to revolution originated with the monarch, while parliament saw itself as the defender of a long-established legal state of freedom. No recourse to natural law was necessary for the legitimation of rights of liberty, only the citation of valid, established law. In the Petition of Right, parliament thus enumerated a series of violations of traditional basic rights by the crown and linked this with the demand that the monarch eliminate the current violations of law and in future refrain from further violations in future. The latter is said to have responded with, 'Soit droit fait come est desire'. Thus, like numerous estate-based documents on the continent, the Petition had primarily a law-affirming and contractual character.[14] The monarch and his executive were under obligations, whilst parliament, which had defended the rights, appeared as the entitled branch.

This genesis not only explains why the Bill of Rights contained primarily rights of parliament and only secondarily individual rights; it also explains why the scope of the rights of liberty essentially remained unchanged. The revolution was not fought against, but rather for the current law and the freedoms it guaranteed. Parliament had proved itself the guarantor of freedom, and the majority of those interested in freedom saw themselves represented by parliament. Consequently, there was no need to secure freedom against parliament. Rather, as the representative of those advocating freedom, it could dispose of rights of liberty without violating the law. Legally ratified limitations of freedom were understood as self-limitation on the part of the rights holders. For the character of basic rights of the English declarations of rights, it thus follows that they laid special juridical emphasis on common law at particularly liberty-sensitive points to grant them an additional, though not paramount, guarantee. They restricted the executive apparatus of the state, but not state power as such, in which parliament participated. Thus, Stourzh is justified in saying that although the rights of liberty were made fundamental in England, no constitutionalization occurred.[15] The step towards basic rights was prepared, but never carried out.

### 2. America

Rather, it was the English colonies in North America which succeeded in transforming statutory rights of liberty into constitutional rights. This circumstance raises the question as to the difference between the colonies and the mother country with respect to basic rights. This cannot be explained through a lesser legal status. Rather, from their founding, the American colonists lived under the English legal order and thus also enjoyed the rights of Englishmen embodied

---

[14] Cf. G. Oestreich, 'Vom Herrschaftsvertrag zur Verfassungsurkunde' in Vierhaus (n. 9), p. 45. The items that were newly channelled in hereby are emphasized by L. G. Schwoerer, *The Declaration of Rights 1689* (Baltimore: Johns Hopkins University Press, 1981). For a modern understanding, cf. E. Hellmuth, 'Die Debatte um die "Bill of Rights" im 18. Jahrhundert' in Birtsch (1987) (n. 1), p. 117.

[15] G. Strourzh, 'Vom aristotelischen zum liberalen Verfassungsbegriff' in F. Engel-Janosi et al. (eds), *Fürst, Bürger, Mensch* (Vienna: Verlag für Geschichte und Politik, 1975), p. 120.

in common law and solemnly affirmed in the documents of the seventeenth century. Their participation in this legal order did not engender any perception of a liberty deficit on the part of the colonists, but rather a feeling of superiority over the European continent, characterized by estate and feudal structures and governed as a police state. Without feudal law and the limitations of the estates that had been left behind in Europe, and with unlimited resources which promised a wealth of opportunity to the bold and hard-working, America possessed a social order that, though based on a slave economy, more closely approximated bourgeois ideals than any European country, including England. Thus, America did not itself provide an environment for legal reform; rather, the reform postulates developed under European natural law could be regarded as the description of the American reality.

This did not change until the colonists were confronted with the deficits in the English protection of liberty, which in the motherland had become perceptible only for a short time. This occurred when the British Parliament resolved to impose special taxes on the American colonies following the expensive Seven Years War. In the dispute that followed, the colonists, as the English did to their monarch a century before, cited the rights of Englishmen which also applied in America, particularly the principles of equality and 'no taxation without representation'. The mother country responded to this argument by referring to the principle of parliamentary sovereignty and the 'virtual representation' of the colonists by the members of the mother country. On the strength of this fiction, the burdens placed on them were regarded as self-imposed and therefore legitimate. This position was unassailable from the perspective of positive law; it was the weakness of this argument of positive law with respect to the basic precepts of English constitutional law that forced the colonists to refer to 'inalienable rights', with which the Declaration of Independence,[16] in a formal reference to the Petition of Right, justified breaking with the motherland in terms of natural law.[17]

In the reconstitution of legitimate state power that became necessary in the wake of the revolutionary break, the Americans resorted to English legal principles, of which they continued to approve. As noted early on, the catalogues of basic rights of the colonies, which had now advanced to states, scarcely contained a right that would not have applied in England.[18] For these rights however, which often had already been enumerated in the settlement contracts and colonial charters, the justification on the basis of pre-state natural law ascribed to them during the revolution were retained. The rights of Englishmen were thus transformed into human rights with the same civil-rights content. But above

---

[16] Text reproduced in S. E. Morison (ed.), *Sources and Documents Illustrating the American Revolution and the Formation of the Federal Constitution 1764-1788* (New York: Oxford University Press, 2nd edn, 1965), p. 157 et seq.

[17] Cf. J. Habermas, 'Naturrecht und Revolution' in his *Theorie und Praxis* (Neuwied: Luchterhand, 1963), p. 52; Dieter Grimm, 'Europäische Naturrechte und Amerikanische Revolution' (1970) 3 *Ius Commune* 120; C. L. Becker, *The Declaration of Independence* (New York: Harcourt, Brace and Co., 1922).

[18] Cf. Pound (n. 9), p. 65.

all, in view of the experiences with British parliamentary sovereignty, they were placed above popular representation, and now restricted public power in all its forms, without exception. In this way, America expanded the English rights of liberty to include the element of supremacy, and soon thereafter further secured them through a separate entity for their assertion, a supreme court, which received its decision-making criteria from the constituent power of the people and realized this in the face of all constituted powers. It is this occurrence of 1776 that signals the decisive break between the older and the newer forms of legal guarantees of liberty and marks the advent of the modern history of basic rights.[19]

### 3. France

France lacked a comparable tradition of catalogued rights of liberty that needed only to be expanded in their function and elevated to the level of the constitution in order to attain the character of basic rights. Rather, the monarch claimed a comprehensive power of control over society, and the legal relationships of the subjects were based on the inequality of estates, external determination, and duty. However, when France found itself in the same situation as America some years later, thinking in terms of basic rights had already become possible. Admittedly, the similarity was restricted to the revolutionary overthrow of the old state power and the necessity of reconstitution. On the other hand, the initial situation differed greatly from the American case. While the American colonists had long since enjoyed the liberal order and merely defended it against threats from the mother country and subsequently secured this in the form of basic rights after winning independence, in France this order was a political postulate of a self-aware, economically powerful, and critically reasoning bourgeoisie which saw itself restricted by the existing order in terms of their influence and experience and, from the mid-eighteenth century on, increasingly pushed for changes. Thus, the order which the Americans defended had to be created in France in the first place.

Here as well, a state financial crisis, to be alleviated by tax increases, presented the lever. Those affected opposed the plans of the weakened monarchy by asserting the right of consent of the estates, which had not been exercised for over 170 years.[20] In this, the nobility and the bourgeoisie, which unlike in England had not formed any identity of interest otherwise, agreed. However, the nobility was thinking of an assembly of the estates established according to the principles of the sixteenth century, whilst the bourgeoisie demanded a makeup that reflected the altered balance of power within society. In this conflict, positive law was on the side of the nobility, so that the bourgeoisie could

---

[19] Cf. G. Stourzh, 'Die Konstitutionalisierung der Individualrechte' (1976) *Juristenzeitung* 397; W. P. Adams, *Republikanische Verfassung und bürgerliche Freiheit* (Neuwied: Luchterhand, 1973); B. Schwartz, *The Great Rights of Mankind. A History of the American Bill of Rights* (New York: Oxford University Press, 1977).

[20] Cf. E. Schmitt, *Repräsentation und Revolution* (Munich: Beck, 1969).

only justify its demand on the basis of the superior position of natural law, which, as previously in America, developed its revolutionary potential. The *cahiers de doléances*, with which the communities instructed their representatives for the assembly of the estates, and a virtual sea of pamphlet literature of the *prérevolution* are replete with demands based on natural law.[21] After the king approved the recall of the Estates General with concessions to the third estate and the latter had declared itself a National Assembly in a revolutionary break from applicable public law, the political prerequisites for the realization of bourgeois demands was created. It became possible to enact the concepts of order based on natural law as positive law.

Unlike in America, however, this task was not resolved by establishing a guarantee of basic rights as an umbrella to secure the social order. Rather, a bourgeois order first had to be created before it could be secured through basic rights. Still, the National Assembly did not choose to reform the legal order first and then guarantee the results through basic rights, but rather placed the drafting of a catalogue of basic rights at the top of the reform effort with the resolution of 14 July 1789. This decision was not without controversy in the National Assembly.[22] The objections are revealing of the character of securing liberty through basic rights. One reservation centred on the concept of the necessity of a catalogue of rights of liberty in principle. Deputy Crenière objected to the various drafts of basic rights, asserting that there was just one basic right, namely the participation of each individual in the formation of the general will. This was the radical democratic position of Rousseau, which was not compatible with the material limitations of majority decisions. By contrast, the majority of the deputies, like the representatives of the American colonies before them, found that individual freedom could also be threatened by elected popular representatives. Consequently, they reasoned, basic rights had to protect individuals from legislators at endangered points.

The other much more strongly supported objection related to the sequencing of the reform steps. According to this, priority was to be accorded to eliminating the existing order with its inequalities and privileges, its repressions and restrictions on commerce, and replacing it with a new one founded on freedom and equality. This meant giving priority to reformation of civil law, criminal law, and trial law, while the task of securing new conditions in the form of basic rights appeared as a secondary problem. On the contrary, the majority of the National Assembly insisted on the priority of basic rights, thus asserting that these represented not only the guarantees for the existence of the bourgeois social order with respect to the state, but also contained the fundamental principles which needed to be established if the reform of ordinary law was to be

---

[21] Cf. e.g. P. Goubert and M. Deni (eds), *Les Français ont la parole. Cahiers de doléances des États généraux* (Paris: Julliard, 1964); W. Schmale, 'Rechtskultur im Frankreich des Ancien Régime und die Erklärung der Menschen- und Bürgerrechte' (1986) 14 *Francia* 513; S.-J. Samwer, *Die französische Erklärung der Menschen- und Bürgerrechte von 1789/91* (Hamburg: Hansischer Gildenverlag, 1970), pp. 6–92.

[22] See the debate in *Archives parlementaires*, vol. 8 (Paris, 1875), pp. 317–25. See also, Samwer (n. 21), p. 103 et seq.

conducted on the basis of principles. In France as well, basic rights as definitive guidelines and limits of legal reform also claimed to be applicable to all state powers including the legislature. But the French ultimately could not resolve to secure this primacy organizationally through the establishment of a constitutional court on account of their experiences with the courts of the nobility under the *ancien régime*, which held the right to affirm legislation and had used this primarily to promote privileged interests.

The basic concept of universally applicable freedom taking precedence over the state, expressed technically in these basic rights, remained through the different phases of the revolution with their succeeding constitutions.[23] Despite appearances, it lived on in the Directorial Constitution of 1795; the catalogue of basic obligations added to the basic rights here proves on closer examination to be merely an admonishment to obedience to the law and a moral appeal to the citizens' disposition. The break with this tradition did not occur until the rule of Napoleon, who, on the one hand, finally concluded the transition of the social order to the principles of liberty and equality in the *Code civil*, while on the other hand rescinding the guarantees of liberty through basic rights in order to return to absolutist practices under the mantle of a constitution. In this way, the indivisible liberty of the revolution was divided into a continuing private, and a politically reversible liberty. By contrast, the *Charte constitutionnelle* of 1814 chose a middle road. The political achievements of the revolution that made up the legitimation of principle of popular sovereignty were repealed, while the social achievements embodied in the *Code civil* were retained. Accordingly, the *Charte* recognized basic rights relating to the freedom of individuals and their economic pursuits, but none that were politically useful.

## 4. Germany

For the German princes, who had suffered no revolution, the constitutional state only became acceptable in this reduced post-revolutionary form. By contrast, the German bourgeoisie lacked the social prerequisites for compelling them to make greater concessions. Certainly, an educated bourgeois class comparable to the French had developed in the second half of the eighteenth century, primarily in the Protestant north. Accordingly, as well many bourgeois conceptions of order and ever more extensive catalogues of basic rights may also be found in Germany that date from before the French Revolution.[24] Economically, however, Germany consistently lagged behind France, so that the German constitutional demands voiced after the French Revolution and even more so after the Napoleonic Wars, largely lacked the assertive force that a property-owning bourgeoisie would have been able to muster. In Germany,

---

[23] Texts of the French Constitution reproduced in e.g. L. Duguit et al. (eds), *Les constitutions et les principales lois politiques de la France depuis 1789* (Paris: Librairie générale de droit et de jurisprudence, 6th edn, 1943).

[24] Cf. D. Kippel, *Politische Freiheit und Freiheitsrechte im deutschen Naturrecht des 18. Jahrhunderts* (Paderborn: Schöningh, 1976).

economically strengthening society was a process that was driven by the power-policy considerations of the monarchs. Even before the outbreak of the French Revolution, the rulers of the most progressive territories, Prussia and Austria, had initiated social reforms that found their legal expression in the codification drafts of the late eighteenth century.

In their introductory provisions, these drafts also contained individual guarantees of freedom for subjects with respect to the state, which reflected the altered understanding of the state under enlightened absolutism.[25] They increased the security of individual personhood and property, but did not permit intellectual freedom, not to mention political participation. Still, the character of basic rights is occasionally attributed to them. However, when one applies the criteria developed at the outset to these rights, they fulfil the character of basic rights even less than the English declarations of rights. Even if one overlooks the fact that these rights, although they relate to the individuals' status as subjects and thus relativize the boundaries of the estates, did not fundamentally challenge the feudal, estate-oriented society or the absolutist state and thus had little to do with liberty, they lacked above all the character of priority. As guarantees of freedom by an absolute ruler who held the undivided power of the state in his hands, they were self-imposed restrictions that could be revoked at any time; the beneficiaries were entirely without means or protective mechanisms that a system of division of powers provides. For this reason, Kriele characterizes them as merely tolerations, as opposed to basic rights.[26] Following the outbreak of the French Revolution, they were removed from the drafts, which took effect only after a delay, and only after being purged of all intimations of basic rights.

The constitutions that emerged after 1815 in southern Germany[27] and a number of small German states, however, were different. Certainly, none of them were won by the bourgeoisie through struggle as in America or France; they were without exception voluntary grants on the part of the princes, who admittedly were prompted to do so by a multiplicity of motives of state policy. Still, all of them comprised catalogues of rights of liberty and equality far exceeding what was granted under enlightened absolutism. Above all, however, in contrast to the codification drafts of the late eighteenth century, the monarchs relinquished the authority unilaterally to alter these rights. The

---

[25] Cf. for Austria, P. H. Ritter von Harrasowsky (ed.), *Der Codex Theresianus und seine Umarbeitungen*, vol. 5 (Vienna: Gerold, 1886), p. 3; J. Ofner (ed.), *Der Ur-Entwurf und die Berathungsprotokolle des Österreichischen Allgemeinen bürgerlichen Gesetzbuches*, vol. 1 (Vienna: Alfred Hölder, 1889), p. v; for Prussia, see *Entwurf eines allgemeinen Gesetzbuches für die Preußischen Staaten* (6 vols.) (Berlin: bey George Jacob Decker, 1784–1788); *Allgemeines Gesetzbuch für die Preußischen Staaten* (Berlin: Königliche Hofbuchdruckerey, 1791). Hereunto H. Conrad, *Rechtsstaatliche Bestrebungen im Absolutismus Preußens und Österreichs am Ende des 18. Jahrhunderts* (Cologne: Westdeutscher Verlag, 1961); G. Birtsch, 'Zum konstitutionellen Charakter des preußischen Allgemeinen Landrechts von 1794' in K. Kluxen and W. J. Mommsen (eds), *Festschrift Th. Schieder* (Munich: Oldenbourg, 1968), p. 98.

[26] M. Kriele, *Einführung in die Staatslehre* (Reinbeck: Rowohlt, 1968), p. 98.

[27] Texts reproduced in E. R. Huber (ed.), *Dokumente zur deutschen Verfassungsgeschichte*, vol. 1 (Stuttgart: Kohlhammer, 2nd edn, 1961), pp. 141–200.

right of absolute rule was definitively eradicated through the act of granting a constitution. Thus, regardless of their genesis as a voluntary self-restriction of monarchic power, basic rights became a higher law binding on the power of the state which could only be altered through the process of constitutional amendment. In particular, this binding power also extended to the ordinary legislative power, which consisted of the monarch and the newly established chambers, even though a great deal of uncertainty prevailed with respect to the nature and scope of the restriction. Their adoption in a constitution binding on all state powers marked the transition from legally guaranteed freedoms to basic rights in Germany as well.

Admittedly, this does not mean that their genesis as voluntary grants on the part of monarchs who remained self-legitimated remained an externality. This had an effect on both the justification for and the scope of validity, as well as on content. In the absence of revolutionary assertion, the basic rights of German constitutions avoided any hint of their natural-law origins and declared themselves as positive law that owed its existence solely to the monarch's will. Consequently, they were formulated as civil rights, and not as human rights. This of course did not reduce their anti-feudal thrust, as unlike older freedoms they were not linked to social status or function but to the individual, and thus, for the first time, represented general legal subjectivity in terms of their applicability. In this way, they were poised to eliminate feudal society, whose law had not been immediately and completely rescinded, as earlier in France, but had been designated an exceptional right tolerated for a limited period. However, to the extent that feudal law still remained in force, the principle of liberty that is constitutive for the basic rights could not develop its full effect.[28] This is clearly apparent when the contents of German and western basic rights are compared.

One searches in vain in the German catalogues of basic rights for a general right of liberty, such as is set out before the individual guarantees in Art. 4 of the French *Déclaration*. On the level of individual guarantees, personal liberty and the protection of the private sphere are ensured in a scope comparable to the western constitutions. By contrast, the politically usable basic rights as set out in the French *Charte* of 1814 are only weakly delineated. Freedom of the press prevailed, but with considerable means of restriction, and was soon strangled by the Carlsbad Decrees of 1819; freedom of assembly and association were entirely lacking. In the economic sector, property was protected against state confiscation. On the other hand, as long as the feudal system persisted, there was no comprehensive freedom of ownership that also included free use, encumbrance, sale, division, and bequeathing. Equality was in a similar state.

---

[28] See papers by G. Kleinheyer, M. Botzenhart, and U. Scheuner in H. Quaritsch (ed.), *Von der ständischen Gesellschaft zur bürgerlichen Gleichheit, Der Staat, Beiheft 4* (Berlin: Duncker & Humblot, 1980); U. Scheuner, 'Die Verwirklichung der bürgerlichen Gleichheit. Zur rechtlichen Bedeutung der Grundrechte in Deutschland zwischen 1780 und 1850' in Birtsch (1981), above n 1. p. 376; W. v. Rimscha, *Die Grundrechte im süddeutschen Konstitutionalismus* (Cologne: Heymann, 1973); R. Schulze, 'Statusbildung und Allgemeinheit der Bürgerrechte' in G. Dilcher et al. (eds), *Grundrechte im 19. Jahrhundert* (Frankfurt am Main: Lang, 1982), p. 85; Dieter Grimm, *Deutsche Verfassungsgeschichte*, vol. 1 (Frankfurt am Main: Suhrkamp, 1988), p. 129 et seq.

It too was guaranteed vis-à-vis the state, here guaranteeing equal access to state offices, equal liability to taxes and equal military service. On the other hand, the relationships of citizens to one another were not consistently characterized by legal equality. Consequently, the German constitutions represented a stunted development compared to those of the west. Still, they guaranteed freedom to a degree sufficient to call them fundamental rights.

By contrast, Austria and Prussia, the preeminent German powers which had taken the lead in modernization in the eighteenth century, did not draft constitutions. Following the death of Leopold II in 1792, Austria pursued a rigorous anti-liberal course that precluded constitutional plans from the outset. In Prussia, the sincerely desired constitutionalism failed in the face of the growing forces of restoration following the Congress of Vienna. However, the lack of basic rights does not imply an absence of bourgeois society. When one compares the German states of the *Vormärz* with respect to their convergence with the bourgeois social model, Prussia, though lacking in basic rights, is without doubt more progressive than the southern German constitutional states. Here, liberalization occurred on the legal level, and the constitution was merely to be the crowning act. Thus, the failure of the constitutional project did not impair social liberalism but only its capacity to withstand revisions in the era of the restoration. The situation in Austria was little different; here, the General Civil Code (ABGB), which like the *Code civil* was based on the principles of freedom of ownership, contracts, and bequests, took effect in 1811. Yet the appearance was deceptive, because the promulgation of the ABGB in no way eliminated the estatist-feudal and mercantilist rules, but rather transformed these into special norms, which as such always took priority over the general provisions. In this way, bourgeois society in Austria remained merely a promise.[29]

## 5. Poland

By contrast, Germany's eastern neighbour Poland acquired a constitution for the brief period of its sovereignty. Indeed, the Polish constitution of 3 May 1791[30] is often considered the very first European constitution. Although it followed the French declaration of human rights of 16 August 1789, it took effect prior to the French constitution of 3 September 1791. However, the constitutionalization of Poland stands in unique contrast to that country's social structure, which was much further removed from a bourgeois state than even the backward German states. Poland consisted of a nobles' republic with an elective monarchy at the top and a relatively broad, but only partly prosperous nobility, a narrow, economically undeveloped and politically powerless urban bourgeois class, and a large proportion of serfs. According to everything that is known about the

---

[29] Cf. Dieter Grimm, 'Das Verhältnis von politischer und privater Freiheit bei Zeiller' in his *Recht und Staat der bürgerlichen Gesellschaft* (Frankfurt am Main: Suhrkamp, 1987), p. 212.

[30] German text in K. H L. Pölitz, *Die europäischen Verfassungen seit dem Jahre 1789 bis auf die neueste Zeit, vol. 3* (Leipzig: Brockhaus, 2nd edn, 1833), p. 8.

prerequisites for the emergence of early constitutionalism,[31] this was not the soil in which constitutions or basic rights thrive. The leading nobility enjoyed cooperative freedoms to a much greater extent than their western counterparts, while the bourgeoisie as the social bearer of the urge for liberty through basic rights had not yet recognized its interests, and would certainly not have possessed the power to assert such interests against the will of the nobility. Finally, the monarch also lacked the position of power that would have enabled him to initiate liberalizations in the interests of the state.

When one looks more closely at the Polish constitution, the lack of a catalogue of basic rights is indeed immediately apparent. Nonetheless, this constitution is more than just an organizational statute.[32] Although the emphasis was on the reorganization of the state, the constitution also established provisions that relate to the social structure. When these are examined more closely, however, it becomes apparent that the intent was not to overcome the estatist social order and the feudal agricultural structure in favour of bourgeois freedom and equality. On the contrary, the constitution expressly affirmed the privileges of the nobility. The citizens' legal position improved, yet not through a universalization of freedoms, as was generally the case where basic rights are concerned, but through easier ennoblement, expansion of the rights of habeas corpus previously reserved to the nobility, and the granting of political representation. By contrast, the landowner-peasant relationship was initially merely placed under state oversight, but not altered. That was the price that the noble reform party had to pay to win over the majority of their peers. Thus, state and social reform in Poland dressed themselves in the modern raiment of the constitution, but did not adopt the programme formed in America and France. In this sense, Poland had a constitution, but one that does not permit us to conclude that basic rights applied.

### III. THE FUNCTION OF BASIC RIGHTS REVISITED

#### 1. *Determining the function of the Basic Rights*

These national case studies confirm the relationship between the introduction of basic rights and the creation of bourgeois society. At the same time, it is possible to refine and differentiate this relationship on the basis of the various constellations that are apparent. First, it appears possible to conclude the existence or emergence of a bourgeois society from the degree to which basic rights are recognized in positive law. This is apparent in the cases of America, France, and the southern German states. When basic rights are abrogated, as in Napoleonic and restoration France, that also indicates a decline in bourgeois influence.

---

[31] See Grimm (n. 28), p. 10 et seq.

[32] Cf. G.-C. v. Unruh, 'Die polnische Konstitution vom 3. Mai 1792 im Rahmen der Verfassungsentwicklung der europäischen Staaten' (1974) 13 *Der Staat* 185; W. F. Redaway et al. (eds), *The Cambridge History of Poland* (New York: Octagon Books, 1978), p. 133; A. Gieysztor et al. (eds), *History of Poland* (Warsaw: Polish Scientific Publishers, 2nd edn, 1979), p. 315.

Conversely, no basic rights are to be found where bourgeois society is neither established nor advocated. This is substantiated by the examples of Austria and Poland. However, the converse, that the lack of basic rights indicates the non-existence of bourgeois society, is not valid. The conditional relationship does not appear to work in both directions. Although no basic rights exist without a bourgeois or at least partially bourgeois society, bourgeois or partially bourgeois societies can exist without basic rights. This is supported by the examples of England and *Vormärz* Prussia.

The notion that bourgeois society does not depend on basic rights requires more detailed examination, as it can contribute to a more precise determination of the function of basic rights for bourgeois society. The basic assumption of the bourgeois social order is the ability of society to regulate itself by means of the market mechanism, which in turn presuppose the freedom and equality of all members. Legally, bourgeois society demands first of all the elimination of all norms and institutions that obstruct individual self-realization and privilege individuals or groups while discriminating against others. However, bourgeois society does not operate in a legal vacuum. Rather, the freedom on which it is based requires both protection and organization. The individual spheres of liberty must be limited and at the same time coordinated. The former demands restriction of individual freedom in the interests of general freedom; the latter demands a set of instruments to establish mutual bonds under the condition of free will. Both are typical tasks of private law as that part of the legal order which regulates the relationships between members of society. Without a private law that makes the principles of freedom and equality operational there can be no bourgeois society. Indeed, one may say that bourgeois society constitutes itself through such private law.[33]

However, as it cannot be expected that either the restrictions on the freedom of the individual in the interests of equal freedom for all or the obligations that individuals assume for the purpose of exchanging goods and services will be uniformly respected, precautions are also necessary to secure liberty, with the aid of which boundary violations can be corrected and obligations asserted. Private law is unable to perform this task because as a law for coordinating equal freedom it cannot exercise coercive force. To the extent that coercion is necessary to avert threats to liberty and assert private obligations, bourgeois society requires the state, which possesses the monopoly of force but which may only use this in the interests of liberty. Consequently, private law, which deals with the relationships of individuals, is joined by a further legal area that deals with the relationships between individuals and the state; this is termed public law. In bourgeois society, it manifests itself in the form of criminal law, police law, and procedural law, along with the tax law needed to finance the necessary expenses. Legally, this makes bourgeois society viable. In this way—and

---

[33] Cf. Dieter Grimm, 'Grundrechte und Privatrecht in der bürgerlichen Sozialordnung' in his *Recht und Staat* (n. 29), p. 192; Grimm, 'Bürgerlichkeit im Recht', ibid., p. 11.

this is key—it can be realized on the level of ordinary law. This explains why bourgeois and semi-bourgeois societies can exist in the absence of basic rights.

This then presents the question: what additional benefit do basic rights provide for bourgeois society? The answer is to be found in that element lacking from ordinary law, namely that of primacy. The key to understanding the importance of this elevated priority of rights of liberty is to be found in the reason for its occurrence. As already seen, the occasion for this was the tax policy of the British Parliament, which caused the North American colonists to conclude that the bourgeois maxims of freedom and equality could not necessarily be considered secure under a parliamentary system of legislation. Ordinary law does not offer protection against threats to liberty that originate not from the executive but the legislative branch. Consequently, as long as it is institutionalized solely on the level of statute law, the bourgeois order is unprotected in the face of legislative power and can only continue to exist to the extent that the latter voluntarily subordinates itself to the liberal maxim. If, however, these are not only to depend on the goodwill of the holders of legislative power, but also be legally anchored, this is only possible from the position of higher-ranking law that is also binding on legislative power. And just this is the task which the basic rights perform. They provide an additional guarantee for the bourgeois order established in ordinary law that the state will not merely assert this against private individuals but will itself respect this order.

Yet that does not appear entirely to describe the function of basic rights. They were only able to assume the role of an additional security against relapses or excesses on the part of a state in a bourgeois order that had already been constituted. This was the situation in America at the time of the revolution in 1776. They had achieved their aim through constitutional guarantee for an already existing bourgeois social order. By contrast, the aim of the French Revolution was to assert a bourgeois social order over an estatist-feudalist social structure and a mercantile, dirigistic state practice. Such an aim could not be achieved through constitutional guarantee for ordinary law. Rather, a comprehensive reform of all ordinary law through the process of legislation was necessary. If the reform project nevertheless commenced with the promulgation of basic rights, the function of basic rights must have been other than in America. They too related to legislative power, but not primarily as an obligation to refrain from certain actions. Rather, basic rights were to precede, initiate, and lead the protracted and complex transformation of the legal order to the principles of freedom and equality and preserve the reform legislators from error. Once the reform of ordinary law was concluded, of course, the French basic rights could revert to their guarantee function and reinforce the stability of the attainments of the revolution.

In Germany, since the bourgeois social order did not exist prior to the basic rights, these could not safeguard the former; nor did the bourgeois win this through revolution and then shape the order in accordance with basic rights. Rather, bourgeois conditions were to some extent in the interests of states and were thus imposed top-down to the extent that this served the needs of states. Thus, the focus was never about freedom as an end in itself, but rather as a means to the ends of the state. In southern Germany, the associated legal reforms occurred predominantly under the Napoleonic aegis during the short phase of the Confederation of the Rhine, before constitutions—promoted by high-level bureaucracy to neutralize fickle rulers or unreliable successors to the throne—were established to secure these reforms. Naturally, that did not stop basic rights, even in their abbreviated form, benefitting their holders, and above all it did not prevent holders from understanding them as a programme for fully establishing a bourgeois social order and demanding its realization.[34] The Prussian example illustrates the added value over systems lacking basic rights: here, limited civil freedom derived its support solely from the will of the state but when this was withdrawn, no guarantee for the status quo existed, much less a legal basis for demanding its expansion.

### 2. Severability from Conditions of Emergence

While the bourgeois social model revealed its problematic side as early as the nineteenth century, and today has been forced to give ground to social and welfare-state concepts even in the capitalist countries that did not radically turn away from the bourgeois tradition, basic rights have lost nothing of their esteem. In view of the close relationship between basic rights and bourgeois society, this forces the question as to whether basic rights can be separated from the conditions under which they originated and can be integrated in a social-state type model or whether they tend—unrecognized but persistently—to defend bourgeois interests. The partial answer to this question is provided by the basic rights themselves. One of their essential characteristics, as opposed to older forms of guarantees of liberty, is that they do not tie freedom to estates or grant it as a privilege, but assert its universality. Even though they happened to serve bourgeois ends during the phase of their emergence, this effect did not—like estatist feudal law—proceed from the legal norm itself, but solely from the situation into which basic rights emerged. In short, the bourgeoisie possessed material prerequisites that made formally recognized liberty practically useful, whereas the classes below the bourgeoisie lacked these.

This circumstance was apparent from the start. However, at the time the bourgeois social model was formulated it could still be hoped that, once all barriers to self-realization posed by estate restrictions, corporative structures, state regulations, and privileges were eliminated, obtaining the material basis would merely be a matter of talent and hard work. To this extent, basic rights in their claim to universal validity anticipated the universalization of the bourgeois class. The fields of endeavour they opened up without regard to estate and birth offered everyone the chance to become bourgeois. If this opportunity

---

[34] For the appeal function of basic rights in the nineteenth century, see R. Wahl, 'Rechtliche Wirkungen und Funktionen der Grundrechte im deutschen Konstitutionalismus des 19. Jahrhunderts' (1979) 18 *Der Staat* 321; R. Wahl, 'Der Vorrang der Verfassung' (1981) 20 *Der Staat* 485.

was not utilized, that could be considered personal failure, and thus did not reflect on the justice of the system.[35] When this expectation was disappointed, because the system permitted extensive misery that was both undeserved and inescapable, the universal content of basic rights exceeding the interests of the bourgeoisie was revitalized. They provided the platform from which a material basis could be demanded without which numerous liberties assured by the basic rights were valueless for the poor or were even perverted into instruments of repression in the hands of the wealthy. If all persons were entitled to liberty but its exercise was dependent on prosperity and education, then the protection afforded by the basic rights had to be extended to those prerequisites that were essential for their realization.

Naturally, such a demand could not be fulfilled without restrictions on freedom in the interest of equal liberty, nor without redistributions of wealth in the interest of material liberty. However, this transformed the universal basic rights into a threat to specifically bourgeois interests and consequently provoked bourgeois reactions. Still, these did not manifest themselves in the form of a rejection of basic rights, as is more apparent in Marxism, so much as in a defensive interpretation.[36] First, the liberal means of realizing basic rights, the defence against the state, was separated from its aim of equal personal liberty and elevated to an end in itself, which could then be defended regardless of the consequences for the idea of equal freedom for all. This is documented particularly starkly in the debates on child labour, where legal prohibition was opposed in the name of freedom of ownership, contractual freedom, and parental rights. Subsequently, basic rights were entirely drained of concrete liberty by portraying them as a merely historically explainable, casuistically framed, early form of the principle of the rule of law, which meant that the state could only intervene in the freedom and property of the individual on the basis of law. This denied that the basic rights contained any meaning that extended beyond the status quo and called for the creation of concrete freedom. Thus reinterpreted, they did indeed serve the property interests of the bourgeoisie in an era in which the Fourth Estate began to organize its interests politically.

This is important for the question at issue, as it shows that basic rights became dedicated to the defence of bourgeois interests because they were interpreted in a certain way, and not because of the basic rights themselves. Thus, it appears only consistent that corrections to the Basic Law from a social-state perspective are derived not from the content of the basic rights but from their function. Under these circumstances, basic rights do not fail on account of an innate prejudice in favour of bourgeois interests. Rather, their future depends on whether a consensus can still be built around their aim of equal individual

---

[35] Cf. Dieter Grimm, 'Die sozialgeschichtliche und verfassungsrechtliche Entwicklung zum Sozialstaat' in his *Recht und Staat* (n. 29), p. 138.

[36] See the Marxian attitude esp. in K. Marx, 'Zur Judenfrage' in his and F. Engels' (eds), *Werke*, vol. 1 Institut für Marxismus-Leninismus beim ZK der SED (Berlin: Dietz, 1970), p. 347 at p. 363 et seq; for the basic rights interpretation, cf. Dieter Grimm, 'Die Entwicklung der Grundrechtstheorie in der deutschen Staatsrechtslehre des 19. Jahrhunderts' in his *Recht und Staat* (n. 29), p. 308.

freedom which found legal expression in them. In this context, freedom means the priority of self-determination over external determination, the scope to create an individual life plan and establish parameters that promote this, but always according to the principle of equal entitlement for all. This necessarily entails restrictions on liberty, which are ever more numerous in a society that is becoming ever more closely interwoven and risky due to scientific and technological progress. But the postulate of liberty retains priority insofar as all restrictions must be legitimated by the ultimate end of equal freedom and function as contributions to this end.

If we continue to assume a basic social consensus for such a concept, securing this through basic rights retains its validity. Their importance has even increased due to the more intensive contact between the state and society and the increased dependence of individuals on state services. Without them, personal liberty would be entrusted solely to the willingness of governmental bodies to recognize it and the readiness of the population to defend it. But there would be no concrete, legally enforceable standards for political action. This would be a significant loss, because freedom within the social order is threatened less by spectacular acts of destruction than by structural changes in the conditions for the realization of liberty and by the accumulation of minor infringements on freedom.[37] Furthermore, the relative autonomy of the various subsystems of society would lack protection. The relevance of this autonomy to liberty is that it supports society's level of performance, which the limited governing capability of the state cannot currently maintain through political control.[38] Above all, basic rights act in this way to prevent the state from accumulating power against which the individual guarantees of liberty would have little chance of prevailing even if they were not constitutionally curtailed.

Nevertheless, basic rights are able to fulfil their function only by adapting to evolving state activity and emerging threats to liberty without being constantly amended. This entails a shift in function with respect to the bourgeois initial phase. At that time, they were intended as the keystone that secured an existing condition of liberty against encroachment by the state. This was true for the American Bill of Rights from the outset, and for the French declarations once the orientation function was exhausted on completion of the legal reform. Naturally, the underlying expectation was that the condition of liberty, once achieved, could be secured once and for all through defensive basic rights. This assumption has proved to be mistaken. The freedom-oriented society constantly produces threats to liberty, whether through an accumulation of social power or through the risks created by scientific and technological progress. The orientation function of basic rights, originally considered temporary, thus becomes a permanent mission. To this extent, the component of basic rights

---

[37] For the one, see the boldly titled analysis by A. Roßnagel, *Radioaktiver Zerfall der Grundrechte* (Munich: Beck, 1984); for the other, see Dieter Grimm, 'Verfassungsrechtliche Anmerkungen zum Thema Prävention' in his *Die Zukunft der Verfassung* (Frankfurt am Main: Suhrkamp, 1991), p. 197.

[38] Cf. N. Luhmann, *Grundrechte als Institutionen* (Berlin: Duncker & Humblot, 2nd edn, 1974).

that transcends the status quo is today more important than the guarantee component. The basic rights function becomes a warning mechanism with respect to freedom deficits of applicable law and operates as a dynamic principle of adaptation of the law. One should not fail to observe that this dynamic aspect of basic rights comes at the expense of legal certainty and binding force, but this will not be examined here.[39]

---

[39] See Dieter Grimm, 'Grundrechte und soziale Wirklichkeit' in W. Hassemer et al. (eds), *Grundrechte und soziale Wirklichkeit* (Baden-Baden: Nomos, 1982), p. 39.

# The Concept of Constitution
## in Historical Perspective

### I. DEVELOPMENT TREND

In the second half of the eighteenth century, a general trend towards the juridification of state rule may be observed which also affects the concept of 'constitution'. Originally an empirical term used to comprehensively describe the political condition of a state, 'constitution' increasingly loses its non-juristic components, is narrowed to the legally structured condition of a state and, following the transition to modern constitutionalism, merges with the law that regulates the establishment and exercise of state rule, thus metamorphosing from a descriptive to a prescriptive term. In the course of this development, it is possible to discern some features that are characteristic of the change in meaning in political language since 1770. The concept of the constitution becomes normatively charged and ideologized. Accordingly, only an order that demonstrates specific formal or substantive qualities may be termed a 'constitution'. Thus elevated, the term no longer requires a semantic object, but stands for itself. 'Constitution' then also temporalizes itself such that it becomes a target term that transports specific expectations that historically are yet to be fulfilled. Yet the legally restricted concept of constitution never achieves undisputed rule. Not only do opponents of modern constitutionalism attempt to preserve the older meaning of the constitution, which thereby becomes itself politicized, but even after consolidation of the constitutional state, the question as to the determining factors underlying the legal constitution re-emerges as soon as that constitution fails to fulfil the expectations placed in it. The focus is then directed back to the more comprehensive politico-social constitution. In the Weimar Republic, the relationship between the two occupies the centre of the constitution discussion, until national socialism decides the issue entirely against the normative constitution.

Constitutionalism: Past, Present, and Future. First Edition. Dieter Grimm. © Dieter Grimm 2016. Published 2016 by Oxford University Press.

## II. THE ORIGINS OF CONSTITUTIONALISM

### 1. *The Pre-revolutionary Terminology*

At the same time that North America and France conduct two successful revolutions to enact modern constitutions, 'constitution' ('Konstitution', 'constitutio') is still understood in Germany to mean a law promulgated by the emperor, without reference to its significance or object. Norms regulating the exercise of political rule are termed 'fundamental laws' ('Grundgesetze', 'leges fundamentales'). 'Verfassung' is used in an empirical, and not in a normative sense and relates to the condition of a state. This condition can be understood as the product of historical developments, actual conditions, and legal determinations. It can also be shaped solely by the fundamental laws. It is in this narrower sense that it is generally understood by social-contract theories. Within the three-part contractual schema preferred in Germany, consisting of the agreement to leave the state of nature and unite to form a state (pactum unionis); the determination of the form of government (pactum ordinationis); and the declaration of submission to the ruler (pactum subiectionis), the second contract is referred to as a 'constitutional contract' ('Verfassungsvertrag'), and its object as 'the constitution of the state'. 'The contract which determines the constitution is termed the constitutional contract. The provisions contained therein make up the basic laws of the society.'[1] Constitutional contract and basic laws thus appear as two sides of the same coin: whereas the constitutional contract focuses on the process, the fundamental laws describe the product. The constitution is then the political condition of the state as created by contract and determined by basic laws. A similar structure may be found in the public law theory of the Holy Roman Empire, whereby contracts between the emperor and the imperial estates usurp the place of the pactum ordinationis. As they are contractually based, the fundamental laws preserve the constitution from unilateral alteration by the ruler. 'Supreme authority itself takes shape only through these laws; they can thus not derive from it. Consequently, the supreme authority too ... never has a right over the fundamental laws of the state, but rather it is only the people as a whole who can make a change therein.'[2] 'One must therefore distinguish between two powers within the state, the active supreme authority, which is established by the basic constitutions, and the fundamental authority of the people as a whole, from which the former originates and which remains quiescent until the basic constitutions are in question, or until the state is in the most immediate danger of extinction.'[3] As a consequence of this understanding of the constitution there is no state without a constitution. Rather, wherever

---

[1] Johann A. Schlettwein, *Die Rechte der Menschheit oder der einzige wahre Grund aller Gesetze, Ordnungen und Verfassungen* (Gießen: Krieger, 1784), p 364.

[2] Johann H. G. v. Justi, *Natur und Wesen der Staaten als die Quelle aller Regierungswissenschaften und Gesetze* (Mitau: Steidel, 1771; reprint: Aalen: Scientia, 1969), p. 91

[3] Ibid., p. 99.

a state exists, there is a constitution, and where a constitution is lacking the state of nature prevails. By contrast, entirely different contents of constitutions are possible. The contractual figure makes constitutional questions decidable. With respect to the possible forms of government, this doctrine adheres entirely to the Aristotelian schema. The definition of constitution does not develop a specific proximity to any form, nor does it exclude one. Equally, it is not bound to a documentary form. In these points, modern constitutionalism goes different ways.

## 2. The Meaning of 'Constitution' in England

Modern constitutionalism developes in England, but is not carried to its logical conclusion there. In the English-speaking world,[4] a 'constitution' originally denotes a formally enacted law, but with the involvement of the Parliament in the legislative process, this meaning has gradually been usurped by the word 'statute'. The manner in which rule is exercised is termed the 'form of government'. In the seventeenth century, however, 'constitution' appears in a new sense, in part synonymous with 'form of government', but in part synonymous with 'fundamental laws'. In a Parliamentary debate in 1610 on new tax demands of James I, Whitelocke asserts that the king's resolutions violate 'the natural frame and constitution of the policy of this kingdom.'[5] This expression, in which the constitution does not yet stand alone, but requires an object, the policy (in the sense of the 'body politic') recurs in a reply to Parliament written for Charles I in 1642 in which he cites the 'ancient, equal, happy, well-poised and never-enough commended Constitution of the Government of this Kingdom', and a little later refers to the 'excellent Constitution of this Kingdom'.[6] The use of 'constitution' in the plural increases after the outbreak of the Civil War in that same year, in the sense of 'fundamental laws'. The expression 'constitutions' probably benefits from the heightened formality compared to the more pedestrian 'laws'. In 1643 an anonymous work, 'Touching the Fundamental Laws, or Politique Constitution of this Kingdom',[7] is published. In the charge of 1649,

---

[4] Cf. Gerald Stourzh, 'William Blackstone: Teacher of Revolution' (1970) 15 *Jahrbuch für Amerikastudien* 184; Gerald Stourzh, 'Vom aristotelischen zum liberalen Verfassungsbegriff' in Friedrich Engel-Janosi et al. (eds), *Fürst, Bürger, Mensch* (Wien: Oldenbourg, 1975), p. 97; Gerald Stourzh, 'Staatsformenlehre und Fundamentalgesetze in England und Nordamerika im 17. und 18. Jahrhundert' in Rudolf Vierhaus (ed.), *Herrschaftsverträge, Wahlkapitulationen, Fundamentalgesetze* (Göttingen: Vandenhoek & Ruprecht, 1977), p. 294; Gerald Stourzh, *Fundamental Laws and Individual Rights in the 18th Century Constitution* (Claremont, Calif.: Claremont Institute for the Study of Statesmanship and Political Philosophy, 1984).

[5] James Whitelocke, cited in Joseph R. Tanner, *Constitutional Documents of the Reign of James I. A.D. 1603-1625* (Cambridge: Cambridge University Press, 1961), p. 260; cf. Charles H. McIlwain, *Constitutionalism, Ancient and Modern* (Ithaca, NY: Cornell University Press, 3rd edn, 1966), p. 25.

[6] [Charles I.], Answer to the 19 Propositions of Both Houses of Parliament (London 1642), printed in Corinne C. Weston, *English Constitutional Theory and the House of Lords 1556-1832* (London: Routledge & Paul, 1965), p. 263.

[7] Cited in John W. Gough, *Fundamental Law in English Constitutional History* (Oxford: Clarendon Press, 2nd edn, 1961), p. 99.

Charles I is accused of violating the 'fundamental constitutions' of the king-dom.[8] By contrast, Cromwell's constitution, written in 1653 after the king's exe-cution and the abolition of the monarchy, is not termed a 'constitution'. Rather, it is called 'The Government of the Commonwealth of England, Scotland, and Ireland, and the dominions there unto belonging', in common usage the 'Instrument (in the sense of "document") of Government'.[9] Locke, however, expressly calls the draft constitution for North Carolina of 1669 'Fundamental Constitutions of Carolina'. This document combines both usages of 'constitu-tion' in the statement that the 120 'Fundamental Constitutions' were to remain 'the sacred and unalterable form and rule of government in Carolina for ever.'[10] 'Constitution' is first used in an official text in connection with the abdication of James II in 1688. The king is accused of seeking to 'subvert the constitu-tion of the kingdom'.[11] Since the Glorious Revolution, the 'British constitution' in the singular has been a fixed feature of common parlance. The expression now always refers to the fundamental rules for the organization of the state. A violation of these has consequences. The normal legal remedies exist for dealing with 'ordinary public oppression', which according to Blackstone is the case when 'the vitals of the constitution are not attacked'. However, when the oppression aims 'to dissolve the constitution, and subvert the fundamentals of government', also termed 'unconstitutional oppressions', then the people have the right to resist.[12] The American colonists are to invoke this right just a few years later.

### 3. The Establishment of Modern Constitutionalism in North America

In line with the usage that had developed in England after the Glorious Revolution, the North American 'Colonial Forms of Government' or 'Colonial Charters' are not infrequently referred to as 'constitutions' around 1750. In contrast to England, the term here admittedly refers to binding, written legal norms defining the powers and limits of local state power compiled in a formal document. After the outbreak of disputes with the mother country in 1764, the colonists apply this conception to the English constitution, which they initially invoke in defence of their rights: 'In all free states the constitution is fixed, and the supreme legislative derives its power and authority from the constitution, it cannot overleap the bounds of it without destroying its own foundation.'[13] It is

[8] The Sentence of the High Court of Justice upon the King, January 27, 1649, printed in Samuel R. Gardiner (ed.), *The Constitutional Documents of the Puritan Revolution 1628-1660* (Oxford: Clarendon Press, 3rd edn, 1968), p. 372.

[9] Instrument of Government, December 16, 1653, ibid., p. 405.

[10] John Locke, *The Fundamental Constitutions of Carolina, March 1, 1669, Works*, vol. 10 (1823; reprint 1963), p. 198.

[11] William Blackstone, *Commentaries on the Laws of England I, 3* (1765) (London: Strahan, Cadell and Prince, Oxford, 10th edn, vol. I, 1787), p. 211.

[12] Ibid., I, 7, pp. 237, 244.

[13] Massachusetts Circular Letter to the Colonial Legislatures, February 11, 1768, printed in Merill Jensen (ed.), *American Colonial Documents to 1776* (London: Eyre & Spottiswoode, 1955), p. 715.

the refusal of the mother country to accept this constitutional understanding that compels the colonists to break with the English crown and establish their own state power. In this process, continuity with colonial tradition means that this has to happen in the form of a constitution. This, however, differs from the English version in three respects. Firstly, a constitution must be set down in writing, because 'a constitution ... has not an ideal, but a real existence; and wherever it cannot be produced in a visible form, there is none.' Secondly, the constitution must originate from the people and be beyond the reach of state power: 'A constitution is a thing antecedent to a government, and a government is only the creature of the constitution. The constitution of a country is not the act of its government, but of the people constituting a government.'[14] These two prerequisites become such basic characteristics of the term 'constitution' that Paine is able to deny the existence of an English constitution entirely on account of the lack of a constitutional document and in view of the Septennial Act of 1716, in which Parliament had extended its legislative period without recourse to the people.[15] Thirdly, in light of the revolutionary experiences, the constitution exceeds a mere 'form of government' and must include material restraints on state power in the form of basic rights. The constitution acquires its true significance specifically from their protection. Thus, the Concord (Massachusetts) Town Meeting of 1776 declares 'that a Constitution in its proper idea intends a system of principles established to secure the subject in the possession and enjoyment of their rights and privileges, against any encroachment of the governing part.'[16] It is true that the first declaration of human rights, that of Virginia, is still outside the constitution, which is framed as a separate document entitled the 'Constitution or Form of Government'. But soon the declaration of rights becomes a part of the constitution. Pennsylvania, for its part, asserts: 'We ... do ordain, declare and establish the following Declaration of Rights and Frame of Government, to be the constitution of this commonwealth.'[17]

### 4. The Reception of the American Constitutional Conception in France

When the break with traditional state power occurs in France somewhat later, the juridified, formalized, and content-laden concept of the constitution prevails. This was not predicted under the French theory. Certainly Montesquieu and de Lolme had enhanced the reputation of the liberal English constitution,

---

[14] Thomas Paine, *The Rights of Man* (1791), *Writings*, Moncure D. Conway (ed.), vol. 2 (New York 1902; reprint 1967), p. 309.

[15] Ibid., p. 311.

[16] Concord Town Meeting Demands a Constitutional Convention, October 21, 1776, printed in Samuel E. Morison (ed.), *Sources and Documents Illustrating the American Revolution 1764-1788 and the Formation of the Federal Constitution* (1923) (Oxford: Clarendon Press, 2nd edn, 1953), p. 177.

[17] The Constitution of Virginia, June 6, 1776, ibid., p. 151; The Constitution of Pennsylvania, September 28, 1776, ibid., p. 162.

whereby they certainly had the traditional concept of the constitution in mind.[18] Rousseau, too, operates entirely within conventional parameters where the constitution is concerned. He divided laws into 'loix civiles', 'loix criminelles' and 'loix politiques' or 'loix fundamentales' and asserts these latter were the ultimate laws 'qui constituent la forme du gouvernement'. But, he adds that the 'veritable constitution de l'Etat' is based on a fourth group of laws: 'Je parle des moeurs, des coutumes, et sur-tout de l'opinion'.[19] It is Vattel who first makes the constitution and legal norms congruent when he defines 'constitution' as a 'règlement fondamental qui détermine la manière dont l'autorité publique doit être exercée'.[20] For Vattel, such a 'règlement' can only originate with the nation, but is not bound to any specific content or form. It is not until during the revolution that the constitution acquires these features. Sieyès plays the decisive role here. For Sieyès, rule can only be legitimated as authority invested by the people. The mandatory relationship makes a constitution necessary. 'Il est impossible de créer un corps pour une fin sans lui donner une organisation, des formes et des lois propres à lui faire remplir les fonctions auxquelles on a voulu le destiner. C'est ce qu'on appelle la constitution de ce corps. Il est evident qu'il ne peut exister sans elle. Il l'est donc aussi que tout gouvernement commis doit avoir sa constitution.'[21] By contrast, the people also exists without a constitution on the basis of natural law and always stands above the constitution as the 'pouvoir constituant'.[22] By means of the constitution it distributes and restricts the assignment of rule and secures its own natural rights. Analogous to this, Mounier reports on behalf of the constitution committee of the National Assembly that 'constitution' is understood as none other 'qu'un ordre fixe et établi dans la manière de gouverner' or, if one likes, 'l'expression des droits et des obligations des différents pouvoirs'.[23] This accommodates the older concept of the constitution as the form of government, but identifies it with the legal norms that determine it and bound to document form. But a further feature of the constitution is that this order originates from the people. 'Quand la manière de gouverner ne dérive pas de la volonté du peuple clairement exprimée, il n'a point de constitution; il n'a qu'un gouvernement de fait.' Furthermore, the order must set boundaries to state power. 'Si cette autorité n'a point de bornes, elle est nécessairement arbitraire, et rien n'est plus directement opposé à une constitution

[18] Charles de Montesquieu, *De l'esprit des lois I I,6* (1748), Oeuvres compl., T. 2 (1951; 1976), p. 405; Jean L. de Lolme, *Constitution de l'Angleterre; ou, État du gouvernement anglais comparé avec la forme républicaine et avec les autres monarchies de l'Europe* (Amsterdam: Harrevelt, 1771).

[19] Jean J. Rousseau, *Du contrat social 2, 12* (1762), Oeuvres completes vol. 3 (Paris: 1964), p. 393.

[20] Emer de Vattel, *Le droit des gens ou principes de la loi naturelle 1, 3, § 27* (1758), M. P. Pradier-Fodéré (ed.) vol. I (Paris, 1863), p. 153.

[21] Emanuel Sieyès, *Qu'est-ce que le Tiers-État?* [Paris, 1789], Roberto Zapperi (ed.) (Genf: Droz, 1970), p. 179.

[22] Ibid., p. 181.

[23] Jean-Joseph Mounier, Speech of July 9, 1789, *Archives parlementaires de 1787 à 1860*, Jean Madival et al. (eds), Iᵉ sèr., vol. 8 (Paris, 1875), p. 214.

que le pouvoir despotique.'[24] Ultimately, the order must be based on human rights.[25] In Art. 16 of the Declaration of Rights, this receives expression in the concept of the constitution, which in the debates is no longer fundamentally opposed, as follows: 'Toute société, dans laquelle la garantie des droits n'est pas assurée, ni la séparation des pouvoirs déterminée, n'a point de constitution'.[26]

### 5. Evolution of the Meaning of 'Constitution' in Germany

Following the promulgation of modern constitutions in its western neighbours, the term 'Konstitution' in Germany loses its old meaning of imperial law and, without displacing these terms entirely, acquires the meanings of 'constitution of the state', 'constitutional contract', 'form of government', or 'fundamental laws'. The change is both rapid and extensive. In 1788, Roth's dictionary, *Gemeinnüziges Lexikon*, still defined 'constitution' as 'the character of a thing, e.g. a body, a disposition, etc., equally a law and a regulation'.[27] The first examples of usage of 'constitution' in the new sense appear one year later.[28] By 1798 this concept is so entrenched that the dictionary *Conversationslexikon mit vorzüglicher Rücksicht auf die gegenwärtigen Zeiten* restricts itself to the definition 'embodiment of fundamental state laws'.[29] The modern expression is preferred when speaking of the new constitutional documents, especially those of France. In 1792 Humboldt entitles an article in the magazine *Berlinische Monatsschrift* 'Ideas on state constitution (Verfassung), occasioned by the new French Constitution'.[30] However, the term is also applied without hesitation to the old contents. Many authors come to divide 'state law' into 'constitutional law' and 'governmental law', whereby the former concerns itself with the subject of 'state power'[31] or 'forms of government',[32] while the latter relates to the exercise of state power. Numerous commentators place the constitution within the familiar contractual paradigm. It can then stand for the conclusion of the contract, as in Kant, who defines 'constitution' as 'the act of the general will, whereby the multitude becomes a

---

[24] Ibid.  [25] Ibid., p. 216.

[26] Constitution Française, September 3, 1791, Art. 16, printed in Günter Franz (ed.), *Staatsverfassungen. Eine Sammlung wichtiger Verfassungen der Vergangenheit und Gegenwart* (München: Oldenbourg, 1964), p. 306.

[27] Johann F. Roth, *Gemeinnüziges Lexikon* vol. I (1788), p. 93, Art. Constitution.

[28] Wigulaeus X. A. Freiherr von Kreittmayer, *Grundriß des Allgemeinen, Deutsch- und Bayerischen Staatsrechts* (1770), vol. I (Munchen: Lentner, 2nd edn, 1789), p. 14; Johann G. Schlosser, *Briefe über die Gesetzgebung überhaupt, und den Entwurf des preußischen Gesetzbuchs insbesondere* (Frankfurt: Fleischer, 1789), p. 119.

[29] *Conversationslexikon mit vorzüglicher Rücksicht auf die gegenwärtigen Zeiten*, vol. I (Leipzig: 1796), p. 288, Art. Constitution.

[30] Wilhelm v. Humboldt, 'Ideen über Staatsverfassung, durch die neue Französische Konstitution veranlaßt. Aus einem Briefe an einen Freund', August 1791, *Berlinische Monatsschrift* (1792), p. 84.

[31] Nicolaus T. Gönner, *Deutsches Staatsrecht* (Augsburg: Kranzfelder, 1805), p. 4; Justus C. Leist, *Lehrbuch des Teutschen Staatsrechts* (1803) (Göttingen: Schneider, 2nd edn, 1805), p.1.

[32] August L. von Schlözer, *Allgemeines StatsRecht und StatsVerfassungsLere* (Göttingen: Vandenhoek & Ruprecht, 1793), p. 14.

people'.[33] Similarly, for Behr, 'the multitude lives in a state of nature until it reunites to form a civil unit by means of a constitution ("Verfassung")'.[34] However, the term is more often used to refer to a form of government created by contract. Thus, Eberhard cites the necessity of legally determining the relationships of rule in a society. This law 'must establish the manner in which sovereignty is to be exercised, and this manner is its constitution'.[35] Unlike the American and French models, the 'constitution' here remains separate from its legal expression. As with the earlier concept of 'Verfassung', the term relates to the political condition of the state. Most authors define 'constitution' as 'the totality of all essential provisions ... that relate to the organization of sovereignty by its necessary subject and the nature in which they are to possess such'.[36] Thus, though in contrast to Eberhard the constitution is raised to the normative level, but is also not identical with its legal form; rather, it remains a collective term for various norms joined by a common object, and is thus equivalent to the basic laws. This is stated most clearly by Feuerbach: 'The laws that determine the *Verfassung* are the (positive) basic laws (*leges fundamentales*): the totality of the same is the constitution.'[37]

## 6. Defensive Uses of 'Constitution'

After 1789, numerous authors also describe the Imperial Verfassung as a 'constitution'. In his essay 'Über die Güte der Deutschen Staatsverfassung', Häberlein presents the amendment of the 'current constitutions' as the most important contemporary feature. He expressly cites France, Sweden, and Poland.[38] With respect to the empire, he emphasizes that it 'already has a Verfassung', and then goes on to assure his readers: 'Yes, it is certain that our constitution can be numbered among the best.'[39] Such statements are often driven by the intention of preventing revolution. The aim is to show that Germany has already long possessed the blessings that France had to win through revolution. Thus, Reinhold explains that a coincidence is itself sufficient for overthrow once a 'Staatsverfassung' has become 'dilapidated'—but that Germany had not reached this state. 'Due to a fortunate constitution, more than any other great nation, we are secured against the most insidious of all diseases of a state body.'[40]

---

[33] Immanuel Kant, *Zum ewigen Frieden*, 2nd. part (1795), AA vol. 8 (1912; reprint 1968), p. 352.

[34] Wilhelm J. Behr, *Über die Notwendigkeit des Studiums der Staatslehre besonders auf Akademien nebst einem vorausgeschickten Grundrisse eines Systems derselben* (Würzburg: Rienner, 1800), p. 81.

[35] Johann A. Eberhard, *Ueber Staatsverfassungen und ihre Verbesserung*, H. 2 (Frankfurt, Leipzig: 1794), p. 35.

[36] Johan C. Majer, *Allgemeine Theorie der Staatskonstitution* (Hamburg: Bohn, 1799), p. 19.

[37] Paul J. A. Feuerbach, *Anti-Hobbes, oder über die Grenzen der Höchsten Gewalt und das Zwangsrecht der Bürger gegen den Oberherrn*, vol. I (1798; Darmstadt: Wissenschaftliche Buchgesellschaft, 1967), p. 34.

[38] Carl F. Häberlein, 'Über die Güte der deutschen Staatsverfassung', *Deutsche Monatsschrift*, vol. I (1793), p. 3.

[39] Ibid., p. 4.

[40] Carl L. Reinhold, *Briefe über die Kantische Philosphie*, vol. I (1790; Leipzig: Reclam, 1923), p. 15.

Wieland, who in 1790 defended the French Revolution against its critics, also provides an example of this attitude. For him, the revolutionaries had rightly operated on the premise that the 'immeasurable boon of a free constitution cannot be had at too dear a price'.[41] Two and a half years later, he explains the absence of revolution in Germany with the quality of the German constitution. 'The German people would have been transformed from a simple spectator to an actor' if it did not already possess in large measure the achievements that France had to attain by force. 'The domestic tranquillity that we ... have enjoyed to date in our German fatherland provides a great deal of evidence for the good side of our constitution.'[42] This denies a fundamental difference between the French constitution and the German Imperial Verfassung. Both are merely variants of a uniform concept of constitution. The features that characterize the French constitution do not appear necessary to the definition. Some commentators even present their lack as an advantage, as when Dalberg terms the Imperial Verfassung 'a permanent Gothic structure which was not erected according to all the rules of construction, but in which one may safely dwell.'[43] Under these circumstances, the postulate that states cannot be differentiated according to the presence or absence of a constitution remains unaltered. Turning decidedly away from France, Eberhard says not only a 'nation that has recorded its basic laws in written monuments has a legally valid state constitution'.[44] Citing John Adams, he adds that a constitution 'is not the paper or parchment on which the agreement is written', but 'the totality of the basic laws according to which a people ... is governed'.[45] Of course, he overlooks the fact that John Adams insisted on precisely this documentary form.

### 7. The Formal Constitution as a Condition for Freedom

However, more and more voices are to be heard asserting that a formal constitution on the French model is necessary to realize the idea of the contract. Thus, Wedekind, for whom a popular resolution is the prerequisite for the constitution, says, 'A country can therefore certainly have a form of government, but it does not acquire a constitution until the rules according to which it is to be governed may be considered a contract entered into voluntarily by its citizens which the people has ratified in its constituting assemblies.'[46] The norms here

---

[41] Christoph M. Wieland, 'Unparteiische Betrachtungen über die Staatsrevolution in Frankreich' (1790), *Sämtliche Werke*, vol. 31 (Leipzig: Göschen, 1857), p. 86.

[42] Christoph M. Wieland. 'Betrachtungen über die gegenwärtige Lage des Vaterlandes' (1793), ibid., p. 222.

[43] Carl von Dalberg, *Von Erhaltung der Staatsverfassungen* (Erfurt: Keyser, 1795), p. 14.

[44] Eberhard (n. 35), H. 2 (1794), p. 15.

[45] John Adams, *An Answer to Paine's Rights of Man* (Dublin: Byrne, Moore and Jones, 1793), p. 16.

[46] Georg Wedekind, 'Die Rechte des Menschen und Bürgers, wie sie die französische konstituierende Nationalversammlung von 1791 proklamierte' (Mainz, 1793) in Heinrich Scheel (ed.), *Die Mainzer Republik I. Protokolle des Jakobinerklubs* (Berlin: Akademie-Verlag, 1975), p. 766.

are thus no longer based on the contract, but are the contract itself. The contract merely represents the necessary manner of their formulation. Wedekind thus takes issue with the assumption under natural law that the constitutional contract can also be tacitly concluded. This proposition now receives increasing criticism. Pörschke describes this construction as 'a temptation to random craving for the property of others'.[47] 'The legend of tacit contracts of peoples' gave 'the rulers ... a golden opportunity.'[48] Bergk refers to tacit contracts as 'artefacts of evil, because they do not respect people as a free and autonomous entity'.[49] Heydenreich states succinctly: 'All contracts are express in nature.'[50] Under these circumstances, the contract must lead to norms set down in writing. The formal requirements find their justification in the content that constitutions are intended to promote—namely individual liberty. The deficiency of the 'republics of antiquity' is revealed in the fact that they did not secure liberty through 'constitutions'.[51] By contrast, Bergk calls the 'legal constitution ... the bastion of civil liberty ... No citizen of a state without a legal constitution is free.'[52] For Weiss, rights are uncertain even in a legally organized state if the state power is concentrated in the chief of state. In such a case, he observes, preservation of law depends solely on the good will of that individual. As an antidote, he recommends that 'the nation must ... also erect its constitution outwardly.'[53] The constitution and its legal form are thus made congruent. Bergk therefore is inclined to speak of the 'legal constitution', in one instance even of 'constitution laws' that contain imperative legal and political norms.[54] For this reason, Zachariä prefers to distinguish the state constitution in the older sense as a legally determined form of government from a narrow concept of the constitution that refers to the 'laws according to which the state as a moral person exists and acts'.[55] To illustrate this difference, Majer in 1799 went so far as to assert that 'the epitome of all circumstances apparent in the same [the state]', that is the Verfassung in the older sense, can no longer be termed a 'constitution', but rather as the 'status quo',[56] while the term 'constitution' is reserved for the legal norms governing state power.

---

[47] Karl L. Pörschke, *Vorbereitungen zu einem populären Naturrechte* (Königsberg: Nicolovius, 1795), p. 26.

[48] Ibid., p. 169.

[49] Johann A. Bergk, *Untersuchungen aus dem Natur-, Staats- und Völkerrechte mit einer Kritik der neuesten Konstitution der französischen Republik* (1796; Kronberg: Scriptor-Verlag, 1975), p. 81.

[50] Karl H. Heydenreich, *System des Naturrechts nach kritischen Prinzipien*, vol. 2 (1795; Bruxelles: Culture et Civilisation, 1969), p. 105.

[51] Bergk (n. 49), p. 239.　　[52] Ibid., p. 45.

[53] Christian Weiss, *Lehrbuch der Philosophie des Rechtes* (Leipzig: Gräff, 1804), p. 252, § 428.

[54] Bergk (n. 49), pp. 45, 290.

[55] Karl S. Zachariä, *Über die vollkommenste Staats-Verfassung* (Leipzig: Fleischer, 1800), p. 11.

[56] Majer (n. 36), p. 21.

## 8. Material Enrichments of the Concept of the Constitution

Already, behind the formal requirements that now begin to be associated with constitutions, material demands had become apparent. In summary, they generally appear under the term 'free constitution'.[57] Analogous to Art. 16 of the French Declaration of the Rights of Man, individual rights and the separation of powers also form the criteria for freedom in Germany, along with popular representation. Insofar as the quality or reasonableness of the constitution can be made dependent on the existence of these features, the material demands stand within the traditional doctrine of the best state Verfassung and thus add nothing to the concept of the constitution. In some cases, however, in variance from tradition, the term *Verfassung* is withheld from a form of government where freedom is not secured in this way. Thus, Wedekind derives the concept of the 'constitution' directly from individual rights. He understands the 'constitution' as 'a covenant of the citizens to secure their human and civil rights according to certain laws or regulations'. Legal guarantees of human rights are thus a part of the concept of the constitution. 'No state in which the preservation of human rights is not ensured, or in which the separation of powers is not precisely defined, can boast of possessing a constitution.'[58] Wedekind of course is not the only author to advocate individual rights in the late eighteenth century, but the first to link them with the constitution in this way. For Bergk, 'neither just laws nor a good ruler alone' secure the rights of the people. Rather, 'civil liberty' is only ensured through a constitution that separates powers. 'No state in which feudal laws are in force, in which no civil code applies equally to all, and in which the government cannot be forcibly compelled to perform its duties, and where therefore no constitution has been implemented that makes law possible and effective and restrains self-interest through the separation of powers, enjoys civil liberty.'[59] The separation of powers implicitly includes the idea of popular representation. Particularly at the dawn of the nineteenth century, and especially in the Prussian constitutional discussion, constitution is frequently identified with popular representation. Stein's memorandum on the cabinet organization of 1806 includes the passage: 'The Prussian state does not have a constitution, supreme power is not divided between the ruler and the representatives of the nation.'[60] Dahlmann asserts that in the absence of a body of popular representation 'everything constitutional ... is just empty smoke and mirrors'. In his opinion, constitutions of this nature are 'half- and quarter-constitutions'.[61]

---

[57] Wieland (n. 41), p. 81.     [58] Wedekind (n. 46), p. 766.     [59] Bergk (n. 49), pp. 38, 41.

[60] Karl Freiherr vom und zum Stein, 'Denkschrift "Darstellung der fehlerhaften Organisation des Kabinetts und der Notwendigkeit der Bildung einer Ministerialkonferenz"', 26/27 March 1806, in his *Briefe und amtliche Schriften*, vol. 2/1 (Stuttgart: Kohlhammer, 1959), p. 208.

[61] Friedrich C. Dahlmann, 'Ein Wort über Verfassung' (1815), in Hartwig Brandt (ed.), *Restauration und Frühliberalismus 1814-1840* (Darmstadt: Wissenschaftliche Buchgesellschaft, 1979), p. 105.

## 9. The Right to Amend the Constitution

Where constitution is identified with a specific form and specific content, so that the absence of these features is equivalent to the absence of a constitution itself, there is no doubt that a constitution may, even must, be enacted. By contrast, if a constitution emerges together with the state, as the majority still assumes, the enactment of a constitution appears to be only an amendment to the constitution, which poses the question as to under what prerequisites and within which limits this is legitimate. The German literature after 1789 deals with this topic to an exceptional extent, as this relates to nothing less than the legitimacy of the revolution. 'Do the people have the right to arbitrarily alter the condition of its state?'[62] Fichte asks in his defence of the French Revolution, and subsequently returns to this question repeatedly. His answer: A constitution that contradicts the principles of reason must be altered; a rational constitution may not be altered.[63] However, he distinguishes between an immutable core and alterable modifications. Changes require 'absolute unanimity', as each individual chose to join the state because they desired a specific constitution, and therefore cannot be compelled to accept changes against their will.[64] By contrast, Kant allows even 'changes to the (flawed) constitution' solely with the consent of the sovereign, and thus 'through reform' and not 'through revolution'.[65] This is because Kant equates 'constitution' with 'state'. Resistance to the sovereign would thus dissolve the civil constitution or the state itself. Compared to this, a defective constitution appears as the lesser of two evils. The only reasonable way to constitutional improvement is through constitutional reform.[66] However, this in every case relates to the provisions of the existing constitution. Naturally, the decided adherents of the fundamental power of the people cannot readily accept this. Bergk is thus moved to distinguish between 'uprising' and 'revolution'. The 'uprising' occurs in opposition to a government acting unlawfully, thus leaving the 'constitution' untouched. By contrast, a 'revolution' is defined with respect to the constitution and understood as a 'complete revision of the principles of the constitution'. This too is permissible as a consequence of the fundamental power of the people, but it also underscores the 'obligation' to adopt a 'new constitution'.[67] However, as the French Revolution unfolds, the warnings against this path grow increasingly louder. Schlözer, who

---

[62] Johann G. Fichte, 'Beitrag zur Berichtigung der Urtheile des Publikums über die französische Revolution' (1793), in *Complete Edition of the Bavarian Academy of Sciences*, I. Abt., vol. I (Stuttgart: Frommann-Holzboog, 1964), p. 219

[63] Johann G. Fichte, 'Das System der Sittenlehre nach den Principien der Wissenschaftslehre' (1798), in *Complete Edition* I. Abt., vol. 5 (1977), p. 216.

[64] Johann G. Fichte, 'Grundlage des Naturrechts nach Principien der Wissenschaftslehre (1796), in *Complete Edition*, I. Abt., vol. 3 (1966), p. 458.

[65] Immanuel Kant, *Metaphysik der Sitten, Rechtslehre*, part. 2, 1. *Allgemeine Anmerkungen* A (1797), in *Complete Edition of the Prussian Academy of Science*, vol. 6 (1907; reprint 1968), p. 321.

[66] Eberhard (n. 35), H. 1, p. 63; H. 2, p. 2.      [67] Bergk (n. 49), p. 119.

elaborately justifies his change of heart, says, 'Tearing out an old, unbearable constitution at the root is not the same as adopting a new, fortunate one.'[68]

### 10. Implications for Social-contract Theory

The material enhancement of the constitutional idea that may be observed in the more recent doctrine of natural law frequently involves contradictions that contain the seeds of their own resolution. The more the content of the constitution is determined by natural law, the less convincing is its contractual justification. The original purpose was to present various constitutional contents as feasible options. If the interest in legitimation of freedom of choice declines and the focus is instead on realizing a specific normative constitutional model, contract theory loses its utility. The contract, which must lead to a specific result which, once achieved, may no longer be altered, makes conclusion of a real contract superfluous. Ultimately, the constitution is no longer the result of a covenant, but of necessity. Schelling is the first to explicitly formulate this idea. He calls the legal constitution the necessary 'condition of liberty', and concludes from this that the emergence of the general legal constitution may not be left to chance.[69] Not much later, Fries is even more outspoken: the legal relationships of every society can be determined by the contract of unification and submission with regards to which it depends on the will of each individual whether or not he wants to be a member. As long as the purpose of society is arbitrary, this does not emerge until the fundamental contract has received the consent of all. This relationship, however, does not obtain for the state. The purpose of the state is to constitute public law, as a decisive judgment of justice and injustice, equipped with sufficient power to compel the obedience of each individual. Since this purpose necessarily applies for each individual in the society, everyone should participate in joining the state. Thus, the purpose of the state is determined not by the free choice of its members but by a law of necessity; here nobody becomes a member through an act of free choice, but with necessity through law as soon as they wish to live among members of the state. It is therefore not a contract of unification, but a commandment of law which determines the purpose of the society and requires that it be joined.[70] This introduces an important future issue. The question becomes merely: how is the formula 'with necessity through law' defined? In his *Rechtsphilosophie*, Weiss notes in passing, immediately after presenting contract theory in a conventional manner: 'According to the constitutions of real, existing states, the constitutional contract cannot

[68] August L. von Schlözer, 'Französische Revolution' in *Stats-Anzeigen*, vol. 14 (Göttingen: Ruprecht, 1790), p. 498.

[69] Friedrich Wilhelm Joseph Schelling, *System des transcendentalen Idealismus* (1800) in his *Werke*, vol. 2 (1927; reprint 1965), p. 582.

[70] Jakob Fries, *Philosophische Rechtslehre und Kritik aller positiven Gesetzgebung* (Jena: Mauke, 1803), p. 77.

always be assumed to be concluded at the start. In such cases, the structure of the constitution depends solely on the arbitrary will of the monarch.'[71]

## III. THE ERA OF CONSTITUTIONAL BATTLES

### 1. *The Basic Positions*

In the first half of the nineteenth century, the constitutional question escalates to become the dominant domestic political issue in Germany. 'It is today in particular the age of constitutions,' observes Rotteck.[72] The Napoleonic wars, which had spurred the people to an awareness of their importance, greatly heightened expectations. 'Virtually all classes of inhabitants,' writes Hatzfeld in 1815, 'believe that they have won a constitution through their sacrifices.'[73] The opponents of constitutionalism also commonly argue their position in the name of the constitution. Thus, 'Verfassung' and 'constitution' are not reliable indicators for the respective positions. The proponents of formal constitutional documents in the liberal tradition use both terms. Conversely, the defenders of the status quo often appropriate the term 'constitution' to disarm them. They then insist on a constitutional process which before the introduction of the constitution can only be the traditional, estate-based process, so that the modern term is used to prevent the propagation of its meaning. Under the heading 'constitution', the Brockhaus Encyclopedia of 1830 notes: 'Constitution. I. As a tendency of our era, there is no word that is so closely related to the movements of our time, indeed that by itself so completely sums up its character, as the word "constitution". Yet there is also no word where there is so little agreement respecting its meaning. One party understands it to mean nothing other than that which currently exists, while the other uses it to refer to something that is yet to be created. One side sees only a constitution where a series of arbitrary articles is promulgated respecting the various branches of public power, its formation and its limits and is equipped with conventional forms of national representation, while the other side asserts that the true constitution is above all human caprice and that it is everywhere naturally present in the manner in which a people of deeds is ruled, as this is the result of the history and development of that people, of which nothing may be altered without annihilating public order. This divergence of concepts reflects the conflict which, though it has always existed among the nations, is now becoming more acute, as adherents of the two opposing viewpoints have become more equal both in numbers and, primarily, in their intellectual force, and because at the same time the

---

[71] Weiss (n. 53), p. 216, § 367, remarks.

[72] Carl von Rotteck, *Lehrbuch des Vernunftsrechts und der Staatswissenschaften*, vol. 2 (Stuttgart: Franckh, 1830), p. 172.

[73] Franz L. Fürst von Hatzfeld, 'Verfassungsentwurf, March 20, 1815', cited in Reinhart Koselleck, *Preußen zwischen Reform und Revolution. Allgemeines Landrecht, Verwaltung und soziale Bewegung von 1791 bis 1848* (Stuttgart: Klett, 2nd edn, 1975), p. 212.

condition of the peoples has indeed become more oppressive from the one side over the last 30 years, while they themselves on the other hand have become more sensitive to all pressure. They thus perceive a diffuse urge to escape from present circumstances, and the idea from which they expect a remedy to their complaints now presents itself to them under the name "constitution".'[74]

## 2. *Constitution as a Principle of Progress*

In view of the minimal revolutionary potential in Germany, the realization of the constitutional idea here was dependent on initiatives from above. The earliest and most serious willingness in this direction appears in Prussia following the collapse of 1806. In the chapter 'Fundamental condition of domestic affairs or internal condition of state law' of his Riga memorandum,[75] Altenstein cites the deficient Prussian constitution as the main reason for the military defeat: 'Lacking was the energetic union of all forces of the individuals for a joint purpose.... The Verfassung had nothing that could have prompted a general participation of the nation in the promotion of a purpose that was not even made clear to it.'[76] And elsewhere: 'As soon as the state [i.e. Prussia] entered into war against another state capable of achieving just the opposite end (namely the greatest possible expression of force) through its constitutional order, it must necessarily lead to the defeat of the former, and this will continue to be the case as long as the Verfassung... is not changed.'[77] To be sure, every constitutional change is the 'result of human actions'.[78] But the actions are driven by a 'world plan' that leads humanity to ever greater progress. In this world plan, the respective constitution is 'a stage through which the human species must pass, yet a stage which it should soon exceed and in which it may not remain forever'. If this necessity occurs, 'then the constitution changes of its own accord, if it is not arrested by fetters that make such response impossible'.[79] In this way, Altenstein overcomes the controversy respecting the feasibility of constitutions. The constitution requires a guiding intervention, but this must accord with the zeitgeist and promote further progress, not the overthrow of the constitution. Overthrow only becomes inevitable when the constitution is held back, contrary to the 'zeitgeist'. 'The highest ideal of the constitution is that not only the potential for progress, but even the occasion for it, is inherent in every provision of same.'[80] Here, 'constitution' is not merely the actual overall condition of a state within the meaning of the older concept of the constitution, nor the totality of public law norms in accordance with the legal theory of constitution. Rather,

---

[74] Allgemeine deutsche Real-Encyclopädie für die gebildeten Stände, vol. 2 (7th edn, 1830), p. 829, Art. Constitutionen.

[75] Karl Freiherr vom Stein zum Altenstein, 'Rigaer Denkschrift "Über die Leitung des Preußischen Staats" September 11, 1807' in Georg Winter (ed.), *Die Reorganisation des Preußischen Staates unter Stein und Hardenberg*, part. I, vol. I (Leipzig: 1931), p. 389.

[76] Ibid., p. 393.    [77] Ibid., p. 395.    [78] Ibid., p. 389.    [79] Ibid.    [80] Ibid.

Altenstein expressly warns against entrusting the constitution to the 'jurist', who will 'assume the status quo to be an unalterable norm or, should he fixate on legislation without changing his entire nature, will act arbitrarily.'[81] Altenstein is most likely to approach the idea of a 'constitution' as a legally formed state, but at the same time exceeds it in two respects. First, the constitution does not define a specific condition, but is open towards the future. Secondly, it does not restrict itself to the form of government, but brings together state and society under a principle of individual and social improvement that endows the process with meaning.

### 3. The Constitution of the Administration

In the course of the reforms, however, the term 'constitution' seems to lose this level of meaning. The term 'constitution' virtually never appears in the so-called constitutional memoranda and draft constitutions. Instead, these speak of national representation, rationally founded estates, and the like. Nor does the royal promise of a constitution of 1810 expressly mentions this term. Rather, the term appears in an entirely different context. On 16 December 1808, the *Publikandum betreffend die veränderte Verfassung der obersten Staatsbehörden* (Decree on the New Constitution of all High Authorities of the State) is enacted. Among other things, this decree states that 'the purpose of the new constitution is to give the greatest possible unity, power and agility to the administration'. It also raises the prospect of more specific regulations on 'organization and constitution' of the 'State Council' and a reorganization of the provincial, financial and police authorities. This, and the 'amended constitution of the highest administrative authorities', is intended to enable execution of 'the fundamental principles of improved state administration' and thus place the 'happiness of the state' on a new, sustainable basis.[82] This reflects Stein's conviction, stated in 1806: 'As the Prussian state does not have a state constitution, it is all the more essential that a government constitution is formed according to correct principles.'[83] This reference, characteristic of the reform phase, reveals that in Prussia after 1806, the primary constitutional concern was that of administration.[84] The reforms which were intended to achieve comprehensive renewal were not, as in France, the work of civil society, which established the state to this end. Rather, they were promulgated as an act of state administration itself, which first had to educate civil society and required an organization suitable for this purpose. The government

---

[81] Ibid., p. 390.

[82] 'Verordnung über die veränderte Verfassung aller obersten Staatsbehörden in der Preußischen Monarchie', October 27, 1810, in *GSLg. f. d. Königl.-Preuß. Staaten* (Berlin: Gesetzsammlungsamt, 1810), p. 3; 'Publikandum, betreffend die veränderte Verfassung der obersten Staatsbehörden der preußischen Monarchie, in Beziehung auf die innere Landes- und Finanzverwaltung', December 16, 1808, in Stein, *Briefe und Schriften*, vol. 2/2 (Stuttgart: Kohlhammer, 1960), p. 1001, 1007.

[83] Stein (n. 60), p. 208.     [84] Koselleck (n. 73), p. 217.

constitution was the prerequisite for the state constitution and the organization of administration was the fundamental issue of constitutional policy.[85] The 'constitutional Verfassung', as Vincke termed it with significant redundancy, was postponed, to one day mark the crowning achievement securing this benevolent administration.[86] The term 'Verfassung' is not regularly applied in the constitutional sense to the state as a whole again until after the Napoleonic wars and the conclusion of administrative reform. Koppe goes so far as to say that it is 'Prussia's calling to serve as a shining example for all tribes of the German fatherland in the constitution it will enact and the manner in which it will enact and justify it.'[87] In this era in which political claims are being lodged, Verfassung, constitutional document, and constitution mean a codification of specific legal positions, the law that secures the legal status of the people against state power. In his constitution memorandum of 1819 Humboldt writes: 'The security that the people obtain through a constitution is a double one, that deriving indirectly from the existence and the effectiveness of the estates, and that which is a part of the constitution and issues directly from it.'[88] By this he means the basic rights.

## 4. *Constitution as a Means of Securing Liberty*

In the *Vormärz* period, the liberty-securing aspect of the constitution gains the ascendency, with only the extreme left equating constitution with popular sovereignty. Compared with the period before the Napoleonic Wars, constitutional debate takes on a much more bombastic tone. It is no coincidence that religious terms are used. In 1819, the periodical *Der Baierische Verfassungs-Freund* presents its readers with a 'confession of faith'[89] asserting that 'an eternal progression of mankind toward a model of perfection' would culminate in 'a representative constitution'. In 1823, the magazine *Konstitutionelle Zeitschrift* runs a German 'constitutional catechism' in which the principles of constitutionalism are repeated in a question-and-answer format.[90] Feuerbach sees a chance for liberty only where it 'is secured by a constitution'.[91] For Welcker, the constitution is not 'just some minor point, but rather the main issue for

---

[85] Ibid., p. 215.

[86] Ludwig Freiherr von Vincke, 'Zwecke und Mittel der preußischen Staatsverwaltung, welche dieselbe verfolgen, deren dieselbe sich bedienen dürfte, (1808) in Ernst von Bodelschwingh, *Leben des Ober-Präsidenten Freiherrn von Vincke*, vol. 1 (Berlin: Reimer, 1853), p. 379.

[87] Johann G. Koppe, *Die Stimme eines Preußischen Staatsbürgers in den wichtigsten Angelegenheiten dieser Zeit* (Köln: DuMont-Bachem, 1815), p. 67.

[88] Wilhelm von Humboldt, *Denkschrift über Preußens ständische Verfassung*, February 4, 1819, paragraph 7, AA, vol. 12 (1904; Berlin: De Gruyter, 1968), p. 228.

[89] *Der baierische Verfassungs-Freund*, vol. 1 (München: Fleischmann, 1819), p. 3.

[90] 'Entwurf eines Verfassungs-Katechismus für Volk und Jugend in den deutschen konstitutionellen Staaten' in Johann C. Freiherr von Aretin (ed.), *Konstitutionelle Zeitschrift* 2 (1823), p. 321.

[91] Anselm von Feuerbach, 'Über teutsche Freiheit und Vertretung teutscher Völker durch Landstände (1814) in his *Kleine Schriften vermischten Inhalts* (Nürnberg 1833; reprint Osnabrück: Zeller, 1966), p. 79.

political freedom and its realisation, yes, even this freedom itself'.[92] Even the more prosaic Dahlmann uses grand language in speaking of the constitution. He asserts that everything he says in praise of it may not be understood 'as if a good constitution would automatically make a state happy, or infallibly prevent political crimes and errors; however, it enhances the likelihood for the happiness of a people, and elevates the same to a higher level of value in every respect than a constitution-less people can ever achieve. The constitution is like that mythical spear that heals the wounds it has made.'[93] This metaphor could be considered to apply to the monarchs, to make the constitutional limitation of their power palatable to them, as a more dependable security of their throne.[94] It is not without a certain shrewdness, however, that the pamphlet, *Bauern-Conversationslexikon*, guides its readers beyond this point. 'Constitution', as this publication observes innocently enough at first, is 'how public matters should be carried on.' By this standard, the pamphlet continues, Russia has no less of a constitution than the United States of America, so this definition is obviously not sufficient. 'When in recent times the peoples of Europe have demanded a constitution, they have meant the limitation of princely power.' This type of constitution, it continues, is widely considered the best. 'Reason and experience, however, show that it is pitiful. The constitutions in Europe are, as one may say, a new rag sewn onto an old dress.'[95] Here, the democratic constitution becomes the true one. Siebenpfeiffer advocates a republican constitution, 'because it realises the boldest dreams of the finest people of all time, because it is rationally imperative, desired from by the purest patriots, expected by all enlightened citizens, and because it is waiting to be born in the present time.'[96]

## 5. The Necessity of a Constitutional Document

In the course of the constitutional demands, the formal qualities of the constitution gain noticeably in importance. At this time, its written nature is not yet commonly considered a defining feature of constitutions. However, the advantages of a 'constitutional document' are asserted on all sides. 'A constitution based solely on tradition thus has no solidity simply by virtue of the form of its existence,' according to Karl Adolf zum Bach. By contrast, the document guards against 'every possible forgetfulness, every deviation and contravention

---

[92] Carl T. Welcker, 'Art. Grundgesetz, Grundvertrag' in Carl von Rotteck and Carl Welcker (eds), *Staats-Lexikon oder Encyklopädie der Staatswissenschaften*, vol. 6 (Altona: Hammerich, 2nd edn, 1847), p. 166.

[93] Dahlmann (n. 61), p. 107.

[94] Johann C. Freiherr von Aretin, *Staatsrecht der konstitutionellen Monarchie*, vol. 1 (Altenburg: Literatur-Comptoir, 1824), p. VI.

[95] Bauern-Conversationslexikon, Art. Constitution, Flugschrift der Frankfurter 'Union' (Männerbund), Feb/March 1834, in Brandt (n. 61), p. 436.

[96] Jacob P. Siebenpfeiffer, *Zwei gerichtliche Vertheidigungsreden* (Bern: Literatur Comptoir, 1834), p. 426.

through the permanent, clear letter of the record.'[97] This formal documentation, he comments, is also useful for the monarch, as 'the solidity and security
implicit in the constitution' would 'revitalise adherence to rulers and public
spirit.'[98] But some authors also mention unsuitable rulers: 'The state does not
perish should the accident of birth happen to put a weak prince upon the throne
... and its fortune is not dependent on a favourite nor on a clique at court.
The constitution stands for itself and gives ... the state and the prince a solid
support.'[99] At this point it is not yet common to see a fundamental difference
between 'written and unwritten constitutions'.[100] Krug, an advocate of 'written
constitutions' even goes so far as to strenuously object to an identification with
the question: 'What justifies you in emphasizing the concrete form instead of
the type?'[101] By contrast, the documentary form is for Schmitthenner a higher
level of constitutional development. Originally just 'a system of observances
in which the people's concept of the state is joined with fixed external legal
norms, ... the constitution gradually passes from the form of legal customs
to that of the formal contract and written law.'[102] With respect to the written
form, several authors draw the line between 'constitution' in the broader or narrower sense or between 'Verfassung' and 'constitution'. According to Zoepfl,
the Verfassung can be based on tradition or positive, documentary establishment. The expression 'constitution' or 'charta' is used to denote the latter.[103]
Pölitz makes the documentary form the selection principle in his comparative
discussion of constitutional law, and writes: 'Under constitutions in the more
modern sense of the word, we understand the written documents that contain
the totality of legal conditions on which the internal life of an existing ... state
is based, according to the necessary interaction between the individual parts
of this life.'[104] For some authors, however, the written nature becomes a defining feature of constitutions. In his *Staatslehre*, Ekendahl expressly discusses 'the
necessity of a written constitutional document for a people that has become
mature enough for freedom',[105] and Buhl attacks the disparagement of the form
with the argument that in constitutional matters 'the form is the matter'.[106]

---

[97] Karl A. zum Bach, *Ideen über Recht, Staat, Staatsgewalt, Staatsverfassung und Volksvertretung ...*, part. 1 (Köln: Rommerskirchen, 1817), p. 60.

[98] Ibid., p. 63.     [99] Johann F. Benzenberg, *Ueber Verfassung* (Dortmund: Mallinckrodt, 1816), p. 211.

[100] See Wilhelm T. Krug, *Dikäopolitik oder neue Restaurazion der Staatswissenschaft mittels des Rechtsgesetzes* (Leipzig: Hartmann, 1824), p. 255.

[101] Ibid., p. 252.

[102] Friedrich Schmitthenner, *Grundlinien des allgemeinen oder idealen Staatsrechtes* (1845; Hamburg: Metzner, 1966), p. 415.

[103] Heinrich Zoepfl, *Grundsätze des allgemeinen und des constitutionell-monarchischen Staatsrechts* (Heidelberg: Winter, 1841), p. 123.

[104] Karl H. L. Pölitz, *Das constitutionelle Leben, nach seinen Formen und Bedingungen* (Leipzig: Hahn, 1831), p. 1.

[105] Daniel G. Ekendahl, *Allgemeine Staatslehre*, part 1 (Neustadt/Orla: Wagner, 1833), p. 100.

[106] Ludwig Buhl, 'Die Verfassungsfrage in Preußen nach ihrem geschichtlichen Verlaufe' in Johann C.I. Buddeus (ed.), *Deutsches Staatsarchiv*, vol. 3 (Jena: Frommann, 1842), p. 222.

## 6. Constitution as the Product of Historical Development

However, as anticipated by Schelling and Fries, a strong counter-movement is formed specifically in opposition to the framed, written constitution. Yet where these commentators emphasized the point that entry into the state and thus possession or non-possession of a constitution could not be arbitrary, the new opposition denies that the specific content of the constitution is subject to planned determination. It is Hegel who paves the way for this understanding of the constitution. This is closely related to his concept of the state. Those who conceive of the state as an aggregation of individuals for the purpose of securing freedom and property attain only a 'superficial state—a state out of necessity and rationality',[107] which Hegel terms 'civil society'. By contrast, the true state is the moral commonwealth without which neither individuals nor the community can achieve their higher purpose. This state is 'per se reasonable',[108] its constitution 'not merely a framed one; it is the work of centuries, the idea and awareness of reason, insofar as this is developed within a people. Therefore, no constitution is simply created by subjects ... The people must have the perception of its right and condition toward its constitution, otherwise the latter can exist formally, but have neither meaning nor value.'[109] If, by contrast, the constitution is based on a form of individual will, even when generalized, it depends on random factors, 'and the further simply understandable consequences that destroy the essential, immanent divinity and its absolute authority and majesty.'[110] While the advocates of the 'law of reason' associate arbitrariness and randomness with the organic constitution, these here become characteristics of framed constitutions. 'What do the ... shouters demand who babble to the peoples of new constitutions? Only the minor matter that all states should dissolve themselves and then constitute themselves anew.'[111] By becoming an expression of a concrete historical being, the constitution admittedly loses its normative function and inadvertently falls into legitimation of the existing order. It is thus no coincidence that in his influential constitutional essay, Gentz comes out in favour of the historical, condition-based concept of constitution and classes 'estate-based constitutions' as orders that emerged 'out of the fundamental elements of the state that exist naturally and not created by human hand,' and 'without violating existing rights, continually approach perfection by the same means by which they formed', while the 'representative constitutions' appear as 'the fruit of external force or arbitrariness', which are only necessary in the event of civil

---

[107] Georg W. F. Hegel, 'Grundlinien der Philosophie des Rechts oder Naturrecht und Staatswissenschaft im Grundrisse' (1821) in *Complete Edition*, vol. 7 (1928), p. 263, § 183.

[108] Ibid., p. 329, §258; cf. ibid., p. 344, § 265.     [109] Ibid., p. 376, § 274, addition.

[110] Ibid., p. 330, § 258.

[111] Johann C. Freiherr von Aretin, *Abhandlungen über wichtige Gegenstände der Staatsverfassung und Staatsverwaltung mit besonderer Rücksicht auf Bayern* (München: 1816), p. 54.

wars and usurpations.[112] The 'constitution' can then be defined as the joining of the 'political elements of the state according to an arbitrary principle'.[113]

### 7. Imposed and Contracted Constitutions

It is obvious that the historical, evolutionary concept of the constitution cannot be reconciled with the theory of the constitutional contract. The latter's rational, constructive approach towards the constitution remains an undiminished object of criticism throughout the first half of the nineteenth century. But the advocates of the constitutional contract themselves fell into justification difficulties as constitutional theory and political reality diverged. In May 1818, the Bavarian constitution, the first modern constitution of a major German state, was enacted. However, it was imposed rather than contracted, which Aretin, Behr, and Schmelzing regard as a defect.[114] Behr, however, quickly arrives at a pragmatic attitude when he asks: 'Who would want to sacrifice the nature of the matter on account of a defect in the form of its genesis? ... What Bavarian would want to trade places with a Prussian or a *Badenser* right now, who are still looking forward to the long promised constitution of their state with a shy, uncertain gaze.... Or do we have cause to envy the Wurttembergers, who have ventured along the path of contractual determination of the principles of the state?'[115] In 1824, Aretin succeeds in reconciling theory and practice: The 'imposed constitution' is also essentially arrived at through agreement, as it only becomes a true constitution through acceptance by the people.[116] Welcker, the most determined advocate of later contractual theory, subsequently adopts this construction. 'The state' as a 'society' of free individuals emerges 'through contracted laws. Its laws, like all laws of society, are contracts,' either direct contracts, which are then termed 'fundamental contracts' or indirect contracts concluded by 'bodies', which he terms 'laws in the narrow sense'.[117] Under these circumstances, Welcker concludes, 'A constitution that is simply imposed is not a constitution at all.'[118] In view of the realities of the situation, Welcker must confront the question of whether in case of a non-contracted but unilaterally imposed constitution a

[112] Friedrich von Gentz, 'Über den Unterschied zwischen den landständischen und Repräsentativ-Verfassungen' (1819) in Brandt (n. 61), p. 219.

[113] Ibid., p. 221.

[114] Johann C. Freiherr von Aretin, *Gespräche über die Verfassungs-Urkunde des Königreichs Baiern*, no. 1 (München: Thienemann, 1818), p. 9; Wilhelm J. Behr, *Staatswissenschaftliche Betrachtungen über Entstehung und Hauptmomente der neuen Verfassung des baierischen Staats* (Würzburg: Nitribitt, 1818), p. 10; Julius Schmelzing, *Einige Betrachtungen über den Begriff und die Wirksamkeit der Landstände, nach den Prinzipien des allgemeinen und natürlichen Staatsrechts* (Rudolstadt: Verlag der Hof-, Buch- und Kunsthandlung, 1818), p. 11.

[115] Behr (n. 114), p. 10.    [116] Aretin (n. 94), p. 11.

[117] Carl T. Welcker, *Grundgesetz und Grundvertrag. Grundlagen zur Beurtheilung der Preußischen Verfassungsfrage* (Altona: Hammerich, 1847), p. 6.

[118] Carl T. Welcker, 'Octroyirte und einseitig von der Volksrepräsentation entworfene und vertragsmäßig unterhandelte Verfassungen' in Rotteck/Welcker (n. 92), vol. 11 (1841), p. 751.

'constitutional legal status is non-existent or impossible'.[119] However, he hastens to assure the reader that such constitutions are no less valid or sacred than contracted ones, precisely because they are in reality also contracted. 'The riddle is resolved in that only the document can be imposed.' For Welcker, these are initially only 'constitutional proposals: mutual, contractual, free and honest acceptance and assurance are what make them a constitution'. For him, this requirement is already fulfilled when the 'people', as occurred in Baden, welcomes 'the offered constitutional document … with joy and gratitude'.[120] The contradiction between contracted and imposed constitution is thus eliminated, if only at the price that the constitutional contract can once more be concluded tacitly.

## 8. The Liberal Turn from the Contractual to the Legislative Creation of Constitutions

The easily declared, but hard to justify, willingness of liberal authors to overlook the defective genesis of new constitutions if their content appeared acceptable once again puts the spotlight on the function of the constitutional contract. It obviously does not exhaust itself in the requirement of a specific form for the emergence of a constitution. Rather, under the conditions of the absolutist state, the contractual construction offered the possibility of according constitutional relevance to the interests of the subjects and to criticise the constitutional conditions of the ancient regime on this basis. In reality, it thus focused on content and not genesis. Under these circumstances, as Kant clearly recognized, it is not necessary to actually conclude a contract. The constitutional idea instead functions only as 'a touchstone for the legality of every public law'.[121] Consequently, it had political significance for future constitutions. In consideration of the already achieved constitution, new problems, namely the implementation and securing of the constitution, took precedence. Unlike Welcker, Rotteck emphasizes this issue. In particular, he is concerned with shielding the constitution, once granted, from unilateral amendment or revocation by the princes. Precisely this was permitted under Haller's definition of the 'constitution', which for him consisted of 'laws' which the prince 'issues for himself, maxims according to which he declares himself willing to act, which he alone has to follow and which essentially do not concern his subjects at all'.[122] Rotteck opposes this by distinguishing between the 'pouvoir constituant' and the 'pouvoir constitué'. These are identical only under absolute monarchy and simple democracy. However, as soon as the 'autocrat' issues a constitutional law, he ceases to be an autocrat. For Rotteck, constitutional laws

---

[119] Ibid., p. 752.    [120] Ibid., p. 752.

[121] Immanuel Kant, 'Über den Gemeinspruch: Das mag in der Theorie richtig sein, taugt aber nicht für die Praxis', II, Folgerung (1793), *Complete Edition* vol. 8, p. 297.

[122] Carl L. von Haller, *Restauration der Staats-Wissenschaft*, vol. 2 (Winterthur: Steiner, 1817), p. 182.

are characterized specifically by the fact that they restrain the constituted power. 'Thus, in their idea they derive from a will which in its nature is higher than this power and conceived preceding its establishment, namely that of the constituting authority, which is nothing other than the society itself.' However, if the absolute monarch enacts a basic law, 'he has acted as the constituting power, i.e. as representing this power, and can now, as constituted ruler, no longer revoke that which he as constituting instance has created'.[123] From this consideration, Rotteck arrives at the conclusion, until then upheld only by the opposing side, that, to be precise, the contractual category is only suitable for the disposition of private rights, but is not applicable to the constitution.[124] Even for Mohl, who after all annotates a contracted constitution, that of Wurttemberg, the form of the constitution is the 'law' and the 'contract' is only its historical cause for emergence.[125]

## 9. Conservative Approaches to the Constitutional State

From the conservative side, Stahl lays the groundwork for a convergence of viewpoints. Like Hegel, he rejects the liberalist state defined only in terms of safeguarding freedom and property. For him, the state is a moral institution that gives effect to God's will in the world, if not with unlimited power, then certainly entirely in accord with the equally God-given individual freedom. 'The constitution is then not merely a reciprocal relationship between individuals (the rulers and the ruled), but rather the relationship of an institution above them, the coherence of this institution in itself.'[126] It binds the ruler as well as the subjects. To effect this bond, Stahl considers formulating the constitution in the form of 'laws' appropriate. They 'naturally distinguish themselves from other laws because they contain the basis for the entire state, the prerequisite for all government, the holiest rights of the nation.' Thus, they enjoy particular safeguards. 'The epitome of such laws ... is termed the basic law of the state. With regards to its content, it is now usually termed, constitution, constitutional law, Verfassung.'[127] Basic laws of this type are nothing new, although initially they were few in number and not secured by additional means. Constitutional law, in this view, was thus not specified to the same degree as 'civil law'. To remedy this, Stahl advocates the written constitutional form and institutional guarantees. He sees the latter in popular representation. Where this exists, he speaks of a 'constitution in the specific contemporary sense of the word'.[128] But this does not entail the idea that constitutions can be framed arbitrarily. 'As the constitution

---

[123] Carl von Rotteck, 'Charte, Verfassungs-Urkunde, Freiheits-Brief', Rotteck/Welcker (n. 92), vol. 3 (1836), p. 405.

[124] Ibid., p. 407.

[125] Robert von Mohl, *Das Staatsrecht des Königreiches Württemberg*, vol. 1 (Tübingen: Laupp, 2nd edn, 1840), p. 71.

[126] Friedrich J. Stahl, *Die Philosophie des Rechts nach geschichtlicher Ansicht*, vol. 2/2 (Heidelberg: Mohr, 1837), p. 35.

[127] Ibid., p. 101.       [128] Ibid., p. 102.

is formed from the beginning within the state itself, and not framed with intent and deliberation, the natural consequence is that no entirely new constitution should be framed at once thereafter, but rather the constitution should develop with the public circumstances and the national recognition of the same, in part through gradual alteration of the tradition, in part through individual laws as prompted by the occurrences of life. These are the historical constitutions.'[129] Stahl recognizes, however, that circumstances, such as breaks in tradition, can occur that make a new constitution necessary. Constitutions of this nature do not only give expression to a constitution, but in some cases establish it. Stahl calls these 'reflected Verfassungen or constitutions in the proper sense'.[130] This of course does not eliminate the fundamental difference to liberalism. For Stahl, the state as a moral institution is always the primary element, the constitution the accretion. The state thus cannot be established by the constitution: it only has the function of securing and developing the order of an already existing state.

### 10. *Constitution in the Material and Formal Sense*

Below these fundamental differences, a broad consensus exists on a more technical level, particularly among scholars of positive constitutional law. It is generally recognized that the object of the constitution is the form of the state ('Staatsform'). For all authors 'state form' means the determination of the holder of supreme power ('form of rule'), and most include the modes of exercise ('form of government') as well. The latter include in particular the basic rights. Zöpfl presents one example of a standard definition: 'The constitution is the epitome of legal principles that apply within a state with respect to the form of rule and government, i.e. with respect to the organization of state power and the rights of the people and their mutual relationship.'[131] With respect to the form of rule, the Aristotelian trisection applies. The form of government is generally divided into limited or unlimited state power. A certain embarrassment may be observed in Prussia in connection with this classification. 'There are no … actual basic laws here', finds Ostermann, before going on to characterize the Prussian constitutional system as a 'representative, non-constitutional … system'. Although, unlike an 'absolute monarchy', popular representation exists, but, unlike in 'constitutional monarchies', this has only an 'advisory voice'.[132] How the supreme power has to act within the boundaries set for it is not a matter for the constitution but the administration. 'Administration' means, more comprehensively than today, the entire activity of the state in the pursuit of its ends. This results in the differentiation between 'constitutional law and administrative law.' 'Constitutional law is the epitome of those rights and obligations that accrue to the sovereign (the government) toward the people (the governed). Administrative law [is] the epitome of those

---

[129] Ibid., p. 105.    [130] Ibid., p. 106.    [131] Zoepfl (n. 103), p. 123.

[132] Wilhelm Ostermann, *Grundsätze des preußischen Staatsrechts* (Dortmund: Krüger, 1841), pp. 31, 59, 13.

legal norms according to which the government is to exercise the rights and obligations accruing to it.'[133] It is then of course obvious that this concept of 'constitution' is not always in accord with the content of the constitutional document. On the one hand, administrative law is mentioned in the constitutional statute, but on the other hand there is constitutional law outside of the constitutional statute. For this reason, Rotteck amends his constitutional definition derived from the object to include 'the determination of the persons or bodies by whom, and the forms or manners by which, the supreme power of the state is to be exercised', and adds a second condition that 'comprises everything determined on the fundamental level': 'This latter concept is also the more common one, and the one that more closely corresponds to practical need; while the other, which excludes all material regulations [i.e. not related to the form of government], appears purer from a scholarly perspective.'[134] This distinction between 'constitution' in a material and a formal sense resolves many long-standing conflicts.

## IV. CONSOLIDATION AND CRISIS OF THE LEGAL CONSTITUTION

### 1. *Abandonment of Natural Law*

In 1868, Held distinguishes between four common interpretations of the term 'constitution': '1) the entire condition of the organized unity of the state with inclusion of the associated non-juridicial moments; 2) the totality of the legal stipulations and institutions relating to the constitution; 3) that part of constitutional law which contains the constitutional institutions; 4) a written, constitutional basic law including all amendments made to it having the same character.' He then adds: 'On the continent, at least, the term is customarily used in the latter sense.'[135] The reason for this habituation is the fact that the constitutional state had asserted itself once and for all with the revolution of 1848. As a consequence, a number of older controversies about the notion of constitution come to an end. The most remarkable feature is the disappearance of justifications based on natural law. Already in Frankfurt's *Paulskirche*, the representatives arguing on the basis of natural law were in the minority. This realistic attitude continues into the second half of the nineteenth century. A liberal such as Twesten remarks in 1859 that an entirely new understanding of history and a fruitful interest in reality is awakening everywhere. In the wake of these, 'the empty declamations, the arbitrary constructions of abstract concepts which have repeatedly led to the criticism that the doctrines of the state appear good in theory but are unsuitable in practice, are falling silent'. They

---

[133] Ibid., p. 55.    [134] Rotteck (n. 72), vol. 2, p. 172.

[135] Joseph von Held, *Grundzüge des Allgemeinen Staatsrechts oder Institutionen des öffentlichen Rechts* (Leipzig: Brockhaus, 1868), p. 315. Braunschweig called his modern constitution of 12 October 1832 antiquated: 'Die neue Landschaftsordnung' in Ernst R. Huber, *Deutsche Verfassungsgeschichte seit 1789*, vol. 2 (Stuttgart: Kohlhammer, 1960), p. 60.

had served well in overcoming the old society. 'Since they essentially achieved their purpose, these concepts have gradually fallen into disrepute.'[136] The contract silently fades from most works of the latter half of the nineteenth century. Nowhere does it represent the sole legitimating origination form for the constitution. Ahrens, who after 1848 includes an extensive 'constitutional doctrine' in his *Natural Law*,[137] notes that the contractual form 'best [corresponds] to the uniformly justified and dignified position [of] state power [and] popular representation', but adds: 'The contract, however, only designates the form of the emergence and existence of the constitution, which according to its end of being generally binding, assumes the character of a law.'[138] By contrast, Held rejects the contractual category as entirely unsuitable for the constitution. State and state power, he observes, always exist before rules governing their exercise are developed.[139] On this basis, Zorn later asserts that 'in constitutional terms, all constitutions ... [are] imposed ... The concept of a contracted constitution is not construable in terms of constitutional law.'[140] Whereas before 1848 the aim was to reinterpret imposed constitutions as contracted, efforts are now directed towards making the contracted constitutions imposed, so that the priority of state power is preserved.

## 2. Constitutional Positivism

On the other side, the feasibility of constitutions is no longer challenged in principle. That is entirely natural for the *Paulskirche*. 'Finally, and I place particular value on this,' states Beseler as reporter for the constitutional committee for basic rights, 'our task is to constitute'.[141] It no longer appears necessary to specify what is to be constituted. The expression has attained an independent, and not merely attributive, meaning. On 3 April 1848, after resolving to convene a 'constituting national assembly', the *Vorparlament* decides 'that the resolution for Germany's future constitution shall be entrusted solely to this constituting national assembly elected by the people.'[142] After his election to the chair of

---

[136] Carl Twesten, *Woran uns gelegen ist. Ein Wort ohne Umschweife* (Kiel: Schwers, 1859), p. 21.

[137] Heinrich Ahrens, *Naturrecht oder Philosophie des Rechts und des Staates* (1839/46), vol. 2 (Wien: Gerold, 6th edn, 1871), p. 355.

[138] Ibid., p. 358.

[139] Joseph Held, *System des Verfassungsrechts der monarchischen Staaten Deutschlands mit besonderer Rücksicht auf den Constitutionalismus*, vol. 1 (Würzburg: Stahel, 1856), p. 304; cf. Joseph Eötvös, *Der Einfluß der herrschenden Ideen des 19. Jahrhunderts auf den Staat* (Leipzig: Brockhaus, 1854); Robert von Mohl, *Geschichte und Literatur der Staatswissenschaften*, vol. 1 (Erlangen: Enke, 1855), p. 109.

[140] Philipp Zorn, *Das Staatsrecht des Deutschen Reiches*, vol. 1 (Berlin: Guttentag, 2nd edn, 1895), p. 35.

[141] Carl G. Beseler, 'Rede vom 4.7.1848' in Franz Wigard (ed.), *Stenographischer Bericht über die Verhandlungen der Deutschen Constituirenden Nationalversammlung zu Frankfurt am Main*, vol. 1 (Frankfurt: Sauerländer, 1848), p. 701.

[142] 'Officieller Bericht über die Verhandlungen zur Gründung eines deutschen Parlaments. Beschluß vom 3.4.1848' in *Verhandlungen des deutschen Parlaments*, vol. 1 (Frankfurt: Sauerländer, 1848), p. 172.

the national assembly, Gagern proclaimed: 'We have the greatest task to perform. We are to create a constitution for Germany, for the entire realm. The appointment and the authorisation to this creation lie in the sovereignty of the nation.'[143] The most frequently used metaphors for this task and objective are 'build', 'building', and 'construction'. Certainly, construction cannot begin without prerequisites, as 'new constitutions are guaranteed to prevail only when the issue from the innermost conditions of the people for whom they are intended, have their roots in the national views and needs and attempt to achieve the possible and attainable under the given conditions'. However, this does not imply a waiver of the claim to actively shape the constitution, as the draft immediately makes clear: 'It cannot be our purpose to simply whitewash the old building or push in a new beam; a restructuring of our existing constitution is required, with new elements, new foundations.'[144] After 1848, conservatives also begin to increasingly reconcile themselves with 'made' constitutions. With respect to the imposed Prussian constitution, Leopold von Gerlach notes, 'It is entirely clear to me that the Lord has taken the right path with this constitution document.'[145] Although the Count of Westphalia, interior minister during the Reaction, cites the 'constitutional principles arising from the revolution' as foremost among the harm and dangers for Prussia, he does not agree with the monarch's desire to replace the 'paper wipe' with a 'royal carte blanche', but instead advises, like Radowitz, the king's confidant, to make corrections through constitutional amendment and constitutional interpretation.[146] Minister President Manteuffel informs Friedrich-Wilhelm IV that although the constitution represents as certain weakening of the monarchy, its unilateral revocation would mean an even greater weakening.[147] The conservative motto is thus no longer opposition to, but rather 'improvement of the constitution'.[148]

---

[143] Heinrich von Gagern, 'Rede vom 19.5.1848' in Franz Wigard (ed.), *Stenographischer Bericht über die Verhandlungen der Deutschen Constituirenden Nationalversammlung zu Frankfurt am Main*, vol. 1 (Frankfurt: Sauerländer, 1848), p. 17.

[144] 'Ausschuß-Bericht über die deutsche Reichsverfassung', 20 October 1848, ibid., vol. 4 (1848), p. 2722.

[145] Leopold von Gerlach, Notiz vom 14.12.87, cit. in Ernst Ludwig von Gerlach, *Aufzeichung aus seinem Leben und Wirken 1795-1877*, ed. by Jakob von Gerlach, vol. 2 (Schwerin: Bahn, 1903), p. 34; cf. also ibid., p. 31.

[146] Ferdinand Graf von Westphalen, 'Denkschrift von 24.10.1852' in Heinrich von Poschinger (ed.), *Friedrich Wilhelm IV. Denkwürdigkeiten des Ministerpräsidenten Otto Freiherr von Manteuffel*, vol. 2 (Berlin: Mittler, 1901), p. 262. For the king's intentions, see Leopold von Gerlach, 'Tagebuchnotiz vom 27.5.1852' in *Denkwürdigkeiten*, ed. by his daughter, vol. 1 (Berlin: Hertz, 1891), p. 770; further Joseph Maria von Radowitz to Friedrich Wilhelm IV., March 5, 1853, in Walter Möhring (ed.), *Nachgelassene Briefe und Aufzeichnungen zur Geschichte der Jahre 1848-1853* (Osnabrück: Bibliotheks-Verlag, 1967), p. 415.

[147] Otto Freiherr von Manteuffel, 'Denkschrift für Friedrich Wilhelm IV. von 1855' in Heinrich von Poschinger (ed.), *Unter Friedrich Wilhelm IV.*, vol. 3 (Berlin: Mittler, 1901), p. 98.

[148] Ibid., p. 100.

*3. Constitution as an Expression of Power Structures*

In his 1861 reflections, Lasker sees only 'repression and destruction' as the result of Prussian constitutional policy: 'Every contradiction in the constitution [was] painstakingly defined and expanded into opposites in principle; new contradictions [were] introduced; the reserved laws were formulated in an evil, ambiguous spirit or omitted entirely; the clear provisions of the constitution were criticised and traded on; the old public law deployed in the struggle against the new, and always victory on the same side.'[149] Through this development, liberalism comes to understand that the effectiveness of a constitution is not automatically established as a consequence of its legal validity. In explaining this discrepancy, Lorenz von Stein notes as early as 1852 that 'constitutional law does not emerge from the law of statutes, but from the law of conditions.'[150] In Prussia, these only permit a 'sham constitutionalism'. Before Stein, in view of the rapid succession of French constitutions, Saint-Simon had arrived at the conviction that the forms of government are less important than property, whose 'constitution' forms the real basis of the 'édifice social'.[151] This view is adopted and popularized by Lasalle.[152] Lassalle compares the aspiration with the reality, starting with the concept of the constitution as the 'basic law of a country', and considers this to mean 'an active force that necessarily makes all laws and legal institutions enacted in this country what they are'.[153] This 'active force' however is not to be found in the constitutional statute, but in political and social power. 'A king who is obeyed by the army and the cannons—that is a part of constitution'.[154] 'Messrs Borsig and Egels, all the great industrialists—they are a part of constitution,'[155] and so forth to his conclusion: 'We have thus now seen ... what the constitution of a country is, namely: the actual power relationships existing in a country.'[156] Thus, once again the older, condition-related concept of 'constitution', which had been gradually displaced by the advance of constitutional documents, emerges from behind the juridicial one, now defined more precisely as a social-economic power constellation. Admittedly, Lassalle also considers the triumph of the legal constitution the result of altered power relationships. However, the legal constitution remains dependent on the actual one. It can only attain validity to the extent that it coincides with the power relationships. 'It does not matter what is written on the sheet of paper if it

---

[149] Eduard Lasker, 'Wie ist die Verfassung in Preußen gehandhabt worden?' (1861) in his, *Zur Verfassungsgeschichte Preußens* (Leipzig: Brockhaus, 1874), p. 8.

[150] Lorzenz von Stein, 'Zur preußischen Verfassungsfrage' in *Deutsche Vierteljahresschrift*, vol. 1 (1852) (Darmstadt: Wissenschaftliche Buchgesellschaft, 1961), p. 36.

[151] Claude-Henri de Saint-Simon, 'L'industrie ou discussions politiques, morales et philosophiques' vol. 2 (1817), *Oeuvres*, vol. 2 (1869) (Paris: Edition Anthropos, 1966), p. 82.

[152] Ferdinand Lassalle, 'Über Verfassungswesen' (1862), in Eduard Bernstein (ed.), *Gesammelte Reden und Schriften*, vol. 2 (1919; reprint Berlin: Cassirer, 1967), p. 25. See also Friedrich Engels, 'Die Lage Englands' (1844), *Marx Engels Werke*, vol. 1 (Berlin: Dietz, 1956), p. 572.

[153] Lassalle (n. 152), p. 31.     [154] Ibid., p. 33.     [155] Ibid., p. 36.     [156] Ibid., p. 38.

contradicts the real situation, the actual power relationships.'[157] Lassalle's understanding of constitution is adopted by the emerging discipline of sociology. Max Weber defines 'constitution' as 'the nature of the actual power distribution in a commonwealth that determines the possibility of influencing the actions of the commonwealth through regulations.'[158]

### 4. Fundamental Order or Partial Order

The Prussian constitutional conflict can be considered a test case for Lassalle's power theory. Legally, only the correct interpretation of individual constitutional articles was at issue. Behind this, however, one can make out two different concepts of a statutory constitution. For the liberals, the constitution caused a complete break with pre-constitutional state law. Previously, Lasker explains, 'all authority of the king [was] an expression of unlimited, absolute power. When the constitution overcame that unlimited nature, the source from which new authority flowed was stopped up. The constitution had to endow the king anew with the authority necessary for the good of the state.'[159] And just a little later: 'The powers of the king are a positive creation of the constitution.'[160] The constitution appears here as a legitimating basis for the actions of the state. It leaves no scope for extraconstitutional authority. By contrast, the conservative school of public law seeks to deny the break and to prove the continuity of state law. For Kaltenborn, 'the constitution of a German country' does not begin with the 'constitutional document', it only 'enters into a new stage ... In particular, the position of the German prince as the bearer of state power is not legally created by the constitutional document, but only determined in greater ... detail and limited.'[161] In this view, the constitution appears to be merely a modifying partial order. Where it does not expressly restrict the monarch, he retains possession of original state power. Under these circumstances, the 'constitutional document' is only 'law to the extent that it applies to the subjects; insofar as the conditions of the crown are regulated, the constitution cannot be law, because law presupposes at all times a person or power in the state that stands above the one for whom the law is promulgated.'[162] For this reason, Seydel starts his *Bayerisches Staatsrecht* with the 'ruler' and only then follows with the 'constitution', where he essentially discusses the estates and the administration.[163] Bornhak sums up this concept of the constitution.

---

[157] Ibid., p. 57.

[158] Max Weber, 'Wirtschaft und Gesellschaft. Grundriß der verstehenden Soziologie' (1911/13; 1921), ed. by Johannes Winckelmann (Tübingen: Mohr, 5th edn, 1976), p. 194.

[159] E. Lasker, 'Fragen des Staatsrechts' (1862/63) in his *Verfassungsgeschichte* (n. 149), p. 373; cf. also E. Lasker, 'Wie ist die Verfassung in Preußen gehandhabt worden?' (1861), ibid., p. 9.

[160] E. Lasker, 'Der König der Verfassung' (1863) in his *Verfassungsgeschichte* (n. 149), p. 385.

[161] Carl von Kaltenborn, *Einleitung in das constitutionelle Verfassungsrecht* (Leipzig: Tauchnitz, 1863), p. 340.

[162] Hugo Gottfried Opitz, *Das Staatsrecht des Königreichs Sachsen*, vol. 1 (Leipzig: Roßberg, 1884), p. 38.

[163] Max von Seydel, *Bayerisches Staatsrecht* (1884), vol. 1 (Freiburg: Mohr, 2nd edn, 1896), pp. 169, 346.

Whereas 'the republic can only enter into legal life through and with its constitution', the monarchy always presupposes the existence of the state person, who is unaffected by the enactment of the constitution. Consequently, the 'first constitution of a republic is … the only basis of public law . . , the constitution of the monarchy' is by contrast only a partial order. The one may be termed a 'constitution', the other merely a 'constitutional document'.[164]

## 5. Precedence of the State Over the Constitution

The precedence of the state over the constitution expressed by these scholars continues to gain ground over the second half of the century, and becomes dominant after the founding of the empire. This marks the completion of the shift in perspective that started in the revolutionary year of 1848. The events of that year taught the bourgeoisie that it could not establish national unity through its own efforts. The nation state did not emerge until governments took this up as their task. The willingness to leave this task to them had increased due to the fear, also inspired in 1848, that the recalcitrant proletariat could not be fended off without cover from the monarchical state. This left its mark on the constitution, which now assumes defensive functions. Kaltenborn opines that 'particularly in our era of turbulent political ferment and development, [it is] an undeniable necessity' to have 'a documentary formulation' of public law 'as a solid foundation for all further development and as a secure barrier against a yearning for unconscionable innovations.'[165] The aim is no longer to interpret state power on the basis of the constitution, but to interpret the constitution on the basis of state power. It is not the basis, but rather an addition. Consequently, with few exceptions,[166] legal scholarship consistently refers to its treatises as 'state law' (*Staatsrecht*), and the constitution appears merely as a non-exhaustive part of it. In assigning the precedence to the state and not the constitution, the doctrine of public law is in accord with the founder of the empire. Speaking before the Reichstag, Bismarck declares: 'For me, there has always been only one compass, a single North Star, by which I steer: salus publica! … The nation comes first of all, its external position, its independence, our organisation such that we as a great nation in the world may breathe freely. Everything that may come after that, liberal, reactionary, conservative constitution – gentlemen, I freely admit, that comes second, that is an institutional luxury for which there is time once that house is completed and securely standing… Let us first build a structure that is solid, secure against the outside, tightly joined inside, bound by the national tie, and then ask me my

---

[164] Conrad Bornhak, *Allgemeine Staatslehre* (Berlin: Heymanns, 1896), pp. 37, 46.

[165] Kaltenborn (n. 161), p. 342.

[166] E.g., Joseph Held, *System des Verfassungsrechts der monarchischen Staaten Deutschlands mit besonderer Rücksicht auf den Constitutionalismus*, vol. 2 (Würzburg: Stadel, 1857), p. 50.

opinion as to how the house may be furnished with more or less liberal constitutional fittings.'[167] The growing conflation of constitution with ordinary law becomes the juridicial expression of this attitude. As with every ordinary law, the constitution is an emanation of the pre-existing state power, and not its basis. The difference lies ultimately only in the greater difficulty of amendment or, as Laband says, the greater 'formal force of law'.[168] It is generally forgotten that the formal force has its justification in the importance of its content, as Gerber was still aware.[169]

## 6. Identity of Constitution and Constitutional Law

In 1870, Lorenz von Stein wrote: 'The main concepts and legal principles of the constitution have been thought through more or less to their conclusion … Even the conception that every positive constitution does not emerge from a legal idea, but it always contains the currently prevailing social order that has become state law, that it derives above all from the distribution of possession and that its history is the history of the order of humanity based on the order of possession and labour is no longer challenged. Our era, itself in possession of such a constitution, has understood how to formulate its principle completely and build its system. Very little is in doubt here, all in all; the decision as regards individual questions can safely be left to the natural development of forces and actualities.'[170] The theory of public law confirms this impression in its own way. After the founding of the empire, positivism prevails rapidly and lastingly, indicating that the constitution no longer posed political problems, but merely legal ones. The conditional relationship between the legal and actual constitution re-emerges briefly only once: in the question of the basis for the validity of the constitution of the North German Confederation and the imperial constitution. The foundation of these two states presented German public law theory with an unusual situation in that it was not an already existing state which later limited itself by constitutional means, but rather that a new state was established on the basis of a constitution. To resolve this problem, most scholars resort to an actual constitution that precedes the legal one. Jellinek considers the effort to constitute the emergence of a state juridicially to be in vain. 'All processes by which … the creation of a state' takes place 'are facts that can be comprehended historically, but not by using a legal formula'.[171] And further: 'The most significant moment in the conception of the state is that it is an order, and an order prior to an order is a contradiction. Consequently, the first order,

---

[167] Otto von Bismarck, Rede vom 24.2.1881, *Die gesammelten Werke*, vol. 12 (Berlin: Stollberg, Verlag für Politik und Wirtschaft, 1929), p. 194.

[168] Paul Laband, *Das Staatsrecht des Deutschen Reiches* (1883), vol. 2 (Tübingen: Mohr, 5th edn, 1911), p. 72.

[169] Carl F. von Gerber, *Grundzüge des deutschen Staatsrechts* (1865) (Leipzig: Tauchnitz, 3rd edn, 1880), p. 7.

[170] L. von Stein, *Handbuch der Verwaltungslehre* (1870), vol. 1, *Der Begriff der Verwaltung und das System der positiven Staatswissenschaften* (Stuttgart: Cotta, 1888), p. 1.

[171] Georg Jellinek, *Die Lehre von den Staatenverbindungen* (Wien: Hoelder, 1882), p. 264.

the first constitution of a state, cannot be derived further in legal terms.'[172] In his *Staatslehre* Jellinek explains in greater detail that 'every permanent association' requires 'an order according to which its will is formed and executed, its area delineated and the position of its members in it and to it regulated. Such an order is called a constitution.'[173] Consequently, he reasons, state and constitution are necessarily associated with each other. However, a constitution does not necessarily need to be a legal order. 'The presence of an actual power that maintains the unity of the state is sufficient for the minimum of constitution that the state requires for its existence.'[174]

## 7. Procedural Dissolution of the Constitutional Statute

Carl Schmitt later said of the positivistic theory of state law of the empire that it did not develop a constitutional theory at all. Schmitt sees the most important reason for this in 'the feeling of political and social security of the pre-war era'.[175] If this is true, then the question as to the constitution must again be posed fundamentally in the Weimar Republic, as the Weimar Constitution did not prove to be the expression of an existing unity, remaining instead an object of controversy over its entire existence. And indeed, after an extreme exaggeration of the juridicial concept of the constitution by Kelsen, this period witnesses a no less determined relativization of the same, particularly by Smend and Schmitt. With his title alone, *Constitution and constitutional law*, Smend distances himself from the normativistic restriction of the concept of constitution without thereby adopting the empirical equation of constitution with actual power relationships. 'The constitution' serves 'life in which the state has its vital reality, namely its integration process. The purpose of this process is always to create the totality of life of the state anew, and the constitution is the legal regulation of individual aspects of this process.'[176] For Smend, the necessity of an 'orientation of the constitution of the state as an integration order according to the value of integration' follows from this.[177] This suggests that constitutional interpretation, unlike the interpretation of ordinary law, is largely detached from text and juridical method; it relates to the success of integration. 'This mandated success may often be achieved by the flow of political life through pathways that are not precisely constitutional: the fulfilment of the integration task mandated by the value-based legality of the spirit and the articles of the constitution will then better correspond to the purpose of the constitution, in spite of these deviations, than a more literally faithful constitutional life that, in terms of success, is more lacking.'[178] Consequently, constitutional norms strictly

---

[172] Ibid., 266.

[173] Georg Jellinek, *Allgemeine Staatslehre* (1900) (Darmstadt: Wissenschaftliche Buchgesellschaft, 3rd edn, 1960), p. 505.

[174] Ibid.    [175] Carl Schmitt, *Verfassungslehre* (1928) (Berlin: Duncker & Humblot, 1954), p. IX.

[176] Rudolf Smend, *Verfassung und Verfassungsrecht* (München, Leipzig: Duncker & Humblot, 1928), p. 78.

[177] Ibid., p. 84.    [178] Ibid., p. 78.

bind constitutional life only in exceptional cases. 'It is simply the immanent and natural sense of the formulated constitution that possesses this elasticity and autonomously supplements and modifies its system.'[179] Admittedly, this no longer permits a fixed boundary to be drawn between law and reality. In radical opposition to positivistic state law doctrine, Smend asserts that, 'as positive law, the constitution is not merely a norm, but also reality; as a constitution it is integrating reality.'[180]

## 8. Decisionistic Dissolution of the Constitutional Statute

Unlike Smend, Carl Schmitt does not resolve the written constitution in favour of an ongoing process, but rather a one-time decision. The object of his 'constitutional theory' is a 'positive concept of constitution', which is defined as an 'overall decision as to the nature and form of political union'.[181] He formulates this positive constitutional concept in the context of a prior distinction between 'constitution' in the absolute and the relative sense. The 'constitution in the absolute sense' designates 'a (real or imagined) whole', either 'the overall condition of political union' or 'a unified, closed system of highest and ultimate norms'.[182] The first case relates to being, the second to an ought. However, the ought finds its justification in the being, because it presupposes a will as origin. If, on the other hand, 'a series of laws of a certain type' is termed a 'constitution', one may only speak of a relative constitutional concept. It does not refer to a uniform 'whole', but to an internally unconnected multiplicity of norms that can only be considered as belonging together according to formal criteria such as their occurrence in the same law or their greater difficulty of amendment. 'Constitution and constitutional law are treated as the same in such case.'[183] Although Schmitt does not make the connection himself, the positive concept of the constitution must be regarded as a subset of the absolute, while the constitutional statute must be characterized as relative. However, the two are not unconnected. Rather, 'constitutional statutes' apply 'only on account of the constitution and presuppose a constitution'.[184] 'The essence of the constitution' thus lies 'not in a law or a norm', but in the overall decision as to the nature and form of political union. The aim of this distinction is 'to direct' the attention of jurists from the 'constitutional statute' to the underlying 'political decision'. 'Viewed correctly, those fundamental political decisions are also the decisive and positive factors for a positive jurisprudence. The further regulations, the enumerations and demarcations of competences in detail, the laws for which the form of the constitutional statute was chosen for whatever reason are relative and secondary to those decisions.'[185] As a consequence, in the case of conflict, the informal political fundamental decision prevails over its formal legal expression. However, with this Schmitt not only draws attention to the social

---

[179] Ibid., p. 79.    [180] Ibid., p. 80.    [181] Schmitt (n. 175), p. 20.    [182] Ibid., pp. 3, 7.

[183] Ibid., p. 3.    [184] Ibid., p. 22.    [185] Ibid., pp. 23, 25.

and political structure underlying the statutory constitution. He also surrenders the advantages of legal control of power. The constitutional statute only binds the political actors according to the standards of the fundamental decision.

## 9. Normative and Existential Constitution

Hermann Heller's *Staatslehre*, which like Schmitt and Smend distinguishes between 'constitution as social reality' and 'autonomous legal constitution', but unlike these seeks to avoid dissolving the constitution in dynamic or decision,[186] does not appear until after the fall of the Weimar Republic in the Netherlands. In terms of constitutional theory, the final phase of the Weimar Republic is dominated entirely by Carl Schmitt, who now completes the qualification of constitutional law begun in his *Verfassungslehre*, thus supplying the opponents of the Weimar constitution with ammunition. In his essay *Der Hüter der Verfassung* ('The guardian of the constitution') from 1931, he analyses 'the concrete constitutional situation of the present day'.[187] This 'constitutional situation' is not placed within the conceptual context of his *Verfassungslehre*, and obviously does not fit in there, as it is identical neither with the (absolute) constitution nor with (relative) constitutional law, but differs from both. Huber thus sees in this essay 'the second major piece of [Schmitt's] constitutional theory', after overcoming the formal constitutional concept of positivism in *Verfassungslehre*.[188] According to this, the 'true constitution' is 'not merely a normative, but also a real, existential constitution'.[189] This eliminates from the concept of the constitution not only those components that cannot be regarded as fundamental decisions, but those fundamental decisions that no longer have any reality. One year later, Schmitt, in *Legalität and Legitimität*, attempts to show that there are no legal impediments to a 'restructuring of the constitution'.[190] According to this, legality is not a general postulate of every legal order, but only the specific form of legality that the parliamentary legislative state has developed. Where this no longer functions, legality has lost its standing. The forms of the constitution therefore do not bind those who seek to defend its substance. Huber praises this as 'a sign of political responsibility of a German scholar of state law that in this threatening situation, Carl Schmitt ... has revealed the constitutional nullity of the demand for legality.'[191] In the situation of 1932, however, Schmitt does not even consider it possible to rescue the entire substance of the constitution.

---

[186] Hermann Heller, *Staatslehre* (Leiden: Sijthoff, 1934), pp. 249, 259.

[187] Carl Schmitt, *Der Hüter der Verfassung* (1931) (Berlin: Duncker & Humblot, 2nd edn, 1969), p. 71.

[188] Friedrich Landeck [i.e. E. R. Huber], 'Verfassung und Legalität, Deutsches Volkstum' (1932) 14 *Halbmonatsschrift für das deutsche Geistesleben* p. 734.

[189] Ibid. Similarly, see Friedrich Grüter [d. i. Ernst Forsthoff], 'Krisis des Staatsdenkens' (1931) 13 *Halbmonatsschrift für das deutsche Geistesleben* p. 173.

[190] Carl Schmitt, 'Legalität und Legitimität' (1932) in *Verfassungsrechtliche Aufsätze aus den Jahren 1924-1954. Materialien zu einer Verfassungslehre* (Berlin: Duncker & Humblot, 1958), p. 343.

[191] Landeck [Huber] (n. 188), p. 734.

Rather, he views the Weimar Constitution as a conglomerate of two contradictory fundamental decisions, the value-neutral organizational part based on majority decisions and the values-based basic rights part. 'If, in the understanding that the Weimar Constitution is two constitutions, one must now choose one of these constitutions', the parliamentary legislative state must be sacrificed in favour of the 'substantive order. If this is successful, the idea of a German constitutional structure shall have been saved.'[192]

## 10. *The End of the Normative Constitution*

It may not be suspected that Schmitt meant by the 'German constitutional structure' the system of national socialism. Once the national socialists came to power, however, he writes, under the title 'Ein Jahr nationalsozialistischer Verfassungsstaat' ('One year of the national socialist constitutional state'): 'Liberalism celebrated its greatest triumph in the assertion that a state without a liberal constitution has no constitution at all ... It is all the more necessary to decisively emphasise right from the start that every constitution has its own constitutional concept.'[193] The national socialist state, he asserts, also has a constitution, which differs from the liberal constitution not only in its content, but also in its form. In his textbook on state law, Huber describes it with the sentence: 'The new constitution of the German Reich ... is not a constitution in the formal sense.'[194] Schmitt even expressly warns against giving a liberal form to *völkisch* content. 'It would be neither politically correct nor in accordance with the spirit of national socialism if the National Socialists were led astray for a moment to believe that they had to match the Weimar constitution at least in terms of the form of a comprehensive regulation laid down in a document with a different document with national socialist content.'[195] What is important is not the promulgation of a 'pseudo-constitution' like the Weimar Constitution, but to 'politically decide ... the true constitutional conditions in all important points'.[196] Admittedly, Hitler himself had announced in his government declaration of 23 March 1933 that a constitution would be framed 'that links the will of the people with the authority of true leadership. The statutory legalisation of such a constitutional form will be ratified by the people itself.'[197] But national-socialist legal scholarship makes it clear that the constitutional statutes or any constitutional document are never 'real constitutions' but only 'emanations and manifestations of an unwritten constitutional core'. The true constitution, they maintain, actually resists normative codification, because it is an order of

---

[192] Schmitt, 'Legalität' (n. 190), p. 344.

[193] Schmitt, 'Ein Jahr nationalsozialistischer Verfassungsstaat, Deutsches Recht' (1934) 4 *Zentral-Organ des Bundes Nationalsozialistischer deutscher Juristen* p. 27.

[194] Ernst Rudolf Huber, *Verfassungsrecht des Großdeutschen Reiches* (1937) (Hamburg: Hanseatische Verlagsanstalt, 2nd edn, 1939), p. 54.

[195] Schmitt (n. 193), p. 27.   [196] Ibid., p. 28.

[197] Adolf Hitler, 'Regierungserklärung vom 23.3.1933' in Max Domarus (ed.), *Hitler. Reden und Proklamationen 1932-1945*, vol. 1/1 (München: Süddeutscher Verlag, 1965), p. 232.

being, not of ought, which bears its legitimacy within itself. 'It is in no way an epitome of express provisions, of written legal principles, of fixed organizations and institutions. The core of the constitution is the unwritten, living order in which the political commonwealth of the German people finds its unity and wholeness.' Since this constitution does not have any benchmark function for political reality, it does not depend on the formal qualities of the legal constitution. Indeed, the informality seems almost a prerequisite for ensuring that 'the fundamental order does not congeal, but rather remains in constant, living flux. Not dead institutions but living basic forms make up the essence of the new constitutional order.'[198]

## V. OUTLOOK

Following the experience of the failed Weimar democracy and national-socialist dictatorship, the legal constitution has been restored and additionally secured. In particular, the establishment of a constitutional court with broad authority has given the legal constitution previously inconceivable significance in the political process. In this way, the constitution operates in the public consciousness almost exclusively as a norm. At the same time, this enhanced claim to validity of the constitution has also heightened awareness for deviations from the legal target condition which are usually considered under the aspect of constitutional reality, in which elements of the empirical concept of the constitution reappear. In spite of the increased significance of the legal constitution, however, it must not be overlooked that conditions have fundamentally changed. The legal constitution emerged as a means for asserting and securing the bourgeois social model, which assumed that society was capable of guiding itself and only required the state as the guarantor of individual freedom and social autonomy. Under these circumstances, the constructive problem consisted in restricting the state to the guarantee function and in tying its activities to the interests of bourgeois society. This task was of a limiting and organizational nature and as such found an adequate solution in law that obligated the power of the state itself. Since the premise of self-guidance has proven to be incorrect, the state is again expected actively to create a just social order. The tasks of the state are once more material. At the same time, the state is becoming dependent on social forces that possess politically relevant resources in the pursuit of its objectives. The legal constitution pays for these changes through a loss in significance. For one thing, the new problems are no longer negative and organizational, but instead positive and material in nature. Constitutional law can guide their solution, but not solve them. Additionally, the constitution surrenders its claim to comprehensively regulate the exercise of political power; to the extent that non-state forces share in political decision-making it becomes a partial order. As awareness of this context grows, the significance of the political-social constitution on which the legal constitution is based will once again increase.

---

[198] Huber (n. 194), p. 55.

# PART III

# CONCEPTS AND FUNCTION

# The Function of Constitutions and Guidelines for Constitutional Reform

## I. THE STATE OF CONSTITUTIONAL THEORY

The reform of the Basic Law cannot be explored without first answering two preliminary questions: what are constitutions supposed to do and what are they able to do? Naturally, these two are closely related, because the objective cannot be determined without considering the potential for realization, while the realization potential can only be assessed in light of the objective. Consequently, the first question takes priority, but always subject to correction through the second. The answers to these questions provide a frame of reference for evaluating proposed improvements. In this way, constitutional reform can be liberated from the one-sided orientation towards short-term experiences. Although these stimulate the will to reform, they do not determine the result. This reduces the danger of a reform that merely heals real or alleged shortcomings but without any perspective.

Presently [i.e. 1972], the prerequisites for such a well-founded reform discussion are not sufficiently established. This is because the Federal Republic of Germany lacks a constitutional theory. This lack has often been deplored, but hardly resolved.[1] Constitutional studies are still occupied in liberating public law and the associated scholarship from the legacy of the nineteenth century.[2] In many respects, the relevant questions for contemporary constitutional theory, not to mention a theory of the state, are only just emerging; an answer is still far away. Equally, the interaction between constitution and political reality has as yet been inadequately researched. Although most jurists have taken notice of this interaction, they largely lack the tools necessary for obtaining concrete insights. Indisputable but superficial insights, such as the assertion that the vitality and effectiveness of the constitution derive from its ability to integrate powerful and spontaneous

---

[1] See H. Dau-Lin, 'Formalistischer und anti-formalistischer Verfassungsbegriff' (1932) 61 *Archiv des öffentlichen Rechts* 29. After the war, esp. H. Ehmke pointed to this gap: *Wirtschaft und Verfassung* (Karlsruhe: C.F. Müller, 1961), p. 3 et seq. In Switzerland, K. Eichenberger raised the demand for a constitutional theory in (1968) 87 *Zeitschrift für schweizerisches Recht* NF 441.

[2] Cf. Ehmke (n. 1). This is evidenced by the subjects of public law habilitation theses in recent years.

contemporary forces and to advance specific present features into the future, are characteristic of the current situation.[3]

The assistance of the political scientists, to whose metier this actually belongs, is not forthcoming.[4] A political science oriented towards the history of ideas and institutions, which long predominated in Germany, devotes itself to the question of meaning rather than reality. The more recent trend, which either adopts medium-term American theoretical approaches or resorts to the Marxist tradition and which has marginalized those who only a few years ago were heralded as innovators,[5] in most cases conveys the impression that, when seeking to explain political reality, law can be neglected. It is either subsumed under empirical assiduousness or treated as an appendage of the socioeconomic system. This has at least once again brought into focus the contingency of norms. But an advance is possible only if the constitution were not only considered as a product, but taken seriously as a determinant.[6]

It goes without saying that these gaps in research cannot be remedied in a single paper. At the very least, however, a consciousness of the frame of reference should be restored and, using the means at hand, the frame of reference must itself be established to the extent possible.

## II. THE STRUCTURE OF THE PROBLEM AND DEVELOPMENT OF THE CONSTITUTION

Historically, constitutions are a product of the conflict between the liberal bourgeoisie and the absolute monarchy. The bourgeoisie was seeking to emancipate the production and commercial sphere from hierarchical direction and to guarantee the predictability of state power. To this end, it demanded the limitation of princely competence to questions of security and order as well as participation in state decision-making concerning issues of freedom and property. These demands were justified on the basis of natural law and were to be secured through positive law. The means was the constitution, which regardless of how it came to be in each individual case had a contractual character. It typically contained basic rights

---

[3] See K. Hesse, *Die normative Kraft der Verfassung* (Tübingen: Mohr, 1959), p. 11; K. Hesse, *Grundzüge des Verfassungsrechts der Bundesrepublik Deutschland* (Karlsruhe: C. F. Müller, 5th edn, 1972), p. 18. Despite the titles of the following, these works do not affect this assessment on the state of research: D. Schindler, *Verfassungsrecht und soziale Struktur* (Zürich: Schulthess, 1932, 4th edn, 1967), K. Loewenstein, 'Verfassunsgrecht und Verfassungsrealität' (1952) 77 *Archiv des öffentlichen Rechts* 387; H. Spanner, 'Die Rolle der Verfassung im gegenwärtigen politischen und sozialen Leben' (1956) VII *Österreichische Zeitschrift für öffentliches Recht* 9.

[4] This assessment is confirmed by K. Loewenstein, *Verfassungslehre* (Tübingen: Mohr, 2nd edn, 1969), p. 159 and F. Ronneberger, 'Verfassungswirklichkeit als politisches System' (1968) 7 *Der Staat* 411 at 420. Luhmann is an exception here but he does not explicitly deal with the constitution. Special mention should be made of the political science habilitation thesis of H.-H. Hartwich, *Sozialstaatspostulat und gesellschaftlicher status quo* (Cologne: Westdeutscher Verlag, 1970).

[5] Cf. Dieter Grimm, 'Politische Wissenschaft als normative Wissenschaft' (1956) *Juristenzeitung* 434. For an orientation on the current state of the discussion see F. Naschold, *Politische Wissenschaft* (Freiburg: Alber, 1970).

[6] H. Heller, who is often referred to by critical political theorists (see e.g. W.-D. Narr, *Theorie der Demokratie* (Stuttgart: Kohlhammer, 1971), p. 135), has always emphasized this: see his *Staatslehre* (Leiden: Sijthoff, 1934), pp. 250, 269. Regarding this issue after the war, see esp. Hesse, *Normative Kraft* (n. 3).

to define the social sphere of freedom, on the one hand, and rules regulating the holders and modalities of the exercise of state power on the other. In particular, it provided for representational bodies to communicate civic interests to the state, a guarantee that the state complied with the decisions of these bodies, together with the establishment of independent courts as a complementary safeguard.

The end and the means corresponded. The political demands were of such a nature that they could be met most effectively by constitutional law. As the just social order was anticipated as flowing from an absence of legal obligations, the only task of the constitution was that of drawing boundaries. If it had merely to negatively limit actions instead of positively guiding them, its provisions would be both highly generalizable and directly applicable. Law was established and the desired effect achieved in a single step. Thus relieved of specifics, the formal constitution of a state of law possessed a highly level of validity. The relationship between the state and society seemed to be conclusively regulated and, for the first time, politics were subject to law.

The constellation from which these constitutions emerged no longer exists. Politically, the idea of popular sovereignty has acquired validity, so that the task is no longer to limit a pre-existing monarchical state power but to constitute a democratic one. The constitution thus loses its contractual character, becoming an element of self-organization of society. Socially, the Industrial Revolution created problems that were not taken into consideration in bourgeois-legal constitutions. For one thing, new power centres and mechanisms of oppression emerged in the social sphere allegedly free from rule which escaped a constitution that was focusing exclusively on the relationship between the state and the individual. Secondly, the sphere dominated by the individual contracted radically, so that today the individual can no longer secure his existence by his own efforts. And with this, the conditions which suggested justice could emerge from the free interplay of societal forces disappeared. Formal guarantees of freedom did not automatically achieve the ends that, optimistically, were associated with them. The defensive attitude with respect to the state has transformed into one of expectation. Social justice and individual security must now be realized through deliberate planning.

All constitutional achievements of the nineteenth century are affected by this shift towards material issues. This has first become visible in the sphere of basic rights. The formal security of freedoms has reached an apogee, but it is their material foundation that makes them usable. In the course of this development, equality of rights is increasingly expanding into equality of opportunities. Although less noted by jurists, the same phenomenon is also occurring in the organization of the state. Here, confidence in procedural protection is declining. Procedural guarantees cannot be used as a guarantee of truth, as was hoped in the eighteenth and nineteenth centuries.[7] This has often been noticed with

---

[7] Cf. N. Luhmann, *Legitimation durch Verfahren* (Neuwied: Luchterhand, 1969), pp. 20, 148. Jurisprudence is often the last stronghold of this opinion: see e.g. C. Starck, *Der Gesetzesbegriff des Grundgesetzes* (Baden-Baden: Nomos, 1979), pp. 169, 171.

regard to legislation but it also affects elections, the principle of representation, the concept of pluralism, the division of powers, and more. Once considered the basic characteristic of democracy, the impact of elections has become problematic, and according to the findings of election researchers, it will become increasingly difficult 'to justify democratic political systems solely by pointing to the existence of "free elections"'.[8] While formerly the existence of elected popular representation appeared to guarantee that the interests of the general population were communicated to the government, we must today deal with the question as to how representatives can be reconnected with the general public.[9] Formerly, the reconciliation of interests was considered to result from the free competition of opinions and societal forces as a matter of necessity; today, we recognize the difficulties in articulating basic interests and the distortion in the contest between even organized interests.[10] Further examples can be cited. They demonstrate that current political problems cannot be resolved by setting boundaries because they are of a material nature. They require positive action. Though constitutions can order these, they cannot effectuate them. The target condition is not created simply through the promulgation of a norm; it depends on intermediate steps.[11]

This 'environmental change' must necessarily have driven the 'rule of law' constitution into a crisis. This has been obvious since the end of the First World War and continues today, as is indicated by the lack of a constitutional theory. Despite valuable individual insights, the attempts undertaken in the Weimar Republic to arrive at a new concept of the constitution largely failed.[12] Smend's insight into the necessity of transforming constitutional law into political action led to a one-sided overemphasis on process and largely robbed the constitution of its relative stability and thus its normative quality. Carl Schmitt's thesis of the constitution as a 'total decision as to the nature and form of political union',[13] which is but disguised as law, identified constitution with politics and thereby surrendered any rational understanding of a legal constitution. Kelsen's normativism was so far removed from specifics that the concept of the constitution

---

[8] W.-D. Narr and F. Naschold, *Theorie der Demokratie* (Stuttgart: Kohlhammer, 1971), p. 195 (and more generally p. 92 et seq., p. 164 et seq.).

[9] See e.g. P. Bachrach, *Die Theorie demokratischer Elitenherrschaft* (Frankfurt am Main: Europäische Verlagsanstalt, 1970); F. Scharpf, *Demokratietheorie zwischen Utopie und Anpassung* (Konstanz: Universitätsverlag, 1970), p. 36 et seq.; U. Jaeggi, *Macht und Herrschaft in der Bundesrepublik* (Frankfurt am Main: Fischer, 1969), pp. 19, 130.

[10] See Narr and Naschold (n. 8), pp. 141, 204.

[11] E. Forsthoff highlighted the incongruence between contemporary political problems and constitutional law. But cf. R. Bäumlin, *Staat, Recht und Geschichte* (Zürich: EVZ, 1961); R. Bäumlin, 'Was läßt sich von einer Totalrevision erwarten? (1968) 87 *Zeitschrift für schweizerisches Recht* NF 386.

[12] See H. Kelsen, *Allgemeine Staatslehre* (Berlin: Springer, 1925); H. Kelsen, *Reine Rechtslehre* (Leipzig: Deuticke, 1934); R. Smend, *Verfassung und Verfassungsrecht* (Munich: Duncker & Humblot, 1928); C. Schmitt, *Verfassungslehre* (Munich: Duncker & Humblot, 1928). Only H. Heller, *Staatslehre* (Leiden: Sijthoff, 1934) is of lasting significance.

[13] Schmitt (n. 12), p. 20.

no longer provided any solution to actual problems. All this is now familiar, and need not be examined here.[14] Following Kelsen, Smend, and Schmitt, many authors have only been able to interpret the crisis as the downfall of the constitutional idea.[15] These works often possess a high analytical value, but lose significance because they lead only to complaint rather than inquiring into the developmental potential the constitution possesses.

## III. FUNCTION OF THE CONSTITUTION

The following instead examines whether the constitution is tied to the conditions of the era of its emergence, or can be separated from these sufficiently so that it can continue to be serviceable today. If the answer is negative, the only conclusion remaining is that constitutions have been perverted to a means for concealing power by claiming to tame it. If one initially examines the outward appearance, it is striking that the constitutional idea has grown beyond its countries of origin and become a globally recognized concept. The most remarkable aspect of this is that even the socialist states, which consider themselves the radical antithesis of the bourgeois rule of law-state (*Rechtsstaat*), have not dispensed with constitutions.[16] As far as may be seen, the constitution has not been declared obsolete in academic writing.[17]

If one seeks elements that continue to support the constitutional idea today, one comes first to their organizational part. The need to organize public power has grown rather than decreased since the early nineteenth century.[18] The challenge is no longer to restrict a pre-existing subject of rule that is deemed legitimated by divine right, but rather to create legitimate bearers of rule and assign them their authority. In this way, constitutions establish the state as a unit of action. They provide the criteria for distinguishing legitimate from illegitimate claims to rule. All constitutions, both historical and current, contain provisions that establish the bodies and processes for the formation and assertion of political will. Admittedly this says nothing about the real centres of power within the state. Yet, these power centres have to follow rules if their will shall become binding and enforceable. Moreover, the formalization of power is today less of

[14] See Heller (n. 12), pp. 194, 249; Schindler (n. 3); W. Kägi, *Die Verfassung als rechtliche Grundordnung des Staates* (Zürich: Polygraphischer Verlag, 1945; reprint 1971); H. Ehmke, *Grenzen der Verfassungsänderung* (Berlin: de Gruyter, 1953); P. Badura, 'Verfassung' in W. Heun et al. (eds), *Evangelisches Staatslexikon* (1966), p. 2352.

[15] See esp.: Kägi (n. 14); Loewenstein, *Verfassungslehre* (n. 4), p. 157; K. Loewenstein, 'Gedanken über den Wert von Verfassungen in unserem revolutionären Zeitalter' in A. Zurcher (ed.), *Verfassungen nach dem Zweiten Weltkrieg* (Meisenheim and Glan: Hain, 1956), 210; G. Burdeau, 'Zur Auflösung des Verfassunsgbegriffs' (1962) 1 *Der Staat* 289. E. Forsthoff's views will be explained later in the chapter.

[16] See I. Kovács, *New Elements in the Evolution of Socialist Constitutions* (Budapest: Akadémiai Kiadó, 1968), pp. 15, 71.

[17] Even the pessimistic Burdeau (n. 15), does not go this far.

[18] See Hesse, *Normative Kraft* (n. 3), p. 6; Badura (n. 14), p. 2343; U. Scheuner, *Verfassung*, in Görres-Gesellschaft (ed.), *Staatslexikon* vol. VIII (Freiburg: Herder, 6th edn, 1963), p. 117; H. Krüger in E. von Beckerath et al. (eds), *Handwörterbuch der Sozialwissenschaften* vol. XI (Stuttgart, Tübingen and Göttingen: Fischer, Mohr and Vandenhoeck & Ruprecht, 1961), p. 72.

a concession than ever. The highly complex industrial society cannot be governed without planning and division of labour. This does not preclude strong leaders, but it does preclude the return to cameralism. However, it would be wrong to regard the organizational provisions of the constitution as more or less arbitrary rules of the game.[19] No organization is entirely objective-neutral. Beyond rationalization, which every form of organization adopts, distinctions can be drawn between structures in which actual power is transformed more or less directly through law, and more or less compelled to operate transparently. The much-maligned 'formal' rule of law-state, whose deficiencies are not to be denied, has certainly always performed such services.

The situation is different for the second traditional component of constitutions, the fundamental rights to freedom. Directed solely at the state, they were not capable of completely fulfilling their emancipating mission. Under the influence of Marx, who was the first to note this defect,[20] socialist states radically turned away from negative basic rights.[21] In the western countries, the idea of a pre-existing sphere of absolute freedom of the individual, in which law could only be seen as an 'intervention', is no longer asserted. However, the necessity for private spheres is not seriously disputed. On the other hand, no one doubts any longer that a just system cannot be established purely on the basis of limitations imposed on the state. The bourgeois constitutions establishing the rule of law were powerless in the face of social injustice. The formal guarantees which they instituted are thus not to be revoked, but rather provided with a material foundation.[22] In constitutional law, this insight led to the introduction of participatory rights, and in constitutional law scholarship to a reinterpretation of the basic rights from rights to protect the individual against the state to principles for shaping society. The development of these approaches has met with considerable political resistance. And their justification has also been challenged in scholarship. Although the social role of the state is affirmed in the conservative camp and emphasized on the left as essential for survival for the so-called late-capitalist system,[23] doubts exist as to whether social activities of the state can be regulated through constitutional norms.

Forsthoff vehemently disputes this possibility,[24] but his position is ambivalent. On the one hand, he assumes that the bourgeois constitution establishing

---

[19] See F. Naschold, *Organisation und Demokratie* (Stuttgart: Kohlhammer, 1969).

[20] K. Marx, 'Zur Judenfrage' in his and F. Engels' *Werke*, vol. 1 Institut für Marxismus-Leninismus beim ZK der SED (ed.) (Berlin: Dietz, 1970), p. 347.

[21] See e.g. G. Brunner, *Grundrechte im Sowjetsystem* (Cologne: Verlag Wissenschaft und Politik, 1963).

[22] The literature is extensive: see e.g. P. Saladin, *Grundrechte im Wandel* (Bern: Stämpfli, 1970); P. Saladin, 'Die Funktion der Grundrechte in einer revidierten Verfassung' (1968) 87 *Zeitschrift für schweizerisches Recht NF* 131; U. Scheuner, 'Die Funktion der Grundrechte im Sozialstaat' (1971) *Die Öffentliche Verwaltung* 505; further P. Häberle, 'Grundrechte im Leistungsstaat' (1972) 30 VVDStRL 43.

[23] Cf. E. Forsthoff, *Der Staat der Industriegesellschaft* (Munich: Beck, 1971), p. 71; W. Müller, 'Die Grenzen der Sozialpolitik in der Marktwirtschaft' in G. Schäfer and C. Nedelmann (eds), *Der CDU-Staat* vol. I (Frankfurt am Main: Suhrkamp, 1969), p. 14.

[24] E. Forsthoff, 'Begriff und Wesen des sozialen Rechtsstaats' (1954) 12 *VVDStRL* 8; E. Forsthoff, 'Die Umbildung des Verfassungsgesetzes' in H. Barion et al. (eds), *Festschrift für Carl Schmitt* (Berlin: Duncker & Humblot, 1959),

the rule of law can be separated from its originating conditions so that it can prevail in the present. On the other, it is in his view so closely tied to those conditions that it is unable to accommodate new content. For him, constitution is always a rule of law (*rechtsstaatliche*) constitution and nothing else. In justifying this, Forsthoff argues that unlike the constitutional norms pertaining to the rule of law, which apply directly, duties to take action and participatory rights always require legislative mediation and this depends on what is possible and appropriate in each case. Consequently, they lack validity in legal terms.[25] With this argument, Forsthoff does not reject the social state, for which he himself prepared the scholarly groundwork. He only insists that it cannot be realized on the level of the constitution, but only by means of legislation and administration. Constitutions may not promulgate a specific social programme; rather their only task is to 'ensure the security of the form of the state and the existence and legal certainty of the citizens of the state'.[26] Consequently, he condemns the reinterpretation of the catalogue of basic rights as a system of values as an attack on its legal character and he describes the social-state clause in the German Basic Law as a proclamation with no legal significance.

In this way, the Basic Law is broken down into a normative and a declamatory component by a pre-existing concept of constitution,[27] and the question as to the possible further development of the idea of the constitution is cut off *a limine* by the identification of the constitution with its rule of law component.[28] Forsthoff accepts these consequences as historically inevitable: as domestic policy today emphasizes compensation and redistribution, a constitution entirely devoted to the rule of law loses its central role and is able to integrate state action only in a fragmentary manner.[29] The dispute thus focuses on the normative quality of principles and imperatives in constitutions.[30] Forsthoff's view suggests that only regulations that are directly applicable to cases are legal norms. Characteristically, he prefers to speak of constitutional *law* and he emphasizes the organizational part as exemplary[31]—a view in which he accords

---

p. 35; E. Forsthoff, 'Der introvertierte Rechtsstaat und seine Verortung' (1963) 2 *Der Staat* 385 (all these essays are reproduced in his *Rechtsstaat im Wandel* (Stuttgart: Kohlhammer, 1964)). Most recently, Forsthoff (n. 23), p. 6.

[25] E. Forsthoff, *Die Verwaltung als Leistungsträger* (Stuttgart: Kohlhammer, 1938).

[26] E. Forsthoff, *Lehrbuch des Verwaltungsrechts,* vol. 1 (Munich: Beck, 9th edn, 1966), p. 62.

[27] This seems a high price, especially for Forsthoff, who argues strongly for interpretating the constitution traditionally, see Forsthoff, 'Die Umbildung des Verfassungsgesetzes' (n. 24), p. 150: 'Interpretative Rangstufen sprengen die Rechtsordnung als Gefüge mit unbedingtem Geltungsanspruch auf.'

[28] For the methodological validity of this reasoning, see A. Hollerbach, 'Auflösung der rechtsstaatlichen Verfassung?' (1960) 85 *Archiv des öffentlichen Rechts* 248; see further K. Hesse, 'Der Rechtsstaat im Verfassungssystem des Grundgesetzes' in K. Hesse et al. (eds), *Staatsverfassung und Kirchenordnung: Festgabe für Smend* (Tübingen: Mohr, 1962), p. 78 (n. 27). On the relationship between the social state and the constitution see E. Forsthoff (ed.), *Rechtsstaatlichkeit und Sozialstaatlichkeit* (Darmstadt: Wissenschaftliche Buchgesellschaft, 1968); D. Suhr, 'Rechtsstaatlichkeit und Sozialstaatlichkeit' (1970) 9 *Der Staat* 66; Hartwich (n. 4), p. 283.

[29] Forsthoff, 'Begriff und Wesen des sozialen Rechtsstaats' (n. 24), p. 51.

[30] The same controversy arose in socialist constitutional law: see Kovács (n. 16), p. 417.

[31] Cf. e.g. Forsthoff, 'Die Umbildung des Verfassungsgesetzes' (n. 24), esp. p. 148.

with Hennis, who understands the constitution as an 'instrument of government' and the incorporation of objectives as an overburdening.[32]

Forsthoff's view appears too narrow. Legal norms are pluri-functional. Jurists tend to raise the dispute resolution function to the absolute level. Systems theory, by contrast, emphasizes the alleviating function of norms.[33] Legislation removes issues from the realm of debate and makes them binding. Imperatives thus reduce decision-making burdens by creating a framework for decision-making authorities. They thereby function as premises for decisions, rather than as issues to be decided.[34] Legal provisions can attain this status on many levels: by extracting a principle from the dispute, while leaving its concretization open; or also by concretizing the principle so that only its application to the individual case remains to be resolved. The scope for action thus narrows from level to level. This reductive function is also fulfilled by those constitutional provisions that are only indirectly applicable. Consequently, contrary to Burdeau,[35] they are more than mere 'suggestions'. The fact that they require specification and development says nothing about their normative quality, but only about the reduction level: they are addressed primarily (not exclusively) to the legislature. This consideration also ought to prompt Hennis, who is concerned about the overloading of parliament,[36] to expand his concept of the constitution. Thus, contrary to Forsthoff, normative and programmatic rules should not be considered contradictory. They merely differ in degree. This is also confirmed by recent research into judicial interpretation which shows how little even traditional types of legal norms are directly capable of subsumption; they merely predetermine the rule that matches the specific case.[37]

But the constitution also performs an alleviating function in the application of law and endows it with meaning. Since legal material is a product of many epochs, systems, and interests, neither unity nor order inhere in it. Yet unity and order are elements of the idea of law.[38] As the capacity for changing the law is in short supply,[39] other ways must be found to infuse unity and order into provisions which by their nature are subject to disparate interpretations. This

---

[32] W. Hennis, *Verfassung und Verfassungswirklichkeit – Ein deutsches Problem* (Tübingen: Mohr, 1968), pp. 19, 36. Cf. the reviews by E.-W. Böckenförde, 9 *Der Staat* (1979) 533 and K. Hesse, 96 *Archiv des öffentlichen Rechts* (1971) 137.

[33] Cf. Luhmann (n. 7), pp. 42, 143, 195.      [34] Ibid., p. 195.

[35] G. Burdeau, 'Zur Auflösung des Verfassungsbegriffs' (1962) 1 *Der Staat* 298.

[36] W. Hennis, 'Der Deutsche Bundestag 1949-1965' (1966) 215 *Der Monat* 29; W. Hennis, 'Zur Rechtfertigung und Kritik der Bundestagsarbeit' in H. Ehmke et al. (eds), *Festschrift für Adolf Arndt* (Frankfurt am Main: Europäische Verlagsanstalt, 1969), p. 150.

[37] See e.g. Hesse, *Grundzüge* (n. 3), p. 20 et seq.; M. Kriele, *Theorie der Rechtsgewinnung* (Berlin: Duncker & Humblot, 1967), p. 50; H. Ehmke, 'Prinzipien der Verfassungsinterpretation' (1963) 20 *VVDStRL* 55.

[38] See C.-W. Canaris, *Systemgedanke und Systembegriff in der Jurisprudenz* (Berlin: Duncker & Humblot, 1969), p. 16. See my review in 171 *Archiv für die civilistische Praxis* (1971) 266.

[39] See Luhmann (n. 7), p. 149.

is achieved by the constitution, and in particular by its basic principles, which reduce the scope for interpretation and specify the direction of interpretation. In Germany, this also applies to the social-state clause, because it makes those areas of the legal structure which, like the German Civil Code, have their origins in the spirit of the nineteenth century, capable of supporting the democratic and social state.

If the result is that it is also possible to find a constitutional answer to current political and social problems, this does not mean that the converse is true, that is, that no social state is possible under a constitution based entirely on the rule of law. Rather, the social state has its own political inevitability,[40] and can thus more easily dispense with guarantees under constitutional law than other objectives of the state. Political acclaim is today obtained primarily by promising and distributing resources and this motivation is stronger than any constitutional guarantee. But dispensable does not mean superfluous. This is illustrated by the Austrian case, where a bourgeois, legalistic constitution coexists with a social state practice, and is mastered only with difficulty by the legal means available—a problem that is exacerbated by a purely positivistic constitutional scholarship and judicature.[41]

Only a constitution which grows beyond its formal and legalistic stature can occupy a central position in political and social life.[42] Not only does the dependency of individuals on the state administration increase, but also their dependency on the social groups that represent their interest. The interpenetration of state and society grows through planned economic, environmental, research and educational policies, on the one hand, and by the permeability of the state bodies to social groups resulting from the need for information and consensus on the other. Under these conditions, the constitution can no longer restrict itself to organizing the state apparatus and limiting state power. It must order not only the state, but society as well. In this way, a convergence with the socialist understanding of the constitution occurs.[43] And besides, this transformation is not as radical as it appears at first glance. The bourgeois-liberal constitutions not only designed the institutions of the state but also established a model for society. The difference lies in the means. Under the liberal constitution, a just order was to emerge from normative

---

[40] Forsthoff, 'Die Umbildung des Verfassungsgesetzes' (n. 24), p. 173; Forsthoff (n. 23), p. 79; Narr and Naschold (n. 8), p. 118; W. Kaltefleiter, *Wirtschaft und Politik in Deutschland: Konjunktur als Bestimmungsfaktor des Parteiensystems* (Cologne: Westdeutscher Verlag, 2nd edn, 1968).

[41] See P. Pernthaler, 'Die Grundrechtsreform in Österreich' (1969) 95 *Archiv des öffentlichen Rechts* 31.

[42] Badura (n. 14), pp. 2344, 2354; Scheuner (n. 18), p. 117; K. Hesse, *Grundzüge* (n. 3), p. 10; K. Hesse, 'Rechtsstaat' (n. 28), p. 86; Bäumlin, *Staat, Recht und Geschichte* (n. 11), pp. 11, 15; Bäumlin (1968) NF 87 *Zeitschrift für schweizerisches Recht* 377; Eichenberger (n. 1).

[43] This is precisely what from a socialist perspective is perceived as the differentiating moment: see Kovács (n. 16), pp. 71, 98. For the German Democratic Republic, see K. Sorgenicht et al. (eds), *Verfassung der Deutschen Demokratischen Republik: Dokumente und Kommentar*, vol. 1 (Berlin: Staatsverlag der Deutschen Demokratischen Republik, 1969), p. 51. A. Hollerbach, 'Ideologie und Verfassung' in W. Maihofer (ed.), *Ideologie und Recht* (Frankfurt am Main: Klostermann, 1969), 44 (who refers to the constitution as a 'theory of the entire society').

abstinence. Today, it must once again be established actively. The traditional components of the constitution retain their functions of power-limitation and rationalization. But they must derive their legitimacy from material provisions. Every exclusion of an important sphere of society would thus result in a loss of legitimacy.

The fact that the constitution thereby becomes more programme-oriented, and loses direct applicability to a corresponding degree, lies in the nature of the matter. Although normative and therefore binding, one must become accustomed to regarding the constitution essentially as a blueprint.[44] This is also the way to overcome the constitutional type that predominates in German constitutional history, and which was concerned above all with registering the political forces that happened to be influential at the time.[45] As a normative framework of meaning, the constitution should be regarded more as something that ought to be achieved rather than something that is already in being. This is not the decline of the constitutional idea, but its realization under altered conditions. What is dramatized as a decline reveals itself as the replacement of a specific concept of constitution. Insofar as the hypothesis of decline is supported by the assertion that the constitution was respected more highly in the past, it is sufficient to cite Bagehot, who as long ago as 1867 distinguished between the 'dignified' and 'efficient' parts of a constitution.[46] Numerous additional historical counter-examples could also be cited. If a constitution overestimates its capacity, it can of course provoke violations and disregard; which is a topic to be discussed in the next section.

## IV. CAPACITY LIMITS OF THE CONSTITUTION

Norms do not stand by themselves. Like all legal provisions, constitutional provisions are not self-sufficient, but are intended to have an effect; in other words, they depend on their being executed. Execution entails a process of interaction between norm and reality, in which both take on concrete form.[47] The relative strength changes from area to area. Matters created by the law itself are obviously easier to regulate than those that it encounters. The reality to which the constitution refers is the most resilient, because it demonstrates a particularly strong inherent dynamic. A further weakness lies in the lower degree of enforceability, as the organization for law enforcement is the object of regulation here, and has no other organized power above it. Consequently, and if at all possible, constitutional law must itself contain the prerequisites for its own realization.

The connection to reality and the need for execution of the constitution give rise to a series of capacity limits that cannot be exceeded without

---

[44] This was emphasized esp. by Scheuner (n. 18), p. 118 and Bäumlin, *Staat, Recht und Geschichte* (n. 11), p. 24. Yet it is precisely this that Forsthoff, Kägi, Burdeau et al. reject.

[45] See Hennis (n. 32), p. 16. This tendency often recurs today: see e.g. G. Burdeau, 1 *Der Staat* (1962) 392.

[46] W. Bagehot, *The English Constitution* [1867] (London: Collins, 1963), p. 3.

[47] See esp. Schindler (n. 3); Hesse, *Normative Kraft* (n. 3); Hesse, *Grundzüge* (n. 3), p. 25.

consequences. They must be taken into account in revisions of constitutions. The most important ones are practical constraints, systemic barriers, and the willingness of parties to cooperate. Its systematic elaboration would require research into the conditions of effectiveness of constitutional norms under analysis of constitutional history. This is lacking. However, some knowledge is available. For example, the effect of practical constraints is visible in the relationship between parliament and government.[48] As much as the framers of the constitution sought to concentrate legislation in parliament, under the conditions of a democratic party state in the industrial era, the focus necessarily falls on the government. Constitutional provisions that, for instance, were intended to withhold from government the right of initiative would have no effect.[49] The establishment of a complete countervailing bureaucracy for parliament would be in vain. Equally, the often-criticized committee practice proves to be not a misguided development, but a consequence of social complexity that compels the legislature to technocracy and specialization. By the same token, the tendency towards centralization is the result of constraints which the precepts of federalism oppose in vain, as the issue of environmental protection illustrates.

Furthermore, constitutional law runs up against systemic barriers. Although it is true that constitutions play a role in constituting the system, they are also its product—particularly when they do not complete a revolution. Unlike the practical constraints, they can be overcome, but with fundamental reforms rather than individual actions. The paradigm of the German Federal Republic is scarcely known. It is thanks to the 'left-wing' political science and sociology that this question has been raised. To date, answers have been extremely general and poorly supported empirically. To put the matter briefly, and thus above any suspicion because it is not only put forward by the left, it may be said that today the fate of the economy determines the fate of the commonwealth. And since the state, as the entity entrusted with the general welfare, has little power to direct the economy, it is partially at the mercy of economic forces.[50] This system is not constitutionally stipulated, nor is it unconstitutional. But the normative assertion of the social-state principle—for instance from a concept of social assistance and correction to a comprehensive economic reform[51]—would reach its actual limit here.[52]

[48] Dieter Grimm, 'Aktuelle Tendenzen in der Aufteilung gesetzgeberischer Funktionen zwischen Parlament und Regierung' (1970) I *Zeitschrift für Parlamentsfragen* 454.

[49] Such attempts failed under the French Constitutions from 1791 and 1795: see M. Deslandres, *Histoire Constitutionnelle de la France*, vol. 1 (Paris: Colin, 1932), pp. 98, 386. Also the American Constitution does not prevent the government from drafting bills itself and having them tabled in Congress by a willing congressman: see e.g. G. Galloway, *The Legislative Process in Congress* (New York: Crowell, 6th edn, 1964), p. 9.

[50] Cf. Forsthoff (n. 23), pp. 24, 57; C. Offe, 'Politische Herrschaft und Klassenstrukturen – Zur Analyse spätkapitalistischer Gesellschaftssysteme' in G. Kress and D. Senghaas (eds), *Politikwissenschaft* (Frankfurt am Main: Fischer, 1972), p. 135. See also Narr and Naschold (n. 8), pp. 118, 131, 157.

[51] See Hartwich (n. 4), p. 12; Müller (n. 23), p. 46.

[52] Narr and Naschold (n. 8), pp. 17, 141; J. Hirsch, *Wissenschaftlich-technischer Fortschritt und politisches System* (Frankfurt am Main: Suhrkamp, 1970), p. 61; Eichenberger (n. 1), p. 453.

The lack of any sanction behind the constitution makes it more dependent on the consent of the people who are to obey it. Whereas two hundred years ago it was held that institutions could replace virtue, today a greater awareness of the necessity of a 'will to constitution'[53] is emerging. However, the consensus is scarce and must not be strained. This limits the constitution in three ways. It must take existing forces and ideologies into account, since political groups can be tamed by law, as has been achieved, for example, through the German law on political parties, and even greatly restrained, but once they reach a certain level of strength it cannot be neutralized. 'Militant democracy' must restrain itself: in any case, it can only defend itself against those that are weak. For the same reason, controversial issues that make up the essentials of the constituting forces must remain unresolved. To do otherwise would permanently endanger the basic consensus which enables the constitution to function. This is why, even though this is suggested by its definition, the constitution will seldom be comprehensive: gaps may turn out to be survival conditions.[54] Finally, constitutions possess only a limited range. The political decision-making process is always made up of more factors than a normative regulation is able to, or even should, take into account. Strictly speaking, the constitution does not regulate the formation of state decisions, but only defines the modes to be observed and the entities that must be involved for a decision to be valid as a state decision.[55] For the normal case, there is no question that this in turn affects the quality of the decision. However, it is virtually impossible to combat by legal means cryptopolitical or even extraconstitutional forces that gain influence through legal entities. This reveals, for instance, the limits of regulation of lobbying activities.

Boundary violations can result in a partial ineffectivity of the constitution. But partial ineffectivities are capable of discrediting the constitution as a whole. Yet the mere existence of a so-called constitutional reality is not evidence of boundary violations. Certainly the popular dichotomy of constitutional law and constitutional reality appears too coarse for the understanding of complex interrelationships. Hennis, to whom we owe the proof of the fruitlessness of this approach,[56] sees its origin in the German tradition of codifying an existing power constellation by means of the constitution. Once norm and reality have been synchronized in this manner, developments can only be viewed with hostility. One arrives at the same attitude by approaching the constitution with the expectation that it can regulate the entirety of politics. In reality, a constitution that sets out principles of a just state and social order instead of recognizing balances of power is unable to exist with just execution of the constitution, but rather demands independent political action under the constitution. Any

---

[53]  See Heller (n. 12), pp. 250, 269; Hesse, *Normative Kraft* (n. 3), p. 12; Krüger (n. 18), p. 77.

[54]  Heller (n. 12), p. 257; K. von Beyme, *Die verfassungsgebende Gewalt des Volkes* (Tübingen: Mohr, 1968), p. 65; Eichenberger (n. 1), p. 453.

[55]  Luhmann (n. 7), pp. 175, 189.

[56]  Hennis (n. 32); Heller (n. 12), pp. 255; Hesse, *Normative Kraft* (n. 3), p. 6; Scheuner (n. 18), p. 118.

attempt to completely juridify politics would be in vain, and not only in technical, but in fundamental terms: politics as a source of law necessarily transcends positive law.[57] Accordingly, constitutional reality is a necessary corollary of the normative constitution, not its opposite.

## V. GUIDELINES FOR CONSTITUTIONAL AMENDMENTS

Even constitutions that remain within the limits of their capacity may require amendment. Yet it is said of constitutional amendments that they undermine confidence in the constitution.[58] Such a verdict is never supported empirically and it so removed from the factors that give rise to constitutional amendments that it need not be discussed further. Constitutional norms differ from other legal norms in degree, not in principle. Even if one wanted them to be considered as expressions of timeless ideas—which could only be true of just a few constitutional articles—they remain historical expressions of these ideas, and can be rendered obsolete. Furthermore, the changing social reality gives rise to a constant need for new norms. Although this affects statute and regulatory law more than the constitution, the latter is not unaffected. Inalterability is only to be had at the price of meaninglessness or stagnation. The more specific the content of a constitution, the more strongly it is subject to the passing of time.[59]

There is a direct relationship between the precision of a constitution and the need for amendment. Conclusions respecting the usefulness or detriment of constitutional amendments thus cannot be arrived at abstractly, but only with respect to the nature of that constitution and its social environment. For this reason, the admonitory references to the US Constitution are of little value. Its stability may be explained through its thematic restriction and low level of precision rather than any particularly highly developed understanding of the nature of constitutions. It is just these characteristics that also facilitate the American veneration of their constitution: everyone can see themselves reflected in it. In this way, it develops a considerable politically integrative force, but its normative power appears limited. The optimum balance between the permanence and precision of constitutional provisions has scarcely been a subject of theoretical research to date.

Thus, if constitutions are not immune to the ravages of time, then a constitution which is constantly circumvented or which prevents overdue reforms does

---

[57]  Dieter Grimm, 'Recht und Politik' (1969) *Juristische Schulung* 505.

[58]  This does not require detailed references. As a recent example one may cite W. Weber, according to whom frequent amendments discredit the constitution: Weber, 'Das Problem der Revision und einer Totalrevision des Grundgesetzes' in H. Spanner et al. (eds), *Festgabe für Theodor Maunz* (Munich: Beck, 1971), p. 453. But it is also noted that most of the twenty-nine amendments of the Basic Law had taken place silently and unnoticed by the public.

[59]  Cf. Heller (n. 12), p. 257; W.-J. Gansdorf van der Meersch, 'De l'influence de la Constitution dans la vie politique et sociale en Belgique' (1954) *Revue de l'Université de Bruxelles* 172.

more damage to the idea of the constitution than constitutional amendments.[60] Naturally, this says nothing as to the scope of changes. Rather, the limits of constitutional amendment must also be derived from the concept and function of the constitution. This is where the real issue arises: the task of constitutional scholarship is not to prevent constitutional amendment to the greatest possible extent, but to distinguish legitimate reform projects from illegitimate ones, to separate the necessary from the superfluous. General guidelines for this process should first be established.

Since its creation, the abiding aim of the constitution is the limitation of power. Consequently, constitutional amendments whose purpose is solely to increase power or facilitate the exercise of power generate concerns. Greater concentrations of power or the elimination of barriers require an objective beside themselves. Naturally, such objectives exist. Thus, the rearmament of the German Federal Republic, which was made possible by constitutional amendment, greatly enhanced the power of the state. Yet however one may adjudge the action politically, the aim was not to increase domestic political power. Rather, the amendments served the defence of the nation and the integration of the Federal Republic in the western alliance. However, this aim itself can in turn be examined to verify its legitimacy. By contrast, the German government's bill to modify the law establishing the Constitutional Court in 1955[61]—which, while not formal constitutional law, is generally considered to be material constitutional law—had the recognizable intent of circumscribing the competence of a state organ that had become an irritant to the government.[62] To prevent misunderstandings, it should be emphasized that a reduction in the power of constitutional courts, for example through the elimination of judicial review, can also be legitimate in a Western-style democracy. However, it must be justifiable by reference to some standard other than the powers of the government.

Further barriers derive from the normative character of the constitution. The constitution does not describe the reality, but rather specifies a goal-oriented state. Accordingly, it is oriented towards the future and seeks its fulfilment and completion in reality. Anyone seeking a description of the existing political system must consult political science, not read the constitution. Constitutional framers who seek to reflect reality condemn themselves to continual amendment of their constitution. Thus, there is no sense in noting changes in political or social reality or of understanding norms and institutions that were not considered by the constitution but do not conflict with it.[63] Hennis rightly attacks

---

[60] R. Bäumlin, 87 *Zeitschrift für schweizerisches Recht* (1968) 383; Hesse, *Normative Kraft* (n. 3), p. 16; H. Krüger, 'Verfassungswandlung und Verfassungsgerichtsbarkeit' in Hesse et al. (eds), *Staatsverfassung und Kirchenordnung* (n. 28), p. 151; Spanner, *Verfassung* (n. 3), p. 31; U. Scheuner, 'Das Grundgesetz in der Entwicklung zweier Jahrzehnte' (1971) 95 *Archiv des öffentlichen Rechts* 366.

[61] BT-Drucks. 178/55.

[62] See H. Laufer, *Verfassungsgerichtsbarkeit und politischer Prozeß* (Tübingen: Mohr, 1969), p. 170.

[63] Cf. those cited at n. 60; also see Hennis (n. 32), p. 19. Further, Heller (n. 12), p. 249; Krüger (n. 18), p. 74; Eichenberger (n. 1), p. 451.

the German tendency to consider the constitution a 'political land registry'.[64] Consequently, he opposes plans to anchor the lobbies in the constitution, as has happened with respect to political parties. In fact, a simple constitutional recognition of lobbies would have an affirmative, and not a limiting effect. But of course, recognition is not the same as attempting to normatively regulate forces that have to date been unfettered.

As a structure of norms, the constitution not only depends on political and social input; it must also be interpreted and developed on an ongoing basis. The framers of the constitution must accept that their product takes on a life of its own, and even acknowledge that the stabilizing effect of norms derives precisely from their ability to emancipate themselves from the intentions of their creators. It would thus be not advisable to amend a constitution if a problem can be solved through interpretation. That approach will generally be easy with respect to basic rights; the principle of proportionality applies and constitutional amendment is a last resort. The decision on this matter depends on whether interpretation has reached its limits, leading to the distinction between the making and the application of law disappearing. This is a matter for legal hermeneutics and will not be discussed further here. But sometimes the division of labour fails because courts or legal scholarship resolve a problem poorly, or not at all. In such cases, the framers of a constitution may not be condemned to inaction. In such a situation they present an authentic interpretation, rather than amending. This is not a matter of division of powers, but rather of highest responsibility for maintaining the state and social order. Thus, the predominant opinion rightly does not raise any objections against authentic interpretation.[65]

Finally, the priority of the constitution sets boundaries to constitutional amendment. It contains those norms that are considered fundamental for forming the state and society and should give structure and direction to the shorter-term business of legislation and administration. At the same time, this function underscores the greater permanence of constitutional law. The quality of its content lends the constitution a greater validity and durability, although conversely these qualities do not elevate a norm to constitutional law. Objects of momentary interest are therefore as unsuitable for addressing in the constitution as rules of minor importance. This would transport the necessity of instantaneous amendment into the constitution itself. One might also consider whether such articles should be repealed on the occasion of a revision of the constitution.[66]

In conclusion, constitutional amendments are appropriate only when the constitution conflicts with practical constraints and this makes violation of its own provisions likely, or when the constitution prevents desirable developments and

---

[64] Hennis (n. 32), p. 17.

[65] Cf. T. Maunz, G. Düring, and R. Herzog (eds), *Grundgesetz* (Munich: Beck, 2nd edn, 1963), Art. 79, recital 13.

[66] For indications see W. Strauss, 'Zwanzig Jahre Grundgesetz' in W. Strauss, A. Hollerbach, and U. Scheuner, *Totalrevision des Grundgesetzes?* (Karlsruhe: Badenia, 1971), p. 19.

thereby undermines its inherent legitimacy. Constitutional amendment is thus constitutional improvement. Those demanding amendment must substantiate this by three means: first, through legitimation of the aim; secondly, by demonstrating that that aim conflicts with individual constitutional norms; thirdly, by showing that the solution can be effected by constitutional law and does not exceed its capacity. This excludes fundamental provisions of the constitution from amendment, as otherwise the result would be a new constitution and not constitutional improvement. The problem of legal limits of constitutional amendment has been adequately discussed and is not taken up again here.[67] The guidelines developed here make no claim to dogmatic validity, but rather derive from constitutional theory.[68]

---

[67] See H. Ehmke, *Grenzen der Verfassungsänderung* (Berlin: Duncker & Humblot, 1953).

[68] A second part of the original paper, which extends the discussion by examining specific plans for reform of the German Basic Law in the early 1970s, is not reproduced here.

# Integration by Constitution

## I. THE NORMATIVE AND SYMBOLIC EFFECTS OF CONSTITUTIONS

When we speak of the integrative function of constitutions, we are referring to the extra-legal effects of a legal object. It is essential to keep these two levels apart. The object—the constitution—is a special set of legal norms that differ from others in terms of their subject matter and status. With regards to subject matter, these norms regulate the creation and exercise of political power. With regards to status, they take precedence over all other legal norms. The effect—integration—is an actual process by which the members of a polity develop a sense of belonging together and a collective identity that differentiates them from other polities. In this sense, integration may be viewed as the condition for both unity and the collective capacity for action, in polities that do not endeavour to forcibly eliminate the plurality of opinions and interests existing in every society.

The question is whether constitutions can have such an integrative effect—and, more specifically, whether we can expect a European constitution to foster the integration of European Union (EU) citizens. The answer depends on how social integration is seen as taking place.[1] According to *action theory*, social integration is primarily promoted by values and norms that are acquired in a socialization process and influence the behaviour of a society's members. According to *systems theory*, the constraints that are imposed by the society's various functional systems play the decisive role and determine individual behaviour to such an extent that little room is left for norm-related motivation. Depending on one's approach, the integrative effect of constitutions must be sought either in the area of systems development and coordination or in that of value determination. There is, however, a link between these two approaches if one admits that systemic constraints do not completely determine the fulfillment of social functions but rather leave space in which normatively influenced attitudes gain significance.[2]

---

[1] Bernhard Peters, *Die Integration moderner Gesellschaften* (Frankfurt am Main: Surhkamp, 1993); Jürgen Gebhardt and Rainer Schmalz-Bruns (eds.), *Demokratie, Verfassung und Nation. Die politische Integration moderner Gesellschaften* (Baden-Baden: Nomos, 1994).

[2] Dieter Grimm, 'Welche Elite für welche Gesellschaft?' in Eduard J. M. Kroker (ed.), *Bürgergesellschaft. Was hält unsere Gesellschaft zusammen?* (Frankfurt am Main: Societäts-Verlag, 2002), p. 81.

As the embodiment of the highest-ranking norms, the constitution is primarily intended to produce normative effects. It constitutes the public power of a society that has resolved to form a political entity, and it determines how this power is to be organized and exercised—naturally in the expectation that in so doing it best serves the needs and convictions of the polity. As a result, constitutions always claim that the political order established by them is 'good' and 'just'. For the public authorities that it forms, the constitution functions as a standard of behaviour. For the controlling organs and the general public it functions as a standard of judgement, allowing them to see whether behavioural codes have been observed or violated. Violations of the constitution may, of course, still occur. However, the constitution allows for a distinction to be made between lawful and unlawful claims to power or acts of governance, and it regulates the consequences of any unlawful exercise of power.

This results in a variety of advantages that make the constitution one of human civilization's great achievements.[3] One principal advantage is that it enables political power to be exercised not despotically, but according to a set of rules. These rules make state actions predictable and give citizens a fundamental feeling of security in their dealings with office-holders and public authorities. Another advantage is that—because of the distinction between the rules for political decision-making and the political decisions themselves—certain fundamental values and procedures are excluded from day-to-day political debate and employed instead as a common basis for rival political forces. This allows society to resolve political conflicts peacefully and to replace governments without the use of force. Finally, by distinguishing between long-term principles and day-to-day decisions, the constitution regulates how a society adapts to changed conditions and thus ensures continuity in change.

Precisely due to these advantages, which a constitution offers as the basic legal framework of politics, and due to its goal of creating a 'good' order, a constitution is subject to expectations that extend far beyond its normative regulatory function. The constitution is expected to unify the society that it has constituted as a polity, regardless of the difference of opinions and conflicting interests that exist in all societies. The constitution is regarded as a guarantee of the fundamental consensus that is necessary for social cohesion.[4] If a constitution is successful in this respect, it can even help shape a society's identity. The constitution then serves as a document in which society finds its basic convictions and aspirations expressed. This is what one has in mind when, next to its normative function, an integrative function is attributed to the constitution.

---

[3] Niklas Luhmann, 'Verfassung als evolutionäre Errungenschaft' (1990) 9 *Rechtshistorisches Journal* 176; Peter Häberle, *Verfassungslehre als Kulturwissenschaft* (Berlin: Duncker & Humblot, 1998), p. 28. See further, Ch. 1 of this volume.

[4] Hans Vorländer, *Konsens und Verfassung* (Berlin: Duncker & Humblot, 1981); Hans Vorländer (ed.), *Integration durch Verfassung* (Wiesbaden: Westdeutscher Verlag, 2002). Cf. Ulrich Haltern, 'Integration als Mythos' (1997) 45 *Jahrbuch des Öffentlichen Rechts NF* 31.

Yet, the normative and the integrative functions are fulfilled on different levels. The processes of constituting, legitimizing, and regulating public authority take place on a juridical level. The constitutive function is specific to the constitution; it is the very thing it is designed to do—namely, to create and regulate public authority that did not previously exist or did not exist in the same form. The same is true of its legitimizing function. The constitution defines who is entitled to wield political power. The constitution's function as a standard of behaviour and judgement is no different. The constitution sets out this standard, conferring upon it a legal validity that does not depend on whether or not the standard is actually followed. Individual violations of a law do not invalidate it. Its effect consists in allowing people to determine what behaviour is lawful or unlawful and attaching legal consequences to these qualifications.

The question is whether the integrative function of a constitution is of the same nature. Is this function an inevitable product of the constitution's very existence? Scepticism appears justified. A recently published book entitled *What Holds Society Together?*[5] does not even mention the constitution as an integrative factor. Indeed, history offers many examples of constitutions that have failed to contribute to social integration. A prime example is the Weimar constitution, which not only failed to integrate, but even drove Germans apart during the transformations following the First World War. On the other hand, one cannot deny the considerable integrative power of many constitutions. The best example of this is the American constitution, which is seen by many as the veritable embodiment of the American myth.[6]

While constitutions—provided they are intended to operate as legally binding texts—automatically produce normative effects, their integrative influence is a different matter. Taken together, the examples of Weimar and the United States (US) show that this influence can, but need not, exist. The reason is that the process of social integration does not unfold on a normative level. Integration takes place in the real world. It is a social process that can be linked with the constitution but is not controlled by it. This limitation is generally characteristic of legal norms. Laws can influence, but never determine, such processes. Even if, in the absence of voluntary compliance, legal rules are implemented by force, the law can only order the use of force. But since the command is executed in the real world, it will only be successful if office-holders are willing to follow the law, and if they are able to break the resistance of those affected by it.

In contrast to real actions that are made compulsory by law and which can be imposed, if necessary, by force, legal orders fall short when it comes to integration as a collective mental process. A norm that would require a constitution

---

[5] Wilhelm Heitmeyer (ed.), *Was hält die Gesellschaft zusammen?* (Frankfurt am Main: Suhrkamp, 1997); see also Heitmeyer (ed.), *Was treibt die Gesellschaft auseinander?* (Frankfurt am Main: Suhrkamp, 1997).

[6] William Y. Elliott, 'The Constitution as the American Social Myth' in Conyers Read (ed.), *The Constitution Reconsidered* (New York: Harper & Row, 1938), p. 209; Hans Kohn, *American Nationalism* (New York: Macmillan, 1957), p. 8; Samuel P. Huntington, *American Politics: The Promise of Disharmony* (Cambridge, Mass: Belknap Press, 1981), p. 30; Frank J. Schechter, 'The Early History of the Tradition of the Constitution' (1915) 9 *American Political Science Review* 713.

to have an integrative effect would be a norm without regulatory value. Even more so, a legal norm requiring citizen integration by constitution would be in vain. Thus, a constitution can fail to have an integrative function despite its legal efficacy. This failure need not result in disintegration, since the constitution is not the only integrative factor of political communities. Other factors such as the nation, religion, history, culture, and the threat from a common foe have a more reliable integrative effect than the normative constitution, and may therefore liberate it from extra-legal expectations.

The EU, however, is at a particular disadvantage compared with nation states because the non-legal integrative factors within its borders are poorly developed or lacking altogether. This explains the current desire for a constitution. The stakes become particularly apparent when we ask why a constitution is currently considered so urgent even though the EU has managed for fifty years without one. The fact that the EU has existed for so long without a constitution does not mean it has not had a basic legal framework—quite the opposite. It has had one from its very inception. However, in contrast to the basic legal framework of nation states, the EU's legal foundation does not consist of a constitution, but of international treaties. If these treaties have at times been described as a constitution, we must see this as an analogy rather than a reality. The treaties fulfill many legal functions that, in nation states, are assigned to the constitution.

Yet, for some time now, many have viewed this basic legal framework as requiring reform. There are mainly two reasons for that. Since the upheavals of 1989–1990, the role of Europe on the stage of world politics has transformed, but its restricted capacity to act in the area of foreign and security policy has left it poorly equipped to face the challenges. It was, above all, the admission of ten new member states in May 2004 that made structural reform necessary in EU bodies and decision-making processes. For a long time now, there has also been a call for a clearer definition of the jurisdiction of the EU and its member states. The Governmental Conference that negotiates changes to the treaties foundered on precisely this point. Therefore, it assigned the creation of a draft to a Convention—a model that had proved successful with the EU Charter of Fundamental Rights, which was solemnly proclaimed but not given legal effect in 2002.

It is important to notice, however, that the need for institutional reform does not imply the transition from treaty to constitution. Just as all previous changes to the legal foundation of the EU were carried out within the framework of its treaties, the required reforms could have been achieved by changing the treaty texts as well. None of the essential or desirable reforms depended on the translation of the treaties into a constitution. Neither the content of the regulations nor their rank in the hierarchy of norms would have differed in a constitution. From a legal viewpoint, the form of a treaty does not exclude any reform measure; neither does the form of a constitution add anything to the legal validity of the reforms. Hence, legal considerations do not make a constitution necessary.

For this reason the Governmental Conference left open the question 'treaty versus constitution' in its assignment to the Convention.

This means that there must be other reasons for the demand for a constitution that won out in the Convention. Since these reasons had nothing to do with legal necessity, we must search for them on the integrative level. A crucial factor has been the EU's undeniable weakness when it comes to legitimating itself. The European project is losing support and is met with growing scepticism among its citizens. A divide is opening up between economic and political integration on the one hand, and social integration on the other. Eurobarometer surveys[7] reveal that the majority of EU citizens now believe that the EU's disadvantages outweigh its advantages. The turnout at the elections to the European Parliament left the impression that EU citizens do not view the EU as their 'business'. Brussels is synonymous with weak rather than close ties to its citizens.

The EU and its member states cannot remain indifferent to these developments. To be sure, there are some who assert that the integration of systems in Europe is so far advanced that the EU is not dependent on social integration. Yet, today's problems are no longer only economic, but also political in nature and cannot be resolved on the basis of the functional constraints of market integration alone[8] (as the question of Turkey's accession and the enlargement of the EU have shown). The lack of social integration is increasingly proving to be an obstacle to further integration. It makes EU citizens ever less willing to support unification, to accept majority decisions that go against their national interest, and to show the kind of solidarity to all of Europe that is typically shown to nation states. The various national governments, which determine the fate of the EU in the European Council while answering only to their national constituencies, cannot entirely ignore this sentiment.

Not completely blind to these matters, the EU has, for quite some time, been pursuing an identity policy that places Europe at the focus of appealing image advertisements and endeavours to sell the idea of the EU by symbolic means. The EU's flag and anthem are part of this campaign.[9] Efforts to secure a European constitution must also be seen in this context. The constitution has a positive connotation and is well suited to mobilizing support. Although the majority of EU citizens no longer view the EU in a positive light, surveys reveal that a majority are in favour of a European constitution.[10] Consequently, it is not the constitution's legal functions that are of central importance—these

---

[7] European Commission (ed.), *Eurobarometer No. 25*; Christine Landfried, *Das politische Europa* (Baden-Baden: Nomos, 2002), p. 108.

[8] Jürgen Habermas, *Die aktuellen und die langfristigen Herausforderungen der EU* (unpublished manuscript, on file with the author).

[9] Ulrich Haltern, 'Europäische Identität' in Ralf Elm (ed.), *Europäische Identität: Paradigmen und Methodenfragen* (Baden-Baden: Nomos, 2002), p. 57; Ulrich Haltern, 'Pathos and Patina: The Failure and Promise of Constitutionalism in the European Imagination' (2003) 9 *European Law Journal* 30.

[10] European Commission, *The Future of European Constitution*, Flash Eurobarometer 159, February 2004; Olivier Beaud and Sylvie Strudel, 'Démocratie, Fédéralisme et Constitution' in Beaud et al. (eds), *L'Europe en voie de Constitution* (Brussels: Bruylant, 2004), p. 12.

could as well be fulfilled by treaties. Rather, the constitution is viewed as crucial because of its anticipated emotive benefits and thus its integrative value.

## II. THE PRECONDITIONS FOR A CONSTITUTION'S INTEGRATIVE POWER

In this context, one central fact about constitutions—that their integrative (as opposed to their legal) function may not necessarily set in—takes on added significance. This raises the question of exactly when constitutions produce an integrative effect and when they miss the mark. It is easier to ask this question than to answer it. Although the integrative function of constitutions has recently attracted greater interest, it has yet to be sufficiently examined.[11] The existing theories—which are rudimentary at best—are not supported by empirical data. The comparative historical studies needed to fill this gap have not been undertaken. Under these circumstances, though it is possible to show, to a limited extent, the factors contributing to a particular constitution's success (assuming it has proved integrative in concrete cases), little is known about the general conditions that must be met for integration to be successful.

This chapter cannot compensate for the lack of research. For now, the answers will have to remain rather abstract, and can be substantiated only by using specific examples. A starting point is the observation that a constitution's legal effectiveness is no guarantee of its integrative power, and that the preconditions for this power must be sought in extra-legal spheres of society. In general, one might say that a constitution will only have an integrative force if, within its area of application, it stands for more than what it is in juridical terms, that is, more than a mere legal text. The quality that allows a constitution to exceed its legal efficacy is its symbolic power. A constitution will have an integrative effect if it embodies a society's fundamental value system and aspirations, if a society perceives that its constitution reflects precisely those values with which it identifies and that are the source of its specific character.[12]

Consequently, integration by a constitution depends on how the constitution is perceived. This perception is only loosely related to its legal quality. To be sure, a constitution's integrative effect is not totally independent of its legal validity—it is improbable that a society will draw its identity from a constitution that, from the very start, is not intended to be valid or which can be permanently ignored, with no consequence, by those in power. Yet the fact that

---

[11] Vorländer, *Integration* (n. 4); Haltern, 'Integration' (n. 4); Gebhardt and Schmalz-Bruns (n. 1); Jürgen Gebhardt (ed.), *Verfassung und politische Kultur* (Baden-Baden: Nomos, 1999); Jürgen Gebhardt, 'Verfassung und Symbolizität' in Gert Melville (ed.), *Institutionalität und Symbolisierung* (Cologne: Böhlau, 2001), p. 585; Gary S. Schaal, *Integration durch Verfassung und Verfassungsrechtsprechung?* (Berlin: Duncker & Humblot, 2000); André Brodocz, *Die symbolische Dimension der Verfassung* (Wiesbaden: Westdeutscher Verlag, 2003); Günter Frankenberg, *Autorität und Integration. Zur Grammatik von Recht und Verfassung* (Frankfurt am Main: Suhrkamp, 2003); Günter Frankenberg, 'Tocqueville's Question: The role of a constitution in the process of integration' (2000) 13 *Ratio Juris* 1.

[12] Hans Vorländer, 'Integration durch Verfassung?' in Vorländer, *Integration* (n. 4), p. 9.

a constitution functions legally does not mean that it will have any integrative power.[13] Because their integrative power is ensured less by the legal quality of their regulations than by the way in which the members of a constitutionally formed polity perceive them, constitutions can acquire or forfeit integrative power without prior textual changes to, or different interpretation of, their content.

In contrast, there is a much closer link between a constitution's integrative power and the polity's order it constitutes and to which it gives both legal expression and a generally binding character. As a normative text embodying this order, a constitution can confer identity only as long as the system it has established is perceived as being a 'good' one.[14] If the society living under this system does not see the system as good, it will reject the very constitution that gives the system a binding character and protects it with its instruments of power. In this case the constitution no longer contributes to a society's integration and in the end fails even in fulfilling its legal function. This was the fate of the Weimar constitution.[15]

As a rule, the perception of a system as 'good' presupposes a high degree of inclusivity. The more people in a society identify with its constitution, the more its power to create social integration will grow. Open wording in a constitution fosters this process. It helps to prevent competing ideas about the meaning of the text from undermining the citizenry's identification with it. Consequently, we may correctly claim that a constitution's symbolic power increases with its interpretative ambiguity,[16] although its legally determinative power decreases to the same degree. Of course, this can only refer to slight shifts in the balance. On the one hand, there is no such thing as a legal norm that does not need to be, or cannot be, interpreted. On the other hand, when they are applied to concrete cases, all legal norms must be given an unambiguous reading relevant to each case.

The question of application is again relevant to social integration. If a constitution fails to exert authority in the real world of politics, not even a concept of order perceived as 'good' will be able to confer identity-building power upon the constitution. This is why constitutions that are linked to an authoritative instance such as a constitutional court (or a general court with the power of judicial review) for the enforcement of constitutional provisions have a greater

---

[13] Constitutions of this type are often called 'symbolic constitutions', cf. Marcello Neves, *Symbolische Konstitutionalisierung* (Berlin: Duncker & Humblot, 1998); Neves, *Verfassung und Positivität des Rechts in der peripheren Moderne* (Berlin: Duncker & Humblot, 1992); Brun-Otto Bryde, *Verfassungsentwicklung* (Baden-Baden: Nomos, 1982), p. 27. The symbolic constitution in this sense should not be confused with the symbolic effects of normative constitutions.

[14] Vorländer (n. 12).

[15] Detlef Lehnert, 'Desintegration durch Verfassung?—oder wie die Verfassung der Nationalversammlung von 1919 als Desintegrationsfaktor der Weimarer Republik interpretiert wurde' in Vorländer, *Integration* (n. 4), p. 237.

[16] Brodocz (n. 11); Brodocz, 'Chancen konstitutioneller Identitätsstiftung. Zur symbolischen Integration durch eine deutungsoffene Verfassung' in Vorländer, *Integration* (n. 4), p. 101.

chance of promoting integration than those that leave compliance up to government.[17] Even so it would be rash to assume that constitutional courts can fill the gap when the constitution lacks sufficient symbolic force and does not offer society identification potential.

In order for integration by constitution to happen, our accumulated knowledge suggests that the circumstances under which a society is founded play a crucial role. Bruce Ackerman, in particular, has emphasized the significance of the 'constitutional moment' for a constitution's integrative and identity-building force.[18] He uses this term to refer to those rare moments that stand out from the usual course of politics, moments in which the desire to revise the principles of social order or the conditions of rule triumphs and is anchored in constitutional law. In fact, the great majority of both historical and currently existing constitutions have been drafted for the establishment or re-founding of polities. Historical ruptures within societies frequently play a critical role here: they primarily take the form of triumphant revolutions toppling despised foreign rulers or oppressive regimes, but occasionally also a country's resurgence following a catastrophic collapse.[19]

However, a 'constitutional moment' must not be understood as the *conditio sine qua non* for successful, integrative constitutions. There are constitutions with great integrative power that have not emerged during such moments. One example is the new Swiss constitution (billed as an 'update' of the old). Conversely, we know of constitutions that have emerged in a 'constitutional moment', but did not gain any integrative capacity. The numerous French constitutions are vivid examples. A 'constitutional moment' creates favourable conditions for effective, integrative constitutions in cases in which a society continues to recognize itself in a historical moment, and thus the emergent constitution creates a link between past and present.

The US exemplifies the triumphalist model of the 'constitutional moment'. The history of the US began with a successful revolution against its mother country, and culminated in the foundation of an independent state. These acts found expression in two founding documents: the Declaration of Independence (1776) and the Federal Constitution (1787). Both are important to the collective memory of the US and symbolize the origins and development of that country's polity. While the Declaration of Independence stands for the casting-off of foreign domination, the founding of a new polity—based on self-government,

---

[17] Helge Rossen-Stadtfeld, 'Verfassungsgericht und gesellschaftliche Integration' in Gunnar Folke Schuppert and Christian Bumke (eds), *Bundesverfassungsgericht und gesellschaftlicher Grundkonsens* (Baden-Baden: Nomos, 2000), p. 169; Schaal (n. 11); Brun-Otto Bryde, 'Integration durch Verfassungsgerichtsbarkeit und ihre Grenzen' in Vorländer, *Integration* (n. 4), p. 329.

[18] Bruce Ackerman, 'Constitutional Politics/Constitutional Law' (1989) 99 *Yale Law Journal* 453; Bruce Ackerman, *We the People: Vol. 1 Foundations* (Cambridge, Mass: Belknap Press, 1991); Bruce Ackerman, *We the People: Vol. 2 Transformations* (Cambridge, Mass: Belknap Press, 1998); 'Symposium: Moments of Change' (1999) 108 *Yale Law Journal*, Special Issue, 1917–2349.

[19] Cf. Bruce Ackerman, 'The Rise of World Constitutionalism' (1997) 83 *Virginia Law Review* 775; Louis Henkin, 'Revolutions and Constitutions' (1989) 49 *Louisiana Law Review* 1023; Ch. 2 of this volume.

liberty, and the rule of law—finds expression in the Constitution. The day on which the Declaration of Independence was adopted has become a national holiday, devoted to the annual commemoration of the founding of the nation. Integration, however, is primarily achieved through the Constitution. There is no other polity in which the constitution plays such an important role in social integration as the US.[20]

This has something to do with the difference between structure and event. The adoption of the Declaration of Independence is an event that people can commemorate on national holidays, just as the storming of the Bastille provides a focal point for commemorating the French Revolution. But the Declaration of Independence and, therefore, the American Revolution were legitimized by values which, expressed in the Constitution, would subsequently form the basic principles of a new order. Only through the Constitution as a normative text did the new order assume permanence and acquire a legally valid form. The Constitution remains valid, with relatively few changes, even today. It blends with the founding myth of the US and keeps the myth alive in people's minds. The Constitution embodies convictions that unite all Americans independently of their origins and traditions. And this unity is fostered by the pithiness and openness with which the Constitution was formulated.

With the exception of the period of bloody civil war between the Northern and the Southern states, Americans have always revered their Constitution. Even in the early years, this reverence was expressed not only in religious metaphors but also in festivals and rituals borrowed from religion. There are two factors that have been largely responsible for this reverence. First, the US, as a land of immigrants, could not offer the same identification potential as fully fledged nation states: prior to the adoption of the Constitution no nation existed. Furthermore, for anyone emigrating to the new country, emigration meant breaking with their own tradition. The new tradition began with the Constitution, which distinctly stands for people coexisting in freedom with respect for one another's differences. Second, America's constitutional jurisdiction ensured from the very start that people would always recognize the importance, as well as the social and political relevance, of the Constitution.

The Federal Republic of Germany may serve as an illustration of the catastrophe model, since its constitution was the product not of a successful revolution, but of a profound defeat. Germany had lost much of its territory, and what remained was divided into two states hostile to each other. The country was burdened with guilt about their National Socialist past. Consequently, in postwar Germany—as in the US (albeit for different reasons)—traditional identification factors did not exist. The nation was out of the question, because it was divided. Its history was off limits, as it was closely associated with the Holocaust. And culture could not enter the equation, because it was needed as

---

[20] Michael Kammen, *A Machine That Would Go of Itself: The Constitution in American Culture* (New York: Knopf, 1987); Jürgen Heideking, 'Der symbolische Stellenwert der Verfassung in der politischen Tradition der USA' in Vorländer, *Integration* (n. 4), p. 123.

a unifying bond for the divided nation. Where other nation states had a sound basis for integration and identity, postwar Germany faced a vacuum.

At the same time, a long phase of undisturbed economic growth turned the Federal Republic into a prospering economic power and stable democracy. Its success was increasingly accredited to the Basic Law. In contrast to Weimar, whose constitution was held responsible for the collapse of the first republic, the Basic Law was identified with the rise of the Federal Republic of Germany. Adopted in reaction to national socialism, the Basic Law symbolized not only Germany's return to the fold of civilized nations, but also a superior alternative to communism. In Germany, as in the US, the introduction of a constitutional court with far-reaching competences meant that Germans, for the first time in their constitutional history, were able to perceive the constitution as a relevant document that gave each individual the means to defend their fundamental rights against the state authorities. This, in turn, reinforced the legal efficacy of the constitution, without which the symbolic effect is unlikely to emerge.[21]

The Basic Law was thus able to fill the vacuum of identification factors. Its popular esteem grew from decade to decade, as the dedications expressed at the various jubilees testify. From the 1970s on, it even became a model for many states that had liberated themselves from dictatorships of every ilk. These states saw in the German constitution a guarantor of economic prosperity and political stability, and borrowed from it when they drafted their own constitutions. Nothing describes the German situation more aptly than the expression (which has no parallel in any other country) 'constitutional patriotism'.[22] It is a phrase with which people on both the left and the right could identify. Thus, it became an expression of the fact that, in a society deprived of its basis for national identification, the constitution was the document that represented the achievements and cherished values of the West German society.

This is in no way altered by the fact that in Germany—as in the US—the meaning of certain constitutional norms, and the demands these norms place on government in specific situations, were frequently the subject of heated debate and the source of profound conflicts. Unlike discord in the Weimar Republic, conflicts in the Federal Republic did not revolve around the constitution as such, but around different interpretations of a constitution that was fundamentally accepted. For when people argue over the correct meaning of a constitution and refer back to it in political and social conflicts, they are basically affirming the constitution through these very conflicts. When such conflicts arise, the constitutional court—which operates at a distance from politics—has the opportunity both to assert the constitution's authority over the political

---

[21] See further Ch. 7 of this volume.

[22] The original sources are Dolf Sternberger, 'Verfassungspatriotismus', *Frankfurter Allgemeine Zeitung*, 23 May 1979, p. 1; Jürgen Habermas, *Eine Art Schadensabwicklung* (Frankfurt am Main: Suhrkamp, 1987). See also Josef Isensee, 'Die Verfassung als Vaterland' in Armin Mohler (ed.), *Wirklichkeit als Tabu* (Munich: Oldenbourg, 1986), p. 11; Jürgen Gebhardt, 'Verfassungspatriotismus als Identitätskonzept der Nation' in his *Verfassung und politische Kultur* (n. 11), p. 15.

branches of government and to anchor it more firmly in the minds of the population. Even though disputes over the interpretation of the constitution sometimes divide society, they do not generally affect the constitution as such.

### III. THE INTEGRATIVE POTENTIAL OF THE EUROPEAN CONSTITUTION

Proceeding from these findings, we can now return to the European constitution and ask ourselves, considering the lack in legitimacy of the EU, whether the constitution is likely to become the integrative power that it is expected to be. In order to answer this question, it is helpful to bear in mind that the need for institutional reform does not render a constitution necessary since this need can be fully satisfied within the framework of the existing treaties. All the changes that appear desirable or necessary to the constitution can be inserted into these treaties. Under these circumstances, the success of the projected constitution—which the Convention found so urgent—depends on whether or not the document, once it has come into force, fulfills the expectations placed in it on the symbolic level, and thus compensates for the lack of a natural basis for integration. This would be similar to what the American constitution managed to do in a country of immigrants, and the Basic Law in a divided Germany.[23]

Of course, no one can predict what will happen with any degree of certainty. The symbolic effect of a constitution is not given with its promulgation. This effect will ultimately be the result of people attributing meta-legal meaning, achievements, and aspirations to the legal text—all of which can change over time. In 1949, nobody expected the Basic Law to have such integrative power. The general public did not show any great interest in it when it was being drafted and came into force. Many legal experts initially took a sceptical and critical view of the Basic Law. Hence, with regards to the European constitution, one can but ascertain whether the preconditions for successful integration by the new document are more or less favourable. Thereby, its efficacy at the legal level, as the prerequisite for its being effective at the symbolic level, can be taken for granted. There is no reason to assume that it will be appreciably less effective than the current legal basis of the EU, even though the simplification and transparency originally hoped for have not been achieved in every respect.

The EU resembles the US as an immigration country and a formerly divided Germany, inasmuch as the Union cannot rely on traditional means of integration. In both countries, this lack offered the constitution an opportunity to fill the gap. Yet, there is no automatism at work. Whether or not this will actually happen depends on a variety of additional conditions. In particular, both constitutions that were so successful in integrating society emerged from a 'constitutional moment' in Ackerman's sense, in order to distance themselves from a past that was viewed with disdain, and to shape a new idea of political order

---

[23] Haltern, 'Pathos and Patina' (n. 9).

which was then made legally binding. Thus created, both constitutions have become symbols of the polities' foundations and lasting successes. These were attributed to the constitutions.

In contrast, the document drawn up by the Convention in 2003 is not a striking symbol of the historical realization of European unity. We are neither witnessing the foundation of the European project nor a new beginning after a radical historical break. On the contrary, European integration is a process of gradual expansion and consolidation. The stages of this process are marked by the accession of new member states and amendments to the treaties. But none of these stages displayed the typical features of a 'constitutional moment'. To be sure, the Maastricht Treaty of 1992 did stand out among the various stages of European unification inasmuch as it made the public aware, for the first time, of the degree of communitization already attained. Until then, integration had escaped public notice and was basically achieved on administrative and judicial paths. However, growing public interest did not give the EU greater legitimacy, but only made its weak support visible. Since Maastricht, the number of EU citizens who see the Union as 'a good thing' has been falling.[24]

It is important to remember, however, that the process of establishing a constitution has gone hand in hand with the expansion of the EU to include ten new members, most of whom, until 1989, had had very different social orders than their western counterparts. Yet, the EU had accepted new member states in the past without people ever viewing this process as a 'constitutional moment'. Moreover, the expansion of 2004 is not regarded as a triumph of the European cause, as it might have been in 1989—a year that would have undoubtedly supplied the preconditions for a 'constitutional moment' and for elevating the constitution to symbolic status. In view of the weak economies and unstable democracies in many of the new member states, the older members tend to view current developments with concern. Additionally, people in the new member states evidently do not feel that they are witnessing a memorable moment, as indicated by the level of participation in the European elections soon after these new countries had acceded to the EU. It is too early to say whether this will change in the future.

To be sure, the process of European integration has achieved something which, considering Europe's painful history, should not be underestimated: one can be almost certain that, owing to their high degree of integration, it is very unlikely the EU member states will ever wage war on one another again. Yet, almost sixty years after the end of the Second World War, and nearly fifty years after the founding of the European Communities, this achievement is now taken for granted to such a degree that, hardly anyone is likely to attribute it to a European Constitution agreed upon in 2004. Even though the expression 'constitutional moment' should not be taken literally, and even though a good ten years passed between the Declaration of Independence and the adoption

---

[24] Landfried (n. 7).

of the Constitution in the US, it would be stretching things to see a connection between two events that are separated by sixty years.

In other respects, too, we are witnessing the birth of a constitution at a moment in time that does not seem suitable to the making of a memorable myth. A 'constitutional moment' in Ackerman's sense is not in sight. Even those who think that the year 2004 has the stuff of which 'constitutional moments' are made must refer to developments in an uncertain future.[25] At present, the transition from the EU's current legal system, which is founded on international treaties, to a document called a constitution appears to be but one more stage among many on Europe's path from a single market to a political union, in much the same way that the Single European Act and the Maastricht Treaty were also stages in this development, without acquiring symbolic character or fostering European identity.

The text of the constitutional document does not lend itself to produce symbolic effects either. It is true that, as a single text, it represents a step forward from the previous legal basis, which was spread over a number of different documents. However, it is cumbersome compared with an integrative constitution. Apart from its two preambles, the draft by the Convention comprises 465 articles, as well as five protocols and three declarations. In contrast, the US Constitution (including later amendments) has twenty-seven articles; the Basic Law contains 183 articles (including amendments); the Portuguese constitution, the longest of any EU member state, contains 299 articles. Hence, the European constitution is very long, detailed, and technical. It is difficult to grasp the interplay of organs, the allocation of competencies between the Union, and the member states, as well as the decision-making procedures.

To be sure, this appraisal does not proceed on the assumption that the citizens of a state know the wording of their constitution. This is not even the case in the US. Yet, as a rule, citizens have some idea of the guiding principles on which their constitution is based. They even remember the precise wording of certain memorable notions and use them to support arguments when necessary. Whether or not the ideas contained in a constitution are memorable or not depends, of course, on the way they are phrased. National constitutions, especially those that owe their origins to a 'constitutional moment', tend to contain such formulations. The text preserves something of the pathos of a 'constitutional moment'. Such formulations are few and far between in the Convention draft, which has not cast off the complicated language of the diplomatically negotiated treaties and is, in fact, identical in wording with them over long stretches.

Fundamental rights, which of all parts of a constitution are most conducive to producing integrative effects, are not likely to achieve much either. After all, they do not mark the end of a period of unfreedom and despotism in a Europe

---

[25] Neil Walker, 'After the Constitutional Moment' in Ingolf Pernice and Miguel Poiares Maduro (eds), *A Constitution for the European Union* (Baden-Baden: Nomos, 2004), p. 23; Ingolf Pernice, 'The Draft Constitution of the European Union. A Constitutional Treaty at a Constitutional Moment?' ibid., p. 13.

deprived of basic rights. Despite the absence of a written charter of fundamental rights, the EU has long since enjoyed protection of fundamental rights
through the European Court of Justice, based on the European Convention
of Human Rights and the member states' catalogues of fundamental rights.
Moreover, the Charter of Fundamental Rights offers citizens of the EU a third
catalogue of human rights (in addition to the national one and the European
Convention adopted by the Council of Europe) to protect them from public
authority. This is also true for the citizens of the new member countries. In
federalist states such as the Federal Republic of Germany, the charter actually
constitutes a fourth catalogue that citizens can invoke.

Ultimately, the new document raises the question whether it really deserves
to be called a constitution.[26] According to the standard set by the American and
French Revolutions as the origins of modern constitutionalism, it is in the constitution that a society determines the form and content of its political unity.
In so doing, society exercises its right to self-determination vis-à-vis the ruling
order, thereby demonstrating that it is sovereign and the sole source of public
authority. It is for this very reason that constitutions are normally adopted by
the people, or at least attributed to them as origins of all public authority, while
state organs derive their existence and powers from the people and exercise
these in their name. The basic legal order of the EU, by contrast, has neither
originated in a decision made by its citizens, nor is it attributed to them. It is a
matter for the member states to contractually agree upon a basic legal order,
which is then ratified by each member state. This is not an act of self-determination, but of external determination.

To be sure, it is by no means impossible that the constitution of a political
entity comes about on the basis of a treaty prepared by its founders. This is,
indeed, the standard procedure when several states combine to create a greater
political whole. In this case, a treaty is merely the mode of constitution-making.
The founding treaty is, at the same time, the final international treaty providing
the legal basis of the new political entity. With the adoption of the treaty, its
character as treaty is consummated. From now on, the new political entity dis-
poses itself of this legal basis, which thereby becomes their constitution. This is
apparent in the provisions relating to constitutional amendments. If the constitutional treaty is the last treaty under international law and subsequent amendments are decided upon by the entity so constituted, the basic legal order is a
constitution. If the member states still retain the power to make amendments
by way of concluding treaties on the basis of international law, the basic legal
order remains a treaty in nature and does not become a constitution.

What is the situation with respect to the European constitutional treaty? In
contrast to the previous text, the one now agreed upon distinguishes between
drafting constitutional amendments and passing decisions on them. In the preparatory phase, an ad-hoc Convention is to be summoned regularly to draft

---

[26] Dieter Grimm, 'Verfassung—Verfassungsvertrag—Vertrag über eine Verfassung' in Beaud et al., *L'Europe
en voie* (n. 10), p. 279.

the text. During the decision-making phase, everything remains as it was before: The Governmental Conference which is not an organ of the EU has to approve the draft unanimously—with or without amendments—and then submit it to the member states for ratification. This is in no way changed by the fact that in some countries, the people themselves are to decide whether the treaty is to be adopted or not. For in this case the 'people' are not the citizens of the EU, and their decision is not a decision upon the constitutional system of the EU. The people are the citizens of different nation states, deciding on whether or not their state is to approve the signed treaty.

Neither is this qualification altered by the fact that the governments of the member states that negotiate the treaty at the Governmental Conference are democratically elected by their citizens, so that one could conclude that the basic legal order is ultimately attributable to the EU's citizens.[27] Here too, the people are only involved as citizens of nation states; and only inasmuch as they elect the national parliament and, in some countries, the president. It is therefore fictitious to claim that all decisions made by the elected organs are results of the popular will. The document remains in the hands of the member states. Measured against a somewhat meaningful notion of a constitution this document cannot be considered a constitution. One could not credibly begin the European constitution with those famous words introducing the US Constitution: 'We the people,' with which every American is familiar.

For all these reasons, it will be difficult—at least in the near future—for the new constitutional treaty to produce integrative effects. There is nothing to be seen for which it could stand other than its legal validity. This obviously does not diminish its legal value. From the legal viewpoint, and all criticism notwithstanding, it is an improvement in both form and content over the present legal basis of the EU. But the fact alone that it will function more or less well on the legal level does not elevate it to the symbolic level. Since this depends on the non-legal effects of the constitution, it would require emotional associations that do not exist. Consequently, the desire for a transition from treaty to constitution, namely to promote social integration, still lacks a solid basis in reality. At present, there is little reason to expect that the constitutional treaty will make up for the EU's legitimacy deficit, anchor the Union in the hearts of Europe's citizens and, in so doing, play an integrative role and help to create identity.

---

[27] See Ingolf Pernice, 'Multilevel Constitutionalism and the Treaty of Amsterdam: European Constitution-Making Revisited?' (1999) 36 *Common Market Law Review* 703.

# INTERPRETATION

# Fundamental Rights in the Interpretation of the German Constitutional Court

## I. FUNDAMENTAL RIGHTS AND CONSTITUTIONAL JURISPRUDENCE

Fundamental rights in Germany are older than the Basic Law. But only under the Basic Law did they gain the full and unprecedented effect which they enjoy today. The increased importance pertains less to their content than to their legal force. Fundamental rights had been weak in the 150 years before the Basic Law and were even suspended completely during the Nazi era. From this experience the framers of the Basic Law drew the conclusion that it was not enough to enact a Bill of Rights, but that it was also necessary to support the rights institutionally. So they established the Federal Constitutional Court. The eminent role of fundamental rights today would be unimaginable without this Court's jurisprudence.[1] Its case law has become a model for several countries which gave themselves liberal constitutions of different kinds after the end of totalitarian or authoritarian regimes.[2] However, the establishment of a constitutional court alone is not a sufficient explanation for the increased role of fundamental rights. Additional factors were a more sophisticated understanding of the meaning and function of fundamental rights, the opportunity to develop understanding through the decision of cases, and the readiness of the addressees of fundamental rights to adhere to the decisions of the constitutional court. Following a short examination of the history of fundamental rights prior to the Basic Law, which is essential to understand their current role, these factors will be the focus of this chapter.

---

[1] For an overview, cf. Donald P. Kommers and Russell Miller, *The Constitutional Jurisprudence of the Federal Republic of Germany* (Durham: Duke University Press, 3rd edn, 2012), p. 59; Peter Badura and Horst Dreier (eds), *Festschrift 50 Jahre Bundesverfassungsgericht* (Tübingen: Mohr Siebeck, 2001).

[2] See e.g. the remark by László Sólyom, the first president of the Hungarian Constitutional Court established in 1989, that the German constitutional jurisprudence was 'nearly overwhelming' for his court: László Sólyom and Georg Brunner, *Constitutional Judiciary in a New Democracy* (Ann Arbor: University of Michigan Press, 2000), p. 5.

Constitutionalism: Past, Present, and Future. First Edition. Dieter Grimm. © Dieter Grimm 2016. Published 2016 by Oxford University Press.

## II. THE DEVELOPMENT OF FUNDAMENTAL RIGHTS PRIOR TO THE BASIC LAW

Fundamental rights were already included in most constitutions of the German states in the *Vormärz* era, the period before the revolution of 1848. But there were clear differences between these fundamental rights and their counterparts in the birthplaces of modern constitutionalism in North America and France.[3] The most important reason for these differences is grounded in the diverging genesis: whereas the American and French constitutions were established through a natural law-inspired revolution against traditional rulers, German constitutions were not. Rather, they were granted voluntarily by the monarchs of the various German states—not motivated by a spirit of constitutionalism, but by the interest in dynastic self-preservation. Therefore, German fundamental rights denied the natural law origin of fundamental rights which had been the legitimating paradigm for the American and French Revolutions. Neither were they regarded as human rights. They were guarantees which the monarchs granted their subjects in the form of positive law. Fundamental rights were voluntary limitations of state power, which not only preceded the constitution, but which was also independent of any consensus. Consequently, fundamental rights catalogues started with provisions regarding citizenship and the protection they offered remained far behind fundamental rights in America and France. They were limited to certain private liberties, whereas political freedoms—with the exception of the freedom of the press—were missing.

Even in this reduced form—compared to modern constitutionalism—fundamental rights had only limited force. The main reason was the lack of any derogating power vis-à-vis pre-constitutional law. After the enactment of the constitution, infringements of liberty and property of citizens required a statutory basis for the respective measure. But such statutory bases existed. They had originated in the era of the police state (*Polizeistaat*) and were not indebted to the liberal ideas which were the root of fundamental rights. Of course, these statutes could be amended; and the parliamentary assemblies, which were established by the constitution, constantly pushed for those amendments. But legislation required the consent of the first chamber, which consisted of the privileged classes, and of the monarch, who initially had the sole right to initiate bills. Therefore, the demands of the elected representations of the people for a 'realization' of fundamental rights (the expression 'realization' [Verwirklichung] was frequently used) mostly failed due to the objections of the first chamber and the monarch. Thus, fundamental rights largely remained promises. In addition, parts of them would soon be superseded by the Carlsbad Decrees of the German Federation, which completely extinguished freedom of the press. Constitutional scholars, who were predominantly liberal, continued

---

[3] Dieter Grimm, *Deutsche Verfassungsgeschichte 1776 bis 1866* (Frankfurt am Main: Suhrkamp, 3rd edn, 1995), p. 110.

to interpret them counterfactually in a liberal way and thereby formed the basis for criticism of the situation. But they were not able to change it.

The change was brought about by the *Paulskirchenverfassung*, to which several victims of the Carlsbad Decrees made significant contributions. The National Assembly had started its work by drafting a catalogue of fundamental rights, which came into force in December 1848 before the enactment of the whole constitution. Like the American and the French constitutions, the *Paulskirchenverfassung* was fought for by citizens and it was based on the principle of sovereignty of the people. Therefore, its understanding of fundamental rights reflected the interests of the citizenry rather than the monarch. Consequently, the catalogue of fundamental rights was expanded in comparison with fundamental rights of the *Vormärz* era. Furthermore, they were equipped with precedence vis-à-vis statute law. Additionally, the constitution aimed at establishing a constitutional court with the power of judicial review of legislation including the power to strike down statutes that violated fundamental rights. But the fundamental rights of the *Paulskirchenverfassung* also did not have a natural law background. Due to the second revolutionary wave, which went beyond reform interest of the bourgeoisie and also made social and egalitarian demands, the majority of the National Assembly shied away from the revolutionary potential which a natural law foundation of fundamental rights might entail. Similarly, the motion to include social rights in the constitution failed.

The *Paulskirchenverfassung* never came into force: the planned constitutional court was not established and the Bill of Rights was repealed in 1851 after the victory of Restauration. This did not put an end to the issue of fundamental rights in general because the constitutions of several states which had been amended or created during the revolution included catalogues of fundamental rights that were similar to the fundamental rights of the *Paulskirchenverfassung*. But they were not secured by constitutional courts because such courts were deemed to be incompatible with the monarchical principle which had again become binding for all member states of the *Deutscher Bund* (German Confederation) after its revival. The interest of the bourgeoisie in fundamental rights now decreased, partly due to the revolutionary experience and the unfulfilled demands of the fourth estate, and partly due to the liberalization of statutory law, which began in the 1860s and fulfilled many hopes previously connected to fundamental rights. The decreasing interest soon had an effect on the interpretation of fundamental rights. After the foundation of the German Empire, whose constitution did not contain a Bill of Rights, fundamental rights on state level were interpreted in a minimalist way. Thereby, they lost their liberal spirit and—finally—also their legal effectiveness to a large extent.[4]

In their interpretation of fundamental rights during the German empire constitutional law scholars started from the assumption that fundamental rights

---

[4] Cf. Dieter Grimm, 'Die Entwicklung der Grundrechtstheorie in der deutschen Staatsrechtslehre des 19. Jahrhunderts' in his *Recht und Staat der bürgerlichen Gesellschaft* (Frankfurt am Main: Suhrkamp, 1987), p. 308; Walter Pauly, *Der Methodenwandel im deutschen Spätkonstitutionalismus* (Tübingen: Mohr, 1993).

could be restricted by statute law. This led to the conclusion that they ranked not above, but below statute law. However, they could not be repealed by statute but only by constitutional amendment. Thus, as in the *Vormärz* era, infringements of liberty and property of citizens required a statutory basis. Yet, the legislator was not bound by fundamental rights when creating this. Consequently, the only effect of fundamental rights was to prevent infringements of fundamental rights by the executive branch without a statutory basis. Exactly the same effect was also regarded as resulting from the principle of the rule of law, to which all constitutions adhered. Hence, fundamental rights did not seem to be necessary to achieve this effect. Therefore, constitutional scholars concluded that fundamental rights were nothing other than a relic of previous times in which the rule of law had not yet been fully developed. Fundamental rights were seen as an old-fashioned casuistic formulation of the rule of law. As such, fundamental rights were regarded as having no function. Due to the existence of the rule of law, fundamental rights could as well be missing without any practical legal effect.[5]

This did not deter the National Assembly, which drafted a new constitution on a democratic basis after the overthrow of the monarchy in the 1918 revolution, from formulating a catalogue of fundamental rights to which it attached high importance. The catalogue not only included liberty rights, but also social and economic rights. Nevertheless, constitutional scholars continued to interpret the new fundamental rights in the old fashion.[6] Fundamental rights did not limit statute law: statute law limited fundamental rights. Social rights were denied any legal effect by claiming that they did not directly entitle citizens to certain benefits, but needed to be concretized by legislation. Therefore, in spite of their inclusion in the constitutional text, fundamental rights were only seen as political statements of intent without legal effect. The younger generation of constitutional scholars in the Weimar Republic criticized this attitude of the positivistic school and started to establish a material understanding of fundamental rights according to which they should also bind the legislature. But this understanding did not prevail before the collapse of the Weimar Republic and the Nazi regime disposed of all constitutional commitments.

### III. STATUS AND EFFECT OF FUNDAMENTAL RIGHTS UNDER THE BASIC LAW

After the end of the Second World War, the authors of the Basic Law were largely influenced by the complete disregard of fundamental rights during the Nazi regime. Likewise, they were mindful of the minimal impact of fundamental rights in the nineteenth century and in the Weimar Republic. They therefore

---

[5] The weakness of fundamental rights was not typical only for Germany; it could be found in all European states and ended only with the establishment of constitutional courts or courts with the power of constitutional review in the twentieth century.

[6] Christoph Gusy, 'Die Grundrechte in der Weimarer Republik' (1993) *Zeitschrift für Neuere Rechtsgeschichte* 163.

regarded the protection of fundamental rights as a concern with highest priority. They had the strong intent to use constitutional law in order to prevent the repetition of the history of the Weimar Republic and the so-called Third Reich. This entailed several innovations in the Basic Law of 1949. Symbolically, the significance which the Parliamentary Council (*Parlamentarischer Rat*) attributed to fundamental rights was shown by the fact that they were moved from the end of the constitution to its beginning. The decision to guarantee human dignity by Art. 1, s.1 of the Basic Law (GG) had not only symbolic, but also immediate legal effect. This provision formed the basis of all fundamental rights and gave them a purpose. Human dignity was declared to be *unantastbar* (inviolable). This expression appears nowhere else in the Basic Law.[7] In addition, human dignity not only had to be respected by the state, it should also be protected against attacks from third parties. With Art.1, s.2, a slight hint of pathos of natural law became part of a German catalogue of fundamental rights. This sections reads: 'The German people therefore [due to human dignity; D.G.] acknowledge inviolable and inalienable human rights as the basis of every community, of peace and of justice in the world.'

Art.1, s.3 explicitly declared fundamental rights to be 'directly applicable law' and to be binding on all branches of government. This rejects the old idea that some fundamental rights had no legal character at all while those to which a legal character was conceded would not have the ability to bind the legislature. At the same time, the Parliamentary Council did not repeat the Weimar attempt to enact social and economic rights. Out of fear that Germany might not recover soon from the war the authors of the Basic Law contented themselves with the classic liberties, but combined them with the objective that the Federal Republic of Germany should be a social state. The ability to infringe fundamental rights by statute was restricted by Art. 19, s.2, according to which the *Wesensgehalt* (essential content) of a fundamental right may not be touched. Art. 79, s.3 finally provided that the principles of Arts 1 and 20 may not even be altered by a constitutional amendment, thereby indirectly also guaranteeing the existence of fundamental rights. Finally, the Parliamentary Council established the Federal Constitutional Court as an institution that should be able to review the constitutionality of all state acts—including those of the legislature—and that it should have the power to strike down all state acts that violate the Basic Law. Further developments were in the hands of this court, which could draw ideas from constitutional scholarship.

When the Basic Law came into force in May 1949, this enactment was seen neither as a special moment in German history, nor as creating expectations for a better future. West German politicians had embarked upon the constitutional

---

[7] The term 'unverletzlich' = inviolable is often used in connection with fundamental rights, whereas a literal translation of 'unantastbar' would be 'intangible' and a better translation might be 'sacrosanct'. In English translations both terms appear as 'inviolable', which obscures the difference. See Dieter Grimm, 'Dignity in a Legal Context' in Christopher McCrudden (ed.), *Understanding Human Dignity* (Oxford: Oxford University Press, 2013), p. 381.

project only reluctantly because they feared cementing the division of the country by founding a West German state. The population of the defeated, destroyed, and divided country showed little interest in the drafting of the constitution. Journalists and experts made unfavourable forecasts for the future of the Basic Law. Sixty-five years later, the Basic Law has become the most successful German constitution of all time. No German constitution has been longer in force than the Basic Law. None achieved a higher significance for the political process and for the societal order. None enjoyed a higher appreciation by the public. None was more frequently chosen as a role model for other countries which had freed themselves from dictatorial regimes and wanted to establish a democratic order.[8] All of this is summed up in the unusual combination of two words: *Verfassungspatriotismus* (constitutional patriotism).[9]

In hindsight, it is often said—especially during anniversaries of the Constitution—that the Basic Law has proven its value in practice. This appraisal is mostly connected with a comparison with the Weimar constitution, which is mostly regarded as a failed constitution. Judgements about the practical success of a constitution do not pertain only to the quality of the text. Although it is improbable that a 'bad' constitution can prove its value, it is not certain that a 'good' constitution will prove its value just because of its legal quality. The assessment that a constitution has proven its value in practice is a judgement about its impact and this is not only determined by the text. A basic requirement for impact is adherence to the constitution by relevant actors. For this to happen it is not sufficient that the organizational structure of the state corresponds with the constitutional provisions. It is also necessary that the various organs act in accordance with formal and substantive norms of the constitution. Several examples from the past and the present show that this cannot be taken for granted.

The value of a constitution furthermore depends on the challenges with which it is confronted and on the answers which are gleaned from the constitution as a reaction to these challenges. These answers are not independent of the text, but neither are they completely determined by it. The meaning of a constitutional norm in a concrete situation must be determined by interpreting the text. It must be possible to trace the result of this interpretation back to the text, but it is admissible to do so through long chains of reasoning. Such chains are increasingly necessary the more challenges appear which were not foreseen by the authors of the text and could not have been foreseen during the drafting of the provisions. The gap between the general and abstract formulation of legal norms on the one hand and the concrete situation, which has to be

---

[8] For the importance of German constitutional jurisprudence, see David Robertson, *The Judge as a Political Theorist* (Oxford: Oxford University Press, 2010).

[9] See Jan-Werner Müller, *Constitutional Patriotism* (Princeton: Princeton University Press, 2009); Dieter Grimm, 'Verfassungspatriotismus nach der Wiedervereinigung' in his *Die Verfassung und die Politik* (Munich: Beck, 2001), p. 107; Dieter Grimm, 'The Basic Law at 60 – Identity and Change' (2010) 11 *German Law Journal* 33 at 36, 45.

assessed with regards to legal norms, on the other, can only be bridged by way of interpretation. However, due to this gap, the interpretation of legal norms inevitably also means a partial creation of legal norms.

Legal interpretation is certainly no question of intuition. It is guided by a certain method. However, this method is not predetermined in a binding way. Even a provision that tried to prescribe a certain method would again be open to interpretation. Therefore, normative reference points for textual interpretation are possible, but not an authoritative determination of a certain method. There will always be competing methodological concepts. It may happen that the methodological dispute is more intense than a dispute about the meaning of constitutional provisions. Constitutional scholarship during the Weimar Republic offers illustrative material.[10] This phenomenon can be explained by the fact that a particular interpretative method does not constitute a neutral instrument for finding a predetermined meaning of the normative text. Interpretative methods rather have their own selectivity and thereby prejudice the results.[11] Therefore, the value of a constitution heavily depends on the question of who has the power to determine the 'correct' interpretation authoritatively and which method is used in doing so. In this respect, the decision for or against a constitutional adjudication is of crucial importance.

However, it would be wrong to believe that a constitutional court starts its work with a complete vision of the constitution and a canon of interpretive methods. Courts are bodies whose personnel change constantly and whose output depends on the cases which they get to decide. Their task is to decide cases and not to develop a constitutional or methodological theory. This does not mean that decisions are not guided by theory or method. On the contrary, theory and method ensure consistency of the interpretation of fundamental rights, even without a formal principle of *stare decisis* that exists in common law countries. But theoretical and methodological assumptions form the background knowledge for deciding a case rather than an independent element of a decision. They are also not formally determined. The dominant theoretical assumption and methodological practice of the case law of a court can only be ascertained in retrospect by looking at the entire jurisprudence.

## IV. THE STRUCTURE OF FUNDAMENTAL RIGHTS AND THE NECESSITY OF A THEORY

Theory and method play a larger role for the interpretation of fundamental rights than for the interpretation of the structural provisions of the constitution, of norms of the Civil Code, or of the Civil Procedure Code.[12] This is caused by

---

[10] See Michael Stolleis, *Geschichte des öffentlichen Rechts in Deutschland*, vol. 3 (Munich: Beck, 1999), p. 153.

[11] Cf. Dieter Grimm, 'Methode als Machtfaktor' in his *Recht und Staat der bürgerlichen Gesellschaft* (Frankfurt am Main: Suhrkamp, 1987), p. 347.

[12] See Ernst-Wolfgang Böckenförde, 'Grundrechtstheorie und Grundrechtsinterpretation' (1974) *Neue Juristische Wochenschrift* 1529.

the special character of fundamental rights, which differ from ordinary legal norms in a way which is highly relevant to their interpretation and application. Ordinary legal norms first describe certain factual conditions like situations, procedures, or conduct in a general and abstract way, and then mandate legal consequences whenever these factual conditions exist. The classic legal norm has an 'if–then' structure: it contains a condition and a consequence. Norms of this type can also be found on a constitutional level: if the Chancellor does not get a majority in a confidence vote in Parliament, the Federal President may dissolve the Bundestag.

Fundamental rights are different. They do not have the usual degree of concretization of typical legal norms. They do not have the usual 'if–then' structure. They are not based on the model of condition and consequence. The typical fundamental right provision declares a certain conduct (e.g. to express a particular opinion) or a certain state (e.g. physical integrity) or certain social institutions (e.g. media, science, arts) to be 'free'. At the same time, it empowers the legislature to limit this freedom. Thus, in contrast to other legal norms, fundamental rights do not determine the desired legal situation. They promise more than they can deliver. The extent of the freedom can only be ascertained by knowing the statutes which limit this freedom. Above that, even the determination of the potential scope of the freedom (disregarding statutory limitations) is highly dependent on an interpretation of the respective fundamental right because it only briefly names the object of constitutional protection. Most fundamental rights use just one word to describe their object: press, religion, art, profession, property. Therefore, the definition is left to the law enforcer. Moreover, in contrast to other legal norms, the clauses that empower the legislature to limit a fundamental right contain a very open wording. It is clear that every infringement of a fundamental right requires a statutory basis, but what the legislature may or may not do exactly is only vaguely described.

For these reasons, the application of fundamental rights demands not only a definition of the protected subject matter, the scope of the protection, and a definition of the essential content of the fundamental right which may not be touched at all. It also requires a determination of who is protected, against whom the protection takes effect, how far this protection reaches, how the protection takes effect, and what can be qualified as an infringement which triggers the protective mechanism of the fundamental right. Furthermore, the kinds of limitations permitted has to be determined. It is possible that answers to these questions are embodied in the constitutional text. But it is not necessarily so and only rarely does the text answer these questions completely. Therefore, compared to other legal norms, the application of fundamental rights is much more dependent on assumptions regarding their function and regarding the modes, extent, direction, and the intensity of their effect. The sum of all these assumptions, which certainly have to be compatible with the constitutional text, is usually called fundamental rights theory. Such a theory can be simple or sophisticated, coherent, or fragmentary. Nobody enacted it. Therefore, such a theory cannot be 'in force' in the same way as legal norms are 'in force'. Nevertheless, it guides the application of fundamental rights consciously or unconsciously, and it is highly relevant to their practical meaning.

To this discourse, Robert Alexy made a significant theoretical contribution.[13] He distinguishes between two types of norms: principles and rules. Contrary to a popular assumption, the difference between these two types is not constituted by the degree of generality and vagueness of the respective norm. Rather, he understands principles as optimization commands which can be fulfilled to a larger or lesser extent—dependent on what other norms and factual circumstances allow. In contrast, rules can only be fulfilled or not fulfilled. In case of a conflict between rules, it has to be decided which rule should be applied (by meta rules). If a rule is applicable, its command will have to be fulfilled exactly. In case of a conflict between principles, they can be balanced against each other in a way which allows both principles to have effect and to prevail in one case and stand back in another case. Fundamental rights are principles, not rules.

As shown earlier in the chapter, the Basic Law attached to fundamental rights provisions regarding the mode of their effect to a greater degree than older constitutions. The intention was to exclude previous practice guided by a certain theory, such as the assumption that fundamental rights rank below statute law. Nevertheless, the Basic Law does not answer all questions which arise concerning the application of fundamental rights. On a theoretical level, answers to these questions must be delivered by legal scholarship, which can offer practitioners ideas formed independently of individual cases and without decision-making constraints which bind practitioners. On a practical level, the answers must be given by the competent constitutional bodies—in many systems the constitutional court. The answers to the questions which were left open by the Basic Law and which were answered by the Federal Constitutional Court over time have formed a remarkable structure. They have made German doctrine one of the leading fundamental rights concepts in the world. Only the United States (US)—with its significantly older constitutional jurisprudence—is largely unaffected by postwar German fundamental rights theory.

## V. THE DEVELOPMENT OF FUNDAMENTAL RIGHTS IN THE CASE LAW

The Federal Constitutional Court reached its main assumptions relatively early in its history and has strictly adhered to them. In determining whether a fundamental right is violated, the court has used a two tier-approach suggested by the structure of fundamental rights and now practised in many countries. At first, it has to be determined whether a fundamental right has been infringed by state action, which requires an assessment of whether the private conduct that was affected by the state falls within the scope of a fundamental right and whether the state action qualifies as an infringement. In the second step, the court will

---

[13] Robert Alexy, *A Theory of Constitutional Rights* (Oxford: Oxford University Press, 2010), p. 44.

determine whether this infringement can be justified, that is, whether it complies with the limitation clauses of the constitution.

## 1. Wide Scope of Protection

From the start, the court has interpreted the scope of protection of individual fundamental rights generously because the effect of the protection mechanism as a whole is dependent on this definition: everything that does not fall into the scope of a fundamental right does not enjoy constitutional protection. However, the court did not have any problems in interpreting the scope broadly because the determination that a conduct falls within the scope of a fundamental right does not resolve the question whether or not this conduct is permissible. This question is answered in the second step of the constitutional analysis where one has to examine whether the governmental measure can be justified from a constitutional point of view. This can be demonstrated by a quick cross-check: German constitutional scholars and the Constitutional Court regard the 'inviolability' of human dignity as mandating that there may be no infringement of human dignity at all. Every infringement of human dignity amounts to a violation. Under these circumstances, the court has no other option than to define the scope of protection of human dignity very narrowly and to refer all other questions to more concrete fundamental rights.

## 2. Wide Definition of Infringement

The court also adopted a wide interpretation of 'infringement'. The reason follows the same logic: if a state action cannot be deemed to be an 'infringement', examination as to whether it violates the fundamental right is barred. In the beginning, an infringement was defined as a state act that leads to an immediate impairment of the good which is protected by the respective fundamental right and does so in an imperative and intentional way in the form of law. Over time, all these requirements have been softened. Today, infringements are defined as encompassing all state actions which preclude or substantially impede the use of a fundamental right. Therefore, infringements can also include non-imperative measures, unintended consequences of state action, state action that is not framed in legal terms (*Realakte*), and indirect impairments of fundamental rights. Recently, official warnings and recommendations have also been deemed an impairment of a fundamental right.[14] In this way, the interpretation of fundamental rights is adapted to a changing field of state action and to an extended range of welfare state activities.

---

[14] *BVerfGE* 105, 252, and 279 (2002) [English excerpts in *Decisions of the Bundesverfassungsgericht – Federal Constitutional Court – Federal Republic of Germany*, vol. 4, (Baden-Baden: Nomos, 2007), pp. 355 ff.; English summary: Kommers and Miller (n. 1), p. 554].

## 3. Proportionality

The decision in fundamental rights cases ultimately depends on the question whether the examined state measure is constitutional, that is whether the infringement of respective fundamental right is justified. To solve this question, some constitutions, such as Canada and South Africa, put forward a rule that extends to all fundamental rights, that only those measures are justified which are necessary in a free and democratic society. The Basic Law contains a few provisions which apply to all fundamental rights, like the prohibition to infringe upon the essential content of a fundamental right. In addition, the Basic Law has provisions that only apply to particular fundamental rights. Some fundamental rights do not possess any specific limitation clauses at all. For some fundamental rights, the constitutional text simply provides that this right may only be limited by a statute or on the basis of a statute without specifying any requirements for the content of such a statute. This group of fundamental rights encompasses such important rights as the right to life and physical integrity in Art. 2, s.2. If the constitutional text were the only criterion, the protection of these fundamental rights would be relatively weak although—thanks to the existence of Art.19, s.2—it would be stronger than under previous constitutions. The legislature would be able to infringe fundamental rights until it reaches the limit of their essential content.

In contrast to that, the Federal Constitutional Court in its early rulings started to establish additional limits to the limitation of fundamental rights— the so-called *Schranken-Schranken* (limits to limitations). For this purpose, the Court added the unwritten condition that only proportionate limitations of fundamental rights were compatible with the Basic Law. In order to examine the proportionality of a measure, the Court developed a four-step test. In the first step, the purpose of the statutory limitation of the fundamental right must be ascertained, and it must be examined whether this purpose is compatible with the Basic Law. A purpose which is constitutionally prohibited cannot justify an infringement of a fundamental right. The next two steps deal with the relation between means and ends. At first, it has to be examined whether the statutory means is suitable to reach the statutory purpose. Unsuitable means cannot justify an infringement of a fundamental right. Afterwards, it will be examined whether the means are necessary to reach the purpose. If less intrusive means are available to reach the statutory purpose in the same way, the measure will be deemed to be an unnecessary infringement of a fundamental right and therefore unconstitutional. In the last step, the test is detached from the means–end relationship. Here, it will be examined whether the infringement is proportionate in a narrow sense: do the benefits of the infringement for a legally protected good or interest outweigh the disadvantages for the infringed fundamental right?

This test was developed in the last quarter of the nineteenth century by the Higher Administrative Court of Prussia to examine measures by the police in cases where the police had been given discretion with only weak legal constraints. The Federal Constitutional Court elevated the proportionality test to the constitutional level and applied it to legislation. This started in an unspectacular way by an assertion of the Court that statutes had to be proportional and only gradually developed into the doctrinal construction that has just been described.[15] This might explain why the Federal Constitutional Court did not specify how the proportionality principle was derived from the Basic Law. Only after scholarly criticism did it specify the constitutional foundation: the rule of law or the fundamental rights as such. But again, it did not specify how the proportionality principle was derived from these provisions.

Today, the principle of proportionality has extremely high significance. It bears the main burden of the protection of fundamental rights in Germany. When the Federal Constitutional Court strikes down a statute, the reason will mostly be a violation of the proportionality principle. To the same extent, the discretion of the legislature has been decreasing. Because of the proportionality principle, the legislature has much less leeway than before and the test has been adopted almost worldwide, again with the exception of the US.[16]

### 4. Comprehensive Protection of Individual Freedom

While the proportionality principle intensified the protection of fundamental rights, the next step entailed a broadening of the scope of the protection. Like earlier constitutions, the Basic Law does not give a general guarantee of freedom. Rather, it guarantees freedom for certain areas of life or certain kinds of conduct. Usually, these are areas which have traditionally been the object of governmental oppression and which are still susceptible to governmental misuse of power, although it is agreed today that they should be left to the responsibility of citizens or of societal processes. With some exceptions (e.g. the Brazilian constitution contains more than one hundred fundamental rights), there are only a few areas which are awarded the special protection by fundamental rights. Fundamental rights are specific guarantees and relate to areas which are particularly significant for the development of someone's personality and for the societal preconditions for this development.

The Federal Constitutional Court was confronted with the question of the scope of fundamental rights protection in a case regarding the freedom to leave the Federal Republic of Germany. In this case, a former politician of the Christian Democratic Union (CDU) named Elfes, who later harshly criticized the CDU-led federal government on trips abroad (especially in Eastern Europe),

---

[15] The proportionality principle was first mentioned by the Federal Constitutional Court in *BVerfGE* 3, 383 (1954); it was consolidated in *BVerfGE* 7, 377 (1958); 13, 97 (1961); 16, 194 (1963); 19, 342 (1965). Since then it has been used constantly by the court.

[16] See Aharon Barak, *Proportionality* (Cambridge: Cambridge University Press, 2012); Alec Stone Sweet and Jud Mathews, 'Proportionality Balancing and Global Constitutionalism' (2008) 47 *Columbia Journal of Transnational Law* 73; Dieter Grimm, 'Proportionality in Canadian and German Constitutional Jurisprudence' (2007) 57 *University of Toronto Law Journal* 383; Moshe Cohen-Eliya and Iddo Porat, 'American Balancing and German Proportionality: The Historical Origins' (2010) 8 *International Journal of Constitutional Law* 263.

was denied a passport. This raised the question whether Elfes's desire to travel abroad was protected by fundamental rights. Although the Basic Law contains an explicit right to move freely throughout the federal territory, it does not contain a similar right to leave the territory. However, the Court found a way out of this situation by invoking the fundamental right to free development of one's personality (Art. 2, s. 1 GG). According to the Court's interpretation, Art. 2, s. 1 GG protects every possible kind of human conduct which is not protected by special fundamental rights.[17] Consequently, fundamental rights protection no longer contains gaps. Every restriction of the conduct of an individual by the state triggers fundamental rights protection and can therefore be appealed against to the Federal Constitutional Court. It is a different question whether such an extension of the scope of fundamental rights is consistent with their meaning.[18] Despite disagreement, the court has adhered to this extension.

### 5. Fundamental Rights as Values

The next step was the most significant step that the Federal Constitutional Court has ever made. It happened one year after the *Elfes* case. The chairman of the Press Club of Hamburg and prominent advocate of German-Jewish reconciliation, Mr. Erich Lüth, had called for a boycott of the first postwar movie by Mr. Veit Harlan, who had been the favoured director of the Nazis. The affected movie companies therefore sued Lüth in the civil courts, demanding a retraction of the call for boycott. The courts decided against Lüth. They based their decision on s. 826 of the German Civil Code which establishes that a person who, immorally or in a manner contrary to public policy, intentionally inflicts damage on another person is liable to the other person to make compensation for the damage. At that time, it was generally agreed among civil law practitioners and scholars that boycott calls fall under that provision. But Lüth filed a constitutional complaint and asserted that the decisions of the civil courts had violated his right of free speech enshrined in Art. 5, s. 1 GG. Lüth had already made this point during litigation in civil courts, but these courts had stated that fundamental rights could only be applied in the relationship between the state and its citizens, and not in lawsuits between two private parties. Again, this statement was in line with the prevailing opinion regarding the effect of fundamental rights at the time. Fundamental rights, on that view, were subjective rights or entitlements of the individual that applied only vertically, not horizontally, and they had only negative and not positive effect.

Lüth challenged the point that they had only vertical application. In fact, Art. 1, s. 3 GG provides that fundamental rights bind all state powers—but only state power, not individuals. Fundamental rights lead to an asymmetric legal relationship. They give rights to individuals, and they bind the state. They form

---

[17] *BVerfGE* 6, 32 (1957) [English excerpts in Kommers and Miller (n. 1), p. 401].

[18] Cf. my dissenting opinion in the case 'Reiten im Walde', *BVerfGE* 80, 137 (1989) [English summary in Kommers and Miller (n. 1), p. 404].

restrictions on state conduct, and give individuals a remedy against such conduct. Courts are certainly part of state power. But the question whether courts may apply fundamental rights to the relationship between private parties rests upon the previous question whether fundamental rights have any significance for this relationship at all. At the time of the *Lüth* decision, there were only a few voices in legal scholarship who advocated an application of fundamental rights between private parties as well due to the increased significance of fundamental rights since 1949. And also some courts had sporadically applied fundamental rights in lawsuits between private parties—for example, the equality right of Art. 3, s. 1 GG in labour law.

In deciding this question for the first time in the *Lüth* case, the Federal Constitutional Court conducted a thorough examination of the character of fundamental rights in order to derive a solution of the case from this angle.[19] It started uncontroversially by stating that in the first place fundamental rights are subjective rights of the individual against the state. But it then continued to say that this function was not the only one and that fundamental rights are also a legal expression of values which society has deemed to be material to the political and social order and as such are objective legal principles of the highest rank. In this capacity as objective principles, fundamental rights are not limited to the citizen–state relationship. They permeate the whole legal order and do not stop short of penetrating private law.

Due to the explicit provision in the Basic Law that fundamental rights are directed against the state, the Federal Constitutional Court felt barred from establishing a direct effect of fundamental rights among private parties. Their relationship would still be governed by norms of private law—which of course had to be constitutional. But also in private law and thus between private parties, the objective values that are expressed in the Basic Law's fundamental rights take effect. According to the Court, provisions of private law have to be interpreted 'in the light' of the respective fundamental right if the application of private law has restrictive effect on a fundamental right—like in the *Lüth* case. The fundamental right 'radiates' to private law. This effect is reached by a special form of interpretation of ambiguous or open provisions of private law. In interpreting such a provision, the significance of the respective fundamental right has to be balanced against the significance of the legal good that the provision seeks to protect with regards to the concrete case at hand. In the *Lüth* case, the open private law provision that was amenable to interpretation was the word *sittenwidrig* (against public policy/immoral) in s. 826 of the German Civil Code. In this case, the Court decided that, because Lüth's call for boycott did not pursue selfish interests and addressed a question with high public

[19] *BVerfGE* 7, 198 (1958) [English excerpts in *Decisions of the Bundesverfassungsgericht – Federal Constitutional Court – Federal Republic of Germany*, vol. 2/part 1, (Baden-Baden: Nomos, 1998), 1; Kommers and Miller (n. 1), 442]. Regarding the significance of the *Lüth* decision, see Thomas Henne and Arne Riedlinger (eds), *Das Lüth-Urteil aus (rechts-)historischer Sicht* (Berlin: Berliner Wissenschafts-Verlag, 2005); Peter Quint, 'Free Speech and Private Law in German Constitutional Theory' (1989) 48 *Maryland Law Review* 247.

significance, freedom of speech outweighed the economic interests of the film companies that s. 826 of the German Civil Code sought to protect. Thus, the call for boycott could not be qualified as against public policy. Of course, this question could be decided differently in other cases.[20]

The *Lüth* case revolutionized the understanding of fundamental rights in several respects. Before *Lüth*, fundamental rights were only understood as subjective rights against the state; now, they are also regarded as objective principles. Furthermore, fundamental rights now have not only vertical effect (directed against the state), but also horizontal effect (within society). But this horizontal effect is not direct, only indirect by way of interpretation of private law in the light of fundamental rights. Within a short time this 'radiation' of fundamental rights to private law was extended to the whole body of statutory law. Whenever a statute with a restrictive effect on a fundamental right has to be interpreted, the respective fundamental right has to be taken into consideration. This jurisprudence had a particularly significant effect because the German codes (the Civil Code, the Commercial Code, the Penal Code, and the Civil Procedure Code) predate democracy. In the same way that these codes were influenced by fundamental rights, the whole German jurisprudence came under the control of the Federal Constitutional Court, at least as far as the influence of fundamental rights on statute law could reach. This entailed a modernization of the whole legal order without legislative amendments. Such explicit amendments of course also occurred later.

## 6. Fundamental Rights as a Basis for Claims

The open question after *Lüth* was whether fundamental rights in their capacity as objective values could go beyond the traditional 'negative' effect of defending citizens against state action and become the basis for 'positive' claims against the state. The *Lüth* case did not require a statement regarding this question because the fundamental right was used in its defensive function. Since Lüth wanted to defend himself against an infringement of his freedom of speech by civil courts, it was enough to state that civil courts had to take fundamental rights into consideration in private law matters if their decision led to a restriction of a fundamental right. However, since the 'numerus clausus' case of the Federal Constitutional Court, it has been recognized that the objective dimension of fundamental rights can also lead to positive obligations of the state.[21] The background of this case was the introduction of the 'numerus clausus' at German universities which had entailed a temporary rejection rate of around 50 per cent of applicants at the faculties of medicine. Fundamental rights in their defensive function would not have helped in this situation. Even if the court had set aside the rejection due to its violation of fundamental rights, this would not

---

[20] Cf. a case decided on the same day and concerning the same kind of fundamental rights collision: *BVerfGE* 7, 230.

[21] *BVerGE* 33, 303 (1972) [English excerpts in Kommers and Miller (n. 1), p. 679].

have given the applicant a place at the respective medical school. Therefore, the court determined that fundamental rights could also entail positive obligations. On the one hand, the court made clear that the state also has a responsibility for the preconditions of the use of fundamental rights as far as they are within its power. On the other hand, the court stressed that this principle may not lead to maximum demands.

## 7. Duties to Protect

The most far-reaching consequence from the objective dimension of fundamental rights was drawn in the abortion case of 1975 regarding the reform of s. 218 of the German Penal Code. According to this provision, abortions should be allowed in the first three months of pregnancy. From a legal point of view, it was widely agreed that the right to life in Art. 2, s. 2 GG also extended to the foetus. However, with a merely 'negative' understanding of fundamental rights, the reform of abortion law would not have created any problems: the state did not intend to perform abortions or compel anybody to do so. The state only declared abortions by private individuals within the first three months no longer punishable. With this reasoning, the Austrian Constitutional Court had decided that a reform of Austrian criminal law similar to the German reform was constitutional.[22] The Court argued that the fundamental rights of the Austrian constitution originated in 1867 and that at that time fundamental rights had only been understood as defensive rights against the state. Thus, according to the reasoning of the Austrian court, the reform did not infringe the right to life because the state did not take away someone's life.

In contrast to that ruling, the Federal Constitutional Court referred to the concept that fundamental rights not only operate in a defensive way, but also form objective principles.[23] From that, the Court drew the conclusion that the state must do more than just respect the values that are guaranteed by fundamental rights: it has to protect these values against third parties.[24] The authors of the Basic Law explicitly imposed this duty on the state only with respect to human dignity, as the highest of all principles, but not regarding the following fundamental rights. However, the Court gleaned such a duty from Art. 2, s. 2 GG as well, which was read in connection with Art.1, s. 1 GG. In its judgment, the Federal Constitutional Court also prescribed the means by which the legislature had to protect unborn life: Due to the special role of the right to life as the basis of all other fundamental rights, it has to be protected by the strongest means available: through criminal law.

---

[22] Österreichischer Verfassungsgerichtshof, VfSlg. 7400 (1974).

[23] *BVerfGE* 39, 1 (1975) [English excerpts in Kommers and Miller (n. 1), p. 374]; Gerald Neuman, '*Casey* in the Mirror: Abortion, Abuse and the Right to Protection in the United States and in Germany' (1995) 43 *American Journal of Comparative Law* 273.

[24] See Dieter Grimm, 'The Protective Function of the State' in Georg Nolte (ed.), *European and US Constitutionalism* (Cambridge: Cambridge University Press, 2005), p. 137.

Among the justices, there was no disagreement regarding the duty to protect as such. Similarly, this duty was praised by legal scholars in the immediate aftermath of the decision. However, the determination of a specific means of protection by the Court drew heavy criticism inside and outside the Court. It was argued that fundamental rights in their capacity as duties to protect could be fulfilled in more than one constitutionally acceptable way. The choice between these options should therefore be left to the political process. Partly due to this criticism, the Court deviated from this decision in the second abortion case.[25] Today, the legislature is free to choose any means that is suitable and appropriate—with regards to the significance of the fundamental right and to the degree and probability of the threat to this right. These words are reminiscent of the proportionality principle. In fact, in addition to the proportionality principle which prohibits an overreaction by the state, there is now a principle against 'underreaction' by the state regarding the fulfillment of duties to protect. A statute is not only unconstitutional when it goes too far in limiting a fundamental right, but also when it does too little in order to protect a fundamental right. The space between these two ends of the scale is the leeway for political preferences.

The abortion decision was triggered by the abolition of a long-standing criminal law protection of the foetus. But the further development showed that not the abolition of existing laws but legislative inactivity became the main target of the duty to protect. The concept is applied when the legislature does not provide sufficient protection against threats to a fundamental right which emanate from private actors. This is especially the case regarding risks created by scientific or technical advances and their commercial use. The promoters of these advances—researchers and commercial companies alike—usually fight against state regulation in these areas and put forward their own fundamental rights as arguments against such regulation. Their practical influence normally outweighs the influence of those groups who are affected by these risks. In particular, parliaments often back down when it is argued that more regulation would lead to competitive disadvantages of the country as a whole. In such cases, inactivity by the state is not a sign of neutrality, but for partiality in favour of the fundamental rights of those who cause the risks. That is the problem which the concept of the duty to protect seeks to solve. An example is the use of nuclear power. The Federal Constitutional Court demanded that the legislature established a degree of risk prevention which corresponded to the degree and the probability of potential harm.[26]

Even before the duty to protect was born in the first abortion decision, the Federal Constitutional Court had decided that fundamental rights such as the freedom of the press or the freedom of broadcasting not only protect the people in the media sector, but also the freedom of the media as such. This was again based on the idea of fundamental rights as objective principles. In this function,

---

[25] *BVerfGE* 88, 203 (1993) [English excerpts in Kommers and Miller (n. 1), p. 387].

[26] *BVerfGE* 49, 89 (1978) [English excerpts in Kommers and Miller (n. 1), p. 177].

they guarantee a media system which has the chance to be guided only by its own journalistic standards and not be instrumentalized for external purposes.[27] This kind of freedom can be threatened not only from outside, but also from inside—by owners, publishers, journalists. As a consequence, conflicts between the objective guarantee of a free media system and the subjective dimension of the same fundamental right may arise. In such cases, the objective freedom of the media can justify limitations of the subjective freedom of people inside the media system. This mechanism was originally regarded as part of the institutional dimension of fundamental rights protection. Today, it would be seen as a case of the duty to protect. The duty may thus lead to more limitations of fundamental rights. But these limitations are only justified if they enhance the overall freedom of the system.

However, the duty to protect should not be confused with horizontal application of fundamental rights. The concept does not change the fact that only the state is bound by fundamental rights. But the state fulfills this duty not only by refraining from infringing a fundamental right. This was only sufficient as along as dangers to the protected freedoms were just expected from the state. Meanwhile, it is evident that these freedoms can be endangered also and sometimes even more severely by societal actors. Only the state can prevent these dangers effectively. Therefore, fundamental rights demand activity and not merely inactivity of the state. The state assumes a double role: on the one hand, state power is still a potential danger to the protected freedoms and has to be limited by the negative dimension of fundamental rights, and on the other, only the state can protect society against fundamental rights violations by third parties. The positive dimension of fundamental rights requires this protection. Thus, the state is at the same time friend and foe of fundamental rights.

The dangers to protected freedoms that emanate from private parties are mostly the result of conduct which is itself protected by fundamental rights, like the freedom of scientific inquiry or occupational freedom. Therefore, the fight against such dangers is not possible without infringing the fundamental rights of those who cause these dangers. The duty to protect may thus lead to greater rather than fewer limitations of fundamental rights. But these limitations are only justifiable if they enhance the overall freedom within society. There are fundamental rights on both sides. Since they do not have a hierarchical order, they have to be balanced against each other. In this way, balancing, which the development of the proportionality principle has already given an important role in deciding cases of infringements of fundamental rights, has become the most important means for solving conflicts of fundamental rights.

---

[27] Cf. *BVerfGE* 20, 162 (1966) [English excerpts in *Decisions of the Federal Constitutional Court* (n. 19), p. 71; Kommers and Miller (n. 1), p. 503]; also the series of judgments regarding the organization of German television: *BVerfGE* 12, 205 (1961); 31, 314 (1971); 57, 295 (1981); 73, 118 (1986); 74, 297 (1987); 83, 238 (1991); 90, 60 (1994); 97, 228 (1998); 119, 181 (2007) [For English excerpts of the first and third broadcasting cases as well as summaries of other broadcasting cases see Kommers and Miller (n. 1), p. 510; for a long extract from the grounds, see *Decisions of the Federal Constitutional Court* (n. 19), p. 31].

An understanding of fundamental rights in the aforementioned way clearly requires a balancing process because only in this way can it be determined which of the abstractly equally important fundamental rights prevails in the concrete case.

### 8. Fundamental Rights Protection through Organization and Procedure

Due to the ever-changing tasks of the state, the traditional means of protection of fundamental rights no longer suffices. This particularly applies to state activities that serve planning and development functions or risk prevention. The traditional duties of the state to restore public order after an incident were retroactive and targeted at concrete cases. They could therefore be regulated in detail relatively easily. In contrast, the new activities are prospective and comprehensive. They are open to future developments, dependent on changing situations and on different resources. Thus, they cannot be regulated in the traditional if–then mode. Rather, this mode of regulation is substituted by the definition of aims: legal norms prescribe certain aims which the administration should pursue and define certain points which have to be taken into consideration on the way. Within this wide margin of discretion, administrative agencies decide upon their actions independently step by step.

Therefore, it is not enough to protect the individual who is affected by a state measure only by allowing him to appeal against the final results of administrative decision-making (e.g. against the already-built airport, the completed nuclear power plant, etc.). This would bar him from appealing against important interim decisions, although it is often impossible to undo the results of such decisions. This would leave him without an effective remedy. Hence, the Federal Constitutional Court decided that in such cases fundamental rights protection has to start earlier in order to be efficient.[28] This led to the concept of 'fundamental rights protection through procedure'. Not only does the result of an administrative procedure have to be in accordance with fundamental rights, the procedure leading to the results already has to be designed in a way that ensures that fundamental rights can be asserted effectively, for example by including the affected people in the procedure, by giving them information and petition rights. Similarly, in complex institutions like universities or public broadcasting stations, the organization has to be designed in a way that respects fundamental rights. Thus, in addition to 'fundamental rights protection through procedure', the concept of 'fundamental rights protection through organization' emerged.[29]

---

[28] *BVerfGE* 53, 30 (1979) [For a short English summary see Kommers and Miller (n. 1), p. 177].

[29] Cf. the judgments mentioned in n. 20 regarding the organization of German TV stations and *BVerfGE* 35, 79 (1973) [English excerpts in Kommers and Miller (n. 1), p. 531] concerning scientific freedom.

## 9. Interpretation of Particular Fundamental Rights

All interpretative innovations mentioned earlier, which adapted fundamental rights to changing conditions for the realization of freedom, pertain to all fundamental rights. This chapter has not touched upon the development of the interpretation of particular fundamental rights. However, for each fundamental right, one could write a similar analysis to describe the development of its interpretation. In this respect, an examination of the development of the right to free development of the personality in Art. 2, s. 1 GG would be particularly fruitful. In several cases, the Federal Constitutional Court has used this right to extend the scope of fundamental rights protection to areas which are similarly important to the development of the personality of an individual or to the freedom of the social order as those areas which are mentioned explicitly in the catalogue of fundamental rights. In particular, the Court developed a protection of privacy. It found a particularly important expression in two rights which were formally seen as a concretization of Art. 2, s. 1 GG but which are in fact new fundamental rights for matters still unknown when the Basic Law was written: a data protection right called 'right to informational self-determination', and a 'right to confidentiality and integrity of electronic communication systems'.[30] But this will not be examined further here.

### VI. METHOD OF INTERPRETATION OF FUNDAMENTAL RIGHTS

The difference between previous German constitutional orders and the Basic Law is thus evident: presently, fundamental rights are omnipresent in the legal order and in the political and social life of Germany. This would have been impossible but for the Federal Constitutional Court. It would also have been impossible if the Court had continued to use the interpretative methods of earlier times. In this regard, the differences are also significant. Legal positivism, which had dominated jurisprudence and legal scholarship during the Second German Empire and also during the Weimar Republic (although more challenged), did not have many supporters after the experiences with the Nazi regime. Although answers to constitutional questions are still searched for in the constitutional text, the Federal Constitutional Court stated from the beginning that no provision can be interpreted in isolation. Each provision has to be interpreted in the light of the whole constitution. Furthermore, the concept of constitutional provisions as an expression of values is far removed from a literal interpretation of the constitution. With such a concept, the goal of constitutional interpretation is to give the greatest possible effect to these values and to the function which constitutional norms are supposed to play in society under changing conditions.

---

[30] *BVerfGE* 65, 1 (1983) [English excerpts in Kommers and Miller (n. 1), p. 408]; *BVerfGE* 120, 274 (2008) [English summary in Kommers and Miller (n. 1), p. 417].

Such a duty cannot be fulfilled without looking at reality. Therefore, in addition to the reference to values, the reference to reality is a special trait of German constitutional interpretation. It compels courts to analyse reality and be open to insights from cognate disciplines. Due to the fact that social reality as the object of constitutional regulation is changing constantly, constitutional interpretation must be able to deal with these changes in order to preserve its social relevance. For this reason, the Federal Constitutional Court examines regularly whether reality has changed in the area which a legal norm seeks to regulate. It examines whether the effect of this norm is diminished or endangered unless the norm is interpretatively adapted to the new situation. Often this requires an assessment of the consequences of different interpretations for the implementation of the purpose of a norm. Consequently, constitutional jurisprudence regularly takes factual consequences into consideration—guided by the norm which the court has to interpret.[31] In this way, constitutional jurisprudence succeeds in keeping the constitution up to date and ensures that its relevance could be experienced on a daily basis. Thereby, it also strengthens the authority of the Federal Constitutional Court and its high degree of acceptance in the general public. This explains the high readiness of German politics to follow the decisions of the Federal Constitutional Court.

---

[31] Dieter Grimm, 'Entscheidungsfolgen als Rechtsgründe: Zur Argumentationspraxis des deutschen Bundesverfassungsgerichts' in G. Teubner (ed.), *Entscheidungsfolgen als Rechtsgründe* (Baden-Baden: Nomos, 1995), p. 139.

## ⤳ 8 ⤲

# Return to the Traditional Understanding
# of Fundamental Rights?

## I. THE SITUATION

In German postwar basic rights doctrine, the discovery of the principle of proportionality and the development of the objective dimension to basic rights
proved to be the innovations with the most far-reaching consequences. However,
while the principle of proportionality acts within the context of the familiar
defensive protection of basic rights and decisively strengthens the defensive
force of basic rights to ward off state infringements on freedom, understanding basic rights in terms of objective principles opens up entirely new fields of
application. This interpretation of basic rights gradually led to: their extension
to civil law through so-called horizontal effect; inherent benefit entitlements or
participatory rights against the state; obligations of the state to actively protect
liberties secured by basic rights; procedural guarantees for decision-making processes that can result in an infringement of basic rights; and organizational principles for public and private institutions in which persons exercise basic rights.[1]
Further steps could follow. As a result, basic rights have been disconnected from
a one-sided state orientation and rendered relevant for the social order as well,
and they have also been freed from an exclusively defensive function, becoming
a basis for the state's obligations to take action.

It would, however, be erroneous to expect that the negative and the positive
components of basic rights could be aggregated without problems. In fact, the
state's duty to protect a constitutionally guaranteed liberty can generally only
be accomplished by curtailing other liberties or the liberty of other bearers of
rights. The mandates for state action derived from basic rights therefore increase
the number of infringements of basic rights and seemingly lead to an attenua-
tion of their defensive strength. While an exclusively defensive understanding
of basic rights contributes to a stabilization of the social status quo, an assertive
understanding of basic rights promotes change. It is therefore not surprising

---

[1] The leading cases of the German Federal Constitutional Court are: 7 *BVerfGE* 198 (1958) on the third-
party effect (*Drittwirkung*) of fundamental rights; 33 *BVerfGE* 303 (1972) on service- and participation-rights
(*Leistungs- und Teilhaberechte*); 39 *BVerfGE* (1975) on duties to protect (*Schutzpflichten*); 53 *BVerfGE* 30 (1979)
on procedural guarantees (*Verfahrensgarantien*); and 57 *BVerfGE* 295 (1981) on organizational principles
(*Organisationsprinzipien*). [Excerpts in English in Donald P. Kommers and Russell A. Miller, *The Constitutional
Jurisprudence of the Federal Republic of Germany* (Durham, NC: Duke University Press, 3rd edn, 2012.]

Constitutionalism: Past, Present, and Future. First Edition. Dieter Grimm. © Dieter Grimm 2016. Published 2016 by
Oxford University Press.

that the principle of proportionality has established itself as an enhancement of the traditional defensive function without resistance and is practised virtually unchallenged, whereas the interpretation of basic rights as duties to protect has remained controversial and, particularly in recent years, has been under increasing criticism.[2] As in the past, this criticism is based primarily on methodological concerns. The critics blame the conception of basic rights as objective principles for the arbitrary nature of the interpretation and associated loss of rationality in the application of law, and additionally see it as one of the most important causes for the usurpation of political competences by the judiciary, in particular the Federal Constitutional Court.

But there are differences between the older and the younger generation of critics. When examined closely, the methodological objections of the older generation often turn out to be motivated by reservations against an understanding of freedom rights in the light of the social state principle of the Basic Law, which indeed depends on the objective dimension of fundamental rights. Limiting basic rights to defensive protection, which they demanded in the name of the rationality of the application of law, aimed in actuality at protecting certain bourgeois interests. This motive does not seem to play a role for the majority of today's critics. Rather, the social-state objectives of the expanded understanding of basic rights are largely accepted. However, the means of interpreting basic rights as objective principles seems too costly in terms of democracy and legal certainty. Therefore, today as in the past, solemn warnings are sounded which seek to resile from the objective and assertive understanding of basic rights and to limit these to their function as subjective and negative rights. The aim should be to defend individuals against state infringements on liberty, and some critics claim that the problems of freedom within the modern welfare state can be resolved using the traditional doctrine. A paper by Schlink that expressly advocates this path is tellingly entitled 'Freedom through defence against infringement—reconstructing the classical function of basic rights'.[3]

In order to justify the demand that basic rights be applied only defensively, it of course does not matter whether their classical function is thereby restored. But honouring it with this distinction serves to make this position more convincing. It is therefore worth asking whether the defence against infringement is in fact the classical function of basic rights. Even if that is the case, one must assume that there are identifiable social causes for the extension of the function

---

[2] See B. Schlink, 'Freiheit durch Eingriffsabwehr—Rekonstruktion der klassischen Grundrechtsfunktion' (1984) *Europäische Grundrechte-Zeitschrift* 457; B. Schlink, *Abwägung im Verfassungsrecht* (Berlin: Duncker & Humblot, 1976). See further M. Degen, *Pressefreiheit, Berufsfreiheit, Eigentumsgarantie* (Berlin: Duncker & Humblot, 1981); G. Haverkate, *Rechtsfragen des Leistungsstaats* (Tübingen: Mohr, 1983); J. Schwabe, *Probleme der Grundrechtsdogmatik* (Darmstadt: Schadel, 1977). The earlier critical line is penned by Forsthoff in several essays from the early sixties, reproduced in E. Forsthoff, *Rechtsstaat im Wandel* (Munich: Beck, 2nd edn, 1976), esp. chs 3, 5; though see also H. Klein, *Die Grundrechte im demokratischen Staat* (Stuttgart: Kohlhammer, 1974). For a critical examination of Schlink's view see K.-H. Ladeur, 'Klasische Grundrechtsfunktion und "postmoderne" Grundrechtstheorie' (1986) *Kritische Justiz* 197.

[3] B. Schlink (n. 2).

of basic rights. Only when these are known does it become possible to assess the justification for this extension. Likewise threatened losses are revealed if the new functions of basic rights were to be surrendered. Such losses are, of course, not inevitable as problems can usually be solved in more than one way. Consequently, it is necessary to examine the assertion that the dangers to freedom that led to the understanding of basic rights as objective principles can also be mastered using the conventional negative doctrine without the losses in certainty and rationality to which the critics object. If this should prove not to be the case, the question arises as to whether solutions are conceivable that meet the rationality criterion of constitutional interpretation, without thereby leaving urgent liberty problems unaddressed with respect to basic rights.

## II. DEFENCE AGAINST INFRINGEMENT AS THE CLASSICAL FUNCTION OF BASIC RIGHTS?

In the modern understanding, basic rights are a product of the American Revolution.[4] They provided the American colonists' response to the characteristic deficit of English rights of liberty, which were only anchored on the level of ordinary law and therefore offered no protection against restrictions on freedom authorized by Parliament. The latter were considered self-imposed restrictions on the part of the holders of liberty, and as such could not constitute a violation of law. However, the American colonists complained that an English right—no taxation without representation—was violated through a tax burden imposed on them by the British Parliament in which they were not represented. When the Parliament refused to yield, they saw themselves compelled to break with the mother country and, citing natural law, to constitute their own state power. In the course of constitution-making the English rights of liberty that obtained in the colonies were elevated, largely unchanged, to constitutional status and, in light of their experience with the British Parliament, placed above legislative authority. Their juridical significance lay in the fact that they shielded a social order that was already freedom-oriented and liberal against state interventions of the kind previously experienced, by granting those affected a right to injunctive relief asserted through litigation. So the history of their emergence in their country of origin supports defence against infringement as the original function of basic rights.

This picture shifts the moment one looks to the European nation of origin of basic rights, namely France. The French Revolution resembled the American Revolution in that it overthrew the traditional state power by revolutionary means and established a new order on the basis of a written constitution that defined the legitimating conditions for political rule and both established and limited its power. But the two revolutions differed in their starting points and

[4] On the historical functions of basic rights see Ch. 3 of this volume. See further, Dieter Grimm, 'Grundrechte und Privatrecht in der bürgerlichen Sozialordnung' in his *Recht und Staat der bürgerlichen Gesellschaft* (Frankfurt am Main: Suhrkamp, 1987), p. 192.

their objectives. Whereas the American colonies already enjoyed a largely free and liberal social order in the eighteenth century which the mother country had infringed only in a specific instance, the French social order was not characterized by freedom and equality, but by duties and bonds, estate boundaries and privileges. Consequently, it was sufficient for the American Revolution to simply replace the political power and take measures to prevent its abuse, while in the French Revolution replacement of political power was merely the means to an overdue reform of the social order. The Revolution's main objective was a transition to the principles of freedom and equality, which, contrary to the American experience, required a comprehensive restructuring of civil, criminal, and procedural law etc.

In light of this situation, it appears surprising that the French National Assembly decided by an overwhelming majority to begin their reform efforts not with the reform of ordinary law but with the development of a catalogue of basic rights, while the law of the *ancien régime* was only to be replaced by a bourgeois, liberal order after the enactment of the Bill of Rights. This prioritization alone reveals that basic rights here cannot have been meant as purely negative rights. Such a function would have been contrary to the aim of the revolution and would have virtually immunized the old legal order, perceived to be unjust, against a restructuring in favour of freedom. Rather, under these circumstances, basic rights functioned as supreme guiding principles of the social order which imbued the lengthy and complex legal reform with strength and permanence. They did not place restrictions on the state but instead charged it with a duty to take action. Their purpose was to serve as target benchmarks for the legislature in reforming ordinary law in conformity with these basic rights. This is exactly the objective function of basic rights. Only when the social order was reformed to achieve freedom and equality did it become possible in France to reduce basic rights to a defensive function, as was implicit in America from the start.

Although constitutions with catalogues of basic rights emerged in Germany on the level of individual states at the beginning of the nineteenth century, these had not been won through revolution; they had been granted voluntarily by monarchs in response to a number of state-related motivations. They thus fell short of the American and French basic rights. In Germany, basic rights encountered a legal order whose transition from estate-based and feudal principles to bourgeois, liberal principles had been initiated but nowhere completed. In this situation, basic rights had a twofold role to play. In some cases, they served to secure the progress achieved to date; in others, they promised a continuation of reforms. As these were not forthcoming in the restoration climate after 1820, the largely liberally inclined legal doctrine of the *Vormärz* placed the objective character of the basic rights above their defensive significance, and interpreted them as principles to which ordinary law had to be adapted. Realization of basic rights through civil and criminal legislation, procedural and police-law legislation was the primary issue for the *Vormärz* parliaments. It was not until the liberty promised by the basic rights was largely established in ordinary law in the second half of the century that a narrowing of basic rights to their defensive function, which is today considered classical, began.[5]

However, this development was inherent in the logic of liberalism, out of whose conceptual world the basic rights emerged. Once established in law, freedom and equality were to automatically bring forth prosperity and justice by means of the market. Under these circumstances, every intervention of the state in society, which did not serve to protect against interference of the order but which instead pursued controlling ends of its own, would necessarily distort the free interplay of forces and imperil the success of the model. In an actualized bourgeois society, then, the primary function of basic rights was to define a boundary between state and society. Considered from the perspective of the state, these were restrictions on action; considered from the perspective of society they were defensive rights. To that extent, in bourgeois-liberal understanding the objective dimension of basic rights appears as an interim state. Only the defensive effect should ultimately remain. However, the objective law dimension did not on that account wither away, but remained latent. It abided in a state of seeming suspended animation, to come forth directly whenever deviations from the objectives loomed or in the event that the automatic nature of the mechanism was interfered with. Consequently, the defensive function may be termed the classical basic rights function only to an extremely limited extent.

## III. REASONS FOR EXPANDING BASIC RIGHTS PROTECTIONS

The rediscovery of the objective dimension of basic rights follows directly from the failure of the liberal premise that equal legal freedom automatically leads to prosperity and justice, without any positive action on the part of the state. This assumption was shown to rest on multiple prerequisites. Consequently, it is no longer possible to discuss freedom rights without considering their real-world prerequisites.[6] They must also be taken into account in assessing whether the negative understanding of basic rights should today be restored. An older and more recent layer of problems should be distinguished.

---

[5] See Dieter Grimm, 'Die Entwicklung der Grundrechtstheorie in der deutschen Staatsrechtslehre des 19. Jahrhunderts' in his *Recht und Staat* (n. 4), p. 308.

[6] From the German literature, see E.-W. Böckenförde, 'Grundrechtstheorie und Grundrechtsinterpretation' (1974) *Neue Juristische Wochenschrift* 1529; P. Häberle, 'Grundrechte im Leistungsstaat' (1972) 30 *VVDStRL* 43; K. Hesse, 'Bestand und Bedeutung der Grundrechte in der Bundesrepublik Deutschland' (1978) *Europäische Grundrechte-Zeitschrift* 427; Dieter Grimm, 'Grundrechte und soziale Wirklichkeit' in W. Hassemer et al. (eds), *Grundrechte und soziale Wirklichkeit* (Baden-Baden: Nomos, 1982), p. 39; from the Swiss literature see P. Saladin, *Grundrechte im Wandel* (Bern: Nomos, 1982); J. Müller, *Soziale Grundrechte in der Verfassung?* (Basel: Helbing and Lichtenhahn, 2nd edn, 1981); J. Müller, 'Grundrechte und staatsleitende Grundsätze im Spannungsfeld heutiger Grundrechtstheorie' (1978) 97 *Zeitschrift für Schweizerisches Recht NF* 270.

## 1. *The Older Layer*

The older problem layer is designated by the term 'social question'. This refers to the discovery as long ago as the first half of the nineteenth century that multiple freedoms secured by basic rights are of no use to those who lack the material prerequisites to take advantage of them. This insight is so elementary that even liberalism could not miss it. Still, liberalism conceived prior to the industrial era might adhere to the assumption that once the numerous obstacles to action resulting from estate restrictions, feudalism, the guild system, and mercantilism were eliminated, obtaining these means would only be a matter of talent and hard work. Those who, despite the universally open opportunities in a liberal order, failed to acquire possession of the goods needed to make use of basic rights thus demonstrated personal incompetence. Their need could thus be regarded as their own fault and was correspondingly considered not unjust. According to liberal convictions, the principle of equal freedom, which prevented the rule of some members of society over others and permitted obligations between citizens solely on a voluntary basis, provided protection against private exploitation or domination. In this way, everyone had the opportunity to pursue their own advantage, and no one could be compelled to engage in transactions to their own detriment. Thus, voluntary agreement—whatever form it might take—engendered no injustice.

The assumption on which the bourgeois social model rested has proved to be inaccurate. Shortly after its realization, mass poverty emerged which was not down to individual failures, but to structural reasons which could not be overcome through individual initiative. This condition did not arise as a consequence of the Industrial Revolution, but was merely intensified by it. This had consequences for the realization of the equal freedom that basic rights promised, which consisted not merely of the fact that the freedom accorded to all equally was more or less worthless to the part of the population that lacked the means to utilize it. The more decisive effect was that this part of the population became dependent on the prosperous class. Having only their labour at their disposal, those lacking in means were compelled to accept the conditions of the wealthy in order to subsist in a situation in which labour was plentiful. Considered in formal terms, both parties were merely exercising their contractual freedom. Considered materially, one side was in a position to arbitrarily dictate terms, while the other could only accept these or perish. By this means, instead of a just reconciliation of interests, private terms of rule developed in the sphere freed from state rule, thereby enabling one part of society to exploit the other.

This finding is not only applicable under the special circumstances of the emerging industrial era. It is generally valid. A concept of equal freedom cannot be realized independently of the actual conditions for the exercise of freedom. Defensively understood, freedom rights only lead to the goal of a just reconciliation of interests when there is a parity of power in society. Where a material imbalance exists, formally equal freedom rights mutate into 'might is right'.

In such a case, limitation of the state is no longer identical with real freedom. However, parity of power, which represents the implicit prerequisite for the success of the liberal model, does not come about spontaneously. Rather, precisely as a consequence of private autonomy, the system permits the accumulation of social power and in this way continually produces threats to freedom. As a freedom-oriented system, it is thus precarious rather than self-sustaining. Once this is established, the freedom problem, which liberalism believed it could resolve using formal means, re-materializes.[7] Although the maintenance of individual freedom still depends on a limitation of state power, it additionally depends on a never-ending support for freedom and countervailing actions on the part of the state. The re-emergence of the objective dimension of the basic rights is the legal expression of this insight.

Although this effect was recognized in the nineteenth century, it was not then addressed. On the contrary, increasingly sharp divisions along class lines were accompanied by a growing dogmatization of the negative function of basic rights. Defence against the state, which was originally intended as a juridical means of achieving individual freedom, was elevated to the central purpose of the basic rights. It thus became possible to defend one of the greatest wrongs of the early industrial era, child labour, against attempts to restrict it through legislation by citing basic rights of property, contractual freedom, and parental authority while the character of this legislative initiative as protecting basic rights went unremarked. The less the threat which the state represented to bourgeois interests, the more the bourgeois appreciation for the basic rights declined. When the 'fourth estate' began to insist on the aim of basic rights to cover its liberty deficit, their assertive content was denied by constitutional scholars. Towards the end of the nineteenth century basic rights were stripped entirely of their freedom-relevance, diminishing to casuistic formulations of the general principle of the rule of law. They no longer possessed an independent normative significance, let alone that of principles constituting the meaning of the social order.[8]

On the other hand, if the basic laws are taken seriously as the highest material norms of the legal order, then following the emergence of the social question they could no longer be limited to keeping the state at bay; they must extend their protection to the material prerequisites for the exercise of freedom and the threats to freedom originating from society itself. This brings their objective significance back into play. In view of the need to materially underpin individual freedom, this significance assumes the form of a performance and participation dimension and in view of the threats to liberty emanating from societal actors, it finds expression in a new relevance for a private law. In both cases, the duty to act imposed by basic rights is directed primarily towards the legislature, which must distribute the resources and achieve the reconciliation of interests wherever this does not come about through private autonomy. Secondarily, however,

---

[7] See Grimm, *Recht und Staat* (n. 4), p. 45.    [8] Grimm, 'Entwicklung der Grundrechtstheorie' (n. 5).

it also covers the application of law that must assure performance necessary for the basic rights even without a law justifying entitlement. And it must also take into account the significance of the impaired basic rights in interpreting any civil law that curtails basic rights. The (indirect) horizontal effect of basic rights is nothing other than this—today generally recognized—application of basic rights to ordinary law affecting basic rights. When this way of operating is recognized, this horizontal effect loses much of its controversial nature.

### 2. The Younger Layer

The more recent layer of the problem is due to the increasing complexity of social structures and functions, which in turn are driven by scientific and technical progress. This has several effects that impact on basic rights. The first one results from the ambivalence of progress, as each relief of human toil generates new threats and consequential costs to freedoms secured by basic rights, in particular for life and health. As the economic system, which commercially exploits the results of science and engineering and is thereby protected by basic rights, is not equipped with sensors that gauge collateral costs (so long as these do not result in declining profits), the state must compel respect for threatened legal assets that are protected by basic rights. This necessity is expressed in legal doctrine by the state's obligation to protect freedoms secured by basic rights. This protective obligation became established in German case law through a case in which a long-standing protection, the prohibition of abortion through criminal law, was eliminated.[9] But the primary application of this obligation to protect does not arise where existing protection is curtailed, but where protections intended to secure the basic rights are first to be met in view of such novel threats as automated information processing or genetic technology.

A further consequence of scientific and technical progress is the increasing artificiality of human existence, while the scope for the exercise of natural freedoms shrinks accordingly. 'Natural' freedom is a freedom which the holder is able to exercise without the need for any prior performance of a third party. Strictly speaking, this type of freedom that does not depend on prerequisites, does not exist. Considered pragmatically, however, it is possible to distinguish between freedoms whose exercise depends solely on the individual's act of will, and those that can only be exercised within the context of social or state institutions. Freedom of opinion, for instance, is one of the former, while media freedom is among the latter. In the growing fields of 'constituted freedom',[10] the ability to exercise basic rights does not, as is the case for natural freedoms, depend primarily on limitations of the state, but on the state structuring the corresponding areas of life so as to promote freedom. This is the reason for

---

[9] 39 *BVerfGE* 1 (1975).

[10] This is the term used by G. Lübbe-Wolff, *Die Grundrechte als Eingriffsabwehrrechte* (Baden-Baden: Nomos, 1988), p. 75.

the growing mobilization of basic rights as guiding principles for such public organizations as educational institutions or public broadcasting.

On the level of the state, both the deficits of social self-control and technically driven complexity of social structures and functions have led to a qualitative and quantitative change in its tasks. Under the liberal premise of the ability of society to control itself, the state could be content to shield the social order from interference or to restore it following a disturbance. The modern welfare state, by contrast, acquires the task of actively providing for prosperity and justice. Yet this acquisition has not been matched by a concomitant expansion of its dispositional authority over the various functional subsystems of society. Rather, these continue to enjoy an autonomy protected by basic rights and this has an effect on the state's instruments for performing its tasks. While the liberal state was characterized by the imperative intervention in the legal sphere of the party causing a disruption to legal order, the modern welfare state mainly uses indirect means of planning and guidance to prevent crises and to shape society. Since very few of these guidance and planning tools demonstrate the conventional features of intervention in basic rights, they are in danger of escaping the protective mechanisms designed with such intervention in mind. Still, they may have a more sustained effect on freedom guaranteed by basic rights than individual interventions in individual legal spheres, as they determine the parameters of individual freedom itself.

In response, a continual expansion of statutory reservation may be observed.[11] It is becoming ever more apparent, however, that it is able to achieve the anticipated effect of democratic oversight of administration and rule of law-compliance only to a limited extent. Whereas liberal imperative interventions have a specific, bilateral, and retroactive effect, modern state activity develops a broad-based, multilateral, and prospective effect. Consequently, this activity, unlike selective interventions of the liberal state, can be conceptually anticipated only within limits and therefore cannot be normatively handled in terms of offence and legal consequence. The norm type that prevails here, then, is different from that governing administration of intervention. Goals set by the legislature typically take the place of classic conditional programmes. However, the norm must leave both the path towards realizing the goal and necessary means open. In effect, to a large extent the administration is obliged to controls itself. The norm programme can no longer generally prescribe the result of its activity; instead, this is determined by the administrative decision-making process. Insofar as this is the case, the laws leave behind a deficit with respect to protection of basic rights in material legal terms which can be compensated only by proceduralizing the protection of basic rights and extending their impact to the administrative decision-making process. This makes basic rights relevant for all those administrative processes whose results can lead to rights infringements.[12]

[11] See W. Krebs, 'Zum aktuellen Stand der Lehre vom Vorbehalt des Gesetzes' (1979) *Jura* 304; J. Pietzcker, 'Vorrang und Vorbehalt des Gesetzes' (1979) *Juristische Schulung* 710.

[12] H. Goerlich, *Grundrechte als Verfahrensgarantien* (Baden-Baden: Nomos, 1981); H. Bethge, 'Grundrechtsverwirklichung und Grundrechtssicherung durch Organisation und Verfahren' (1982) *Neue*

The extension of the application of basic rights as a consequence of their objective dimension can thus be explained neither as constitutional arbitrariness nor as a passing fad. Rather, every single enhancement of the significance of the basic rights is a response to altered realization conditions of individual freedom and is thus due not to chance but necessity. The objective dimension of the basic rights proves to be the true dynamic element of a legal order which ensures that the latter keeps pace with changing conditions. Without such an expansion of the applicability of basic rights in their capacity as objective law, a gap would appear between the current threats to liberty and its legal protection and this would significantly diminish the importance of basic rights. The new functions of basic rights find their doctrinal resilience in the obligation to protect. Even though this stands alongside other forms of the objective element of basic rights in its historical development, it proves, on close examination, to be its central concept. All other objective components of basic rights merely represent special aspects of the obligation to protect. This is primarily an obligation on the legislature, often without a corresponding individual right. Depending on the threat, the legislature fulfils the protective obligation through material law, specifically regulatory law or procedural and organizational law. In extreme cases, however, the legislature's objective duty to act can also coalesce in the form of subjective entitlements, which must be then fulfilled directly by the administration and the judiciary.[13]

### IV. EFFECTIVENESS OF DEFENSIVE BASIC RIGHTS

Unlike the older criticism of the structural-legal function of basic rights, the more recent criticism no longer disputes the necessity of extending basic rights protection to the altered conditions of realization of freedom. However, it asserts that this protection can be effected by means of the negative function of basic rights, and specifically without sacrifices in rationality and certainty. To assess whether this is possible, it is first necessary to understand the fundamental difference between basic rights in their capacity as subjective rights and as objective principles. In their defensive interpretation, basic rights are designed to fend off state interventions. However else one might define it, the prerequisite for intervention is always state action. Defence against intervention can thus only have an effect when, contrary to a prohibition by basic rights, the state has acted. By contrast, the problems that revived the objective law function of basic rights are typically problems relating to state inactivity, where activity is called for in the interest of maintaining individual freedom. The question thus culminates in whether the state's obligation to act derived from its protective

---

*Juristische Wochenschrift* 1; Dieter Grimm, 'Verfahrensfehler als Grundrechtsverstöße' (1985) *Neue Zeitschrift für Verwaltungsrecht* 865.

[13] See examples given by R. Breuer, 'Grundrechte als Anspruchsnormen' in O. Bachof et al. (eds), *Festgabe Bundesverwaltungsgericht* (Munich: Beck, 1978), p. 89.

duty is amenable to being handled by employing the negative function of basic rights.

The answer cannot be uniform.[14] Certainly, negative rights cannot help where the state has remained entirely idle. However, inactivity differs from those cases in which the state has taken action, but its activity amounts to a refusal to fulfil a claimed entitlement or the rescission of a previous intervention. For example, when a foreigner applies for a residence permit and this is not granted, this refusal can be interpreted as an infringement. If the affected party invokes the defence against infringements embodied in basic rights, for example by citing the protection of marriage and the family, this leads, if the case is made, to a nullification of the refusal. Although he still does not hold a residence permit, it is clear that the refusal was unconstitutional. He has de facto obtained his end. The situation is similar when the legislature eliminates the protection of unborn life under criminal law. Certainly, this is not an infringement in the classic sense: the state neither takes life itself nor does it order the taking of life by a third party. Still, the elimination of criminal penalties can be interpreted as an infringement into the right to life of the unborn. If this is declared unconstitutional, it can be regarded as a restoration of the old protective norm. The objective is also achieved in this case.

Although, strictly speaking, both cases involve claims not to omission but to action based on basic rights—in the first case to an administrative act and in the second to a law—the negative function of basic rights can take effect. However, it must be recognized that as defensive claims, they do not generally fulfil the positive urge, but rather can only create an equivalent state. This is the case when either the natural freedom to act can unfold following annulment of the state act contravening basic rights, so that the enjoyment of a basic right is a consequence of state inaction, or a previously existing protection can continue to exist following annulment of a state action intended to eliminate that protection. However, the proportionality test, which is an essential component of the negative functions of basic rights, shows that the application of the notion of infringement to cases of positive claims has an artificial element. If the 'infringement' consists of the state denying or eliminating what is required by basic rights, the question as to the least invasive means is in all cases an empty one.

Yet, there is also a number of constellations aside from pure injunction in which the defensive protection of basic rights reaches its limits at the outset. For example, if a secondary-school graduate is refused admittance to a higher-education programme, this refusal, like the case of the residence permit, can be interpreted as an infringement. If the applicant then invokes the defensive basic rights protection and succeeds in challenging the refusal, it is settled that the refusal was unconstitutional. However, this does not mean that this student will necessarily obtain a place. If the neighbour of a proposed nuclear power station is denied a hearing during the approval process, this can be interpreted

[14] See Lübbe-Wolff (n. 10).

as an infringement. If she successfully opposes this omission through an action defending against infringement, then it is clear that the omission is illegal. However, she cannot obtain the hearing itself by means of defensive basic rights protection. The difference between these cases and those previously discussed is that the desired success is not the consequence of state inaction. One can thus conclude from these examples that wherever elimination of the intervention fails to restore natural freedom, and the cited basic right can only be exercised where the state has first acted, defensive protection of basic rights will not solve the problem.

The suggestion that constitutional interpretation be restricted to defensive basic rights protection in the interests of rationality is therefore not without its price. For one thing, it is wholly incapable of addressing omissions on the part of the state in the context of basic rights. Also, all social sectors in which individuals can no longer naturally exercise freedom guaranteed by basic rights and are dependent on prior public performance are removed from basic rights protection. That might be acceptable in exchange for the promised enhancement of rationality if these concerned insignificant aspects of an individual exercise of freedom. However, this is absolutely not the case. In view of the increasing artificiality of modern life and the growing dependence of individuals on positive enablement of their exercise of freedom, this would entail the risk that basic rights protection would be reduced to a few scattered residual zones of natural development. In the areas of social life with greater relevance to individual personal development and utilization of life opportunities, on the other hand, the protection afforded by basic rights would become wholly inoperative. Basic rights would then combat only the relatively minor threats to freedom emanating from the period of their emergence, while the more severe threats to freedom in the age of science and technology would no longer be addressed in terms of basic rights.[15]

## V. A POSSIBLE SOLUTION

There thus appears to be no choice remaining except either to restrict the protection of basic rights to minor cases or accept a deterioration in rationality and legal certainty. Before such a choice is made, however, the asserted degradation must be more precisely identified.[16] Once again, the fundamental difference between basic rights as defences against infringement and as positive duties to act must be applied.[17] An infringement of basic rights always consists of an act

---

[15] See Dieter Grimm, 'Verfassungsrechtliche Anmerkungen zum Thema Prävention' in his *Die Zukunft der Verfassung* (Frankfurt am Main: Suhrkamp, 1991), p. 197.

[16] It would be a mistake to see this only when interpreting basic rights objectively. When, in their role as protective rights, assessing proportionality in a narrower sense of appropriateness (*Zumutbarkeit*), this can also lead to a considerable loss of certainty. This is why Schlink, 'Freiheit durch Eingriffsabwehr' (n. 2), p. 461, is being consistent in demanding a waiver of the assessment of appropriateness.

[17] See Lübbe-Wolff (n. 10), p. 37. Further, R. Alexy, *Theorie der Grundrechte* (Baden-Baden: Nomos, 1985), p. 395.

by the state. However, an act is characterized by the fact that it is determinative. If it is found to be unconstitutional, a defined constitutional response exists: the annulment of the act. Admittedly, uncertainties are also possible here, for instance whether an infringement exists and whether this takes the form of a violation. But this is merely an uncertainty common to all applications of law regarding the prerequisites for a legal remedy. The remedy itself, however, is absolutely certain. By contrast, omissions by the state prove to be a non-specific behaviour. Therefore, if it is unconstitutional, no definitive constitutional response exists, only an indeterminate number of constitutional alternatives. Basic rights as positive duties to act thus fundamentally do not determine the legal consequence of constitutional non-fulfilment of a protective obligation.

In these circumstances, one solution might be to limit the court's ruling to determining the duty of the state to act and leave the means and nature of fulfilment to the legislature. That, however, would entail an overly hasty curtailment of the objective content of basic rights. Even as objective principles, basic rights are not devoid of content. They do not merely require that something happen; they stipulate the direction of state action and contain at least a minimum of material content. This minimum can be determined by asking the question as to which state performance or prior action is required to ensure that an individual's basic rights are not fully impaired.[18] The minimum that can be determined in this manner is then directly necessary for basic rights protection, and not merely for their promotion. To the extent that it makes the minimum directly required by the right a positive mandate, legislation is declaratory and not constituting. From this, it also follows that in the event of legislative omission, the judiciary must ensure a minimal basic rights protection. Naturally, this must be restricted to the absolute minimum. The justification for more far-reaching claims is a matter for the legislature alone for no other reason than that, unlike omissions, benefits are finite and under conditions of scarcity basic rights cannot determine resource distribution priorities.

However, cases exist in which the basic rights minimum and the basic rights optimum are identical. University places provide an example. The Federal Constitutional Court has derived an individual right of admission to a place of study where the prerequisites for admission are fulfilled on the basis of basic rights.[19] Nevertheless, half the applicants for a place in medical school in Germany had to be rejected. Thus, the issue was not a specific basic rights deficit, which could have been met without significantly impacting public resources, but a deficient condition of an entire social sector, whose elimination would have entailed exceptional expenditure.[20] This dilemma also could not be ameliorated by proportional cuts, as in the case of monetary benefits. If under these circumstances the courts had recognized a participatory right, the decision would remain without consequences due to a lack of resources or, if

---

[18] See Breuer (n. 13).     [19] 33 *BVerfGE* 303 (1972).

[20] See F. Müller, *Juristische Methodik und politisches System* (Berlin: Duncker & Humblot, 1976), p. 28; Grimm (n. 6), p. 69.

obeyed, create deficits in other areas covered by basic rights. Consequently, the Federal Constitutional Court felt compelled to severely curtail the entitlement and limit to the minimum possible that the individual could reasonably expect from society. Applied judicially, this is a type of inverse proportionality test: the question is whether the state can reasonably be expected to fulfil its protective duty taking into account other basic rights.

In conclusion, one may say that the choice between restricting basic rights to their defensive facet and an arbitrary interpretation of basic rights is not as severe as critics assume. The weak determinative power of basic rights as objective principles weighs on their side of the scales. The exclusion of modern threats to freedom from the protection through basic rights falls on the other side. In view of this, the decision is easy. As has been shown, it is the objective component of basic rights that, as a dynamic principle embedded in the legal order, opens the law to social change and compels the optimization of freedom in the face of changing situations. Admittedly, such optimization is also possible as political decision without the pressure of constitutional duties to act. But in such cases basic rights would only serve as a corrective, and no longer as a motor for political structuring. They would be neutral in the face of a political sphere unwilling to undertake optimizations. As regards weakness in determination, however, the last word has not yet been spoken. The basic rights doctrine here faces the task of formulating the minimum of positive content required by each individual basic right. This simultaneously represents the boundary for extension of the objective component of the basic rights as well as the competence boundary between politics and the judicial system. This would significantly reduce the risk of arbitrary interpretation.

# PART V

# ADJUDICATION

## ⚮ 9 ⚮

# Constitutions, Constitutional Courts, and Constitutional Interpretation at the Interface of Law and Politics

## I. CONSTITUTIONAL ADJUDICATION

Before the end of the Second World War constitutional courts or courts with constitutional jurisdiction were a rarity. Although constitutions had been in place long before, a worldwide demand for constitutional adjudication arose only after the experiences with the many totalitarian systems of the twentieth century. The post-totalitarian constitutional assemblies regarded judicial review as the logical consequence of constitutionalism. In a remarkable judgment, the Israeli Supreme Court said in 1995: 'Judicial review is the soul of the constitution itself. Strip the constitution of judicial review and you have removed its very life.... It is therefore no wonder that judicial review is now developing. The majority of enlightened democratic states have judicial review ... The Twentieth Century is the century of judicial review'.[1] Based on this universal trend, the Israeli Court claimed the power of judicial review even though it had not been explicitly endowed with it in the constitution.

Yet, just as the transition from absolute rule to constitutionalism had modified the relationship between law and politics, this relationship was now modified by the establishment of constitutional courts. As long as law was regarded as being of divine origin, politics were subordinate to law. Political power derived its authority from the task to maintain and enforce divine law, and this did not include the right to make law. When the Reformation undermined the divine basis of the legal order and led to the religious civil wars of the sixteenth and seventeenth centuries the inversion of the traditional relationship between law and politics was regarded as a precondition for the restoration of social peace. The political ruler acquired the power to make law regardless of the contested religious truth. Law became a product of politics. It derived its binding force no longer from God's will but from the ruler's will. It was henceforth positive law. Eternal or natural law, despite its name, was not law, but philosophy.

---

[1] *United Mizrahi Bank Ltd. v. Migdal Village*, Civil Appeal No. 6821/93, decided 1995.

Constitutionalism: Past, Present, and Future. First Edition. Dieter Grimm. © Dieter Grimm 2016. Published 2016 by Oxford University Press.

Constitutionalism as it emerged in the last quarter of the eighteenth century was an attempt to re-establish the supremacy of the law, albeit under the condition that there was no return to divine or eternal law. The solution of the problem consisted in the reflexivity of positive law. Making and enforcing the law was itself subjected to legal regulation. To make this possible a hierarchy had to be established within the legal order. The law that regulates legislation and law-enforcement had to be superior to the law that emanates from the political process. Yet, since there was no return to divine law the higher law was itself the product of a political decision. But in order to fulfil its function of submitting politics to law it needed a source different from ordinary politics. In accordance with the theory that, in the absence of a divine basis of rulership the only possible legitimization of political power is the consent of the governed, this source was found in the people. The people replaced the ruler as sovereign, just as previously the ruler had replaced God. But the role of the popular sovereign was limited to enacting the constitution while the exercise of political power was entrusted to representatives of the people who could act only on the basis and within the framework of the constitution.

Hence, one can say that the very essence of constitutionalism is the submission of politics to law. This function distinguishes constitutional law from ordinary law in various respects. There is, first, a difference in object. The object of constitutional law is politics. Constitutional law regulates the formation and exercise of political power. The power holders are the addressees of constitutional law. Secondly, constitutional and ordinary law have different sources. Since constitutional law brings forth legitimate political power it cannot emanate from that same power. It is made by or attributed to the people. Thirdly, and consequently, the making of constitutional law differs from the making of ordinary law. It is usually a special body that formulates constitutional law and its adoption is subject to a special procedure in which either the people takes the decision or, if a representative body is called upon to decide, a supermajority is required. Fourthly, constitutional law differs from ordinary law in rank: it is higher law. In the case of conflict between constitutional law and ordinary law or acts of ordinary law application, constitutional law trumps. What has been regulated in the constitution is no longer open to political decision and the majority rule does not apply. This does not mean a total juridification of politics. Such a total juridification would be the end of politics and turn it into mere administration. Constitutional law determines who is entitled to take political decisions and which procedural and substantive rules have to be observed in order to give these decisions binding force. But the constitution neither predetermines the input into the constitutionally regulated procedures nor their outcome. It regulates the decision-making process but leaves the decisions themselves to the political process. It is a framework, not a substitute for politics. Finally, constitutional law is characterized by a certain weakness compared to ordinary law. Ordinary law is made by government and applies to the people. If they do not obey, government is entitled to use force. Constitutional law, by contrast, is made by or at least attributed to the people as its ultimate source and it applies to government. If the government does not comply with the requirements of constitutional law there is no superior power to enforce it. This weakness may differ in degree, depending on the function of the constitution. With respect to the constitutive function the structure of public power will usually conform to the constitutional arrangement. With respect to its function to regulate the exercise of political power this cannot be taken for granted. The historical evidence is abundant.

It was this weakness that gave rise to constitutional adjudication, in the United States (US) soon after the invention of constitutionalism, in Europe and other parts of the world only after the collapse of the fascist and racist, socialist and military dictatorships beginning in the 1950s and culminating in the 1990s. Although many of these systems had constitutions, their impact was minimal, and invoking constitutional rights could be dangerous to citizens. In the light of this experience, constitutional courts were generally regarded as necessary to the completion of constitutionalism. If the very essence of constitutionalism is the submission of politics to law, the very essence of constitutional adjudication is to enforce constitutional law vis-à-vis government. This implies judicial review of political acts including legislation. However, constitutional courts or courts with constitutional jurisdiction cannot fully compensate for the weakness of constitutional law. Since the power to use physical force remains in the hands of the political branches of government, courts are helpless when politicians refuse to comply with the constitution or disregard court orders.

But apart from this situation, which is exceptional in a well-functioning liberal democracy with a deeply rooted sense for the rule of law, it makes a difference whether or not a political system adopts constitutional adjudication. Even a government that is generally willing to comply with the constitution will be biased regarding the question of what exactly the constitution forbids or requires in a certain situation. Politicians tend to interpret the constitution in the light of their political interests and intentions. In a system without constitutional adjudication usually the interpretation of the majority prevails. In the long run this will undermine the achievement of constitutionalism. By contrast, in a system with constitutional adjudication an institution exists that does not pursue political intentions, is not subject to election, and specializes in constitutional interpretation in a professional manner. It is thus less biased and can uphold constitutional requirements vis-à-vis the elected majority. Even more important is the preventive effect of constitutional adjudication. The mere existence of a constitutional court causes the political majority to raise the question of the constitutionality of a political measure quite early in the political process and in a more neutral way. It observes its own political plans through the eyes of the constitutional court.

Hans Kelsen, whom the Israeli Supreme Court quotes approvingly in the *Mizrahi* opinion, may have exaggerated when he said that a constitution without constitutional adjudication is just like not having a constitution at all. There is a number of long-established democracies where the constitution matters even though no constitutional review exists. Here constitutional values have become part of the legal and political culture so that there is less need for institutionalized safeguards. But for the majority of states, in particular for those who turned towards constitutional democracy only recently, the constitution would not matter very much in day-to-day politics if it did not enjoy the support of a special agent that enforces the legal constraints to which the constitution submits politics. The small impact of fundamental rights before the establishment of judicial review proves this.

But the existence of a constitutional court alone is not sufficient to guarantee that politicians respect the constitution. Just as constitutionalism is an endangered achievement, constitutional adjudication is also in danger. Politicians, even if they originally agreed to establish judicial review, soon discover that its exercise by constitutional courts is often burdensome for them. Constitutions put politics under constraints and constitutional courts exist in order to enforce these constraints. Not everything that politicians find necessary—be it for themselves or their party, be it for what they deem good for the common interest—can be effectuated if the court finds that it does not conform to the constitution. Politicians therefore have a general interest in a constitutional court that, to put it mildly, is at least not adverse to their objectives and plans. But there is also a specific interest in the outcome of constitutional litigation on which the implementation of a certain policy depends.

The danger is that any political interference with the judicial process would undermine the whole system of constitutional democracy. This is why judges must be protected against political influence or pressure. The dividing line between the various organs of the state drawn by the principle of separation of powers is particularly strong where the judiciary is concerned. Independence of the judiciary is indispensable for the functioning of a constitutional system and is therefore itself in need of constitutional protection. If it is true that constitutional courts are helpless when political actors refuse to obey their orders, it is even more true that constitutional courts are useless when they cannot take their decisions independently from politics. The best protection of judicial independence is, of course, a deeply rooted conviction on the part of politicians that any interference with court procedures is unacceptable, supported by a strong backing for the constitution within society. But this cannot be taken for granted. Rather, special safeguards are necessary. Judicial independence must be guaranteed, not only against any attempt to directly influence the outcome of litigation, but also against more subtle ways of putting pressure on the judiciary. This is why constitutions usually guarantee the irremovability of judges and often a sufficient salary, to mention only a few devices.

A special problem in this context is the recruitment of judges of constitutional courts or courts with constitutional jurisdiction. Since these courts have a share in public power, the judges need democratic legitimation. If they are not elected directly by the people, a circumstance which presents problems of its own regarding judicial independence, some involvement of the elected branches of government in the recruitment process seems inevitable. Yet every involvement creates the temptation to elect or appoint deferential judges. Recruitment of judges is the open flank of judicial independence. A constitutional court that simply reflects political interests will hardly be able to keep the necessary distance from politics. Hence, safeguards against a politicization of the court are of vital importance.

Most countries with constitutional adjudication have special provisions for the election or appointment of constitutional judges. If they are elected by parliament often a supermajority, like the one required for amending the constitution, is prescribed. This means that majority and minority must agree on one candidate, which makes extreme partisan appointments unlikely. Other countries prefer a mixed system of election and appointment by dividing the right to select constitutional judges among different bodies of government. In others, non-political actors are involved in the process, for instance representatives of the legal profession. It may be difficult to determine which system is best. But it is not difficult to see that some barriers against the threat of a politically docile constitutional court must be erected if constitutionalism is to live up to its aspirations.

Judicial independence is the constitutional safeguard against the threat arising from politicians to the judges' proper exercise of their function. It is directed against attempts to induce judges not to apply the law but to bend to political expectations. This is an external threat. But it would be naïve to assume that this is the only threat to which the functioning of the constitutional system is exposed. There is also an internal threat that comes from the judges themselves. It comes in two forms. One is the inclination to voluntarily follow, for what reasons ever, political expectations or even party lines. The other is the temptation to adjudicate according to one's own political preferences or ideas of what is just and unjust rather than following constitutional standards. The constitutional guarantee of judicial independence protects judges against politics, but it does not protect the constitutional system and society against judges who, for other reasons than direct political pressure, are willing to disobey or distort the law.

For these reasons, external independence must be accompanied by internal independence. The constitutional guarantee of judicial independence is not a personal privilege to decide at will, but a functional requirement. It enables judges to fulfil their function, namely to apply the law irrespective of the interests and expectations of the parties to the litigation or powerful political or societal forces. It frees judges from extra-legal bonds, not to give them leeway in their decisions, but to enable them to decide according to the law. The reason for the independence from extra-legal bonds is to give full effect to the legal bonds to which judges are submitted. Submission to law is the necessary counterpart of judicial independence. As with external independence, precautions can also be taken for internal independence.

However, since internal independence is largely a matter of professional ethics and individual character, the possibilities of the law are limited. Gross misbehaviour such as corruption can of course be outlawed and made a crime.

Experience shows, however, that it is difficult to fight corruption within the judiciary when corruption is habitual among politicians and also in society. This seems to be a problem in a number of new democracies. It is likewise justified to criminalize perversion of justice, though it is not easy to clearly distinguish perversion of justice from false or questionable interpretation of the law. This is why convictions because of perversion of justice are rare. But criminalizing corruption and perversion of justice and removing judges from office who committed these crimes is not a violation of the independence of the judiciary.

A more subtle misconduct is the willingness or pre-disposition to interpret the law in a way that is favourable to certain political views or to a party or a candidate for political office, either in general or in an individual case. This usually comes in the guise of legal argumentation that seeks to hide the fact that it is result-driven. This will not always occur intentionally. Self-deception of judges as to the motives of their judicial behaviour is not impossible. The problem is that this type of misconduct does not only appear in a number of new democracies but can also be observed in mature constitutional states. The decision of the US Supreme Court in *Bush v. Gore* in 2000 may serve as an example. There can hardly be a legal sanction in such cases, but there may be harsh public criticism or even a loss of trust in the judiciary to which no court can remain indifferent.

## II. CONSTITUTIONAL INTERPRETATION

Law owes its existence to a political decision and political motives are legitimate in the process of law-making. But in a constitutional democracy the role of politics ends when it comes to applying the law. Application of the law is a matter for the legal system and in this process political motives are illegitimate. For this reason the division between law and politics is of crucial importance. But what if law application, and in particular constitutional adjudication, is in itself a political operation so that all attempts to separate law from politics on the institutional level are thwarted on the level of law application? This is a serious question, and it is a question that should not be confused with the abuse of judicial power which lies in the intentional non-application or misapplication of the law.

Constitutional adjudication is of course inevitably political in the sense that the object and the effect of constitutional court decisions are political. This follows from the very function of constitutional law, which is to regulate the formation and exercise of political power, and the function of constitutional courts, which consists in enforcing this law vis-à-vis politics. Constitutional courts form a branch of government. Excluding political issues from judicial scrutiny would be the end of constitutional review. Hence, the question can only be whether operations that judges undertake in order to find the law and to apply it to political issues are of a political or a legal character.

This question arises because all analyses of the process of law application to concrete issues show that the text of the law is unable to completely determine judicial decisions. One of the reasons is that the law in general and constitutional law in particular is neither void of gaps and contradictions nor always clear and unambiguous; this can hardly be different, given the fact that a legal system is a product of different times, reacting to various challenges, inspired by different interests or concepts of justice, and depending on the use of ordinary language. Filling the gaps, harmonizing the contradicting provisions, rendering them precise enough for the decision of an issue is the task of the appliers of law, in the last resort of the courts, which, in turn, draw profit from the efforts of legal science.

But even if provisions are formulated as clearly and as coherently as possible they can raise questions when it comes to solving a concrete case. This incapacity to guarantee a full determination of legal decisions, even in the case of seemingly clear provisions, is inherent in the law because a law is by definition a general rule applicable to an indefinite number of cases arising in the future. This is why it must be formulated in more or less abstract terms. Consequently, there will always remain a gap between the general and abstract norm on the one hand and the concrete and individual case on the other. The judge has to discover what the general norm means with regards to the case at hand. This is achieved by interpretation, which always precedes the application of the norm. The general norm must be concretized as a more specific rule before the individual case can be decided.

Like the task of filling gaps, harmonizing contradicting provisions, and clarifying vague norms, concretization contains a creative element. Norm application must therefore always to some certain extent involve norm-construction. This is undisputable, though the degree can vary and rests on a number of variables. The most important one is the precision of a norm. A narrowly tailored norm leaves less room for the constructive element whereas a broad or even vague norm requires a lot of concretization before it is fit for application to a case. Usually a constitution will contain more vague norms than, say, the code of civil procedure. This is certainly true for the guiding principles and for fundamental rights, less so for organizational and procedural norms. Another variable is the age of a norm; the older a norm, the larger the number of problems that were not or could not have been foreseen by the legislature, and thus the broader the range of questions of meaning and applicability.

The mere fact that the law does not fully determine judgment in individual cases is not sufficient to turn law application from a legal into a political operation. It remains a legal operation if what the judge adds to the text of the law in the process of interpretation has its basis in the text and can be derived from it in a reasonable argumentative manner. If not it becomes a political one. The task therefore is to distinguish between legal and non-legal arguments, be they political, economic, or religious. This decision can only be taken within the legal system. No other system is competent to determine what counts as a legal argument. Within the legal system the distinction between a legal and a non-legal argument is the concern of legal methodology. By doing so, methodology attempts to eliminate subjective influences from the interpretation of the law so far as possible. This is why the distinction between legal and non-legal operations in the course of law application becomes largely a question of legal method.

Yet, different from the text of the law that is the product of a political decision and thus not at the disposition of judges, methodology is itself a product of legal considerations. It emerges in the process of interpreting and applying the law or is developed in scholarly discourse, but it is nowhere decreed authoritatively. This suggests that various methodologies can coexist, as can different variations of a certain methodological creed. Method is a matter of choice within the legal system. All historical attempts by legislators to prohibit interpretation or to prescribe a certain method have been in vain, since they have themselves been subject to interpretation. But the lack of one authoritative method does not mean that methodology can justify any solution and thus loses its disciplining effect on judges. Just as certain legal orders have their time in history, so too do methodologies. There is usually a core of accepted arguments or operations and a number of arguments or operations that are regarded as unacceptable. The degree to which a method can succeed in eliminating all subjective elements from interpretation is controversial, though there were, and are, methods that claim this capacity.

One historically influential method that promised to eliminate subjective influences was legal positivism, not in its capacity as a theory of the validity of law opposed to all natural law theories, but in its capacity as a theory of legal interpretation. For a positivist in this sense the legal norm consists of its text and nothing else, and the only instrument to discover the meaning of the text is philology and logic, that is, neither the legislative history, nor the motives or the intent of the legislature, nor the values behind the norm, nor the social reality that brought forth the problems the norm was meant to solve and in which it is to take effect, nor the consequences the interpretation may entail. There can be but one correct understanding of a norm and this remains correct as long as the norm is in force, no matter how the context changes.

The problem with positivism was, on the one hand, that it could not fulfil its promise to eliminate all subjective influences on interpretation. Rather these influences were infused into the interpretation in a clandestine way, mostly in connection with the definition of the notions used by the legislature. On the other hand, positivism prohibited an adaptation of the law to social change by way of interpretation. Since the social reality in which the norm was to take effect was regarded as irrelevant for the interpretation, a positivist could not even perceive of social change. Of course, a positivist would not have denied that, because of social change, a legal norm may miss its purpose and produce dysfunctional results. But this was regarded as a matter for the law-maker, not for the law-applier. It was this deficit that largely contributed to the decline of positivism after the far-reaching social change in the wake of the Industrial Revolution and the First World War.

There is yet another influential theory of interpretation that claims to preclude all subjective influences, namely originalism. Different from positivism, originalists believe that only a historical method is the right way to ascertain the meaning of a legal norm. The law-applier must give a norm, in particular a constitutional norm, no meaning other than the one that the framers had had in mind. Sometimes originalism appears in a crude way that excludes the application of a norm to any phenomenon the framers could not have known. If the First Amendment to the US Constitution protects the freedom of the press, this would not allow the law-applicant to extend the protection to radio and TV by way of interpretation. Sometimes originalism appears in a more enlightened form. The law-applier is then permitted to ask whether the framers clearly would have included a new phenomenon had they known it at the time the law was enacted. In this case it would be methodologically permissible to include radio and TV into the protection of the First Amendment by way of interpretation. But like a positivist an originalist is not prepared to acknowledge that there can be more than one sound interpretation of a norm and that the interpretation can legitimately change when the circumstances in which it is applied change.

The problem with originalism is first a practical one. In most cases it is difficult, even impossible, to discern the original understanding or the original intent. It is even more difficult if many persons are involved in the process of constitution-making, many of whom may not have expressed their understanding or intent. For this reason ascertaining the original intent or understanding is often a highly selective process, in which some utterances of actors are singled out and taken for the whole. The second problem is similar to that which positivism encountered. There is extremely limited, or even no, room for adapting legal norms to social change. If social change affects the constitution adversely the only remedy is to amend the text, which can be extremely complicated in a country like the US. The constitution tends to petrify, in opposition to the theory of a living constitution.

Although one would have difficulties in finding positivists or originalists in Germany, these methodologies are by no means of historical interest only. Positivism, or more precisely a crude literal understanding, plays a considerable role in a number of post-communist countries and in parts of Latin America. Originalism has a stronghold in the US in reaction to the activist Warren Court of the 1950s and 1960s. In Germany, the idea that a legal method exists that can exclude any subjective element from the interpretation of legal norms is no longer maintained. The same is true for the majority of American legal scholars. But the consequences drawn from this premise differ considerably in the two countries. A very powerful movement in the US, Critical Legal Studies, is of the opinion that not only law-making is a political operation, but also is the interpretation and application of law, with the only difference being that the legislature operates in a political setting while judges operate in a judicial setting. As a further consequence, the focus of academic interest in the law differs. The question many American jurists tend to ask is: how will the courts decide? The dominant question in Germany would be: what is the correct decision?

In the last resort a different attitude towards the autonomy of the law appears behind the two concepts. While adherence to Critical Legal Studies does not leave much room for scholars to recognize the autonomy of the legal system, in Germany at least a relative autonomy of the law is widely accepted. This concept acknowledges on the one hand that law is a political product. It emerges from the legislative process, where political arguments dominate. On the other hand, once enacted the law is disconnected from politics. It is up to the legislature to decide whether a legal norm remains in force or not. But as long as it is in force its application does not follow political criteria. It is not only a difference in the institutional setting of political and judicial decisions. There is also a specific rationality of the legal system, which differs from the rationality of the political system.

This difference is not without impact on the recruitment and the behaviour of judges. If interpretation and application of the law is regarded as a political operation, the political preferences and affiliations of the judges are important, whereas they do not matter as much when the neutralizing effect of legal rationality is recognized. The degree of politicization of the judiciary is linked to this. It explains at the same time the constant concern of the American constitutionalists as well as the American public with the so-called counter-majoritarian difficulty or the undemocratic character of judicial review, which is more or less absent in Germany and other countries where the establishment of judicial review was a reaction to their experience with non-democratic regimes.

An inside perspective of a constitutional court can confirm the extent to which doctrine and methodology are able to bridge ideological differences. During my term on the bench I could observe that decisions were not necessarily result-driven. Legal arguments mattered and it happened quite often that members of the court changed their mind because of the arguments exchanged in the deliberation. Of course, this observation in one court cannot be generalized. But it certainly shows the importance of requiring judges to give reasons for a decision. It is true that there may be good reasons for different results, but it is also true that not every result can be supported by legal reasons.

Which method guides the German Constitutional Court when it decides constitutional conflicts? Authentic descriptions by the Court itself are rare, and where they appear in an opinion they do not come in form of a systematic and coherent explanation. Courts hardly discuss methodological questions, let alone describe in their opinions which method they followed. The method is practised, not theoretically developed. This means that it must be inferred from the way a court usually reaches its solutions. Easier than a positive statement on which method the court adopts is the negative statement on what it avoids: there are neither positivists nor originalists on the bench in Germany, which means neither that the text of the constitution is neglected nor that historical arguments are absent.

In general terms, the prevailing method can be described as purposive or functional. Constitutional norms are regarded as expressions of values or principles that society wanted to establish on the highest legal level. These values, in turn, inform the concretization of the constitutional provisions that apply to a concrete case. The goal of interpretation is to give utmost effect to these values or principles behind the text. Whenever the meaning of a constitutional provision vis-à-vis a concrete issue is to be determined, the court asks for the objective that a constitutional provision pursues or for the function that it is to fulfil in society. Why shall the media be free? Why does the family enjoy the special protection of the state? Why is parliament limited in delegating legislative power to the executive? Why are political parties obliged to organize themselves democratically and to lay open their finances?

The results of value inquiries matter. It makes a difference whether the idea behind freedom of the media is to give owners and journalists the possibility to disseminate their individual opinions to a larger public or whether it aims to allow owners to make as much profit as possible, or whether it is meant to enable the individual recipient to form his or her opinion and to guarantee that society gets the information it needs in the interest of self-government. In the two first cases media regulation would present a constitutional problem, in the third case it may be a constitutional obligation. If a conflict between constitutionally protected values arises the court does not establish a hierarchy among them but tries to harmonize them in a way that both retain as much as possible of their content. Thus balancing becomes an important tool for the court when it adjudicates fundamental rights issues.

The methodological maxim, according to which the purpose of the constitutional provision at stake shall be given the utmost effect, has a further consequence that characterizes the methodological attitude of the German Court: what the utmost effect is cannot be ascertained without knowledge about the segment of social reality in which the constitutional provision is to take effect. Legal norms are formulated in the context of a certain state of social reality. Next to text and purpose this context is constitutive for the meaning of the legal norm. But different from the text and the purpose, which are determined by the legislature and remain the same as long as the norm is in force, the context is subject to social change. As a consequence, an interpretation that served the purpose best under certain conditions may cease to do so under changed conditions.

If this is so, sticking to the original interpretation can lead to suboptimal results. It can even miss the function of the norm completely and produce dysfunctional results. The court's jurisprudence takes social reality into account in order to ensure that the law keeps up with new challenges and retains its normative force vis-à-vis new problems. The court even goes one step further and asks for the probable consequences of alternative interpretations in the real world and then chooses the interpretation whose consequences are closer to the normative purpose. In this way, it reacts in particular to new threats to constitutionally protected liberties that arise from scientific and technological developments and their commercial use and thus broadens the protective scope of fundamental rights.

In sum, this method endows the constitution with high practical relevance. A number of important doctrinal innovations owe their existence to this approach, such as the principle of proportionality, the horizontal effect of human rights, and the constitutional obligation of the legislature to protect fundamental rights against menaces from private actors or societal forces. They have since been adopted in many new constitutions or in the jurisprudence of many constitutional courts. Yet, it is just this dynamic interpretation of the Court that returns us to the question of the law–politics divide. At what point does a new interpretation amount to an amendment of the constitution? Of course, in a formal sense an amendment requires a textual change of the constitution. This cannot be done by a court. In a more substantive sense, however, changes in the meaning of a given text may have a bigger impact than textual changes.

In sixty years, the Basic Law has been formally amended fifty-two times. Yet, the changes by way of interpretation, particularly in the field of fundamental rights, are certainly of a similar if not greater impact. Is there a borderline behind which interpretation turns from a legal into a political operation? The answer cannot be different from the one given earlier. As long as the interpretation is derived from the text in a legally acceptable way, it remains within the realm of the law. The political consequences may nevertheless be severe. Every new content that a court derives from constitutional norms changes the balance between the political branches of government and the judiciary, mostly in favour of the latter. Sometimes this is called judicial imperialism. But it is necessary to distinguish between intent and effect. The intent of courts usually is to give effect to constitutional requirements. The effect is often a gain of power that corresponds with a loss of power on the side of the legislature. Still it seems very difficult to convince courts not to enforce what for them follows from the constitution.

In this situation many authors resort to judicial self-restraint as a remedy. But self-restraint, as commendable as it might be, is but an appeal to professional ethics, not a legal rule. Descriptively, one can distinguish between active and deferential courts. Prescriptively, no operational criteria are visible. Too many factors are at stake, and often closer analysis shows that an interpretation which looks extremely bold is well-founded under the circumstances in which it was taken. In addition, it is by no means clear that there is a connection between judicial self-restraint and the degree of politicization of courts. The German Constitutional Court, for example, is more active than the US Supreme Court but it is less politicized.

A more promising tool to limit the expansion of judicial power is the amending power. Courts are bound by the text of law. Changing the text belongs to the political power. The political powers can re-programme the judiciary when they disapprove of their jurisprudence. There is, however, one important difference between ordinary courts and constitutional courts.

If the legislature is of the opinion that the interpretation of a law runs against their legislative intention it can change the law with a simple majority. Constitutional courts apply the constitution whose amendment is usually more difficult and for good reasons. Yet, only by amending the constitution can the political branches of government correct or re-programme constitutional courts. Therefore, amendments should not be made too difficult. When they are very difficult, as in the US, the burden of adapting the constitution to new challenges lies on the judges' shoulders and makes them more political. If the judges shy away from carrying this burden, say for methodological reasons like originalism, and the amendment procedure is extremely difficult, it is to the detriment of the normative force of the constitution.

Amendments are an external corrective to the power of courts. But there is also an internal corrective: even if it is true that, what is legally acceptable and what is not can only be defined in the legal system, it is never defined once and for all and judges are not the only actors to take part in the ongoing discussion. It is therefore extremely important that constitutional courts are embedded in a lively discourse in which the division of functions between the political and the juridical branches of government, the acceptability of legal methods, and the soundness of interpretations are constantly evaluated and readjusted. Judicial independence is not in danger when judges pay attention to the reaction their decisions elicit in society.

# 10

## Constitutional Adjudication and Democracy

### I. WORLDWIDE RECOGNITION, PRECARIOUS STATUS

Constitutional adjudication is as old as democratic constitutionalism. But for a long period, the United States of America remained alone in subjecting democratic decision-making to judicial review. While constitutions had become widely accepted by the nineteenth century, it took almost two hundred years for constitutional adjudication to gain worldwide recognition.[1] In the nineteenth century, only Switzerland entrusted its Supreme Court with jurisdiction in the field of constitutional law, and this did not include review of federal legislation. All other attempts to introduce constitutional adjudication failed. This is also true for Germany where the constitution of 1849 provided for judicial review in an ample manner but the constitution adopted by the revolutionary *Paulskirchen* Assembly did not enter into force because, once the revolution had been put down, the monarchs refused their consent.

The reason for the rejection of constitutional adjudication in the nineteenth century was its alleged incompatibility with the principle of monarchical sovereignty which governed most of the European states at that time. When the monarchy collapsed and was replaced by popular sovereignty, as in France in 1871 and in many other states after the First World War, constitutional adjudication was found to be in contradiction with democracy. Parliament—as a representative of the people—should be under no external control. The only exception was Austria which, in its constitution of 1920, established a constitutional court with the explicit power to review acts of the legislature. Austria thus became the model of a new type of constitutional adjudication: that by a special constitutional court. In Austria this court holds a position parallel to other specialized supreme courts, whereas in most other countries which adopted this model in the second half of the twentieth century the constitutional court is placed on top of the judicial hierarchy.

In Germany, the Austrian example and the difficulties of the Weimar constitution of 1919 caused an intensive academic debate on judicial review where Hans Kelsen (who had drafted the Austrian constitution) and Carl Schmitt were

---

[1] See C. N. Tate and T. Vallinder (eds), *The Global Expansion of Judicial Review* (New York: New York University Press, 1995).

Constitutionalism: Past, Present, and Future. First Edition. Dieter Grimm. © Dieter Grimm 2016. Published 2016 by Oxford University Press.

the leading adversaries.[2] Kelsen, departing from his theory of the hierarchy of norms, declared judicial review a necessary element of constitutionalism. If ordinary law was inferior to constitutional law and could claim legal validity only when within the constitutional frame, an institution was needed to determine whether or not the frame had been transgressed. Schmitt, on the other hand, argued that judicial review would mean a loss for both legislature and judiciary. It would necessarily end up in a 'juridification of politics' and a 'politization of the judiciary'. In practice, the narrow competences of the *Staatsgerichtshof* were not enlarged, but on very rare occasions, the Supreme Court (*Reichsgericht*) claimed the power to review federal legislation.

It needed the experience of twentieth-century dictatorship with its disdain for human rights to overcome the old reservations and open the doors for constitutional adjudication. Germany and Italy established constitutional courts in their postwar constitutions. Spain and Portugal followed after their respective revolutions. After the fall of the communist regimes which had been in strong opposition towards any kind of judicial control of state action, with the early exception of Yugoslavia and the late exception of Poland, all former members of the Soviet Union and the Eastern alliance provided for constitutional courts in their legal systems. Constitutional courts also were established in East Asia and in Latin America after the collapse of military dictatorships and also in Africa, most prominently in South Africa after the collapse of the apartheid regime. In other countries in the British tradition, such as Canada, Australia, and India, the supreme courts soon began to exercise judicial review. The same is true for Israel.

There are other states, however, some of them with an undoubted democratic tradition like the United Kingdom and the Netherlands, which still refuse to adopt constitutional adjudication, and quite often they do so on the ground that democracy forbids it. In many former communist countries the newly established constitutional courts are under strong attack, partly from politicians who had favoured constitutional adjudication to cure the old vices but find it cumbersome when applied to their own activities, and partly from the traditional supreme courts which cannot get accustomed to having been relegated. But even in countries where the existence or the scope of judicial review is not seriously challenged, the question of legitimacy of constitutional adjudication and its compatibility with democratic principles is frequently raised. This is certainly true for the United States with its endless debate on the 'counter-majoritarian difficulty',[3] but to a certain extent also in countries like Germany or France, at least when unpopular decisions are handed down.

---

[2] See now the literature collected in Lars Vinx, *The Guardian of the Constitution: Hans Kelsen and Carl Schmitt on the Limits of Constitutional Law* (Cambridge: Cambridge University Press, 2015). For a discussion, see H. Wendenburg, *Die Debatte um die Verfassungsgerichtsbarkeit und der Methodenstreit der Staatsrechtslehre in der Weimarer Republik* (Göttingen: Schwartz, 1984).

[3] See in particular A. M. Bickel, *The Least Dangerous Branch* (New Haven: Yale University Press, 1962).

Thus, the relationship of democracy and constitutional adjudication has remained precarious and subject to heated debate.[4] Some theorists worry that democracy will be paralysed by constitutional straitjacketing. Others fear that the constitutional dike might be breached by a democratic flood. This chapter tries to show that there is neither a fundamental contradiction nor a necessary connection between constitutional adjudication and democracy. Judicial review has a number of democratic advantages, but it also creates some democratic risks. Consequently, the question whether or not a country should adopt constitutional adjudication is not one of principle, but of pragmatics. It requires a balancing of benefits and costs. The answer may vary according to time and circumstances, and each country has to find its own solution. Yet, in view of the precarious situation of democratic constitutionalism in many parts of the world and the direction party politics take in many established democracies, it seems that more arguments speak for rather than against judicial review.

## II. NEITHER CONTRADICTION NOR NECESSITY

### 1. No Contradiction

Constitutional adjudication is just as little irreconcilable with democracy as is constitutionalism itself. It characterizes a democracy in which sovereignty belongs to the people. This is its distinctive element in comparison with other forms of government where a hereditary monarch or an elite are regarded as sovereign or where sovereignty is attributed to God and exercised by His chosen representatives on earth. Democracy does not mean that the people governs itself. The bigger the society and the deeper its functional differentiation, the more it needs an independent system specializing in political matters. Governmental functions are then entrusted to special organs and officials. But these derive their power from the people and exercise it on behalf of the people to whom they remain accountable.

The means of securing the dependence of government on the people is the constitution. The constitution is a direct expression of, or at least attributable to, the popular will. In its constitution the people lay down the principles and form according to which public authority shall be exercised. In order to reach this end, the constitution is endowed with legally binding force and—since it regulates the making and execution of the law by the various state agencies—it is superior to all other law. Thus, the constitution functions as a basis and framework of legitimate power. Subjection of rulers to the conditions laid down by the people is the explicit function of the constitution. It therefore allows a distinction to be drawn between legitimate and illegitimate power claims. The question whether a certain person or a number of persons can duly claim to

[4] See e.g. J. Elster and R. Slagstad (eds), *Constitutionalism and Democracy* (Cambridge: Cambridge University Press, 1988); D. Kennedy, *A Critique of Adjudication* (Cambridge, Mass: Harvard University Press, 1997); U. R. Haltern, *Verfassungsgerichtsbarkeit, Demokratie und Misstrauen* (Berlin: Duncker & Humblot, 1998); M. Tushnet, *Taking the Constitution away from the Courts* (Princeton: Princeton University Press, 1999).

act on behalf of the people and whether or not a certain act is binding for the people is answered by the constitution.

As with every other legal norm, constitutional law obligates those to whom it is addressed. But it is not capable of guaranteeing that the addressees comply with the norms or that—if willing to comply—they correctly understand their meaning. The threat of non-compliance is particularly serious in the field of constitutional law. Different from ordinary law which binds the citizens and is enforced by the state, the addressees of constitutional law are the highest state organs themselves so that no higher authority exists which could enforce the constitution against them. When, in view of this particular weakness of constitutional law, the people provide for a special agency charged with the task of determining the meaning of the constitution in cases of conflict, and evaluating power claims and government acts as to their conformity with constitutional requirements, the existence of this organ and the exercise of the power vested in it cannot be deemed undemocratic.

This is even true when the constitution sets up a purely majoritarian type of democracy. In this type of democracy, the will of the majority governs unconditionally. Whatever the majority decides has binding effect for the community. Constitutions which follow this model and consequently lack all substantial limits to majority decisions nevertheless contain a certain number of procedural requirements whose violation can render a decision invalid. Hence, judicial review remains possible with regards to those formal requirements for the correct formation of the majoritarian will. Constitutional adjudication on procedural grounds can even be exercised when the constitution allows its guarantees to be set aside in a single case, provided that the decision was taken by the majority necessary to amend the constitution (*Verfassungsdurchbrechung* as admitted in the Weimar Republic). The question whether this majority had been attained can be decided by courts.

Moreover, it seems rather difficult to uphold a concept of democracy which is purely formal. First, a concept of democracy based on the majoritarian principle alone is incapable of effectively securing democratic government. It does not prevent the majority from abolishing the majority rule by majority vote. This is what happened in Germany in 1933—an experience that had a strong impact on the legislative history of the Basic Law. Secondly, democracy, even if identified with the majority principle, is difficult to conceive of without some additional guarantees for the functioning of the democratic process. Freedom of speech and information are arguably the most important ones. Protection of the minority is another whose absence would severely curtail the chances for democratic change. Such additional guarantees, when implicated in the notion of democracy, could, of course, be subject to review without any violation of the democratic principle.[5]

[5] This is the route the Supreme Court of Israel took, beginning with the *Kol Ha'am* decision: see *Selected Judgements of the Supreme Court of Israel*, vol. 1, p. 90. See further, D. Kretzmer, 'Democracy in the Jurisprudence of the Supreme Court of Israel' (1987) 26 *Israel Yearbook on Human Rights* 267.

As a matter of fact, rights of that sort, but also others regarding life; liberty; and property; or institutional guarantees, for instance of marriage and family, are expressly contained in most modern constitutions. Today, the question is no longer whether a constitution should contain fundamental rights, but which rights should be included. Next to the classical civil liberties, younger generations of human rights have found entrance into more recent constitutions. All are intended to guide or restrict government activities. Where a bill of rights exists, the legislature is not allowed to do whatever it deems good or necessary for society. There are some pre-established guidelines as to what the common weal requires. The existence of such a bill of rights does not deprive a constitution based on popular sovereignty of its democratic character. If the people decide to check government power vis-à-vis the citizens through fundamental rights, enforcement of such rights against a ruling majority can hardly be regarded as anti-democratic.

However, the problem is that, in cases of conflict, it is always a past majority binding a present majority. Yet this effect lies in the very nature of constitutions. Constitutions extend the consensus of a given society as to the forms and principles of governance into the future and endow it with legally binding force. They lay down general rules for future decision making and thereby exonerate the political process from the burden of constantly having to rediscuss the substantial and procedural premises of political decisions. In addition, the fact that these principles are agreed upon in advance and are distant from an actual controversy make a just solution more likely. Finally, only by general rules can the ultimate end of constitutions, namely to secure a government of laws and not of men, be reached. The proper solution for the conflict between historical and actual consensus is, therefore, not the abandonment of constitutional principles but the permission to amend the constitution.

## 2. No Necessity

While judicial review is not inconsistent with democracy, neither is it indispensable for democracy. Those who take the opposite position and declare judicial review a necessary condition of democracy argue that democratic constitutions are of little or no value without an institution that guarantees government compliance with constitutional provisions. To be sure, this argument can rely on historical evidence. There are plenty of examples of constitutions turning out to be largely ineffective because, in case of conflict, it is impossible to enforce them against reluctant government organs. This is certainly true for most pre-, pseudo- or semi-democratic constitutions. But even democratic governments which are in general devoted to the constitution, may, on special occasions, develop a tendency to disregard constitutional norms which stand in their way in the pursuit of political goals.

On the other hand, there is sufficient historical proof that democratic states can live without constitutional adjudication. Constitutions are not condemned to remain mere paper tigers without specialized enforcement organs. It may be that examples of this assertion are less frequent than examples of the opposite case but they undoubtedly exist. Nobody would deny the democratic character of states like the United Kingdom or the Netherlands which do not support constitutional adjudication. The reasons are manifold. On the one hand, democratic governments will hardly ever be disdainful of the limits drawn to them by the constitution. In particular, the political process usually functions according to the organizational and procedural rules laid down in the constitution. On the other hand, courts are not the only possible guardians of the constitution. The inter-organ control stemming from the separation of powers is one; popular support for the constitution or effective media control are others.

In the last resort, respect for the law in general and the constitution in particular depends on roots that stretch deeper than legal precautions. The willingness to comply with the constitution even if it interferes with one's political plans and even if one is in a position to neglect it without risk is, to a large extent, a cultural achievement. There are societies where this respect is more deeply rooted in citizens than in others. In these societies, democratic politicians will usually be less inclined to neglect the law and the general public will react in a more hostile manner to governmental violations. The risk to loose acceptance is then an additional factor to strengthen the constitution. When after the events of 1989–90, many drafting committees of new constitutions and many newly appointed constitutional judges asked how political compliance with constitutional law and with orders of a constitutional court could be achieved, one had to refer them mainly to the cultural backing which constitutions need and which a constitutional court can never fully replace.

Therefore, Kelsen's position that constitutional adjudication is the logical consequence of constitutionalism can hardly be upheld. Kelsen saw the function of constitutional law in regulating the formation of ordinary law and concluded that this function could be fulfilled only when the constitutional requirements were enforceable against a reluctant legislature. A constitution which regulates the legislative process without caring about the compliance by the legislators lacks, in his view, full legal validity. It is not much more than a 'non obligatory desire'.[6] Strictly speaking, it regards its own provisions about legislation not as binding but leaves them to the disposition of the legislature. Kelsen's reasoning may have some historical evidence. In many political systems, the constitution—in the absence of special safeguards—was indeed not taken seriously. Examples can be found particularly in societies without a firm democratic and constitutional tradition where other safeguards of the constitution are underdeveloped. But it is not true as a general principle.

It is all the less true considering that courts also cannot guarantee government compliance with the constitution. They can only enhance the chance that it be respected. Ineffective courts are as possible as ineffective constitutions. They can, for example, be so closely linked to rulers that their willingness to perceive or invalidate unconstitutional acts is low. Secondly, the already mentioned fact that, vis-à-vis the constitution, addressee and guarantor of the law

---

[6] See Kelsen, in Vinx (n. 2), ch. 2. See further, Dieter Grimm, 'Zum Verhältnis von Interpretationslehre, Verfassungsgerichtsbarkeit und Demokratieprinzip bei Kelsen' (1982) 4 *Rechtstheorie* 149.

fall together, puts courts which enforce constitutional requirements against government organs in a precarious situation. When the highest authorities of the state neglect court orders the courts have no means to enforce respect for the constitution vis-à-vis the rulers. There is no bailiff for constitutional matters. This shows that not only constitutionalism but also constitutional adjudication rests on cultural grounds. Effective judicial review requires a political culture where, in general, court decisions are accepted even by those who are in power, and where public esteem for the constitution is so high that disrespect becomes too costly for politicians.[7]

Hence, political systems with and without judicial review may form different types of democracies. But the characterization of a given political system as democratic or undemocratic does not depend on the recognition of constitutional adjudication. Neither is the existence nor the absence of judicial review a precondition of democracy. Consequently, the decision pro or contra judicial review is not one of principle but of pragmatics. The choice has to be made between different types of democracy, not between democracy and judicial review. The decision requires an assessment of the advantages and disadvantages of judicial review for democratic systems. It is best based on an analysis of the differences between democratic systems with and without judicial review and on an appraisal on whether the disadvantages can be minimized without weakening the benefits.

### III. DEMOCRATIC ADVANTAGES AND DEMOCRATIC RISKS

### 1. *Advantages*

The observation that the government and the political parties acting within government organs tend to form their political will irrespectively of the constitution may serve as a starting point for the comparison. Constitutional provisions rarely guide the perception, processing, and solution of political problems. The question whether a political plan or measure is compatible with the constitution usually enters only at a later stage of the decision-making process. Constitutional law then functions as a subsequent corrective. It is true that political organs when they raise a constitutional question do not dispose of other ways of determining the meaning of a constitutional provision. The legal method is the same for politicians and judges. But the circumstances under which constitutional questions are answered differ. And the circumstances of the political sphere are not particularly favourable to unbiased constitutional answers.

Politicians act in a competitive environment. What counts here is political success and ultimately electoral victory. This creates an inclination to submit constitutional requirements to political needs—not necessarily in the sense that

---

[7] See H. Jacob et al. (eds), *Courts, Law and Politics in Comparative Perspective* (New Haven: Yale University Press, 1996).

the constitution is simply set aside, but in the sense that it is understood in a way favourable to one's political purposes. In contrast, courts operate under a different code. They do not pursue political plans and usually do not depend on re-election. They are specialized in legal adjudication. Law is their primary concern. Their autonomy and independence vis-à-vis political actors allows them to determine the meaning of a given legal text by professional criteria, unaffected by political programs and the imperative of winning elections against other competitors. It is therefore more likely that the intentions of the constitution and not those of the politicians prevail when a constitutional conflict arises.

In a democratic system without judicial review these virtues do not enter into the political play. A system in want of constitutional adjudication is therefore less able to counterbalance the inclination of political actors—even if they are constitutionally minded—to understand the constitution in the light of their political purposes. Moreover, in the absence of an independent arbiter, conflicts about the constitutionality of a given government act will always be decided in favour of the majority, since no one can hinder it from going along according to its understanding of the constitution. As a consequence, the basic consensus among competing political forces laid down in the constitution is in danger of being eroded in the long run. Conflicts within the constitutional framework tend to become conflicts about this framework and may finally affect the stability of the democratic system.

In contrast, political systems with constitutional adjudication enjoy, through the mere existence of a court with the power of judicial review, the advantages of an early and more or less neutral look to constitutional requirements. In such a system, political actors are forced to anticipate the opinion of the court in order to avoid a legal defeat. While arguments of political desirability or usefulness usually prevail in the decision-making process, they are now balanced by legal arguments. The potential of constitutional conflicts is thus minimized. When the anticipatory mechanism fails and conflicts about the constitutionality of political measures arise, judicial review can help to settle them in a manner which leaves intact the integrative force of the constitution. The court decision solves the dispute and creates certainty about the meaning of the constitution. The disputed measure either gains additional legitimacy or is definitely excluded from the range of permitted alternatives.

In addition, judicial review operates as a counterbalance against the tendency of all political forces to rid themselves from their competitors to the largest extent possible. Competition, it should be noted, is the most important motor of democracy and the best means of controlling government. But the controlling effect depends on the existence of equal opportunities for the majority and opposition and hence on safeguards against abuses of majority power to the detriment of the minority. The controlling effect of competition completely disappears when competitors share a common interest. This is the case, for instance, in questions of party financing. Another common interest, at least with the established parties, is the use of their legislative or administrative power to suppress or hamper political newcomers or dissidents within the party.

In areas where party competition fails, courts are the only means of securing the degree of openness that is crucial to democracy.

The same is true for the societal preconditions of democracy. Periodic elections and deliberating parliaments alone do not constitute a democratic system. Democratic government depends on a constant feedback between the governing and the governed. Such feedback only comes about when opinions can freely be formed and expressed and when interests can freely be organized and articulated. Since governments are always tempted to use their power to silence or intimidate critical voices or to favour followers and discriminate against opponents, equal freedom is in need of special guarantees effective against government actions. This need is fulfilled by fundamental rights which have been part of constitutional law from the beginning. But constitutional history teaches that most bills of rights remained a merely symbolic, legally irrelevant part of constitutional law as long as they were not accompanied by constitutional adjudication.

Finally, constitutional adjudication can contribute to the legitimacy of the democratic system as a whole. Apparently, pluralist societies suffer from the difficulty of securing sufficient legitimacy and mustering political motivation in society. This notorious shortage of consensus, legitimacy, and societal engagement may be caused by the fact that it is up to constantly changing majorities to define the common weal. Everything seems contingent. Under such conditions, a constitutional court manages, to a certain extent, to compensate for this deficit by making visible, behind the befuddling contingency of party politics, generally binding principles and norms. Politicians cannot simply give vent to their own or their clientele's interest or follow their momentary ideas. The constitution matters. Its limitations of government power are more than mere promises. Politicians will often find the enforcement of constitutional requirements burdensome or even unjustified in individual cases. But what, in the short run, may look like an obstacle turns out, in the long run, to stabilize the acceptance of political decisions.

## 2. Risks

While it is true that judicial review can strengthen democracy, this does not mean that it presents no democratic risks. These risks, to be sure, do not refer to the possibility of wrong decisions. Every political system knows institutions that have the last say in a given matter, and therefore lives with the risk of 'wrong' decisions. While it is possible to keep them at bay through institutional arrangements, there is no avoiding them completely. The German Constitutional Court owes its existence and ample powers to the legislature's former abuse of its power to have the last word. Rather, the democratic risk lies in the lack of democratic control. After all, the judiciary can set aside the will of the elected representatives of the people without enjoying equal democratic legitimacy and without being equally accountable to the people. The latter is even true for countries where judges are elected, not appointed.[8]

---

[8] For the problems created by the election of judges see S. P. Croley, 'The Majoritarian Difficulty' (1965) 62 *University of Chicago Law Review* 689.

Furthermore, judicial review tends to judicialize political discourse. Political actors are tempted to blame a political programme or a draft law which they dislike as being a violation of the constitution. By doing so they do not only curtail the political part of the discourse where arguments concerning the usefulness, consequences, or price of political plans prevail. They can also impair the constitution, which instead of being the underlying integrative force of the polity becomes a weapon in the political struggle. It becomes one argument, among many others, and is, so to speak, pluralized into the conflictual, controversial market of opinions. Without one integrative document, however, the textualization of the polity would come to an end.[9] Germany, with its long tradition of political controversies masquerading as legal argument, seems to be a major example of this development.

Yet, the lack of accountability and of the democratic control it entails would be of minor importance if judges exercising judicial review could be said to apply general constitutional norms only to individual cases. Since Montesquieu's days, this is indeed the most common justification of judicial independence: judges are bound to the prescribed norms, and their task is to discover the content of these norms and to apply them—a process known as the 'theory of binding norms'. Courts are not entitled to make genuine decisions but to enforce decisions made by others. If this were true, every exercise of judicial review would still entail a loss of power for the democratically legitimized organs. But what is lost is nothing more than the unfettered power to act in breach of the constitution which enjoys higher democratic legitimacy. It is for this reason that judicial review was not considered a democratic problem when introduced in Germany after the Second World War.

Today, it is a truism that legal norms do not and cannot determine judicial behaviour and court decisions in a comprehensive manner. In exceptional cases only does the text of a norm immediately provide the answer to a legal question. Cases like these rarely require litigation. Under normal circumstances, the meaning of a general norm with regards to an individual case has to be determined by interpretation, and interpretation usually leaves room for more than one answer. This is true for legal norms in general. But it applies with particular force to constitutional norms. Constitutions fulfil the function of providing a common basis for political adversaries and thus require a political consensus broader than that underlying ordinary laws. They are also more difficult to amend. For these reasons, constitutions tend to be more open-ended as well as less complete and consistent than ordinary laws. Gaps in scope and content, therefore, need to be bridged through interpretation or concretization.[10]

---

[9] This expression is taken from N. Luhmann, *Gesellschaftsstruktur und Semantik*, vol. 4 (Frankfurt am Main: Suhrkamp, 1995), p. 114.

[10] For the latter see K. Hesse, *Grundzüge des Verfassungsrechts der Bundesrepublik Deutschland* (Heidelberg: C.F. Müller, 20th edn, 1995), p. 24 ss.; cf. E.-W. Böckenförde, 'Die Methoden der Verfassungsinterpretation' (1976) *Neue Juristische Wochenschrift* 2089.

What follows from this is that the application of constitutional norms *in concreto* involves extrapolation beyond the given. The meaning of a provision must be determined in a more or less complicated operation of legal reasoning which sometimes makes it difficult to recognize the boundaries between interpretation and amendment. This is particularly true for the growing number of cases where old norms have to be adapted to new developments, mainly in the field of basic rights. Thus, to maintain that judicial review poses no democratic problem because all that judges do is to enforce prior decisions made by the people is too easy a way out. Application of norms cannot be clearly distinguished from norm creation. Adjudication constitutes a mixture of cognitive and voluntary elements. The norms which bind government are, in the process of interpretation, to a large extent 'made' by the courts.

Compared to, say, the United States Supreme Court, the German Constitutional Court goes pretty far in this direction. Not only does it interpret the various civil rights in such an expansive manner that hardly a state action remains out of the range of judicial control, enabling the Court to act as 'censor of reasonableness of all governmental action'.[11] It also deduces from the bill of rights—besides the government's duty to refrain from certain actions—an obligation of the legislature to actively protect fundamental rights against intrusions from societal forces. It thus uses its competencies not only to invalidate certain government acts, but also to require action where the government was unwilling to act under its own impetus. Thus, in a number of cases, legislation was declared unconstitutional, not because it had gone too far in restricting fundamental rights, but because it had done too little in protecting them against menaces stemming from private parties.

Of course, the creative element permeates not only judicial review, but more or less law application in general. Yet, there is an important difference between ordinary and constitutional law. If the legislature finds the interpretation given to ordinary law by the courts unacceptable, it can alter the legal programme and thereby change the practice of the courts. With regards to ordinary law the legislature thus has the last word. Constitutional law, on the other hand, binds the legislature, and so does the court's interpretation of the constitution. In the case of conflicting views it is the constitutional court, not the legislature, which has the last word. It is true that constitutional courts as well can be reprogrammed, but only by constitutional amendment which is usually difficult to obtain. It is precisely this political element of judicial review that needs to be reconciled with democracy.

[11] D. P. Currie, *The Constitution of the Federal Republic of Germany* (Chicago: University of Chicago Press, 1994), p. 319. For civil rights jurisprudence, see Dieter Grimm, 'Human Rights and Judicial Review in Germany' in D. M. Beatty (ed.), *Human Rights and Judicial Review: A Comparative Perspective* (Dordrecht: Martinus Nijhoff, 1994), p. 267. See further Ch. 8 of this volume.

## IV. AVOIDANCE OF DEMOCRATIC RISKS

### 1. Substantial Approach

Such reconciliation requires a delimitation between the proper domain of the legislature as direct representative of the people and that of the courts as guardians of their fundamental and integrating values. Many criteria for this delimitation have been tried. The most popular one is the difference between law and politics. The courts shall only render legal decisions and abstain from political rulings which, in turn, belong to the legislature alone. Although it is undeniable that law and politics are not identical, the difference between them seems much too imprecise to solve the problem of delimitation. The reason lies in the nature of constitutional law. On the one hand, it forms the body of norms which are designed to bind the legislature when it takes political decisions, and constitutional courts are charged with examining these decisions as to their conformity with these norms. On the other hand, constitutional norms are far from that degree of precision which could give them strictly binding effect force.

The consequence is that constitutional adjudication is inevitably political in a double sense. First, it has tremendous political effects insofar as the courts function as arbiter in genuine political conflicts. They decide whose political will prevails, for instance the one of the legislature or the one of the executive, the one of the majority or the one of the opposition, the one of the federal government or the one of the member states (*Länder*). Furthermore, it ultimately depends on the court whether the legislature is able to realize what it deems politically necessary and whether it has to take action where it would prefer to remain passive. Secondly, in deciding questions of this sort according to constitutional law, the courts are not bound to an extent that would exclude any political element from the decision. Enforcing constitutional law contains an element of political choice which can be narrowed but not completely avoided.

A more precise criterion seems to be the principle of separation of powers. Yet, although all democratic constitutions adhere to this principle because it has proved to be an effective safeguard against absolutism and abuse of power, there is not one single notion of separation which could furnish a universal criterion for delimitation between courts and legislature. Rather, every constitution goes its own way, none being able to strictly separate the various branches of government. When a constitution provides for judicial review, it inevitably gives the courts a share in law-making—a negative one when they are restricted to invalidating acts of parliament, a positive one when they are, in addition, empowered to oblige the legislature to act. But the constitution cannot exactly tell where the power of the legislature ends and that of the court begins. This, in turn, depends on the requirements the constitution contains with regards to the legislative process.

This is why a number of authors pin their hopes on legal methodology. In their view, only those decisions which have been found according to the accepted principles of legal reasoning are legitimate. But, methodology is equally unable to provide a satisfactory answer to the problem of delimiting judicial review. This is not to say that methodology does not matter. It no doubt helps to infuse rationality into the process of interpretation and to bring forth controllable results. Yet, there is usually not one single accepted method, but a plurality of methods, so that choices have to be made which influence the results.[12] Moreover, methodology is not exempt from change, and very often it is the courts that bring forth new methodological variants which later enter into the accepted canon. In sum, methodology lacks the degree of precision and authority which would allow a clear distinction between decisions remaining within the realm of the judiciary and encroaching upon functions of the legislature.

A more precise limitation on the basis of methodology seems possible only by following the theory of original intent much discussed in the United States.[13] Yet, interpretation according to the intent of the framers is both a self-deception and a depreciation of the constitution. The deceptive effect results from insurmountable difficulties in establishing what the framers' original intent was and even more what it might have been had they known of the issue now before the court. The depreciation lies in the fact that the courts, if they applied the method in its strict sense, would have to refuse to answer all problems not foreseen by the framers. The adaptation of constitutional norms to new developments—television, atomic energy, electronic data processing for instance—would be left to constitutional amendments, even in cases where constitutionally protected values are directly affected. The theory, therefore, ends up reducing the importance of the constitution. Consequently, it does not have any followers in Germany inside or outside the Constitutional Court.

In view of these inadequacies, many resort to judicial self-restraint as a way out of the dilemma. Self-restraint, however, is not able to furnish criteria for distinction between the domain of the legislature and that of the courts. It appeals to the professional or democratic ethics of the judges, perhaps also to their self-interest not to undermine their own position which can easily happen when a court goes too far in restricting or pre-determining the political process. But the necessity of such an appeal is the best proof of the difficulty to find workable limits. For, were there borderlines which could guide judicial behaviour, no need for self-restraint would arise. In addition, self-restraint does not help where the courts, by way of constitutional interpretation, find or develop requirements binding the legislature. It would be difficult to convince a judge not to rule what he or she thinks the constitution requires.

---

[12] See Dieter Grimm, 'Methode als Machtfaktor' in *Festschrift für H. Coing*, vol. I (München: Beck, 1982), p. 469.

[13] Cf. A. Scalia, *A Matter of Interpretation* (Princeton: Princeton University Press, 1997); W. Heun, 'Original Intent und Wille des historischen Verfassungsgebers' (1991) 116 *Archiv des öffentlichen Rechts* 185.

## 2. Functional Approach

A more helpful approach to shaping the contours of legislative as opposed to judicial tasks seems to be a functional one. The keywords here are action and control. The constitution structures political action by organizing, guiding, and limiting it. But it does not regulate it to an extent which would reduce politics to mere execution of constitutional orders. Within the framework of the constitution the political organs are free to make those choices which, according to their view, the common good requires. The election decides which of the competing views is preferred by society and which political group may therefore fill the leading positions in the state and carry out its political program. By contrast, courts and especially constitutional courts, are called to control whether the other branches of government, in defining, concretizing, and implementing the political goals, have acted in accordance to the constitutional principles and not transgressed the constitutional limits.

This division of functions which underlies all democratic constitutions allowing judicial review does not affect the power of courts to define what the constitutional provisions mean and how far they reach. This is an integral part of the juridical function. But it generates two other consequences. First, courts lack the power to determine political goals. Their competence is limited to measure goals against constitutional requirements. Beyond the range of constitutional law, the courts' preferences are without relevance. Second, the order of political decision and control must not be reversed. Courts are not called upon to anticipate or design legislative measures but to review them after they have been taken. This presupposes that another government organ must have acted before constitutional control can set in. It does, however, not exempt political omissions from control, provided that a constitutional duty to act exists.

The function of the different organs also determines their equipment. Under the pressure of numerous and complex problems law-making requires a highly differentiated and cooperative system for both perceiving problems and devising workable and effective solutions. As state tasks expand and as the government's capacity to directly intervene into social systems decreases, legislative functions get to be performed in a mediative, rather than authoritative process. For these reasons, legislation today rests, in substance, with the executive branch with its greater expert knowledge and mediative resources. Parliaments have gradually lost their role of drafting laws. Rather, parliamentary procedure finds its main justification in providing transparency and political control. The parliamentary minority can force the majority to disclose and give reasons for its plans and can confront the majority with its own alternative projects. Societal interests get a chance to intervene, and the media may raise viewpoints relevant for the general public and the politicians alike.

Courts have no equivalent instruments at their disposal fit to fulfil this function. They lack the wealth of information and expert knowledge assembled in the other branches of government. Empirical findings are by no means excluded. On the contrary, the so-called legislative facts play an important role in judicial review. But the findings follow a selective principle which is guided by the norms the courts apply. Aspects of effectiveness, expediency, or social consequences of a decision enter into the decision-making process only from a normative point of view. Prognostics of future development which play an increasing role in the legislative process of welfare states cannot be undertaken by the courts. While it may be true that courts, in one case or another, have decided on a more thorough basis of information than the legislature,[14] this cannot offset the general restrictions under which law, in an era of ever-increasing differentiation, must operate.

Among such drawbacks, court procedures count as perhaps the most important. In contrast to parliamentary procedures, they do not, need not, and, perhaps, must not reach a similar degree of transparency or offer equal chances to particpate. The judicial framework makes it impossible to completely disclose and exhaustively discuss underlying points of political or social controversy. The formalized procedure leaves little to no room for non-parties to the conflict to voice their views or introduce their interests. There are no direct feedback-mechanisms between court decisions and societal reactions. Courts are, of course, not beyond public criticism but, not subject to elections, they are much more protected against public protest than political actors. Judicial procedures, therefore, are adequate when it comes to review laws as to their constitutionality or when there is need to remind the legislature of unfulfilled constitutional duties. They are ill-devised, though, to determine political goals or anticipate legislative decisions.

Ultimately, it has to be taken into account that every issue decided in the judicial process is no longer open for decision in the democratical process. Courts concerning themselves with such issues too early deprive the deliberation about social conflicts and the possible solution of its political phase. At the same time, the guiding principles and values of political deliberation—like publicity, transparency, acceptability, and accountability—play a minor role in court procedure, and it is doubtful whether this deficit is offset by specifically juridical values. The possibility that the decision of the court is the better one for the community cannot set aside the functional limits drawn by the constitution. The same is true for the argument that, in case of parliamentary reluctance, a court decision is better than no decision at all. Where constitutional criteria for the 'better' are lacking, politics are free to act or not act and have to bear the responsibility for their behaviour.

It is worth mentioning that the omission of the political phase is often enough in the interests of political organs themselves. It allows them to shift responsibility to the courts for measures that are unpopular or likely to spark off heated debate. This manoeuvre, however, benefits political actors only in the short term. In the long run, it leads to their considerable weakening since social areas once ceded to constitutional review cannot easily be regained for

---

[14] For examples from the jurisprudence of the German Constitutional Court see K. J. Philippi, *Tatsachenfeststellungen des Bundesverfassungsgerichts* (Cologne: Heymanns, 1971).

political decision. This works as follows: the more decisions that are left to the courts, the less room is left for political decision, the less elections matter, and the more difficult the implementation of innovation or major change becomes. In other words, the risk is that judicial review may lean towards securing the status quo, devalue traditional instruments of democracy, and favour the ossification of the political process. In the end, the result may be political blockades and a loss of legitimacy for the polity as a whole.

## V. COMPENSATION OF DEMOCRATIC DEFICITS

Constitutional democracy, by definition, entails a simultaneous commitment to the principles of democracy and constitutionalism. In this combination, the constitution tends to be the weaker part. Constitutional adjudication is an attempt to make up for this weakness. But, as demonstrated, it generates its own democratic problems. When the democratic advantages and disadvantages are weighed in light of the preceding considerations, it seems, however, not impossible to collect the benefits and to minimize the risks of judicial review. Still, there is no guarantee for success. The balance remains a precarious one because, to a large extent, it depends on the judges whether constitutional adjudication and democracy will be reconciled, there being no superior organ which could put the court in its place. Thus, it is understandable, when, in spite of the worldwide expansion of judicial review, some societies trust the political process more than the judicial one.

However, for states where constitutional democracy is a rather new achievement and where the societal preconditions of democratic government are still underdeveloped, or for states where the constitution did not matter for a long time because state agents could disregard it without risking a loss of legitimacy in the population, it will be more difficult to renounce constitutional adjudication than for states with a long and stable democratic tradition and a general respect for the rule of law. In states of the first category, the constitution will normally be in need of an independent agent whose primary concern it is to guarantee compliance with its rules and who thus makes it visible and meaningful for the general public. This may explain why so many countries which only recently turned democratic have opted for constitutional adjudication.

Compared with the question of introducing or renouncing constitutional adjudication, it is of secondary importance whether it is exercised by the ordinary judiciary or by a particular constitutional court. Both systems have their advantages and disadvantages.[15] The hierarchical position of the constitution and the informational resources required by judicial review could speak for a separate constitutional court. On the other hand, the ordinary

---

[15] See M. Cappelletti, *Judicial Review in the Contemporary World* (Indianapolis: Bobbs-Merrill, 1971); from a practical point of view see Dieter Grimm, 'Probleme einer eigenständigen Verfassungsgerichtsbarkeit in Deutschland' in R. J. Schweizer (ed.), *Reform der Bundesgerichtsbarkeit* (Zürich: Polygraphiscer Verlag, 1995), p. 161.

courts may be better prepared to integrate constitutional requirements and ordinary law and thus avoid inconsistencies as well as the permanent issue of where to draw the line between the realm of constitutional and that of ordinary law, and correspondingly to determine the limits between the constitutional court and the ordinary courts. In the last resort, it will probably be decisive how willing and capable the ordinary courts are to open themselves up for constitutional arguments and to interpret ordinary law in light of the constitution.

Yet, there is one consideration which may also stress the importance of constitutional adjudication for countries with a solid democratic system. Constitutional review seems capable of compensating for some of the most dangerous deficiencies of modern democracies. The catchword is professionalization of party politics. Surprisingly, such deficits arise from the principles of democratic accountability and responsive government, which turn out to be double-edged swords.[16] Democratically organized political systems and particularly political parties as their main actors operate under the imperative of winning elections. Electoral success is the prerequisite of bringing one's personnel into leading positions and of making one's political programme enforceable. Hence, from the point of view of political parties, it is reasonable to do everything that helps win the elections and to avoid, at the same time, everything that may endanger this goal.

This imperative has its costs. The tendency to instrumentalize all public spheres where decisions can be taken which may affect the claims of political parties endanger the autonomy of areas where party influence is not legitimate, such as public administration, the judiciary, and public television. The checks and balances provided in the constitution are thereby undermined.[17] In addition, political parties tend to concentrate on short-term success, if possible close to election day, in order to raise their chances. They may even try to fabricate events of success, be they merely symbolic ones, for the purpose of reinvigorating their campaign. The downside, of course, is a neglect of long-term issues and of side-effects likely to occur in the not-so-near future. Furthermore, parties reveal a certain indifference vis-à-vis fundamental societal principles embedded in the constitution when they can exchange them for an imminent gain.

The judicial system operates under entirely different conditions. Its far-reaching lack of accountability and answerability to the public may in this light be its main virtue. Political success is not a relevant parameter. Judges generally do not owe their position to general elections and are not subject to re-election or, mostly, re-appointment. Thus immunized, their autonomy protects them against sanctions in response to unpopular decisions. Usually

---

[16] A more comprehensive analysis of the downside of democratic accountability can be found in J. G. March and J. P. Olsen, *Democratic Governance* (New York: Free Press, 1995), p. 144 ss.; Haltern (n. 4), p. 398.

[17] See Dieter Grimm, 'Die politischen Parteien' in E. Benda, W. Maihofer and H.-J. Vogel (eds), *Handbuch des Verfassungsrechts* (Berlin: de Gruyter, 2nd edn, 1994), p. 599.

they do not need to seek a professional career after retirement from the court. All of this makes them far less dependent on consent than politicians. What becomes clear, in sum, is that such insulation—taken together with professional standards—is the source of judicial authority. It enables the court to insist on respect for the lasting principles on which society rests, and to remind politicians of their long-term obligations, at least as far as they have a basis in constitutional law.

# PART VI

# THE FUTURE

# The Future of Constitutionalism*

## I. ORIGINATING CONDITIONS

### 1. The Bourgeois Social Model

There appears to be no cause for concern regarding the future of the constitution. Emerging in the eighteenth century as a consequence of two successful revolutions and won through bitter struggle in the nineteenth century, the constitution propagated globally in the twentieth century. The number of states that are today governed without a constitution is negligible. Although one must not conclude from this that the constitution is taken seriously everywhere, its universal propagation can be regarded as an indication of the attractiveness of the idea that political rule requires constitutional legitimation and must be exercised on a constitutional basis in order to be recognized by the governed. But in the second half of the twentieth century, compliance with the requirements that constitutional law imposes on the political process has grown as well, thanks to the spread of constitutional adjudication. One may say of Germany that no constitution has ever stood in such high regard or has shaped political reality in such a sustained manner through constitutional court rulings as the Basic Law.

In spite of these indisputable outward successes, however, more and more indicators are appearing that point to a growing inner weakness of the constitution and foster doubts as to its unimpaired capacity to regulate politics. If one considers only the traditional, order-preserving activities of the state to which the constitutional provisions originally referred, such indicators are easy to overlook. But they become immediately apparent when the modern activities intended to promote the general welfare are taken into account. These were not foreseeable when the constitution emerged and although there has been no lack of attempts to adapt the constitution to these altered state activities, their limited success raises the question as to whether the constitution's weakness in this area is due to insufficient adaptability, or because constitutional law is not a suitable instrument for guiding the welfare state and that constitutional amendments and even complete revisions cannot fully recoup its normative power.

---

* The original German text of this chapter contains many notes referring primarily to German sources: they are omitted in this English version.

Constitutionalism: Past, Present, and Future. First Edition. Dieter Grimm. © Dieter Grimm 2016. Published 2016 by Oxford University Press.

The constitution is just as susceptible to such inner erosion as other legal regulations. As a novel historic occurrence that emerged over two hundred years ago under quite specific conditions, the constitution can itself disappear when these conditions no longer exist. The history of law contains numerous examples for such processes. It therefore makes sense to begin our examination into the future of the constitution by verifying its origins. If the conditions to which the modern constitution owes its emergence are known, it is possible to examine whether the changes that have occurred since affect these conditions and are thus able to explain the weakness of constitutional law with respect to the welfare state. However, this also provides a more reliable basis for assessing whether and to what extent the constitution's effectiveness can be maintained under these altered conditions. Since the prerequisites for emergence have been described in detail elsewhere, a brief summary relating to the issue of its future is offered in this chapter.

In terms of its emergence, the constitution is to be seen in the larger context of the transition from the estate-based feudal to the bourgeois-liberal order. The bourgeois social order is to be understood as a model based on the assumption that society is able to achieve prosperity and justice once it is allowed to develop free from external intervention. The medium which was to effect this was the free exercise of the will of formally equal individuals. This permitted every individual to form his or her own opinions autonomously, define their own interests, and adjust their behaviour accordingly, while at the same time compelling them to seek satisfaction of their needs through an accord of will with other, equally free members of society, and which promised to give rise to a just reconciliation of interests precisely because of the absence of external compulsion. This did not preclude social differences, even of individual need, but in the system of individual freedom these could be attributed to personal failure and were accordingly not viewed as unjust.

With this basic assumption, the bourgeois social model placed itself in opposition to the estate-based feudal order, which was based on a presupposed, materially defined idea of the common good, under which the individual was not entitled to liberty. Rather, each individual was assigned his or her place in society, generally established through birth and therefore unalterable, in which he had a specific social function to perform under pre-established conditions. Consequently, the legal status of the individual did not derive from her person but from the estate to which she belonged, and was explicitly characterized not by equality but by inequality. The bourgeois social model was also opposed to the absolute, monarchical state, which held public power by divine or inherent right not derived from any social consensus and, by asserting a superior understanding of the general welfare, claimed the authority to determine both the social order and individual life conduct down to the last detail and realize this through absolute power.

By contrast, the bourgeois social order did not conceive the general welfare as a preordained material standard by which all social life was to be governed, but as an open outcome of the interaction of free exercises of will. This allowed the question of justice to be formalized: it could be solved by enabling individual self-realization, thus dispensing with concrete behavioural requirements. The chief consequence of this reversal was that the various functional areas of society, above all the economy but no less the cultural sector, was decoupled from political control and entrusted to the control of the market so that it could develop according to its own specific rationality criteria by means of individual determinations of will. This autonomy, gained by replacing politics with the market, and considered as guaranteeing performance and justice, was the factor that required a new order in the relationship between the state and society, in which the modern constitution was to play a decisive role.

## 2. The Function of the State

In order to comprehend this role, it is important to understand that the capacity of self-control attributed to society in no way made the state unnecessary. This is related to the susceptibility to disturbances of a system that seeks to arrive at the general welfare by means of individual freedom. In such a system, the possibility that individual members of society will exercise their own freedom to impinge on the equal freedom of others, and thereby neutralize the mechanisms of social self-control, cannot be eliminated. That makes it necessary, on the one hand, to delimit the spheres of freedom of individuals with respect to one another and to secure these boundaries against incursions, and on the other to open up opportunities for cooperation and ensure the fulfilment of obligations voluntarily entered into. However, a society consisting of unconstrained individuals unleashed to pursue their own interests and stripped of all authority to rule cannot guarantee the prerequisites for its own self-control. Rather, it must reconstruct these outside itself, and it does so in the form of the state.

But the state formed in this manner is fundamentally different from the absolutist monarchical state with respect to legitimation and function. It had to relinquish the ruling position that it held under the conditions of a concretely defined and pervasive general welfare. Society, now enabled to prosperity and justice by its own efforts, claimed priority, while the state assumed a subservient position derived therefrom. Theoretically, such a state created to fulfil a social purpose was conceivable since the older concept of the divine establishment of political rule had lost much of its persuasiveness with the schism and had been supplanted by the doctrine of the social contract. However, the doctrine of the social contract, developed in the shadow of religious civil wars, which demanded an unrestrained peacekeeping entity, initially increased the power of the princes, and it was only the elimination of traditional state power by the bourgeois revolutions that created the prerequisite for a planned reconstitution of the political order based on social consensus.

The replacement of consensus-independent, self-legitimating state power by state power requiring consensus and legitimated by those subject to its rule thus led to a constituting act almost by necessity. To that extent, the revolutionary break with traditional state power, as exercised in North America and France, was constitutive for the modern constitution. However, the constitutional act should not be equated to the constitution itself. It is also possible to conceive of unconstrained rule that is derived from and based on social consensus. The older social contract doctrines had proven that with their defence of absolute monarchical power. Yet, absolute power, whether originally or derivatively justified, cannot be reconciled with constitutional regulation. It excludes the distribution of power among different holders and the binding of its exercise on specific principles or procedures. Rather, the ruler's decision-making power is not subject to any legal limitations. Public law is limited to asserting the ruler's omnipotence and regulating succession.

Consequently the need for political rule based on consensus had to be joined with a second change affecting the function of the state before a momentum in the direction of a constitution could emerge. In the face of the bourgeois premise of society's ability to control itself, the state lost its comprehensive responsibility for individual good behaviour and social justice which until then it had claimed for itself. All objectives and preferential decisions, regardless of whether they were of a social, economic, or cultural nature, now fell within the sphere of social autonomy, and this the state was compelled to accept. The state retained only that task which society could not perform on its own, namely defending society against threats to freedom that interfered with the free inter-action of social forces that was expected to guarantee the general welfare. The state established by bourgeois society was stripped of a welfare function and was reduced to ensuring foreign and domestic security. This distribution of tasks is what is meant when the bourgeois order is summed up by the expression 'separation of state and society'.

Certainly, the separation of the state from society changed the task portfolio of the state. However, this change did not affect the method of performing these tasks. The limited function of defence against threats to liberty can only be fulfilled through the use of force. The state even had to hold a monopoly on this, as any intra-societal right of rule would have violated the equal freedom of the social constituents and annulled the self-control mechanism. Consequently, the bourgeois revolution did not eliminate the domestic sovereignty that had developed as the characteristic of the modern state since the sixteenth century and which distinguished it from the medieval order of rule. On the contrary, it shifted the process of sovereignty formation to its conclusion by conveying those rights of rule remaining to the nobility and the clergy under absolutism to the state. At the same time, however, it replaced the monarch with the people as the bearer of sovereignty. Thus, the possession and exercise of the power of rule was no longer concentrated in one hand, but was separated.

This split, and the distributive principle of freedom on the side of society and limitation on the side of the state occasioned by the separation of state and society, presented civil society with a regulatory problem unknown to ear-lier societies. It was not known to medieval society because its rule—not yet functionally specialized in politics and distributed geographically and materially among numerous autonomous holders—was entirely incapable of a specifically rule-related regulation. Nor was it known to the renaissance princely state, because it was capable of regulation, by virtue of its sovereignty but not in need of its absolute character. By contrast, it became necessary to bind once again the functional units of state and society that had been sundered under the premise of self-control but remained interdependent, in a manner which gave the state all the means it required to fulfil its function as guarantor of individual freedom and societal autonomy and yet prevented it from using these for its own control purposes in contravention of liberty.

### 3. The Importance of the Constitution

This problem found its ideal solution in the constitution. As bourgeois society required the state only as a guarantor of its freedom, the challenge was to restrict the state to this function, and to organize it in a way that bound it to the interests of the people in performing its tasks while precluding excesses insofar as possible. In both cases, the aim was not to set specific material objectives or mandatory actions for the state, but to limit and channel its activities. Seen in this way, the regulatory task is formal. Law develops its specific rationality in the resolution of formal tasks. It can attain a relatively strong determinative power and its implementation does not pose particular difficulties. The observance of prohibitive, organizational, and procedural norms is largely a matter of will. When violations occur, they can be handled within the legal system itself, specifically through nullification of illegal acts.

Special issues only arise from the fact that in this case the objects of binding norms are not individuals but the state, in other words the institution charged with formulating and asserting law and equipped with sovereign power to this end. The task cannot therefore be performed by means of laws enacted by the organs of the state. Rather, it requires a legal foundation higher than statute. Consequently, the legal order was divided into two parts: one that originates from society and binds the state, and one that originates from the state and binds society. Naturally, the former had to take precedence over the latter because it granted the authority to collectively make binding decisions, specified the conditions for their legal validity, and made their binding character dependent on these conditions. This describes nothing less than the modern constitution, which as the sum of fundamental norms regulates the establishment and exercise of public power and is thus necessarily superior to all other legal norms that derive from this.

Specifically, the constitution resolved this task by delimiting the area in which society enjoyed autonomy and where therefore the individual's acts of will, and not the will of the state, were decisive. This was the function of basic rights. From the perspective of the state, these represented barriers to action and from the perspective of the individual, defensive rights against state actions. In view of the threat to the freedom of others inherent in individual freedom, however, it was not possible to constitute the limits to state action to be absolute in nature. Rather, the state had to be able to exercise its power even in the sphere of basic rights where this was necessary to protect freedom. In view of the fundamental decision in favour of individual freedom, however, this activity was deemed an 'infringement'. Although essential in order to preserve liberty, infringements in the individual sphere under the protection of the basic rights was regarded as the greatest threat to bourgeois society, as it was not out of the question that power-holders would use it for purposes other than protecting liberty.

Thus, the entire organizational part of the constitution was concentrated on alleviating the danger inherent in infringements. The state is only permitted to intervene in the sphere of basic rights on the basis of statutes. Statutes can only be enacted by the representatives of the populace chosen in free elections, that is, the parliament. This branch thus functions as the bridge between the state and society. It establishes the bounds of individual freedom in a general and abstract manner following public discussion under the scrutiny of the electorate and authorizes the state to defend it in the specific case using its compulsory powers. The state administration is bound to the legally enacted programme. Independent courts can, at the behest of those affected, review whether an infringement adhered to the statutory programme, and in the event of a violation are authorized to annul the administrative act and compensate the affected individual for the damages suffered. In this way, democracy, the rule of law, and division of powers reinforce the substantial protection of basic rights and stabilize the separation of state and society.

Statutory law becomes the pivot of the entire system. The success of this ordering model thus depends on the suitability of the parliamentary statute for constraining the activity of the state. This was, however, favoured by the peculiar activity of the liberal state. Obligated to a predetermined order arising from the free interplay of social forces, it was tasked solely with shielding against interference or restoring order following such interference. On the other hand, the state was expressly stripped of the task of structuring order. Unlike structuring of order, however, the task of preserving order is relatively amenable to determination through law. In terms of its subject matter, the norm can determine relatively precisely and conclusively what is to be considered a disturbance of order, and determine the legal effect of actions that the state must take in response to the prerequisites. As in this system the contact of the state with society exhausts itself in legally regulated cases, the potential threats of the state, and the legally mediated protection are congruent.

The constitution therefore differed from older legal bonds on political rule, which were in no way unheard of even under absolutism. Whereas these bonds limited state power only in isolated respects or in favour of individual groups, the modern constitution asserted a fundamental and comprehensive claim to regulate public authority. Admittedly, this must not be understood as if every political power or initiative required constitutional legitimation from this point on. However, the claim to comprehensive regulation means that all holders of public power required constitutional legitimation, that extraconstitutional holders of sovereign rights would no longer be tolerated, and that every state decision acquires validity only by following the procedures specified under the constitution. This may not have eliminated the power problem, but it defused it so that an unobstructed transformation from power to law was precluded.

## II. CHANGES

### 1. *Market Failure*

From these considerations, we can derive three prerequisites for the emergence of the modern constitution. Above all, it required a unified public power functionally specialized in politics as the possible *object of regulation* by a constitution. However, *need for regulation* of the object of regulation only emerged when public power was no longer considered as given or transcendentally or traditionally legitimated, but derived its right to rule from social consensus and exercised it on behalf of society. To enable the need for regulation to be fulfilled by a constitution, however, a *regulatory purpose* was also required. This focused primarily on the limitation and organization of public power, in other words, on tasks that find their appropriate solution in law. Finally, insofar as statutes functioned as the central control element, this required state tasks that were amenable to legislative control. Social changes that affected these conditions thus could not leave the constitution unaffected.

The changes begin with the fact that the bourgeois social model proved unable to make good on its promises. Certainly, the feudal social structures, which impeded progress and were increasingly perceived as unfair, were swept away along with the constraints of the absolute state. The anticipated unleashing of economic productivity also came to pass. But the just reconciliation of interests that the bourgeois model had also promised failed to materialize. Instead, economically based class barriers formed under the rule of private autonomy and its pillars of freedom of property and contract, which had the effect of dividing society into owners and non-owners. This made possible new dependency and exploitation relationships—freely entered into in law yet compelled by economic circumstance—which could not attribute the resulting poverty of a broad social stratum to personal failure. This arose independently of the Industrial Revolution, which did not cause, but merely intensified, the situation.

It was thus clear that the market mechanism was unable to give rise to a just reconciliation of interests under all circumstances or for every good. To a much greater extent than assumed, the bourgeois social model was also predicated on the assumption that equal legal freedom corresponded with a balance of social power if autonomous regulation of social relationships was to lead to social justice. However, such a balance of power existed neither at the outset of bourgeois society, nor could it have been maintained under the logic of the system. Admittedly, this discredited not the objective of the social order, but only the means of its realization. The bourgeoisie had not reserved freedom for itself, but proclaimed it universally. If this universal entitlement was to be redeemed, the equal freedom that largely existed in law had to be established in fact. This required, first, protection against social threats to freedom, and secondly, a material foundation of freedom that made it usable.

Thus the justice problem became, once again, a material, as opposed to a merely formal, problem. The common good could no longer be considered an automatically occurring result of individual freedom, but rather had to be actively implemented, even under the conditions of freedom. Equal freedom thus depended on limitation of personal autonomy and the redistribution of material goods. Unlike the elimination of feudal obstacles to self-realization and authoritarian constraints and the unleashing of productivity, this task could not be realized by imposing limits on the state. Rather, it could only be accomplished through the application of public power. Consequently, the defensive posture towards the state that had emerged in reaction to monarchical absolutism was transformed through the experience of the Industrial Revolution into an attitude of entitlement towards the state. At issue was a reactivation of the state, admittedly a reactivation whose goal, in contrast to the absolutism of the past, was not to assert a pre-established common good, but rather to make individual freedom real.

Corresponding demands began to be heard in the early nineteenth century, but were met by the resistance of the bourgeoisie, which increasingly identified the aim of equal individual freedom with the means of its realization, limitation of the state, and private autonomy. The greater the influence of the bourgeoisie on the state, the less likely were the prospects for system corrections. The franchise played an important role here as, regardless of the popular sovereignty on which the political order was based, it depended almost exclusively on property criteria or educational certificates, which effectively precluded those interested in a system change from political participation. To this extent, it was only the creation of democracy with a universal, equal franchise that opened the door to the reactivation of the state. Following the initial efforts at the beginning of the nineteenth century, state activity has expanded continually since the end of the First World War, particularly in terms of the accrual of new tasks, the development of new means of performing these tasks, and the emergence of new political actors.

## 2. New tasks: Developing Society

The growth of state tasks stands in the foreground of change. To date, this has been mainly driven by two sources. One can be circumscribed by the word inclusion, the involvement of the entire population in the benefits of all social subsystems. Whereas initially the inclusion-driven expansion of state activities was primarily due to the social costs of liberalization and industrialization, inclusion gradually detached itself from the social question of the nineteenth century and now comprises all conceivable disadvantages suffered by individuals or groups without reaching immanent limits. The second source is to be found in the continuing differentiation of social structures and functions, which on the one hand significantly increases the performance capability of society, but on the other hand makes it much more susceptible to disturbances. The tendency of specialized systems to combine a high sensitivity for their own matters with great indifference to those of others becomes a particular problem. To that extent as well, the state leaps into the breach.

This process has both quantitative and qualitative aspects. Quantitatively, we can (without laying claim to a precise demarcation of eras) identify three stages. In the first stage, which commenced in the nineteenth century, the task of preventing gross abuses of economic freedom was added to that of preserving public order. This task could be performed primarily by imposing legal restrictions on private autonomy. In the next stage, which commenced following the First World War, the state began to take action in cases of social distress and economic bottlenecks and in particular to secure the basic needs of human life. This was achieved primarily through intervention in the economic process and the establishment of state benefit systems and public utilities. In the third, and still relatively recent stage, the state assumed a global responsibility for the stability and development of society in social, economic, and cultural respects. To this end, it primarily employs the planning and control of social developments.

The countervailing tendency of privatization of state tasks has not offset this growth, though in view of the increasing financial and functional overstretch of the state it may be accelerating. Still, one can recognize a shift in the levels on which public tasks are performed. This is entailed by technological and economic developments that lead to increasing international interdependencies and reduce the number of problems that can be resolved within the nation state framework or by means of treaties. States have therefore begun to transfer a series of economic, technological, and military tasks to supranational organizations and assign them the necessary sovereign rights. As a consequence, the resolutions of these organizations are often directly binding on member states, requiring no further transformation. States lose sovereign rights through this process, without the bodies assuming them themselves taking on the quality of a state.

In qualitative terms, the most important change lies in the fact that as a consequence of the materialization of the justice problem, state activity is becoming disconnected from its link to a given, quasi-natural social order which the state must merely defend against disturbances. Instead, the social order itself has become an object of state modification and development. It is not possible for the claim to inclusion to be realized without continual modification of the existing living conditions and social infrastructure and without the redistribution of social wealth, nor can the burdens resulting from technological and industrial progress be managed without altering the parameters for the social subsystems and without rolling over the financial costs. Here, the state is increasingly compelled not only to respond to crises but to anticipate possible undesirable developments and avert them in their early stages through timely and proactive measures. This task is never completed; in a dynamic society it must be constantly pursued.

The state thus emerges from the marginal role it assumed under the aegis of the bourgeois premise of society's capacity of self-control, and from which it was only supposed to emerge when a disturbance in this self-control was manifest or impending. In this way, its activity loses its specific and retroactive orientation and gains a universal, prospective character that was alien to the absolute state on account of its limited structuring options, and to the liberal state due to its limited power to structure society. It is no longer possible to identify any social sectors that lie entirely outside state influence. The influence on social structure is merely a matter of degree. However, this means that both individuals and social subsystems are becoming increasingly dependent on the state. Neither the development of human personality nor the functional performance of the systems can succeed without the prior performance and ongoing support from the state. Under such circumstances, freedom as an unaltered target value of order is to an ever lesser degree natural freedom, and ever more freedom that is conveyed and conditioned by the state.

### 3. New tasks: Security

The shift of state activity from preservation of the status quo to planning for the future is currently acquiring an additional dimension thanks to scientific and technological progress. The use of new technologies, such as nuclear, information, and genetic technology, as well as the utilization of new chemicals, creates risks that in many respects exceed the dangers of the first phase of industrialization. These are often beyond the limits of sensory perception or only reveal their effects after a long latency period or at great distances. At the same time, however, they are assuming a historically unprecedented dimension, extending even to the self-destruction of mankind. Even below this threshold, damage can occur in such an intensity or extent as to be irremediable for the foreseeable future. It is increasingly difficult to localize responsibility for such damage because it accumulates from numerous harmless, microscopic instances or from the simultaneous occurrence of events that are harmless in and of themselves, or that simply could not be anticipated at the time they were caused. At the same time, tested and proven safety concepts are lacking on account of insufficient experience.

In view of the rapid increase in risks and the declining likelihood that individuals can protect themselves through appropriate caution, a change in popular attitudes towards scientific and technical progress has taken place. Whereas previously the advantages counted more than the associated risks, fears for the future are now becoming more prominent. The more apparent it becomes that it is not possible to expect self-limitation or responsibility for consequences within the scientific system that delivers these new inventions, and that the economic system that commercializes these discoveries can only be expected to be sensitive if profit is affected, the more insistently the state is expected to impose external limits of social compatibility on the producers of social risk and to secure the threatened future. Security becomes a primary task of the state, and its legitimacy depends just as much on the fulfilment of this task as on the maintenance of material prosperity, and is already coalescing into a subjective entitlement on a par with human rights.

However, the state cannot fulfil such expectations by resorting to the traditional system of defence against threats, which was formerly adequate for addressing the scientific and technological dangers. Defence against dangers always related to impending threats that could be attributed to an originator, limited in their magnitude and extent, and able to be mastered by means of safety measures and at least compensated by insurance. By contrast, in the absence of empirical knowledge of all sources and consequences of damage incidents, it is not possible to promulgate precise and reliably effective regulations for the prevention of damage due to new technologies. In the absence of unambiguously identifiable originators and geographically and chronologically limitable, or at least remediable, damage, claims for damages and insurance coverage cannot serve to compensate losses incurred. The task of the state thus changes from preserving the status quo and restoring it after a disturbance, to future-oriented risk management that controls the process of scientific and technological change in society.

In fulfilling this task, the state finds itself in a dilemma. In order to hold its own in international competition and afford the increasing costs of inclusion policies, the state is largely tied to the process of scientific and technological innovation. It cannot address the evil at its roots in this manner, and would find it difficult to obtain a consensus for comprehensive prohibitionist strategies in view of the ambivalent nature of progress, and the indisputable and rapidly available advantages as compared to the uncertain and chronologically distant disadvantages. The aim can only be to channel and contain the risks. Further, the associated decisions must be taken under conditions of uncertainty given the lack of information on technological consequences and protective measures. Still, such decisions taken in a context of uncertainty often have consequences that burden future generations for many years to come, or are even irreversible. Nor does a refusal to decide solve this problem, because it allows technological development to run free. This makes it difficult to generate a consensus.

As the technical sources of risks are difficult to master, the state is increasingly shifting to secondary strategies and attempting to minimize the human risks that result from the use or rejection of new technologies. In view of the potential magnitude of the harm, it no longer limits itself to manifest dangers, but expands its attention to include 'dispositional' risks. This lends its activity a fundamentally preventative character. Unlike the prevention function that the liberal state always exercised, the new foresight is no longer focused on preventing a concrete, unlawful behaviour, but rather aims at early detection of possible disturbance flashpoints and danger sources. This causes the state's need for information to massively increase, as the number of potential sources of danger is incomparably greater than the number of acute dangers. In this way, prevention becomes detached from its previous relation to illegal behaviour and is used to avoid unwanted situations of all types. The individual can no longer keep the state at bay simply by behaving lawfully.

## 4. New Instruments

Under the conditions of this preventative transformation of state activity, the forms of state action have also changed. The instruments through which the state performed its classic task of guaranteeing a predefined social order consisted of command and coercion, and the state differed from society precisely in that it possessed these means. They continue to be used for the preservation of order. However, command and coercion cannot easily be applied for the purpose of developing the social order and prevention of crises. This is because achieving these ends does not depend solely on the use of the medium of power, but on numerous other resources which the state itself does not possess and which it cannot control through imperative means. Neither scientific-technological innovation nor economic upswings or cultural behavioural patterns can be achieved through command and coercion. If these ends are added to the tasks of the state, they must be pursued using other means.

But even where the object of state control would admit the use of imperative means, these cannot always be applied. The expansion of the state's tasks and responsibilities is not accompanied by a corresponding expansion of its dispositional authority. Even though the intervention thresholds have been reduced noticeably in accordance with the growing demand for state guidance, nothing has changed with regards to the principle of autonomy of the various social function units. Rather, protected by basic rights, these remain in private disposition and thus follow their own system logic. Thus, in broad areas of its social-structuring activities, the state must dispense with the use of the specific state means of command and coercion. Subject to only weak limits with respect to the assumption and expansion of tasks, the state is still subject to constraints as to how it fulfils these. In this way, a growing gap is emerging between the state's area of responsibility and its area of assertion in all democratic welfare states.

To the extent that the state may not act through command and coercion, it must resort to employing indirect and non-imperative means of fulfilling its tasks. This primarily takes the form of money; a private behaviour that the state wishes to encourage is made attractive using financial incentives, and undesired behaviour is made unattractive through financial deterrents. However, non-imperative control is also realized in the form of information or persuasion. Lastly, the state influences private behaviour indirectly by expanding or reducing the capacities of public services or by altering the legal parameters of private decisions. These forms of control differ from imperative means, including the means of money in such forms as fines and fees, in that the objects of control remain free to choose their behaviour. Undesired behaviour is also legal, but must be paid for with disadvantages, so that it is ultimately a matter of personal calculation whether or not the state's policy prevails.

To the same extent, of course, the private objects of control are released from the position of subjects. They are not under any obligation to obey indirect control. Rather, the state depends on the private actors' voluntary willingness to comply. Consequently, they find themselves in a negotiation situation, which on the part of the state is equivalent to a necessity to negotiate. Political actions become the subject of negotiations in which the private actors can require state compensation for their willingness to comply. The state is not automatically at a disadvantage in these negotiations, as the private decision-makers themselves are dependent on state activities. Insofar as imperative and non-imperative means of control are interchangeable, the private willingness to comply is often enhanced by the announcement of compulsory measures. In many areas, however, the proclamation or enforcement of a statutory regulation is merely used as a trump card in the negotiation to induce the private actors to a compromise.

In recent years, the scope of negotiations between public and private decision-makers has increased so greatly that they can no longer be considered an exception. Rather, the state has institutionalized these, formally and informally, to a great extent. Under these circumstances, the connections are no longer limited to occasional contacts, but are a matter of routine and are already influencing the character of the system. It is acquiring neo-corporatistic characteristics. The content of state decisions is shaped by the negotiating process. The result of negotiation is no longer subjected to any autonomous state evaluation, but ratified as it is. Although the negotiation partners can still be differentiated according to state or social origin, the product of their negotiations cannot be assigned unambiguously to either side. State and society meet on the same level. Recent proposals would fill the resulting vacuum with neutral arbitrators accountable to neither side; examples of this solution are already in place in the United States.

### 5. New Actors

The dependence on consensus and the mandatory character of state rule implicit in the concept of the constitutional state required an opening of the state boundary to society. The popularly elected parliament was to serve as the binding element. However, quite unintended by the constitutions, this mediating model soon gave rise to auxiliary organizations in the form of parties, which, through elections, aggregated popular opinions and interests, distilled them into a political programme, and presented candidates who were to realize this programme in parliament. Under the conditions of legitimate pluralism and the universal franchise, parties became a functional prerequisite of the system, since the people can only exercise their franchise when the range of individual opinion and interest combinations is reduced to a few alternatives suitable for decision-making. In spite of this, parties were long considered extra-constitutional entities that in terms of constitutional law were attributable to society and not subject to the rules that apply to branches of the state.

However, the function of parties does not exhaust itself in preparing for elections. Rather, they occupy the branch of the state recruited by means of election in accordance with the election results, and for the duration of the legislative period can appoint their own leaders to the leadership of the state and make their programme the government's programme. Although their home is society, their destination is the state. The influence of parties is not limited to elected governmental bodies. As in the democratic constitutional state every state function must be directly or indirectly based on democratic legitimation, the parties also gain a foothold in those governmental bodies that are not subject to party competition because they have a say in the appointment of officeholders. This affects primarily state and municipal administrations, but also independent review instances in the form of courts, central banks, data protection officers, and broadcasters under public law, as well as publicly held businesses and utilities.

As a consequence of this development, the formation of political will shifts from state bodies to party committees, where it is centrally controlled. In this process, the governing parties enjoy especially broad influence. Wherever the opposition parties have veto power because certain decisions may only be made by a qualified majority or require the consent of a body which they control, they too are included in the informal decision-making. On account of their dual role as members of both party and state leadership, party members in state positions regularly have special weight. That does not necessarily mean that material decision-making is returned to the state bodies. However, the governmental and institutional boundaries interrupt direct party influence, and this can vary significantly from body to body. Informal 'chains of command' do not run to all bodies, and for institutions with great autonomy influence is only mediated by shared convictions.

Of course, the political parties are no longer the sole mediators between the state and society. The greater the role that the state assumes in shaping society, the more it affects the special interests of social groups. The political parties are often unable effectively to represent such special interests, as they must aggregate and balance different interests in order acquire a broad basis of electoral support. Consequently, since the rejection of liberalism, one also can observe the rapid emergence of a new form of affiliation that under the liberal concept of the state was neither provided for nor necessary: the federations or pressure groups. These associations differ from other voluntary affiliations in that they are focused on the state, because their aim is to influence state decisions to the benefit of the interests they represent. Unlike political parties, however, they are limited to presenting their demands and needs to state bodies. They do not become a part of them, as political parties do.

Thus, constitutions took these associations into account to an even lesser degree than political parties. Rather, under constitutional law, they, like any other club, are a part of society and thus enjoy freedom under the basic rights and are not subject to constitutional constraints. However, the evolution of state tasks and state instruments is matched by a change in the quality of these associations. It is primarily the great business and professional associations, but today also increasingly associations that advocate a specific general interest, that are involved in the negotiation process for state planning and guidance of social development. In their role as negotiation partners in corporative structures, their significance is no longer limited to communicating demands to the state. Rather, they are participants in state decisions just like political parties, though in narrower contexts. Thus, it is no longer possible to draw a clear boundary between the sphere of the state and that of society, either with respect to content or actors.

## III. EFFECTS

### 1. *Need for Regulation*

If, in view of this conclusion, one asks what repercussions these changes have for the possibility of controlling politics by means of constitutional law, it is helpful to compare the originating conditions of the modern constitution and the changes that have occurred since. If first considered in terms of the need for regulation, we discover that the rejection of transcendentally or traditionally legitimated state power that does not derive its right of rule from the consent of the governed, asserted through revolution at the end of the eighteenth century, has been virtually universally accomplished. Political rule by divine right, hallowed tradition, or superior insight is no longer capable of being recognized today. The consent of the governed remains as the sole source of legitimation. The ruling authority of the state is therefore of a derivative, and not an original nature, and is primarily understood as an office bestowed by society.

Under these circumstances, rule cannot simply be assumed: it requires establishment and legitimation. The concept of assigned rule implies a constituting act. It is true that the constituting act need not necessarily result in a constitution. Should rule be assigned unconditionally or under the sole condition of revocation at any time, no further regulation is required. By contrast, if the authority to rule is to be assigned conditionally, the consensus, if it is to be considered legitimate, must cover the conditions under which it is exercised. At a minimum, these conditions comprise organizational and procedural rules respecting the establishment of state power and the making of collectively binding decisions. Such an agreement as to the method of arriving at decisions is often possible even when the content of the decisions is controversial. However, as there is no such thing as a value-neutral organization, it is reasonable to establish a consensus regarding the fundamental aims and boundaries of political rule as well.

No society can escape from this consensual constraint, as otherwise it would be incapable of making decisions or unable to ensure that its decisions were complied with. Admittedly, this does not yet answer the question as to why this consensus should be cast in the form of the normative constitution. One would likely approach an answer if one considered why the constituting act in and of itself does not fulfil this purpose or, put another way, what the normative form adds to the basic consensus respecting the establishment and exercise of rule that precedes it. This reveals three features that the preceding historic-political consensus lacks: certainty, binding character, and normativity. The written formulation of the text of the consensus liberates it from the subjective understanding of the parties involved and endows it with verifiable determinateness. Enriching it with legally normative force frees it from the historical will of its originators and makes it valid over time. Normative codification liberates it from its founding purpose and makes it applicable for later enforcement.

This is associated with significant achievements. The binding written formulation reduces the likelihood of later disagreement as to the content of the consensus. In the event that differences of opinion do occur, normative codification makes it easier to determine what requirements it places on state behaviour in each specific case. The permanence bestowed on the consensus by legal validity relieves politics of the necessity of having to build a new consensus every time which, under the conditions of a need for permanent decision-making in the face of competing decision proposals, would entail insupportable costs. Rather, relief from the need to conduct ever new discussions on the principles of attaining unity is the prerequisite for the political decision-making process. The constitution enables this because its regulations are no longer an issue for, but rather the premise of, politics. By separating fundamentals from individual decisions in this way, the constitution also makes it easier for the defeated parties to accept majority decisions, thus limiting conflict potential.

But the benefits of the constitution go beyond this relief function. It also proves to be the form for monitoring social change. Almost everything is mutable in modern societies but they are able to cope with only a certain amount of simultaneous or abrupt change. By institutionalizing a higher degree of continuity at the level of principles and procedures rather than that of execution and realization, constitutions stabilize the relationship between continuity and change. They achieve this less by preventing change than by increasing the requirements for consensus and justification, impeding the process, or delaying decisions. By adding different time horizons to the political process, they protect society against haste and create the space for social learning. Naturally, the constitution itself cannot be immune to change, and must provide for its own adaptation and amendment. This applies even to eternity clauses such as Art. 79 (3) of the Basic Law, which apply only to normal constitutional amendments but cannot prevent the sovereign from reconstituting the state.

There is currently no functional equivalent to the constitution in its function as a cross-generational stabilizer of a historically determined basic consensus with its relief and oversight effect. It therefore continues to find its greatest support in this function. Repeal of the constitution would thus represent a loss of social peace and controlled change. Naturally, this says nothing as to the degree to which the constitution succeeds in fulfilling these functions under changed conditions. In contrast to the pre-constitutional constraints on political rule, which had merely a modifying, localized, and specific effect on rule, the constitution is designed to formulate the conditions for the legitimacy of rule and comprehensively subject all forms of public power to its rules. The aim is neither the complete juridification of politics nor the annulment of all social power, but to assert that collective obligation can only be engendered by bodies and claimed for decisions that remain within the constitutional framework.

### 2. *Object of Regulation*

The modern constitution relates to the state. The formation of a differentiated state power separate from society and functionally specialized on arriving at collectively binding decisions was the prerequisite for regulation by constitutional law. Particularly on account of the danger to individual freedom and social autonomy inherent in the state monopoly of force, that monopoly was subjected to special conditions that were neither intended, nor necessary, for society. This is not to say that the constitution has no significance for the social order. On the contrary: it defines the principles of this order. But it expresses them by binding the state to them. The state is the object of constitutional regulation and society its beneficiary. The unity of state power, a proposition that appears increasingly dubious empirically, finds its legal basis in the constitution. To that extent, the modern constitution presumes that state and society are different. Conversely, it is not prepared for actors, institutions, and processes that cannot be pinned down to this boundary.

Without expressly intending to, the constitutional state itself has given rise to such hybrids as political parties and associations and social power groups that have moved into this halfway role on account of the changing nature of state activity. Each calls into question the ability of the constitution to regulate politics, though from a purely formal view this remains invisible. Political parties remain outside the state; nowhere does the constitution allocate state entities, offices, or decision-making power to a party. Rather, the power of the state is invested in individuals, and always presupposes an act of investiture on the part of the people or an entity of the state legitimated by the people. However, candidacy for elective state offices and a great number of other public positions is de facto only possible through the agency of a political party. Once in office, however, these officeholders recruited through party politics are subject to the rules of separation of powers with their competence boundaries, guarantees of autonomy, and resulting mutual necessities of cooperation and oversight.

Nonetheless, the principle of a separation of powers, which is constitutive for the constitutional state, is undermined by political parties because, as with recruitment at all levels and functions of the state, parties also acquire influence on institutions that are removed from party competition, so that they can loyally serve changing party governments, like public administration, or exercise controlling functions within the political process dominated by parties, like the judiciary and the media, or can orient themselves at criteria other than the preservation of power, like public enterprises. Above all, parties leap over the constitutionally delineated boundaries because they shift the state decision-making process to the party level and then assert it through their representatives in the bodies of the state. Political parties thus have exercised their influence before the constitutional separation of powers can take effect. No longer do mutually independent state powers hold each other in check; rather it is the political parties which cooperate with themselves in varying roles.

Constitutional law is largely powerless with respect to this development. Its possibilities for regulating the input structures for the state's bodies and processes necessarily remains limited in a democratic system that is dependent on and open to society, while the constitutional requirements for the parties such as party-internal democracy or the disclosure of finances do not reach the separation-of-powers problem. The counterweights to party influence, such as opening representative democracy to popular initiatives or increasing the access barriers of political parties in the non-parliamentary sector can restrain their oligarchic and expansionistic tendencies, but they cannot restore the separation of powers. Rather, their task is assumed in part by the competition between parties and otherwise no longer relates to the functional separation of political forces, social groups, or state bodies so much as to the differentiation in time and arrangement of various legal decision-making processes, where they can develop their power-limiting impact by other means.

In contrast to parties, special-interest associations still do not send representatives to state bodies. If they wish to play a role in them, they must depend on political parties. However, the entities of the state have themselves begun formally and informally to involve them in the process of making and asserting state decisions. Such an involvement of social forces did not affect the state as the object of constitutional requirements as long as they were limited to the preparation of state decisions and did not reduce the decision-making freedom of the state bodies. Yet, what is at stake is not the preparation of decisions, but rather the decision-making itself through negotiation, which can only achieve their end when both sides commit to observing the result. Thus, the state surrenders its sovereignty in the scope of this commitment and allows social forces to participate in the exercise of public power without their being included in constitutional legitimation and responsibility contexts or subject to the constitutional requirements that apply to state bodies.

In contrast to the surrender of sovereignty rights to supranational institutions, for which no general impediment to constitutionalization exists, the domestic diffusion of state power presents significant problems. Constitutionalization of associations in the form of parties are constitutionalized, as is often proposed, could solve the problem of the legitimate communication of interests to the state, but would be unable to alter their character as advocates of special interests. Rather, the weakness that the constitution has already revealed with respect to the commingling of different state levels is here fully evident. Where public power passes over into the sphere of society, the state-oriented constitution cannot follow. Since this neo-corporatism is driven by a social change that is impervious to constitutional prohibitions, we must accustom ourselves to the fact that the system is once again acquiring characteristics of pre-modern polycentric rule that cannot be subjected to constitutional regulation. In spite of its ambition, the constitution no longer binds all holders of public power, but only a part.

### 3. Purpose of Regulation

The constitution focuses on the separation of state and society not only with respect to its object, but also with respect to its purpose. It was supposed to secure the restriction of the state to the function of guarantor for the social order. The functional expansion of the modern welfare state therefore leaves in its wake a constitutional regulatory deficit. In view of the focus of the constitution on infringements, this is evident everywhere the state no longer employs the means of infringements in fulfilling its structuring tasks. No infringement means no necessity of a law, where no law exists the administration is not subject to statutory constraint and the courts cannot review its compliance with the law. However, this deficiency also extends to the area where the state continues to employ infringements. The reservation of statute loses its effect of basic-rights protection when the problem is no longer to regulate isolated infringements of the administration over the basic rights of an individual, but changes in social relationships and structures mandated by the legislature itself that affect large social groups with clashing basic-rights positions.

These regulatory deficits have not gone unnoticed. The constitutional answer to change in the function of infringement is the proportionality principle, which now makes the constitutionality of an administrative act dependent not only on a sufficient statutory empowerment of the administration, but also on whether the empowering law itself does not unreasonably restrict the affected basic right and sufficiently balances the clashing basic rights positions. In the area of non-imperative state action, the concept of infringement has expanded to comprise all effects of state activity that negatively affect the exercise of basic rights, and the reservation of statute has extended to cover all state activities essential to basic rights regardless of the quality of a formal infringement in response to the altered conditions. Above all, however, basic rights themselves are no longer understood solely as negative rights against the state, but also as objective principles that obligate the state to protect basic rights against all sorts of menaces and tie its social-structuring activities to the principles of basic rights.

But the constitution's territorial gains with respect to the welfare state must not be overestimated. Basic rights in their character as objective principles do not develop the same binding force as in their capacity as negative rights. The high binding force of negative rights is due to the circumstance that, as prohibitions of action, they can only be fulfilled in one manner, namely by refraining from action. A violation can thus be remedied only in one conceivable manner: annulment of the corresponding act. Consequently, as negative rights they are immediately applicable and in the case of violation can be asserted by the courts with little difficulty. By contrast, a number of permissible alternatives are available for fulfilling the duty to protect basic rights against non-state actors.

It is then the task of politics to decide on the basis of its priorities and resources how to fulfil the duty to protect. In their character as objective principles, they are thus in need of statutory mediation. As long as this is lacking, they do not constitute an entitlement of individuals, and therefore cannot be asserted in court.

There is of course a further problem relating to the fulfilment of the duty to protect basic rights. Social structuring is almost always a matter of such great complexity that it cannot entirely be conceptually anticipated, and thus is determined only incompletely by law. As a consequence, classical conditional programmes are being increasingly supplanted by 'final programmes' that restrict themselves to setting out the aim of state action and enumerating a few aspects which must be taken into account. But the realization of such programmes depends not only on the will of the entity applying the law, but also on numerous external factors, and must thus remain situationally open. The content and result of that administration's actions can no longer be generally and abstractly predefined by statute. Rather, the administration determines these autonomously in the course of executing the project. The adaptation of basic rights thus proves to be largely an illusory victory for the constitutional state and democracy. The best evidence for this lies in their increasing proceduralization, which aims to compensate for the curtailed substantive protection through participation of the affected individuals in the administrative decision-making process.

But the material protection of basic rights, which has been made to depend largely on the proportionality principle, also has its constitutional and democratic costs, because as a standard for reasonableness and appropriateness it is largely beyond generalization and delivers results only on a case-by-case basis. Insofar as the courts review legislative and executive action through application of this standard, they therefore claim for themselves social structuring, without having been sufficiently equipped or legitimated for this task. The risk prevention task that has emerged in recent years also threatens to reduce the freedom-preserving effect of the proportionality principle. As a relative standard it makes the appropriateness of a restriction of basic rights dependent on the extent of the danger to the basic right being opposed. When this danger is great enough, the intervention threshold can be drastically lowered for other basic rights. In the risk society, it thus becomes conceivable that every single action appears necessary and appropriate as a relatively minor constraint on a highly valued legal good, yet in sum freedom withers. The constitution then finds itself at the margins of society without a single amendment to its text.

The protection of liberty mediated by democracy also comes under pressure, because the accumulation of irreversible decisions compelled by scientific and technological progress tends to make democratic majority change irrelevant. Improved findings or altered power relationships cannot change the situation for the foreseeable future. To the same extent, the democratic principle is nullified. Qualified majorities or popular initiative competencies such as those that are often proposed as compensation for this deficit fail to solve the problem because for existential problems they neither increase the legitimacy of the decision for the losers nor can they justify binding future generations. Now that the constitution is unable any longer to integrate all public power holders in its regulatory framework, we must therefore anticipate that it will also no longer apply to all areas of state activity. It remains to be seen whether a changed understanding of the constitution can remedy this loss of validity or whether the constitution will decline into a partial order.

# ❧ 12 ❧

## Can Democracy by Bargaining
## be Constitutionalized?

### I. INTRODUCTION

The question as to whether *Verhandlungsdemokratie* (negotiative democracy) can be constitutionalized is predicated on two assumptions whose correctness determines whether the question that forms the title of this chapter is meaning-ful. The first assumption is that the political system of the Federal Republic of Germany has acquired characteristics of a negotiative democracy. The second is that the practice referred to as 'negotiative democracy' is not constitutionally regulated but that it should be. I have examined both these underlying assump-tions on various occasions, but have never directly addressed the matter of con-stitutionalization. Thus, this chapter complements earlier analyses on the topic of negotiative democracy or the 'bargaining state'.

### II. WHAT IS NEGOTIATIVE DEMOCRACY?

The term 'negotiative democracy' is used here to designate a political system in which bi-directional private–public negotiation processes emerge that infor-mally arrive at a result which is either implemented in the form of legal norms by the responsible state bodies or is regarded by the negotiating parties as bind-ing without attaining the status of legal validity. The arrangements supple-ment the monodirectional, state-centred decision-making process whose result takes legal form and is binding on all private parties subject to that decision and which, if necessary, can be asserted by means of coercion. Admittedly, this process of negotiation does not become a characteristic of a political system until it occurs to an extent that this phenomenon can no longer be considered an isolated, atypical exception but rather forms an established state practice.

The fact that state actors enter into negotiations at all is not novel. Many negotiations, even though not expressly mentioned in the Basic Law, are a con-sequence of the constitutional architecture. Such is the case in the formation of a government when no party has achieved the majority necessary for electing the chancellor in the Bundestag. Additionally, negotiations are necessary when-ever constitutional norms or other laws make political decisions contingent on a two-thirds majority which no party has alone been able to muster. This is

Constitutionalism: Past, Present, and Future. First Edition. Dieter Grimm. © Dieter Grimm 2016. Published 2016 by Oxford University Press.

the case, for instance, for constitutional amendments or the election of constitutional court judges. Finally, negotiations are inevitable when controversial laws approved by the Bundestag require the approval of the Bundesrat but the majorities in these two bodies differ.

In contrast to these negotiations, which take place entirely within the bounds of state structures, negotiative democracy concerns negotiations between public and private actors. Contacts between public bodies and private subjects of regulation have long been common in the preparatory phase of public decisions and, generally speaking, are in no way questionable in constitutional terms. For one thing, the constitution does not regulate the public decision-making process until a certain point has been reached, leaving the prior phase open, even for private influence. Additionally, constitutional norms or the procedural rules of public bodies often require consultation with affected private individuals. However, this imposes no obligations on the state; the decision is made within its bodies according to the prescribed process.

By contrast, 'negotiative democracy' means that the preliminary phase of public decision is left behind and the content of the decision becomes the object of negotiations with private actors. These negotiations relate to the requirements that the state places on private parties in the interest of the common good, or burdens that it wishes to impose in pursuit of its objects. These are not established unilaterally through the state processes intended for that purpose, but bilaterally with participation of those who are subjects of the decision. For some time now, this process has been apparent on various levels of state activity—deliberative, decision-making, and executive. Negotiations are conducted with these bodies in the establishment of norms by parliament and government, in the execution of norms by the administration, and even in the application of norms by the courts.

In the execution of norms, negotiation is not restricted to the area in which the administration is granted discretion. Rather, it can also be found where strict norm conformance applies, for instance in the determination of taxation or the elimination of unlawful conditions in planning or environmental law. In the area of norm application, negotiation occurs in criminal proceedings. The negotiation concerns the question to which charges the defendant pleads guilty, which ones the prosecution or the court will drop, and what sentence will be imposed. In both cases, the reason for this is generally that the unilateral, sovereign decision needs complex, time-consuming and expensive investigations, so that it appears advantageous to negotiate, which, of course, requires concessions on both sides.

Such negotiations in the areas of administration and justice present significant constitutional problems. However, since they primarily concern issues of due process rather than democracy, these will not be examined here. The democracy problem arises mainly in the area of legislation. The question as to whether a political system can be termed a negotiative democracy can be answered according to the extent to which the behavioural rules that apply to society are negotiated between government representatives and influential special interest groups, rather than by elected representatives in deliberative processes that offer opportunities for broad participation. Therefore the analysis in this chapter will concentrate on this area, though this is not meant to imply that negotiations in the areas of administration and justice present no problems from a democratic perspective.

The impetus for negotiations in the legislative process generally derives from the insight that certain social (usually scientific-technical or commercial) developments need to be regulated. Once the problem has been identified, it is often the state that initiates negotiations with those causing it as to the solution or, if a solution has been developed, clarifies in negotiations the extent to which this is to be realized. However, private actors often preempt the threat of state initiative and voluntarily offer self-limitations, which are then negotiated. On the part of the state, these negotiations are usually conducted by the government. On the private side, the industry associations are generally involved, the enterprises causing the problem less often, and affected third parties even more rarely.

Such negotiations can lead to draft legislation, which is then presented to the parliamentary bodies for ratification. This occurs in particular when the outcomes of negotiation cannot be realized without a law, whether because the solution requires limitations of a basic right of third parties, or because some parties causing the problem are unwilling to comply voluntarily with the negotiated solution. In the past, however, regulations, which are intended to specify legal requirements and which frequently implement them and make them operative, have been the object of such negotiations more often than laws. Although the government requires a prior parliamentary authorization in order to promulgate regulations, the negotiated outcome itself can be made legally valid without parliamentary participation.

An alternative is that the negotiated outcome is not implemented in the form of legal norms but rather that the private party makes a commitment, in response to which the state waives regulation. Here, the statute is no longer the aim of negotiations; it is only brandished as a threat to increase the private party's willingness to make concessions during the negotiation process. For this type of outcome, it has become common to distinguish between agreements that replace, represent, and avoid legal norms. The focus of such agreements is on behavioural standards for private problem originators. On occasion these standards are supplemented with reporting or notification obligations. Some agreements also call for inspections to verify adherence to private promises of 'good' behaviour.

In the case of a private commitment on behaviour in exchange for the state refraining from regulation, the result assumes no legal status. Although it is intended to bind both sides, the agreement does not take a statutory form and thus cannot be asserted in law. Still, the state's option of resorting to legislation enhances the binding nature of the agreement. Naturally, the informality of the agreements does not prevent them from being fixed in writing, whether unilaterally in a letter from the private negotiation parties to their public opposite numbers or bilaterally in a protocol of the negotiation parties. Publication is also not uncommon, sometimes in press statements of one or both parties, occasionally in the Federal Gazette, and at times in the Bundestag's printed materials, when, for example, the negotiations are the subject of a parliamentary inquiry but not reported in the Federal Law Gazette.

A complete inventory of such agrements does not exist. Not even the German government has an overview. The literature generally limits itself to collections of examples, some quite extensive. Despite their incompleteness, they provide an impression of the extent to which this mode of performance of state tasks is utilized, even though only a few negotiations have attracted as much public notice as phase-out of nuclear power or $CO_2$ reduction. The quantitative focus is in the area of environmental protection. This is also the area in which the most extensive catalogues exist, for instance that of the Federal Environment Ministry from 1999. Other areas in which agreements are frequently reached include consumer protection, in particular product safety and product information, product advertising, and healthcare policy.

Even if all contractual agreements in the legislative area were known, the number would still be significantly smaller than the laws and regulations promulgated during the same period. But still, it remains true that legal norms are determined or replaced by agreements in key policy areas. Negotiative democracy is a reality. However, before the question as to the need for constitutional regulation is addressed, we should examine the reasons for the spread of this course of action, as no feasible constitutional response is conceivable as long as these remain unknown. In particular, if the causes are not analysed, there is no possibility to estimate what constitutional measures would fail in the face of inherent necessitiy, and which are likely to prove effective.

The roots of this development may be found in the expansion of state tasks. In its departure from the liberal model, the state has gradually re-assumed overall responsibility for the maintenance and development of society in social, economic, and cultural respects. But this expansion of responsibility was not accompanied by a commensurate expansion of authority and compulsory methods. Rather, the state remained constitutionally obligated to, and therefore bound by, individual freedom and social autonomy. Today, these boundaries are interpreted even more strictly than at the dawn of constitutionalism. Under these circumstances, not everything that is considered a state task can be accomplished using the specific state methods of command and coercion. Three different constellations can be identified.

There is one task segment in which the application of imperative law is objectively impossible because the objects of regulation are not amenable to legal commands. Economic fluctuations, research results, and changes in mentality cannot be ordered. In a second area, the use of imperative methods is objectively possible but not legally permissible, as the basic rights assign the areas to be controlled to the sphere of personal disposition. This does not preclude state regulation. However, regulation can only limit private authority and change the parameters for the pursuit of personal interest, but not disproportionately constrain or even eliminate personal decision-making freedom. Investments, the hiring of employees, and the provision of residential space cannot be ordered.

Finally, there is a third area in which imperative control is objectively possible and legally permissible, but is not exercised because it appears neither effective nor opportune to state actors. The most important reason for the ineffectiveness is that the state often lacks the information necessary for formulating an effective programme for control, while private decision-makers possess this but are not necessarily willing to disclose it. The main reason for being inopportune is that those to be subjected to control can threaten to transfer their activities outside of the jurisdiction of regulation or have possibilities for avoiding compliance with the norm, so that the state is faced with implementation costs that for financial reasons it is reluctant to assume.

In general, wherever imperative means of control fail or are not applied for one of these reasons, the state depends on voluntary compliance of the subjects of control. To ensure this, however, it must resort to equivalences for legal action that provide sufficient motivation. The most common method is financial motivation. Monetary incentives or deterrents are intended to push the objects of control to that behaviour which is in the general interest. This generally takes a statutory form. But compared to imperative law, these are not statutes that impose a certain behaviour on the objects of the norm; rather, the aim is to influence them in their self-determined behaviour by aligning this with advantages or disadvantages.

The more recent instrument consists of pursuading private subjects of control to cooperate with the state. This puts them in a negotiating position with respect to the state which the latter must recognize through concessions in the control programme. Negotiations are the logical means for this, and occur ever more frequently due to the obvious advantages for both sides. Private actors can expect less onerous burdens, while the state saves implementation or incentivization costs. It would therefore be too simple to attribute negotiative democracy solely to an aversion to take responsibility or to laziness on the political side. Under the conditions described above, it has its own inevitability. This does not mean that every negotiation of this type is unavoidable, but certainly that the tendency towards negotiation democracy has structural causes.

## III. IS CONSTITUTIONALIZATION NECESSARY?

There are no constitutional provisions that expressly apply to negotiative democracy. It was not possible to anticipate this practice at the time the Basic Law was drafted and none of the numerous amendments since have taken into account the phenomenon of the bargaining state. For a long time, it was not even noticed. This does not mean that negotiations take place in a legal vacuum since constitutional requirements and prohibitions bind the state in all its manifestations and modes of action. It may not, for example, replace laws with agreements where the Basic Law requires the enactment of legislation. Nor can the state escape its constitutional constraints by shifting to forms of action not provided for under constitutional law.

However, the question arises as to whether these general provisions provide sufficient security, or whether negotiative democracy requires that its particularities are taken into account. This question would be answered quickly if the agreements had no decision-making character with respect to statutes but negotiations of this type fell into the statute preparation phase, which the constitution leaves open, and were thus merely a form of intensified lobbying. However, this could only apply to those cases in which agreements between government representatives and private interests are subsequently submitted to the formal parliamentary legislative process. The parliament is not bound by the agreements arrived at by the government: it can accept, reject, or modify the negotiated draft legislation as it sees fit.

Even in this case, however, one should not overlook the de facto constraint under which majority factions stand. When draft legislation is based on agreements with third parties, parliament lacks fewer alternatives than it would have with respect to normal government bills; amendments are out of the question as they would endanger the entire undertaking. To that extent, the situation is similar to that faced by parliament when ratifying international treaties. It can only either accept or reject such treaties. Amendments are not permitted, as they require the consent of all parties to the treaty. In the case of negotiated draft legislation, the restriction on amendment is not legal, but de facto. But it is no less compulsory for that reason.

But parliament is not involved at all when the agreed provision can be promulgated by the negotiating government in the form of a regulation. The government requires parliamentary authorization for this, but once issued parliament's influence is exhausted. Parliament is entirely excluded when the negotiations lead to a waiver of state regulation, rather than an agreement on the specific content of a norm. To be sure, such a waiver on the part of the government is not binding on parliament, which is free to take up the matter and enact a law as it sees fit. However, this presumes knowledge of the agreement and, where this exists, a majority will to overturn the government's declared waiver of regulation through statutory regulation. This too is extremely improbable.

By the nature of things, therefore, behavioural rules arise in the negotiations between government and private parties that are either implemented in the agreed form as legal norms or derive their binding nature from the participants' mutual desire to adhere to them, without formal legal validity. These differ from other contracts which the state concludes with private parties in that the object of the agreement is the exercise of sovereign authority. The agreement relates to legal norms or their surrogates. To that extent, it seems justified to regard these agreements as functionally and materially equivalent to legislation. Consequently, the private portion of this cannot be adequately understood using influence categories of the type applied in older empirical studies of legislation. It can only be described appropriately in terms of participation categories.

The question then arises as to what constitutional consequences follow. The answer requires a reflection on the purpose of the constitution. Succinctly put, it is the juridification of state power in the interests of individual freedom, democratic rule, and social justice. This juridification is comprehensive in two senses. First, only those who are democratically legitimated and accountable may take collectively binding decisions and exercise sovereign power. Secondly, collectively binding decisions can only claim legitimacy when they have passed through the constitutionally required processes and meet constitutional requirements as to their content.

The constitution thus thrives on a separation of public and private actors. The state alone exercises public power, but in turn is subject to the constitutional constraints. Private actors are subject to state power, but in return enjoy the constitutional guarantees of freedom and protective mechanisms. This separation would be circumvented if the state could exercise the freedom of private entities, but also if private entities could dictate the deployment of sovereign power. Additionally, the constitution lives from the formalization of collectively binding decisions, as otherwise the constitutional provisions would have no basis. This does not preclude informal preliminary phases; rather, it often necessitates them, though they must reckon with the subsequent formalized phases, including review.

With respect to the question of the need to regulate negotiation arrangements, this means that they are not expressly unconstitutional, as there are no applicable constitutional norms that could be violated. Still, they undermine key constitutional principles that contribute to the legitimation of rule. For one thing, the negotiation arrangements give rise to privileged private parties who are not limited to general citizen status, but rather participate in the state will formation without being integrated in the democratic legitimation and accountability context to which the constitution subjugates public power holders. For another, the constitutionally mandated decision bodies and processes are marginalized in the same degree that the state has obligated itself with respect to these private entitites.

The effects have impacts primarily on the main legislative body, the parliament. It is not involved in the negotiations, which are conducted by the government even if they concern the content of legislation. If the negotiation produces draft legislation, only the parliament can enact it; however, the de facto necessities bearing on the parliamentary majority will generally lead to this being adopted unchanged. If the result is a waiver of regulation on the part of the government, this requires no parliamentary involvement at all. It is also unlikely that parliament will undertake to regulate the matter on its own initiative. On the contrary, it sometimes occurs that, instead of preparing its own draft legislation, parliament calls on the government to enter into negotiations with the private originators of problems, as in the case of CFC reductions.

With the abdication of parliament from the negotiation sector, the advantage presented by the parliamentary stage of the legislative process is also lost. This is the public debate, in which proposed regulations must be justified and stand up to criticism, with the consequence that the public can form an opinion and take a position. This is important mainly for those who have not been heard by public actors in the preliminary stage. But even a parliamentary debate following the negotiation usually lacks the power to connect state and social discourse, because the negotiation result is fixed and parliament no longer constitutes a forum in which differing understandings or neglected interests can be meaningfully asserted.

When examining consequences, however, one cannot stop at parliament. Weaknesses also extend to the product of the parliamentary process, the statute, or its informal surrogate, the private assurance of compliance. They generally do not develop the level of general acceptance that has a legitimating effect. After all, negotiations are not conducted with all affected parties, only with veto players. Thus, their interests have a greater likelihood of being considered. This is not due to power accumulated independently of the state, which to a certain extent must be accepted as a consequence of freedom, but to a procedure offered by the state. It thus advances positions of social power that are to be neutralized through the constitutionally regulated legislative process.

Negotiative democracy thus also diminishes the significance of elections. Elections are a fundamental democratic act that determine the representatives of the people, who, on the basis of this legitimation, are authorized to make decisions on behalf of the community as a whole. If these decisions are negotiated instead with private interests, elections no longer determine who influences the decision-making process of the state. Certainly, as voters all are equal. But the desired internal equality of the products of the elected parliament is no longer assured, since a few privileged private entities are not limited to their right to vote and to the organized representation of their interests with respect to the state, but are able to shift the balance in their favour through their involvement in state decision-making processes. The state helps their interests to an enhanced level of consideration.

However, it is not only the principle of democracy that pays a price; the rule of law also pays a penalty. The submission of public power to law and the ensuing individual assurance, as well as judicial remedies against state action, are cornerstones of the state under the rule of law. Both are mediated by statutes, which in turn are subject to review of their constitutionality. Various public bodies can initiate an abstract judicial review, the ordinary courts can initiate a concrete judicial review, and individuals can require a review of laws they find onerous by means of a constitutional complaint. All this contributes significantly to the legitimacy of law under the conditions of legislation guided by party politics with all its well-known deficits.

Where negotiations lead to private assurances of good behaviour in return for state waiver of regulation, there is no object of judicial review. There exists neither a standard for a review of legality through administrative courts nor an object for constitutional-court review. The courts also have no possibility of investigating whether private commitments are complied with, even though the prerequisites for this are unfavourable due to the division between negotiation parties and those subject to the obligation on the private side: the negotiators are commonly the associations, while those subject to obligation are businesses. Often not even the administration verifies whether the obligations are being met. When the outcome of negotiation remains unpublished, media and citizen initiatives cannot close this oversight gap.

Negotiative democracy thus distances itself greatly from the fundamental principles of the constitution. The regulations to which the legislative process is subjected precisely in the interests of participation, deliberation, transparency, and oversight do not cover negotiative democracy. Privileged participation takes the place of generally open participation, negotiation is substituted for deliberation, transparency yields to back-room dealings, and contractual compliance supersedes review. The disciplining effect that derives from the implicit threat of judicial review, and the associated possiblities for corrections that benefit other affected parties, are lost. If one wishes to maintain the constitution's claim with respect to collectively valid decisions, then no doubt can be cast on the need for constitutional regulation. The question is whether this need can be met.

## IV. CAPABILITY OF CONSTITUTIONALIZATION?

When seeking constitutional solutions, it is advisable to eliminate two radical alternatives at the outset. The first is the prohibition of these arrangements. Although they threaten to undermine key constitutional protections, a prohibition does not appear promising as there are structural reasons for the transition to negotiative democracy. Negotiations with private problem originators regarding behavioural standards are a politically rational response to the dilemma which the state faces when it is expected to resolve a regulatory problem without being able or willing to use imperative law to accomplish this task. Where ineffective, unimplemented, or contra-productive law would be the alternative, consensual solutions appear preferable.

The second alternative is the elimination of the causes of negotiative democracy. As they are found in the expansion of state tasks, these would have to be pruned back to their classical-liberal dimensions. If the state reduces itself to safeguarding market mechanisms and public safety, this will obviate most of the problems that prevent it from resorting to imperative law. But the state would violate other constitutional principles, in particular those of the social state. For all the vagueness inherent in this, it does not permit a reversion to laisser-faire liberalism. Additionally, given the complexity of the matters to be regulated even in the classical state mission of public safety, it is difficult to arrive at effective solutions without involving private problem originators.

The only remaining alternative is to adapt the constitution to negotiative democracy. This would legitimate it while making it subject to constitutional discipline. Unless the latter is capable of succeeding, there is no point in pursuing this proposal. Constitutional recognition without regulation would simply shroud the practice in a mantle of legitimacy without reducing the dangers inherent in it. Doubts as to the success of the attempt derive from the fact that negotiation arrangements are orthogonal to the structure of modern constitutions in two respects. First, they cross the boundary between the state and society, which determines the area of application of democracy, the rule of law and basic rights. Secondly, it lives off its informality, while constitutionalism expressly demands formality.

Accordingly, as constitutionalization of negotiative democracy means its acceptance its idiosyncrasies have to be accepted. This considerably reduces the possibilities of constitutional regulation. It is neither possible to nationalize the private participants in negotiations of norms, nor can they be democratically legitimated without at the same time robbing them of their status as bearers of partial interests. It is equally impossible to formalize the negotiations or their results comparable to state legislation if they are to retain their purpose. First, the constitution can only apply on the state side. Secondly, it cannot intervene directly, but only through contextual control. With respect to the necessity and nature of the intervention, it is useful to distinguish between the commencement, execution, result, and review of negotiations.

When negotiations intended to lead to agreements in lieu of legislation are commenced, an obligation to publish as an equivalent to the introduction of draft legislation in parliament is an obvious idea. This could draw public attention to this process and motivate other affected parties who are not included in the negotiations. However, it is precisely the informality of negotiations that makes it difficult to define a threshold for triggering such an obligation. The transitions from the initial overtures to result-oriented negotiation are fluid. Unlike legislation, texts stand at the end, and not at the start of the process. Artificially set thresholds would strip away informality. When conclusion of negotiations is imminent, publication can no longer fulfil its function.

Furthermore, there is a question as to whether objective boundaries exist for the commencement of negotiations with the aim of an agreement in lieu of statute. In one respect, this is easy to answer: the German government can only negotiate within the legislative competence of the federal government. By contrast, there is no necessity to limit its negotiating authority to the area of regulations or decrees. That would disregard legislative reality. The government is the driving force in legislation and holds the power of initiative, and the great majority of bills originate from the government. Nor is such a restriction necessary to preserve the rights of parliament, as in statute-avoiding negotiations the government can control its right of initiative but cannot bind parliament. For the same reason, it also does not require parliamentary permission to negotiate.

The situation becomes more difficult when the question as to the material limits of such negotiations is posed. As one major danger of negotiation arrangements is that not all parties affected by the result can assert their interest in the negotiations, the idea of permitting negotiative solutions only where two negotiating parties with opposing interests are facing each other, and the consequences of the agreement are restricted to them or those they represent, has been considered. However, it is highly questionable whether matters that meet this prerequisite ever become an object of negotiations between public and private actors at all. Even collective-bargaining agreements between employer associations and labour unions, which probably inspired this proposal, have effects that extend far beyond the group of collective-bargaining parties.

Negotiations that the state conducts with private parties in the area of legislation relate entirely to conflicts between particular and general interests. What complicates such negotiations is the fact that interests and negotiating sides are not congruent. In a system in which economic growth is a state task, the particular interests on the private side can always claim to contribute to the general welfare, for instance job preservation, while on the state side client bonds and political self-interest dilute the connection to the general welfare. The aim is thus usually to mediate between particular interests with a general welfare aspect and other aspects of general welfare. For this reason, it seems that the current state of affairs must remain unchanged: an agreement in lieu of statute is only out of place where a statute is required by the constitution.

When negotiations are prepared, the question of access becomes paramount. This question acquires its significance from the circumstance that generally only the parties interested in a waiver of regulation or minimal regulation are represented on the private side, and not those interested in greater limitation. The state speaks for them, but makes their interests subject to the negotiations without granting them a voice. The fact that the private parties also make their interests subject to negotiation does not offset the state's readiness to concede, because the requirements of the general welfare as defined by the state are already based on a weighing of conflicting legitimate interests. Negotiations according to the current model are thus at risk of producing unbalanced results on account of the limited participation and information.

On the other hand, one cannot ignore the predicament to which negotiative democracy owes its development. Negotiations with private actors on behavioural standards obtrude where the traditional toolkit of statutory guidance of behaviour reaches its capacity limit. Under these circumstances, the question arises as to whether the goal of regulation can be achieved more adequately through consensual solutions. The consensus that must be ensured here is that of the private originators of the regulatory problem. Their willingness to broker a consensus is of course sufficiently great only where the alternative of a statutory regulation is still threatening enough that taking the path of negotiation appears worthwhile. Constitutional provisions must not eliminate the conditions for this.

This does not automatically preclude rights of access for representatives of the opposing interests. However, the question is: who can represent these? As these concern negotiations in the area of legislation, the scope of affected parties is not so easily delimited as in the case of the application of laws to specific individuals. The interests opposing those of the private negotiating parties are largely those of society in general. Interests of clean air, healthy food, and safe power plants are those of the general public, which unlike corporate interests cannot be organized in the form of federations. Still, civil movements can take up such general interests. Admittedly, they lack a mandate and compulsory power, but they often possess expert knowledge and the potential for public mobilization.

The existence of such civil movements enriches the democratic process. However, they cannot be easily integrated in the structures of negotiative democracy. Since the purpose of negotiations is only achieved when the problem originators commit themselves to complying with the agreement, the involvement of further participants encourages shifting to preliminary stages and subsidiary forums in which the results are negotiated. The constitution is powerless in the face of such practices. This in turn gives rise to doubts respecting a constitutional order, not to mention the difficulties of defining the prerequisites for participation. Nevertheless, the state side should give these groups an opportunity to express their views, as is common in the legislative process. This does not require a constitutional regulation; the proper place for this is in bye-laws.

With respect to the content of agreements, it is clear that the bargaining state cannot escape its constitutional bonds, in particular its duty to protect basic rights. According to the German Federal Constitutional Court, the state is not only required to refrain from violating basic rights but also has the duty to protect these against dangers from other sources. This is usually accomplished through statutes. How the legislature fulfils these obligations to protect basic rights is a matter of its own political discretion. But the constitution demands a level of protection that is commensurate to the importance of the rights to be protected and the magnitude of the danger. If this protective duty is met through agreements instead of statutes, these too may not violate the prohibition of insufficient action.

Even when negotiations do not result in a formal act, they are eventually brought to a conclusion. The conclusion is successful when the government accepts the binding undertaking of the private side and expressly or tacitly waives statutory regulation. As this is functionally a legislative act, the corresponding rules also apply here. Just as the federal government as a whole holds the right of initiative in the legislative process, the agreement in lieu of statute must obtain the consent of the cabinet, and not merely the negotiating ministry. This is not merely a matter of form. The involvement of the cabinet ensures that the interests of different ministries are taken into account and undesired side effects or consequences in other sectors are avoided as much as possible.

If the agreements are implemented in the form of statute or regulations, neither a knowledge problem nor a legal protection problem exists. It is different in the case of agreements in lieu of statute, which is why they must be published. This is democratically necessary, to ensure that the public and parliament may intervene. Even though parliament will seldom replace the agreement with a law, this at least gives the opposition the opportunity to critically examine the agreement and force the majority to justify its position. Also, defects in execution can lead to changing attitudes. Consequently, the obligation of notice must be extended to compliance with the agreement. As it transpires that nowhere near all agreements are published, an amendment to the constitution to include a publication obligation is far from superfluous.

Additionally, publication is the prerequisite for legal protection. Agreements, like statutes, must be subject to constitutional judicial review. This is at best doubtful under the current law. According to the Basic Law, the object of judicial review is 'federal or state law'. It requires courts to submit 'laws' that are key to their ruling and which they consider unconstitutional to the Federal Constitutional Court for review. However, these agreements are not laws, but informal behavioural standards. Regardless of this, they fulfil the function of law. An express extension of judicial review in the Basic Law to agreements in lieu of statute and a corresponding modification of the various procedural codes thus appears necessary.

Legal protection is the most important compensation for restricted access to negotiations. If this is extended to agreements in lieu of statute, the Federal Constitutional Court can review whether the interests affected, insofar as constitutionally recognized in basic rights or objectives of the state (such as protection of the natural basis for life) have been placed in an appropriate relationship, just as in judicial review of statutes. If there is a deficit here, the court would have to order the Federal Republic (or a state) to fulfil its duty to protect. The nature of this fulfilment would remain a political matter, as always in the fulfilment of protective obligations respecting basic rights. The government can attempt to reopen negotiations and achieve a different result, or it can take the legislative path. But in principle this would require the adoption of certain constitutional amendments.[1]

## V. CONCLUSION

The proposed constitutional responses to the new instruments of negotiative democracy admittedly do not justify the hope that these amount to fully adequate substitutes for the constitutional provisions that regulate the traditional forms of state action. Rather, one must come to terms with the fact that the constitution cannot fully extend its effect to the sphere of private–public cooperation and informal agreements. The binding force of the constitution declines, but this is no reason to lapse into constitutional resignation and fail to utilize the degree of constitutional discipline that can actually be applied to this new form of action.

---

[1] Inserted between Art. 80 and Art. 80a GG: 'Should the federal government arrive at agreements in lieu of statutes with private parties in the area of its legislative authority, the Bundestag and Bundesrat are to be informed of the agreement and compliance therewith.'

Inserted in Art. 93 (1) no. 2 GG after 'federal law or state law': 'as well as agreements in lieu of statute'.

Inserted after Art. 100 (1) sen. 2 GG as a third sentence: 'The same shall apply accordingly where the conformity of agreements in lieu of statute with the Basic Law is concerned.' The latter assumes that legal recourse is open under ordinary law for the case that those affected see their rights violated thorugh the content of or non-compliance with agreements.

# PART VII

# EUROPEANIZATION

# The Role of National Constitutions in a United Europe

## I. THE AIM OF THE CONSTITUTION

The shift in meaning to which national constitutions are subjected in a united Europe can be fully appreciated only by considering the aim that originally inhered in national constitutions. This aim derives from the conditions under which constitutionalism emerged.[1] The modern constitution developed at the end of the eighteenth century as a consequence of two successful revolutions in North America and France, in which the traditional rule was overthrown and had to be replaced by a new one. In this situation, the much older idea that the legitimacy of political rule is based on the consent of the governed acquired practical significance for the first time. Political rule could be derived neither from divine right, nor from the inherent right of the ruler, nor from a superior understanding of the common good, and certainly not from the mere possession of power. It had to be founded on the people.

The difficulty was that the people as bearer of the power to rule lacked the ability to exercise this power itself. It had therefore to be entrusted to representatives. Under the condition of popular sovereignty, political rule became a matter of mandate. Together with another resurgent idea—that ruling authority should not be bestowed unconditionally but only for a specific purpose and a limited period and that, to protect the liberty and equality of individuals, it must be distributed among different holders—this conviction led to the formulation of conditions for legitimate rule, on the basis of which individuals were then appointed to exercise power. Endowed with legal validity, these conditions formed the constitution, whose origin was attributed to the people. In order to fulfil its function, the constitution took precedence over all acts of those entrusted with the exercise of rule.

The ambition of the constitution was thus defined. It constitutes legitimate rule and at the same time regulates its possession and exercise consistently, comprehensively and obligatorily.[2] This does not mean that the content of every act of rule is specified in the constitution, so that rule exhausts itself in execution of the constitution. But it does mean that all authority to rule must derive from

---

[1] See Chs. 1 and 2 of this volume.    [2] Cf. Chs. 1 and 15 of this volume.

Constitutionalism: Past, Present, and Future. First Edition. Dieter Grimm. © Dieter Grimm 2016. Published 2016 by Oxford University Press.

the constitution and conform to the requirements of constitutional law. The holders of power may neither pursue ends prohibited by the constitution, nor employ constitutionally prohibited means or exceed the limits imposed by the constitution. The modern constitution's claim to validity thus prohibits extra-constitutional holders of ruling power and extraconstitutional ways and means of exercising rule. Within the body politic that is constituted by it, the constitution applies universally and exclusively.

Such a form of rule could only be conceived once an object existed that was amenable to systematic and comprehensive regulation by a law which was specifically designed to control political activity. Such an object was lacking in the Middle Ages. In medieval society the rights of rule referred to persons and not territories and were split among numerous mutually independent holders. It therefore lacked a constitution in this sense and could not possibly have had one. It was the concentration of the various rights of rule in a single holder and their crystallization as a uniform power relating to a defined territory, which emerged only at the end of the sixteenth century and was quickly understood as a 'state', that enabled legal regulation by means of a constitution. Historically, the state was the essential prerequisite for the constitution. The modern constitution was the constitution of the state.

Naturally, the fact that the claim of constitutionalism was set out in the first constitutions provided no guarantee that every subsequent constitution would realize that claim. Once the modern constitution had emerged and had acquired a substantial appeal even in countries that had not experienced revolution, it became possible to declare documents as constitutions that realized the constitutional project only partially or not at all. In fact, constitutions existed which were not driven by any serious will to restrain politics. One can term this *pseudo-constitutionalism*. Equally, constitutions were drafted that did not place the power of rule on a new legitimating foundation but merely limited a pre-existing power of rule in one respect or another—that is, they merely modified rather than constituted rule. Constitutions of this nature express *semi-constitutionalism*.

However, no constitution subjected its own state's power to foreign rule or recognized actions of foreign ruling authority as binding within its own territorial area of application. This resulted from the circumstance that states formed the highest-level political units, and claimed the right of self-determination within their territory. Above the states there was no lawless zone. Rather the supra-state level was subject to international law. But international law consisted entirely of treaty law or customary law and thus derived its validity from the will of the states, which bound themselves voluntarily. The highest principle of international law was thus the sovereignty of the state, which assured states of internal autonomy and external independence. Bonds under international law applied only with respect to external relationships and could only attain validity within the state if the state transformed it into national law. Since no capability for asserting international law obligations existed, states were effectively left to their own devices.

The state constitution could thus fulfil its comprehensive claim to regulation because public power was identical to state power and a supra-state public power did not exist. Although a multiplicity of state powers existed, there was only one for each territory, and its authority ended at their borders.[3] This foundation for redemption of the claim to validity of the national constitution became so much a matter of course that it was no longer even mentioned. Rather, it has only become apparent as a prerequisite for the validity of the constitution since states began to establish supranational bodies for the purpose of increasing their problem-solving capacity. Unlike traditional leagues and alliances, these supranational bodies do not simply coordinate state activities; they have also acquired sovereign rights in order to attain common objectives, which they may validly exercise within the states and in response to which states may not cite their right to self-determination.

## II. THE EMERGENCE OF SUPRANATIONAL SOVEREIGN POWER

This is the basis of the change in the significance of modern constitutions. As a consequence of the emergence of supranational power the identity of public power and state power dissolves. The origins of this process predate European integration. The formation of supranational sovereign power began with the founding of the United Nations (UN) in 1945. The member states of the UN not only renounce their right to resolve their conflicts by force (except for self-defence); they also empower the UN to assert this renunciation of the use of force where it is violated, by military means if necessary, but also through civil tools, such as legal proceedings. The UN has thus attained a share of public power. National boundaries have become permeable to acts of public power of the UN. The strict separation between internal and external affairs on which fulfilment of the constitution's claim to comprehensive regulation rested no longer exists.

This development has continued to evolve. In principle, the UN's right to humanitarian intervention is recognized today when a state violates the fundamental human rights of its population or specific population groups. The International Criminal Tribunals of the former Yugoslavia and Rwanda were established on the basis of resolutions of the Security Council, not treaties, and the activities of these bodies are independent of the consent of the affected states. Additionally, rules of international law are taking shape under the umbrella of the UN that claim validity as *ius cogens* independently of the approval of the states and which bind them when they conclude treaties. Outside the UN, but covering most nations, the World Trade Organization has acquired authority to assert trade agreements through a court-like arbitration process that is also not bound by the consent of the affected states.

---

[3] The Bundesstaat is a special case, in which state power is both horizontally and vertically divided, but conflicting power claims are averted through a clear division of tasks and hierarchalization.

Nowhere, however, has this development progressed as far as in Europe. Admittedly, UN interventions, when they occur, can have major consequences. But they do not occur frequently, in part because the great majority of member states do not provide a reason for intervention, and in part because a permanent member of the Security Council exercises its veto. With respect to its object, the UN's sovereign power is not only more restricted than that of the states but also, unlike state sovereign power, it is rarely exercised and only over countries that provide reason for this. Most nations have never been subject to a sovereign action of the UN. That is not so with respect to European integration. The powers transferred to European institutions do not include physical force—this is reserved for the states. But member states are constantly subjected to the effects of European sovereign acts.

A distinction must here be made between the Council of Europe and the European Union. The Council of Europe mainly acts in states through the European Court of Human Rights (ECtHR), whose task is to ensure compliance with the European Convention on Human Rights (ECHR). The ECHR owes its legal validity within the member states to the national ratification that also determines the legal status of the ECHR within the hierarchy of national norms. The ECtHR can review actions of member states for violation of the ECHR but it is restricted to declaratory judgments and does not have the right to reverse state acts in case of violation. The member states' obligation of compliance is one of international law and cannot be enforced by the Council of Europe. In this respect, European human rights protection remains within the framework of traditional international law. However, this is transcended insofar as individuals who assert that their Convention rights have been violated by a member state can initiate action.

By contrast, the authority of the European Union (EU) is much broader. Member states have assigned sovereign rights to the EU which it may exercise autonomously. This affects all branches of state action: legislative, executive, and judicial powers have been assigned. The actions of the EU in the exercise of this authority, including legal norms, are directly valid within member states. According to the jurisprudence of the European Court of Justice (ECJ), they take precedence over national law—even the highest national law, the constitutional law. Although EU law cannot abolish national law, because the two flow from separate sources and a collision norm like Art. 31 of the German Basic Law is lacking, national law that opposes European law may not be applied so long as the latter remains in force. Even though the EU lacks the compulsory means of asserting the validity of its law within member states, this does not alter the fact that within the purview of European law the latter can no longer act in a self-determined manner.

On the other hand, the EU has not yet acquired the right to determine its own legal basis. This consists of treaties under international law that the member states have concluded by unanimous consent. The treaties are not merely the mode for the emergence of the legal basis. Unlike the legal basis of federal states, the legal basis of the EU is not put at the disposal of the Union but remains in the hands of the member states. Only they are authorized to amend it. This requires a further mutual treaty agreement. The member states remain, as one might say, 'masters of the treaties'. Even the failed European constitutional treaty did not seek to change this. This also means that member states autonomously determine which sovereign rights they assign to the EU and how the EU is to exercise them. The EU cannot decide which sovereign rights of the member states it wants to assume. The member states retain *Kompetenz-Kompetenz*.[4] With respect to its legal basis, the EU is externally controlled.

This distinguishes the legal basis of the EU from a constitution, in which a political unit autonomously determines the purpose, form, and content of its political union. If, despite this, treaties are often referred to as the EU 'constitution',[5] this is true in that they fulfil a series of functions which fall to the constitution in a state. They establish the Union, determine its tasks, install its institutions, define its competencies, regulate its procedures, organize its relations to member states, and so on. But the constitution's constitutive element of self-determination, and also the attribution of European power to the Union's citizens as the source of public authority, is lacking. For the same reason, the EU has not yet become a state even though it has long since outgrown the legal format of traditional international organizations to become a structure that transcends the conventional forms of cooperation and for which a suitable term has not yet been coined.[6]

## III. THE NATIONAL CONSTITUTION AS THE FILTER FOR EUROPEAN LAW

The fact that the legal basis of the EU does not derive from the EU itself but from the member states by way of treaty has considerable significance for the importance of national constitutions. It ensures that the constitutions of member states influence the primary law of the EU, not least because member states are bound by their constitutions with respect to the signing and ratification of treaties. For one thing, the procedural requirements of national constitutions can affect the outcome, as became apparent in the context of acceptance of the European constitutional treaty. In France and the Netherlands, for example, the treaty failed to win approval in referendums, even though it would probably have been approved by their parliaments.

---

[4] It is hard to find evidence of a conflicting view, but see: I. Pernice, 'Multilevel Constitutionalism and the Treaty of Amsterdam' [1999] 36 *Common Market Law Review* 710.

[5] The literature on this is extensive: see e.g. A. Peters, *Elemente einer Theorie der Verfassung Europas* (Berlin: Duncker & Humblot, 2001); Armin von Bogdandy (ed.), *Europäisches Verfassungsrecht* (Berlin: Springer, 2003); T. Giegerich, *Europäische Verfassung und deutsche Verfassung im transnationalen Konstitutionalisierungsprozess* (Berlin: Springer, 2003). For my own position see e.g. Dieter Grimm, 'Does Europe need a Constitution?' (1995) 1 *European Law Journal* 282.

[6] For a listing of attempts, see Vivien A. Schmidt, *Democracy in Europe* (Oxford: Oxford University Press, 2006), p. 8 et seq.

Secondly, material constitutional provisions can acquire importance when national constitutions prohibit the ratification of treaties that collide with specific constitutional requirements. To this extent, national constitutions provide a filter for European primary law.

However, this filtering effect cannot prevent every deviation from the national constitution that is associated with the exercise of sovereign rights by supranational organizations like the EU. The state that demanded this would render itself incapable of participating in supranational organizations. As the German Federal Constitutional Court found in its Eurocontrol ruling, every transfer of sovereign rights results is an alteration of the constitutionally defined system of competences and thus in substance a constitutional amendment.[7] If a state does not want to exclude itself from international cooperation associated with the transfer of sovereign rights, it must accept curtailments of its own constitution and must otherwise content itself with defining the prerequisites and limits of such transfers in its constitution and create compensation for intra-state power shifts, such as is achieved by Art. 23 (2)–(7) of the German Basic Law.

The respective provisions of member state constitutions determine what this filter captures and what it permits. In Art. 24, the Basic Law withdrew the German state's exclusive claim to rule right from the outset, opening up the Federal Republic to law from other legal sources. Since then, this has been expanded by an express authorization to participate in the EU in Art. 23 (1) of the Basic Law, which was adopted in 1992. The constitutions of most of the other member states also contain similar authorizations. In some countries, such as France and Ireland, these are merely ad-hoc authorizations to permit ratification of individual treaties which alter European primary law. They exhaust themselves after being exercised once so that each subsequent act of transfer requires another constitutional amendment.

Formally, both Art. 24 (1) and Art. 23 (1) of the Basic Law require a law permitting the transfer of sovereign rights. This is also the rule in the other member states. Some states permit referendums or require them under certain circumstances, for instance in Slovakia for accession and devolution and in Denmark when a simple majority but not the required five-sixths majority is achieved. In the Czech Republic, the Constitutional Court must, prior to ratification, determine that the treaty is compatible with the constitution. Some constitutions require a majority prescribed for constitutional amendments in cases where the content of the treaty deviates from the constitution or makes such deviations necessary. Article 23 (1) of the Basic Law links ratification of treaty provisions which alter or amend the content of the Basic Law to the requirements of Art. 79 (2) and (3) of the Basic Law.

The Basic Law also places substantive restrictions on the transfer of sovereign rights to the EU. Article 23 (1) makes the commitment of the EU to democratic, social, and federal principles according to the rule of law prerequisites

[7] *BVerfGE* 58, 1 (36) (1981).

for Germany's further participation in European integration. That corresponds to the provisions defining the objectives of the state set out in Art. 20, the principles which Art. 79 (3) excepts from amendment. A further requirement is the protection of basic rights comparable to the Basic Law, including the provisions of Art. 1, which are also non-amendable. A further prerequisite is that the EU complies with the subsidiarity principle. Such material conditions for the ratification of European primary law are less common in the constitutions of other member states, but may be found for instance in Portugal and Sweden.

The function of national constitutions as filters on the formation of European primary law is particularly clear where national constitutional courts or supreme courts with constitutional jurisdiction can review treaties as to their compatibility with the national constitution. The point of reference here is the national ratification law. In formal terms, this is the sole object of review. However, as this is without content, the question as to whether the content of the treaty to which ratification refers is reconcilable with the national constitution becomes the matter under review. To prevent an unconstitutional treaty from becoming binding under international law, the Federal Constitutional Court permits petitions for review of a ratification law before promulgation and the following lodging or exchange of ratification documents. In its Art. 54, the French Constitution even permits a treaty to be reviewed before ratification and if it contains unconstitutional elements it may only be ratified following an amendment of the constitution.

It is not only in Germany that the enactment of European primary law depended several times on constitutional review on the basis of the national constitution. In Ireland, ratification of the Single European Act was reviewed notwithstanding a constitutional provision intended to prevent a collision between Community law and national law because the constitution did not explicitly mention the Single European Act.[8] In Germany and other member states, the Maastricht and the Lisbon Treaties were the object of rigorous constitutional scrutiny.[9] The Federal Constitutional Court deemed them compatible with the Basic Law, but used the opportunity to elucidate the limits to integration that derive from German statehood. The Danish Supreme Court promulgated a similar decision.[10] The French Conseil Constitutionnel declared both the Maastricht and Amsterdam Treaties incompatible with the French Constitution, so that these could not be ratified until after a constitutional amendment.[11]

---

[8] *Crotty v. An Taoiseach*, 9 April 1987 (Supreme Court of Ireland).

[9] *BVerfGE 89*, 155 (1993); *BVerfGE 123*, 267 (2009).

[10] *Højesteret*, decision of 6 April 1998, Carlsen u.a. ./. Rasmussen, I 361/1997, UfR 1998, S. 800, I 361/1997.

[11] *Conseil Constitutionnel*, decision of 9 April 1992, Rec. S. 55; v. 2.9.1992, Rec. S. 76; v. 23.9.1992, Rec. S. 94; v. 31.12.1997, Rec. S. 344.

## IV. THE INFLUENCE OF THE NATIONAL CONSTITUTIONS ON THE EUROPEAN LEGISLATIVE PROCESS

The influence of the national constitutions does not end with the declaration and ratification of EU primary law. In an attenuated form, it continues to act on the creation of secondary EU law. The reason for this is that the primary law assigns member states a central role in the Union's legislative process. The EU's unique nature as a federation of states is apparent, among other things, in the fact that the primary legislative body is not the European Parliament, elected by the citizens of the member states, but the Council, which is made up of the governments of the member states. Granted, the Council does not have the right of initiative; this rests with the Commission. Nor is it still the sole legislative body. The Parliament's participation rights have continually expanded, most recently by the Treaty of Lisbon. However, the Parliament can only respond to resolutions of the Council; it cannot itself take the lead. To date, efforts to adapt this structure along a more state-like model have failed.[12]

But the making of secondary law differs greatly from the creation of primary law. The latter is enacted by way of treaties that follow the rules of international law, while secondary law is created through resolutions according to the rules of European primary law. The Council, which enacts the resolution, is not a conference of states but a body of the EU. It exercises competences that have been transferred to the EU and is not bound by the national constitutions. Unlike all other EU institutions, however, it is composed of members of a national state institution, namely the governments of member states. This arrangement enables the Council members to assert their national interests and thus the requirements of their national constitutions in the legislative process. Insofar as their national constitutions obligate them, these acquire an indirect influence on the European legislative process.

The respective constitution determines whether such an obligation exists. To answer this question for Germany, it makes sense first to separate the area in which EU activities are not regulated by European law in their entirety but rather require coordinated action. Until the Lisbon Treaty, this area included the two EU pillars of joint foreign and security policy and home and justice affairs. In this area, the collaboration remained intergovernmental. Today the rescue mechanisms established to solve the financial crisis follow this pattern. The decision-making method resembles that of treaty negotiation under international law and therefore the same behavioural standards apply. The German representatives must insist on the requirements of the Basic Law and thus may not agree to a legislative proposal that would violate the Basic Law.

In the communitized areas the constitutional restrictions on the German government were controversial when it participates in a legislative act of the Council for which within Germany the Länder would be responsible. In such a

---

[12] See Dieter Grimm, 'Vom Rat zur Staatenkammer' in his *Die Verfassung und die Politik. Einsprüche in Störfällen* (Munich: Beck, 2001), p. 264.

case, the Federal Constitutional Court has held that the German government was required to preserve any rights of the Federal Republic in opposition to community legislation and effectively defend these in the EU institutions. It may not simply flout the lack of an EU competence. Only in exceptional cases can urgent foreign or integration policy reasons justify the German government not insisting on its position.[13] The previous decision regarding the petition for issuance of a temporary injunction was even more determinative: insofar as possible, the formation of secondary community law that is not compatible with the German constitution must be prevented.[14]

These principles can be generalized. But the unique nature of the European legislative process cannot be overlooked.[15] Even though secondary EU law is created by resolution and not by treaty, the Council is less a deliberative than a negotiating body. The Council members primarily follow their national interests and the political goals of the national parties that make up their government. Legislation in the Council is often the result of negotiated packages whose creation demands compromises from all sides. Under these circumstances, the national government can only represent their national interests successfully when they have latitude in the negotiations. In terms of the overall result, a rigid constitutional bond can result in a disadvantage for the constitution. However, the Basic Law must remain paramount even in the event of compromises. Individual constitutional positions can only be surrendered in exceptional cases when this enables prevention of greater constitutional harm.[16] Approval of a Union law that contravenes Art. 23 (1) of the Basic Law would never be permissible.

However, a guarantee for compliance with the national constitution only exists where the treaties require unanimity for the enactment of EU law. In this area, one must thus assume that the German government is specifically bound. The requirement for unanimity recognizes the fact that the interests of each individual member state have such weight that this state can prevail over all others, though only negatively: the national constitution can inhibit incompatible EU law, but not compel compatible EU law. Thus, the flexibility and compromising skills required to influence majority decisions do not justify a relaxing of the constitutional stricture. An unresolvable linkage of draft legislation that requires unanimity with one for which a simple majority suffices does not occur in practice, and thus does not require any additional exception to the strict constitutional obligation.

Yet, what is true for the representatives of the German government on the Council applies neither for the Commissioners appointed by Germany nor for the members of the European Parliament elected in Germany. In contrast to

---

[13] *BVerfGE* 92, 203 (1995).    [14] *BVerfGE* 80, 74 (1989).

[15] See Armin von Bogdandy, *Gubernative Rechtsetzung* (Tübingen: Mohr Siebeck, 1999); Hartmut A. Grams, *Zur Gesetzgebung der Europäischen Union* (Neuwied: Luchterhand, 1998); Stefan Kadelbach and Christian Tietje, 'Autonomie und Bindung der Rechtsetzung in gestuften Rechtsordnungen' (2008) 66 *VVDStRL*, 7 and 45.

[16] See also *BVerfGE* 4, 157 (168 f.) (1955).

the government representatives on the Council, the Commissioners are not concurrently members of a German state body. The European and national action levels are not entwined in these bodies. Therefore, the German members are not subject to the obligation of faithfulness to the national constitution when they make decisions in Parliament or the Commission. Art. 14 of the Treaty on European Union (TEU) describes the representatives elected to the European Parliament as representatives of the citizens of the Union. As such, they are not subject to the constitutions of their respective peoples. Article 17 of the TEU grants members of the Commission 'complete independence' and obliges them to pursue the general interest of the Union.

## V. THE PRIORITY OF COMMUNITY LAW

National constitutions are decisive for the transfer of legislative competence to the EU. They can indirectly influence the exercise of legislative competence by the Council. Once created, however, EU law is valid independently of the national constitutions. Yet that does not determine how European and national law play out when the two come into conflict. The Treaty of Rome did not expressly regulate this issue. Nor do the constitutions of the member states, aside from a few exceptions, contain provisions regulating interaction of the two legal orders. This question was not decided by the ECJ until some years after the founding of the European Economic Community (EEC) in a manner that differed from the normal rules of international law and elevated the European Communities to that special status between international organizations and federal states which it still holds today.[17]

In 1963, the Court ruled that Community law is directly applicable in the member states and must be enforced by the national courts.[18] This stripped the national legislature of its role as a gatekeeper with respect to EU law. This was followed one year later by the ruling that Community law takes precedence over national law[19]. In 1970 the Court affirmed this precedence even over national constitutional law.[20] In its decision, the Court noted that the Community cannot fulfil its function if the member states were able to decide on the priority of European law at will, thus challenging its universal validity. In its reasoning, the ECJ assumed that Community law had become independent of its origin in international law and had achieved an autonomous validity, while others assume that the priority of European law is derived from the authorization by the member states.

---

[17] See Karen J. Alter, *Establishing the Supremacy of European Law* (Oxford: Oxford University Press, 2001); J. Weiler, 'The Transformation of Europe' (1991) 100 *Yale Law Journal* 2403; Alec Stone Sweet, *The Judicial Construction of Europe* (Oxford: Oxford University Press, 2004).

[18] *Van Gend & Loos* (1963) Case 26/62.     [19] *Costa v. ENEL* (1964) Case 6/64.

[20] *Internationale Handelsgesellschaft mbH v. Einfuhr- und Vorratsstelle für Getreide- und Futtermittel* (1970) Case 11/70; *Amministrazione delle Finanze v. S.p.A. Simmenthal* (1978) Case 106/77.

With respect to the legal consequences of a collision between national and European law, the ECJ initially tended towards the assumption that Community law voids opposing national law. A member state would then no longer be able to determine its own constitution in a sovereign manner. Sovereignty, which in the constitutional state had already retreated to that of the constituent power of the people, would, even on this level of withdrawal, have been subsumed. Later, the Court adopted the opinion that conflicting European law does not void national law but merely makes it inapplicable.[21] The priority of Community law is not one of validity but of application. If the Community obstacle were to be removed, national law is automatically revived. As a consequence, the ECJ does not invalidate national law,[22] and it leaves the conclusions to be drawn from its interpretations of Community law to the national institutions.

But priority of application also acts as a constraint on national constitutions. The block on the application of national law that contravenes European law grants all state institutions that apply law, both courts and administrative agencies, the authority to review national law for its applicability and ignore it in the event of a conflict. Out of respect for the democratically directly legitimated parliament and in order to avoid contradictory rulings as to the applicability of laws, the Basic Law withheld this authority from the courts, and most definitely from public authorities. The Federal Constitutional Court holds the monopoly on the rejection of German laws. But rulings of the ECJ have put an end to this. Where European law is concerned, it has extended norm control to authorities and courts, thus reducing the position of parliament intended by the Basic Law.

The interpretation of EU law acquires a separate importance for the extent to which its priority of application displaces national constitutional law. In the interpretations of the Commission and the ECJ, the four basic freedoms of Art. 26 of the Treaty on the Functioning of the European Union (TFEU) and their expressions in the treaties have developed a significant dynamic that puts them into a potential conflict with the national understanding of basic rights, and puts the latter on the defensive. Beginning with *Cassis de Dijon*,[23] the ECJ, in the course of realizing the Common Market, interpreted ex Art. 28 EC to mean that products that meet the legal requirements of their country of origin may also be offered for sale in every other member state. Member states are therefore no longer able to uphold their own protective standards, even if these were imposed in order to fulfil their obligations of protecting basic rights.

Since then, the Commission, with the backing of the Court, has adopted an active liberalization policy,[24] which has come to target in particular those institutions of member states that are organized under public law. If these have private competitors, the European institutions regard funding under public law

---

[21] *Ministero delle Finanze v. IN.CO.GE 90* (1998) Case 10/97.

[22] *Jongeneel Kaas v. Niederlande* (1984) Case 237/82.

[23] *Rewe Zentral AG v. Bundesmonopolverwaltung für Branntwein (Cassis de Dijon)* (1979) Case 120/78.

[24] See Martin Höpner and Armin Schäfer, 'Eine neue Phase der europäischen Integration' in Höpner & Schäfer (eds), *Die politische Ökonomie der europäischen Integration* (Frankfurt am Main: Campus, 2008), p. 129.

as a state subsidy, which is prohibited under ex Art. 81 ff. EC when it is deemed to distort competition. The reasons of general welfare that were decisive for the choice of the organizational form under public law are irrelevant because of the Commission's obsession with competition. The consequence is an asymmetry between negative integration that eliminates market obstacles and positive integration that undertakes market corrections. Whereas negative integration occurs in the non-political mode of the administrative or judicial application of law and can be asserted with a stroke of the pen, positive integration requires legislation and is much more difficult to realize.[25]

The constitutional aims of the social state assume the consequences. Granted, member states are not prevented by law from pursuing these. However, the European liberalization policy drastically restricts their possibilities de facto, while the stabilization of the social state on the European level appears virtually hopeless on account of the extremely disparate social security systems of the member states.[26] The price is also paid by national basic rights, which are being increasingly displaced by market freedoms. While on the national level personal, communicative, and cultural basic rights are usually better protected than economic rights, and constitutional courts tend to review laws regulating economic activity leniently, this hierarchy is reversed on the European level. In the field in which the national constitutions grant the legislatures the greatest scope, the interpretation of Community law renders this the smallest.

## VI. THE RESERVATION OF NATIONAL CONSTITUTIONAL COURTS

The ECJ holds that the priority of Community law applies without restriction. The reach of national constitutional courts ends with their review of whether the national constitution opposes a competence transfer to the EU, but the national constitution is irrelevant with regards to the manner in which the EU exercises the transferred competence. In the view of the ECJ, this is true even for the question of whether the EU possesses a certain competence. Admittedly, the Court does not deny that competence violations on the part of EU institutions can occur. However, it insists on the exclusivity of the primary law as a standard for review, for which the Court itself is the definitive interpreter. If a member state believes that the EU lacks the competence to make a certain decision, it can bring an action for annulment before the ECJ. National courts have recourse to the preliminary ruling procedure. According to the ECJ, the national constitutional court has no jurisdiction.[27] It would have to treat such an action as inadmissible.

---

[25] See Fritz Scharpf, *Governing in Europe* (Oxford: Oxford University Press, 1999), pp. 43–83.

[26] See Fritz Scharpf, 'The European Social Model' (2002) 40 *Journal of Common Market Studies* 645.

[27] *Foto-Frost v. Hauptzollamt Lübeck-Ost* (1987) Case 314/85.

Some member states accept this without reservation. Slovakia concedes the precedence of EU law in its national constitution. In Art. 29, the Irish Constitution even expressly stipulates that none of its provisions may be cited in opposition to acts of Community law.[28] The Netherlands Constitution grants a priority over national law to the generally binding provisions of the treaties and resolutions of international organizations in its Art. 94. No corresponding provisions may be found in the constitutions of the remaining member states. Although they are open to international law, as for instance the Basic Law in Art. 24 from its inception and since 1992 specifically for European law in Art. 23, they do not address the issue of precedence. In some of them, however, the national constitutional courts or supreme courts have begun to erect a constitutional barrier against the precedence of EU law.

Specifically, the Italian Constitutional Court, in its decision on *Costa v. ENEL*,[29] denied this precedence on the basis of an international law approach regarding the source of validity of European law. Following the principal decision of the ECJ in this matter,[30] the Italian Constitutional Court reversed itself, but reserved the right to decide on the non-applicability of national law in each individual case of collision.[31] It is this practice that the ECJ struck down in the *Simmenthal* case.[32] Since then, the Italian Court has withdrawn to the position that European law in general takes precedence even over the Italian constitution, but insists that the constitution justifies 'controlimiti'. Precedence applies only insofar as fundamental principles and inalienable human rights are not affected.[33] In France, it is the Conseil d'Etat, not the Constitutional Council, that is the source of sustained resistance.[34]

In 1967, by contrast, the German Federal Constitutional Court declined to review a constitutional complaint against Community law because even 'an absolutely urgent need of legal policy' could not expand the Court's jurisdiction.[35] Seven years later it reversed itself in *Solange I* and, building on the fundamental significance of the basic rights for the legitimation of political rule,

---

[28] Art 29 states: 'No provision of this Constitution invalidates laws enacted, acts done or measures adopted by the State which are necessitated by the obligations of membership of the European Union or of the Communities, or prevents laws enacted, acts done or measures adopted by the European Union or by the Communities or by institutions thereof, or by bodies competent under the Treaties establishing the Communities, from having the force of law in the State'.

[29] *Corte costituzionale*, decision of 5 February 1964, Nr. 14/64, Costa v ENEL e soc. Edisonvolta in *Foro Italiano* 1964, I, p. 465.

[30] *Costa v. ENEL* (n. 19).

[31] *Corte costituzionale*, decision of December 27 1973, Nr. 183/73, Frontini v Ministro delle Finanze, in *Foro Italiano* 1974, I, p. 314.

[32] *Amministrazione delle Finanze v. S.p.A. Simmenthal* (n. 20).

[33] *Corte costituzionale*, decision of 31 March 1994, Nr. 117/94, Fabrizio Zerini, in: Raccolta ufficiale delle sentenze e ordinanze delle Corte costituzionale 1994, p. 785, in *Foro Italiano* 1995, I, p. 1077.

[34] See esp. *Conseil d'Etat*, decision of 22 December 1978, Ministre de l'Intérieur v Cohn-Bendit, Rec. 1978, p. 524.

[35] *BVerfGE* 22, 293 (1967).

claimed authority to review European legal acts against the fundamental rights of the Basic Law so long as the Community level lacked an adequate protection of basic rights.[36] After this decision had prompted the ECJ to more actively develop European protection of basic rights, the Federal Constitutional Court declared in *Solange II* that it would no longer exercise its authority as long as an adequate protection of basic rights on the Community level was assured.[37] However, this claim has not been renounced, only suspended. This review competence is in abeyance for as long as the EU offers sufficient protection for basic rights—and may be revived if this changes.

The EU Charter of Fundamental Rights, proclaimed in 2000 and turned into valid law by the Lisbon Treaty, further strengthens protection of basic rights on the norm level. In terms of its provisions, the Charter is no less ambitious than the Basic Law. On the contrary, it is modelled closely on the Basic Law, and also formulates issues that the Federal Constitutional Court has developed by way of interpretation of the basic rights as independent basic rights and in many areas even exceeds the level of protection afforded by the Basic Law. Adequate protection of basic rights within the meaning of the *Solange* ('so long as') decision, however, also comprises the enforceability of the basic rights in court and their actual assertion by the ECJ. In this respect, however, new doubts arise on account of the trend described earlier. Consequently, the implementation of the Charter does not render the *Solange* decision moot.

By contrast, the Federal Constitutional Court has expressly reserved for itself the right of final decision in questions concerning transgression of competences.[38] It assumes that EU law is valid in Germany on the basis of the order to apply law which the German legislature issued in the ratification law. The question as to whether this order was issued is one of national law, which must be decided by the national courts. Insofar as the national legislature has failed to transfer a competence, EU legal acts rob the German state institutions of their constitutionally granted scope of action in an impermissible manner. Consequently, the Federal Constitutional Court claims the power to forbid the application of such a legal act within the territory covered by the Basic Law. This also applies when the ECJ decides a competence question in favour if the EU but in doing so crosses the line between treaty interpretation and treaty amendment.

The constitutional or supreme courts of Denmark, France, Greece, Ireland, Italy, and Spain have also claimed such an ultimate jurisdiction on competence matters; a trend towards following this example may be seen in further member states.[39] Even though it is generally recognized that the validity of European legal acts in the member states does not depend on their conformity to the national constitution, the statehood or sovereignty of the member states, the

---

[36] BVerfGE 37, 271 (1974).     [37] BVerfGE 73, 339 (1987).     [38] BVerfGE 89, 155 (1993).

[39] For a throrough analysis, see Franz C. Mayer, *Kompetenzüberschreitung und Letztentscheidung* (Munich: Beck, 2000), pp. 140–257, 260. Cf. Monica Claes, *The National Courts' Mandate in the European Constitution* (Oxford: Hart, 2006), p. 385 et seq.

fundamental principles of their constitutions, the competences remaining to the states, and the standard of protection of basic rights are at any rate defended against the claim to comprehensive validity of EU law. It appears only logical that it is the state-level justice system that is erecting this barrier, as the claim to unconditional validity of European law does not originate from the treaties, but is established only by the rulings of the ECJ.

## VII. INTERACTION BETWEEN NATIONAL AND EUROPEAN JUSTICE SYSTEMS

No 'war of the judges'[40] has, as yet, broken out. National constitutional courts no longer resist the precedence of EU law. On the contrary, they help to assert it. In Germany, the recognition of the ECJ as a 'lawful judge' within the meaning of Art. 101 (1) of the Basic Law is a lever for this.[41] As a consequence, a violation of a German court of last resort of the obligation in Art. 267 TFEU to refer is at the same time a violation of the Basic Law, which can be rebuked by the German Constitutional Court. The review competence of the national constitutional courts, by contrast, remains in reserve for severe threats to the basic relationship between member states and the EU and the fundamental principles of their constitutions. In this way, national constitutional courts assert the essential statehood of the member states and at the same time obstruct a 'transformation' of the EU into a state, which many see as the ultimate goal of European integration.

Consequently, the courts in the EU cannot culminate in a single hierarchic peak, as in a state. Just as the national and European levels interact in the setting of norms, there is also a mutual interdependence between the national constitutional courts or supreme courts and the ECJ in which it remains open who has the last word.[42] Certainly, the ECJ can usually assume that its decisions will be respected by the highest courts of the member states in the interests of equal application of EU law. However, it is not in a position to assert the requirements of EU law under any circumstances, as would be possible from a position at the top of a hierarchy. If it wishes to avoid the collision of two opposing decisions of last resort, it must take the decisions of the national constitutional courts into account so as not to run up against insurmountable barriers.

This interplay also characterizes the relationship between the ECtHR and national constitutional courts. Certainly, the ECHR is in a weaker position compared to EU law, because it cannot claim precedence over national law. However, it is not subordinate either. The rulings of the ECtHR are binding on those

---

[40] Claes (n. 39). This expression is first found in the *Cohn-Bendit* case: 'Ni gouvernement des juges, ni guerre des juges. Il doit y avoir place pour le dialogue des juges'. See Mayer (n. 39), p. 154.

[41] *BVerfGE* 73, 339 (1986) (366 ff.). Yet this leverage works only in the final instance of the deciding courts. See Ulrich Haltern, *Europarecht* (Tübingen: Mohr Siebeck, 2nd edn, 2007), p. 337.

[42] See Claes (n. 39); Ingolf Pernice, *Das Verhältnis europäischer zu nationalen Gerichten im europäischen Verfassungsverbund* (Berlin: de Gruyter, 2006).

member states of the Council of Europe against which the proceedings are taken. The Federal Constitutional Court has established this for German courts that ignored the judgments of the ECtHR. It held the disregard of decisions of the ECtHR by German courts to be a violation of the principle of rule of law embodied in the Basic Law.[43] Like the violation of Art. 267 of the TFEU, the failure to take decisions of the ECtHR into account can be challenged before the Federal Constitutional Court. This makes the latter, as the highest national court, the upholder of international law by the national justice system.

Yet, here too reservations are asserted. The Federal Constitutional Court has also explained that consideration does not necessarily mean compliance. National law must yield to the ECHR only insofar as it allows scope for interpretation on the part of the applying institution. Within this scope the national courts have to follow the ECtHR even when this requires the surrender of established national case law. However, where such scope is lacking, whether because the German legal situation does not permit any, or because the compliance with a decision of the ECtHR would lead to a violation of the Basic Law, national law takes precedence over the ECHR. According to the decisions of the Federal Constitutional Court, this applies in particular when relevant national law is a balanced subsystem that reconciles different positions on basic rights, into which the rulings of the ECtHR cannot be inserted.

This in turn compels the ECtHR to consider the national legal situation, particularly national basic rights and national basic rights jurisprudence if it wants to ensure implementation of its decisions. The often neglected Art. 53 of the ECHR offers one tool for this. Under this provision, the ECtHR may not interpret the Convention such that it would limit or impair basic rights that are recognized under national law. This rule becomes especially significant when the Court must review national decisions deriving from civil-law proceedings in which both parties can cite basic rights and the national courts must arrive at a reasonable balance between two basic rights positions of equal rank. If the ECtHR allows the appeal of the losing party in the national proceedings, this necessarily diminishes the national basic rights protection for the party who won in the national proceedings.

However, the ECtHR has no mandate to unify law in Europe. It shall ensure a minimum standard of basic rights that is recognized by all member states of the Council of Europe, not implement the same basic rights standard for all. Particularly when the aim is to reasonably reconcile colliding basic rights positions, sufficient scope must remain for national solutions. The Caroline rulings are an example for this.[44] The various European states arrive at different results when resolving the conflict between freedom of the press and protection of privacy. Whereas in France protection of privacy generally takes precedence, this is typically reversed in the United Kingdom (UK). Guided by the principle

---

[43]  *BVerfGE* 111, 307 (2004).

[44]  See *BVerfGE* 101, 36 (1999)—Per contra EGMR, judgment of 24 June 2004, v. Hannover ./. Deutschland, complaint no. 59320/00, ECHR 2004-VI, and EuGRZ 2004, p. 404; *BVerfGE* 120, 180 (2008).

of practical concordance between colliding basic rights, Germany assumes a position between these two poles. If the ECtHR resolves the tension in favour of one of the extreme positions, it runs the risk that the affected state is unable to comply for reasons deriving from its own constitution.

The different contexts in which national and international courts operate also promote a cooperative relationship between national courts and international courts in a non-hierarchical system. National courts are generally embedded in a denser participation and responsibility context than international ones. Although courts enjoy independence by virtue of their function, this does not remove them from the culturally shaped context within which national law is created and is applied, and which form self-perceptions of the function and practice of judges. National judges additionally operate in a much denser deliberative context, both in the general social and special legal connection, which manifests itself in their decision-making behaviour and keeps them in touch with the society for which they perform their function. International courts lack a comparable matrix that underpins the rule of law. They thus have greater freedom than national judges, and must balance this freedom through greater sensitivity to national characteristics.

## VIII. THE ROLE OF THE NATIONAL CONSTITUTION IN THE IMPLEMENTATION OF COMMUNITY LAW

Finally, national constitutions remain meaningful insofar as the European legislature exercises the transferred competence in such a manner that its norms cannot be directly applied in the member states, but rather require a transformation or completion by national legislatures. This is the case for framework decisions and directives. They either grant the national legislature decision-making discretion or at the very least decision-making scope. The legislature can then use this as it sees fit, but not in violation of the national constitution. The constitutional obligation begins where that of EU law ends. The national institutions cannot dispense with the constitutional obligation by simply saying that they implement European law.

National legislatures had the greatest freedom with respect to framework decisions within the meaning of ex Art. 34 EU. Intended for the third pillar of the EU, the cooperation on matters of home and judicial affairs, these were thus drafted outside of the supranational decision-making structures and consequently lay in the area of international law, not Community law. Framework decisions could thus only be enacted unanimously. The European Parliament had no participatory right, but must only be heard. As an element of international law, framework decisions additionally depended on transformation into national law and were binding only in terms of their ends, while the forms and means were at the discretion of the member states. The national parliament thus had the possibility of rejecting them. The Lisbon Treaty abolished this instrument.

National legislatures have less freedom when implementing European directives. Directives are an instrument of EU policy. They are governed by the rules of EU law and not international law. No transposition into national law is required. The national parliament is bound with respect to the aim but free to choose the means. Insofar as EU law allows it discretion, the binding force of the national constitution again applies. Both the federal allocation of competences and the separation of powers between the legislature and the executive are decisive—as are the national basic rights. These are not considered only insofar as a directive of European law leaves the member states no implementation scope. The national legislature then lacks options for structuring, the exercise of which would make it possible for the basic rights to have an impact.

The Federal Constitutional Court can review whether the national legislative bodies have complied with the constitutional constraint. In the case of framework decisions, this occurred in the constitutional complaint proceedings against the law implementing the European arrest warrant.[45] In this case, the Federal Constitutional Court concluded that the legislature could not deviate arbitrarily from the prohibition against extradition of German citizens to other EU countries, but rather must observe the qualified legal reservation expressed in Art. 16 (2) of the Basic Law and the principle of proportionality. As a law restricting basic rights, the implementation law had to conform to all constitutional constraints and structure the limitations of basic rights agreed on in the framework decision as sparingly as possible. As the Bundestag had enacted the law without having acted in awareness of its scope for action, the majority of judges held the entire law void, causing the Bundestag to reassess the matter completely.

The reviewable nature of the implementation of directives has long been recognized. However, in expanding the *Solange II* decision, the Federal Constitutional Court has now clarified that the intra-state implementation of such directives that set compulsory requirements and leave the member states no scope for implementation is exempt from review as long as adequate protection of basic rights exists on the European level that must be complied with in essentially the same way as those set out in the Basic Law.[46] Previously, this was only recognized for regulations. However, it does not only apply for directives that, like regulations, apply directly in the member states. The sole criterion for review of an implementation law by the Federal Constitutional Court is whether the directive grants the national legislature scope for action.

The national courts and administrative agencies tasked with applying the provisions of an implementation law of a European directive are also bound by the basic rights insofar as these directives grant the national legislature scope for action. However, the national authorities are restricted here, as according to the rulings of the ECJ national legal requirements that implement directives are not divorced from the directive to which they refer—even when they are

---

[45] *BVerfGE* 113, 273 (2005).      [46] *BVerfGE* 118, 79 (95 ff.) (2007).

not directly applicable. This continuing constraint impacts the interpretations, which must be in conformity with the directive.[47] The national law must be interpreted in light of the text and purpose of the directive. The ECJ based this opinion on ex Art. 10 EC. However, by this means it also limits susceptibility to review by the national constitutional court. In the event of a conflict between a directive-compliant interpretation and a basic rights-friendly interpretation, the directive-compliant interpretation prevails, provided that the reduced national basic rights protection is compensated by the protection of basic rights under EU law.

Nor did this change after the EU Charter of Fundamental Rights took effect. It is true that the European basic rights do not apply only for the institutions of the EU: they also extend to all national institutions when they apply EU law. However, the Charter of Fundamental Rights does not impose itself on the national basic rights in the same way that the basic rights of the Basic Law preempt the basic rights in the constitutions of the Länder in accordance with Art. 142. Where the German state executes EU law, it is bound by the basic rights of the European Charter. Where it implements EU law, it is bound by the national basic rights. On account of this rule, the state institutions, courts, and public authorities must comply with different standards of basic rights, depending on whether they are engaged in executing European or national law. However, no gap in the basic rights protection may occur.

## IX. NATIONAL CONSTITUTIONS IN THE BALANCE

The role remaining to the national constitution following the previously discussed developments is determined by the fact that it is the constitution of a state and thus cannot hold any greater relevance than is accorded the state in a united Europe. The importance of the national constitution declines in proportion to the degree to which the state has transferred or lost competences to European institutions. It is reduced to regulating that portion of public power which remains state power. Even to this extent, however, it can no longer fully assert its claim to comprehensive regulation. As the EU largely depends on the member state's administrations and courts to achieve its ends, they act, to a greater or lesser extent, as institutions for exercising EU law—yet, without becoming EU institutions.[48] When they act in this capacity, they must abandon their dependence on the national constitution in the interests of a uniform application of European law in all member states.

But it would be wrong to look only at the debit side of the balance. Through the communitization of formerly exclusively state competences, EU member states simultaneously gain opportunities to exert influence at the European level and through this on the other member states. In exercising its opportunities to

---

[47] *Von Colson v. Land Nordrhein-Westfalen* (1984) Case 14/83.

[48] See for this opinion, J. Temple Lang, 'The Duties of National Courts under Community Constitutional Law' (1997) 3 *European Law Review* 3; Pernice (n. 4), pp. 710, 718, 724.

exert influence, the state is tethered by the national constitution, which thereby extends its area of influence beyond the borders of the state, but encounters the same claim from other constitutions. This necessarily disrupts the influence of an individual constitution. In the area in which European decisions require the unanimous consent of all member states, violations of national constitutions can be averted. At worst, a regulation is not promulgated. However, it is virtually impossible to assert imperatives of the national constitution that can only be fulfilled through action and not omission in those areas where unanimity is required.

EU member states still retain the greatest freedom where they determine their own fundamental order. The constituent power is not subject to any external constraints. It is legally unlimited. In this way the EU differs from a federal state. However, certain exercises of this freedom would represent a break with the Union and lead to withdrawal or expulsion from the EU.[49] If a state wishes to remain in the EU, it can neither invalidate the prerequisites for membership nor reverse the fundamental relationship to the Union in its constitution. The former would be the case if a member state eliminated democracy or surrendered significant elements of the rule of law. However, different variants of democracy and the rule of law remain possible. The latter would be the case for example if a state were to stipulate in its constitution, analogous to Art. 31 of the Basic Law, 'State law overrides European law'.

The freedom is otherwise no longer unqualified. As the intra-state organization and the execution and assertion of EU law remain largely a matter for public administration and the courts of the member states, their structure and competence cannot be a matter of indifference to the EU. The EU places demands on the intra-state organization and the national legal system which are prerequisites for uniform application of EU law. The *Simmenthal* decision of the ECJ,[50] which related to the rejection monopoly of the Italian Constitutional Court, is one example of this. The UK was forced to include interim relief against the Crown in its legal system.[51] Many member states found themselves confronted with the necessity of altering their state liability system for reasons of the effectiveness of EU law.[52] If the relevant regulations are not enacted in the ordinary law of a member state but contained in the constitution, this state as well comes under pressure to adapt accordingly.

With regards to the transfer of competence to the EU, the constitution can of course specify under which circumstances and to what extent the state may participate in the supranational community. However, the exercise of the transferred sovereign rights by the EU is no longer subject to the rules of the national constitutions because that would mean nothing other than differential validity and application in each member state. To preclude this, in a long chain of

---

[49] These two positions are not sufficiently differentiated in Pernice (n. 4), p. 710.

[50] *Amministrazione delle Finanze v. S.p.A. Simmenthal* (n. 20).

[51] *R v. Secretary of State for Transport, ex parte Factortame Ltd.* (1990) Case 213/89.

[52] *Francovich u. Bonifaci v. Italian Republic* (1991) Case 6/90 and C-9/90.

decisions, the ECJ has continually pushed back the influence of the national constitutions in their own area of application. Although some of its decisions have provoked resistance on account of the creeping gain of competences for the EU, overall this line of jurisprudence offered few opportunities for concrete attempts to reverse the policy. This is due to the selective, gradual, seemingly non-political approach, which is the characteristic feature of courts and which only subsequently attracted public attention. It is this judge-driven development that is commonly referred to as the 'constitutionalization' of the treaties.[53]

National constitutional courts only act to push back against the extreme consequence of these efforts, which is the complete subordination of national constitutional law to EU law. But even without this last step, the national constitution can no longer fulfil the expectations originally placed in it. This is true for both its ordering and its legitimation function. With respect to the ordering function, it can no longer fulfil its claim of comprehensively regulating the power of rule within its territory of application. In opposition to this claim, there exists extraconstitutional holders of sovereign power and extraconstitutional ways and means of exercising rule within the territory of the state it constitutes. It regulates the rule exercised there only in part. Analogous phenomena within the states reinforce this trend.[54]

Regarding the legitimation function, the national constitution can no longer fulfil its claim that all rule exercised within the territory of its application derives its legitimacy from the people. Certainly, the power of rule ceded to the EU does not lack a legitimation basis. This consists of the treaties that created the Community and regulate it legally. However, this law does not originate from the people of the state that is subject to this rule. The EU's power of rule derives from the states. The fact that they themselves are democratic does not provide a democratic legitimation for this legal foundation as is the case for constitutions. It also does not guarantee that the people are subject only to those acts of rule to which their own state has consented in a democratic process. It guarantees each member state a right to participate in the legislative process of the EU, but not any affirmation from the people.[55]

## X. EUROPEAN CONSTITUTION AS COMPENSATION?

The significance that the national constitution gains through the greater reach of state power in a united Europe does not offset the loss of significance within its territory of application. The gain in significance is relativized by the necessity

---

[53] See Joseph H. H. Weiler, *The Constitution of Europe* (Cambridge: Cambridge University Press, 1999), p. 19 and Ch. 14 of this volume.

[54] See Chs. 11 and 12 of this volume.

[55] These differences are elided in Pernice (n. 4) for whom it is sufficient that in the origins of European integration there was an act of will and therefore one can assert that the decisions of the Community institution are a result of the will of the people. In this way, there can from the outset be no legitimation problem. See Helge Rossen-Stadtfeld, 'Demokratische Staatlichkeit in Europa: ein verblassendes Bild' (2005) 53 *Jahrbuch des öffentlichen Rechts NF* 45.

of many states, each bound by its own constitution, to work together, while the loss of significance in home affairs manifests itself in full force. Naturally, this does not mean that the loss of statehood that the nation states suffer through the communitization of numerous policy areas is more severe than the gain in problem-solving capability and peacekeeping that go along with it. The EU is without doubt one of the greatest and most promising innovations in political institution-building. However, that does not obviate the question as to whether the loss of significance of the national constitutions can be compensated on the European level.

For a long time, hopes rested on a European constitution. After the failure of the constitutional treaty in France and the Netherlands, this is moot for the time being. However, even before the efforts towards a European constitution, there was no lack of juridification of the public power that the EU exercises. This function, which the constitution fulfils on the state level, was assumed on the European level by the treaties. A constitution was not required for this. What separates the treaties from a constitution in the strict sense of the term is the lack of reference to those subject to rule.[56] It is the member states, and not the citizens of the EU, who are the source of public power. The member states dispose of the legal foundation of the EU, while the Union citizens have nothing to do with this either as active citizens or even as entities to which European public power is attributed. The treaties do not fulfil the legitimation function that derives from the constituent power of people under state rule.

This could of course be changed. Unlike a medieval polity, the EU, which does not fall materially short of the central government of a federal state in terms of its organizational density and scope of competence, is an 'object capable of constitutionalisation'.[57] In order to transform the treaties that currently form the legal foundation of the EU into a constitution, member states would have to surrender their power of disposition over the legal basis of the Union and transfer it to the EU. They would then no longer be 'masters of the treaties'. Rather, the EU itself could determine its own legal foundation, however much power the constituting body of the EU chose to grant to the member states. If the right of self-determination would be exercised by or attributed to the EU citizens as the source of European public power, this would endow the treaties with that element whose lack currently separates them from a constitution.

The question is merely whether such a European constitution could perform comparably to the nation state constitutions and thus offset their loss of significance on a higher level. That depends above all on its ability to provide the EU with the legitimacy and solidarity resources which the nation state has always

---

[56] See Dieter Grimm, 'Europas Verfassung' in Gunnar Folke Schuppert, Ingolf Pernice, and Ulrich Haltern (eds), *Europawissenschaft* (Baden-Baden: Nomos, 2005), p. 177.

[57] See Chs. I and II of this volume.

possessed.[58] Yet, the prerequisites for this are not favourable.[59] Even when we take note of the democratic deficits in the member states, they still have relatively dense civil-society structures, effective mechanisms for mediating between citizens and state institutions, and a broad array of media that maintains the flow of communication between state and society and thus imbues the legitimation and responsibility relationship intended by constitutional law with life so that overall, one could, at any rate, speak of a material, and not merely a formal democracy.

In the EU, by contrast, these social prerequisites for a functioning democracy are only weakly developed or are lacking entirely. Political communication as a fundamental condition of democracy is still largely determined by national interests and habits and stops at the national borders. The economic prerequisites for European media with a widespread impact and a truly European perspective are not likely to exist for a long time. Even when one assumes that European political parties will emerge rapidly following a nationalization of the EU, the communication structures between those in power and the base would remain much less dense than within the states. The willingness to shoulder special contributions out of a feeling of national solidarity, which can always be assumed within a state, will be difficult to foster in a continually growing Union.

Yet a self-supporting Union would require much more of all this than one borne by member states, without any hope of being able to redirect their legitimation and solidarity resources to itself. Expecting this of a constitution would be to overestimate its power. As the roots of the problem are of a social nature, they cannot be resolved through institutional reforms along state lines. Rather, it is to be feared that an EU disassociated from the responsibility of the member states would be cut off from the legitimation provided by them without being able to call on a comparable level of legitimacy of its own. In the end, it would be more remote from the EU citizens than ever. This leads to the conclusion that the basic responsibility of the member states for the EU needs to be increased rather than reduced. A European constitution within the proper meaning of the term would result in just the opposite.

This has consequences for the relationship between national constitutional law and European law.[60] Although national constitutions will never recover their former significance, it must be in Europe's interest to prevent them from falling to the level of state constitutions in a federal system. In an association of states like the EU, all national constitutions are merely partial constitutions that cannot fulfil their claim to comprehensive regulation by themselves but

---

[58] See Ch. 6 of this volume. Ulrich Haltern, 'Europa—Verfassung—Identität' in Christian Calliess (ed.), *Verfassungswandel im europäischen Staaten- und Verfassungsverbund* (Tübingen: Mohr Siebeck, 2007), p. 21.

[59] See Fritz Scharpf, *Reflections on Multilevel Legitimacy*, MPIfG Working Paper 07/3.

[60] See Ingolf Pernice, Peter M. Huber, Gertrude Lübbe-Wolff, and Christoph Grabenwarter, 'Europäisches und nationales Verfassungsrecht' (2001) 60 *VVDStRL* 148–415.

only with the constitution-like legal foundation of the EU. The two are thus dependent on one another. In this sense, it may be appropriate to speak of a 'constitutional association'.[61] However, if the same level of legitimation cannot be achieved for both sides of this association, and instead national constitutions possess the greater reserves of legitimacy, considering this relationship only under the aspect of precedence does more harm than good.[62] This would unnecessarily diminish the achievement of constitutionalism even beyond the inevitable degree.

---

[61] 'Verfassungsverbund', see Pernice et al. ibid; Matthias Jestaedt, 'Der europäische Verfassungsverbund' in Calliess (n. 58), p. 93.

[62] C. Joerges, *Rethinking European Law's Supremacy*, EUI Working Papers, Law 2005, p. 17.

# ⚭ 14 ⚭

# The Democratic Costs of Constitutionalization: The European Case

## I. CONSTITUTIONALISM AND DEMOCRACY

### 1. Interdependence

Democracy and constitutionalism are usually not seen as mutually contradictory. Both emerged simultaneously. The prototypes came into being as democratic constitutions based on the principle of popular sovereignty. Non-democratic constitutions were regarded as a deficient form of constitutionalism. Whenever people fought battles for constitutions the constitutions they had in mind were democratic. Where nations turned from authoritarian or dictatorial regimes to democracy they started by drafting constitutions. How then can constitutionalization put democracy at risk? Before turning to the European case a look at the idea of constitutionalism as it found expression in the beginnings may be helpful.

Modern constitutions were the product of two successful revolutions against the traditional rule, colonial in North America, absolutist in France. These revolutions differed from the many revolts and upheavals of the past in that they did not content themselves with replacing one ruler by another. Rather, they aimed at a different system of rule which they designed before calling individual persons to power. The lack of legitimate public power that the revolution left behind together with the principles that guided the construction of the future regime pointed towards constitutions.

These principles were not invented by the revolutionaries. They had been developed in natural law theory long before.[1] But in spite of its name natural law was not law. It was a philosophical system that did not gain legal recognition before the revolutions. Only after the American colonists and the French middle classes had failed to reach their reform goals—self-rule in North America,

---

[1] See from the rich literature, Bernard Bailyn, *The Ideological Origins of the American Revolution* (Cambridge, Mass: Belknap Press, 1967); Bernhard Groethuysen, *Philosophie de la Révolution française* (Paris: Gallimard, 1956); Wolfgang Kersting, *Die politische Philosophie des Gesellschaftsvertrags* (Darmstadt: Primus Verlag, 1994); Diethelm Klippel, *Politische Freiheit und Freiheitsrechte im deutschen Naturrecht des 18. Jahrhunderts* (Paderborn: Schöningh, 1970); John W. Gough, *The Social Contract* (Oxford: Oxford University Press, 2nd edn, 1957); Ian Shapiro, *The Evolution of Rights in Liberal Theory* (Cambridge: Cambridge University Press, 1986).

Constitutionalism: Past, Present, and Future. First Edition. Dieter Grimm. © Dieter Grimm 2016. Published 2016 by Oxford University Press.

removal of feudalism and liberalization of the economy in France—within the framework of the existing legal order did they resort to natural law to justify the break with the old system and to design a new one.

There were two basic assumptions of natural law theory: that government ought to be legitimized by the consent of the governed and limited by innate rights of the individuals. Yet, these assumptions had only served as a test for the legitimacy of political systems before the revolutions. Political systems were regarded as legitimate if so organized that they could have found the consent of reasonable people. Reason taught that this consent could only be expected if the individuals were not obliged to relinquish their natural freedom when entering into a state. Rather, government was established in order to make natural freedom secure.

In the revolutionary situation these principles became guidelines for political action and thereby transcended philosophical theory. The philosophers themselves were not prepared to design constitutions. They had developed conditions for the legitimacy of government, but not reflected on the means by which they could be implemented. With one exception—Emer de Vattel in his *Droit des gens* of 1758[2]—none of the theorists had pushed the ideas to a postulate for formal, legal, and written constitutions. Forced by the task of reconstructing public authority, the revolutionaries did just this. The ingredients of constitutionalism preceded the revolution, the constitutions themselves were a product of the revolution.

Each central element of the new systems, democracy as well as fundamental rights, called for regulation. The problem with democratic government is that the people are the source of all public authority but cannot govern themselves, as the revolutionaries in North America and France understood well when they put their ideas into effect. Democratic rule was necessarily rule by mandate. The mandate had to be conferred and the conditions of mandatory rule had to be fixed. Different from traditional or absolutist rule, democratic rule needs to be organized before persons are called on to exercise power.

The same is true for limited government. Limits have to be defined and sanctions determined for cases of transgression. Government should be organized in a way that best guarantees individual liberty. As a consequence the revolutionary legislatures in the North American colonies and in France began with the adoption of Bills of Rights even before the constitutions were enacted. From the perspective of the citizens, they were safeguards of individual freedom; from the perspective of government, they were constraints on public power. Public power was legitimate only if it respected and protected the rights of the citizens.

---

[2] Emer de Vattel, *Le droit des gens ou principes de la loi naturelle* (Leiden, 1758), § 27. Cf. Heinz Mohnhaupt and Dieter Grimm, *Verfassung. Zur Geschichte des Begriffs von der Antike bis zur Gegenwart* (Berlin: Duncker & Humblot, 2nd edn, 2002), pp. 91, 105.

The rules had to be binding on government. This required their transformation into positive law. Only the law could make them mandatory and enforceable, detaching them from the historical moment of adoption and the persons who formulated them, and extending them into the future. As a matter of fact, the law develops its regulatory potential best where it organizes and limits human behavior. Law was thus the appropriate means of achieving the revolutionary ends. The contribution of the revolutionaries to a new political order was not the development of the natural law principles, but their transformation into positive law.

A precondition for the norms to fulfil their function was that they enjoyed primacy over all government acts including legislation. Constitutions bring legitimate government into existence and formulate the conditions for the exercise of public power. They thus antedate government and are not at its disposal. The consequence was a distinction between *pouvoir constituant* and *pouvoir constitué*[3] and, accordingly, the division of the law into two parts: one that is attributed to the people and binds government—constitutional law; and one that emanates from the government and binds the citizens—ordinary law. The first part regulates rule-making whereas rule making itself is left to the second part. This distinction is crucial for constitutionalism.

Democratic government and fundamental rights were the goal of both the American and the French revolution. Constitutions were the means to make them effective. However, this does not mean that constitutions are necessarily democratic or committed to fundamental rights. Once the constitution had been invented, it became possible to use the form without subscribing to the substance. One can find constitutions with fundamental rights, but without democracy; one can find constitutions with democracy, but without fundamental rights; and one can even find constitutions that lack both, rights and democracy.[4]

If these constitutions are not mere window-dressing, they may have a limited impact. But they fall short of the achievement of constitutionalism.[5] A constitution that is based on a legitimacy principle other than democracy will put the supremacy of its rules at risk since in cases of conflict the legitimacy principle, be it divine, hereditary, or elitist, will prevail over the limits that the constitution imposes on government. Similarly, a constitution without fundamental rights will put the autonomy of the individual at risk, whose protection is the function of legitimate government. As Jürgen Habermas puts it: democracy and rights are co-equal.[6]

---

[3] First formulated by Emmanuel Joseph Sieyes, *Qu'est-ce que le Tiers État?* (Paris, 1789). See Pasquale Pasquino, *Sieyes et l'invention de la constitution française* (Paris: Editions Odile Jacob, 1998).

[4] See Dieter Grimm, 'Types of Constitutions' in Michel Rosenfeld and András Sajó (eds), *The Oxford Handbook of Comparative Constitutional Law* (Oxford: Oxford University Press, 2012), p. 98.

[5] See Ch. 18 of this volume.

[6] Jürgen Habermas, *The Inclusion of the Other* (Cambridge: Polity Press, 2002).

## 2. Tension

If one wants to enjoy the benefits of constitutionalism fully, democracy and rights must coexist. This is not to say, however, that democracy and fundamental rights are always in harmony and can never endanger the constitutional project. Democracy may undermine rights. Rights may overwhelm democracy. There is a tension in constitutionalism itself as it emerged from the two revolutions. Carl Schmitt even saw these two elements of modern constitutions as contradictory so that ultimately a choice between the two would become necessary.[7] Hence the question: is there a tension or a contradiction?

Tension leaves room for accommodation, contradiction excludes it. This raises the question whether each of them could stand by itself. Democracy, to begin with, has some preconditions. It depends on free elections that, in turn, require free citizens. They must be politically free to form and express their opinions, articulate their interests, and associate in order to invigorate their political influence. Free media are an indispensable condition for political freedom of the citizens. But the citizens must also be free in their private sphere, since political freedom will not thrive without private autonomy. Democracy itself cannot guarantee these preconditions. They depend on the protection by fundamental rights.

Rights also have preconditions. They do not enforce themselves. They are in need of being protected and they have to be limited in order to make the many liberties or the liberties of the many compatible with each other. In short, they depend on governmental power. Yet, governmental power is in itself a threat to individual freedom. How can the two be reconciled? Among the various forms of government, democracy seems to be the form that best serves the autonomy of the individual because it grounds public power on the will of rights bearers and rejects legitimacy principles that trump rights.

Therefore, Schmitt's asserted antagonism between rights and democracy exists only if they are pushed to extremes. Radical democracy is strictly majoritarian. It recognizes only one fundamental right: the right of every citizen to participate in the formation of the political will of the people. All other limits on government are incompatible with this notion of democracy. The minority is unconditionally surrendered to majority decisions. In a radical democracy, constitutions shrink to a number of rules that regulate will formation and execution organizationally and procedurally. Majoritarian democracy is formal democracy.

But just as radical democracy tends to minimize legal rules that limit political action, rights foundationalism, as Bruce Ackerman calls it,[8] tends to minimize democracy. The reason is that all matters regulated on the constitutional level are not open to political decision. What has been decided in the constitution is

---

[7] Carl Schmitt, *Constitutional Theory* (Durham, N.C: Duke University Press, 2008); Carl Schmitt, *Legality and Legitimacy* (Durham, N.C: Duke University Press, 1997).

[8] Bruce Ackerman, *We the People. Foundations* (Cambridge, Mass.: Belknap Press, 1991), p. 10.

not the object but the premise of political decisions. This means also that elections do not matter as far as constitutional law extends. In the end all politics is reduced to executing the constitution. Public power shifts from the people themselves and their elected representatives to the courts.

Both radical versions develop a self-destructive dynamic. Radical democracy may take the form of popular dictatorship. It cannot even defend itself against the abolition of majority rule by majority vote. On the other hand, rights foundationalism reduces the importance of elections and endangers the adaptability of laws to changing circumstances. It therefore risks the constitution hampering democratic change and becoming a barrier to coping with new challenges. The stronger the challenges are, the sooner politics will re-appear on the scene and circumvent or suspend the constitution in order to achieve what they understand as the common good.

There may be, and often is, too little constitutionalism. But it may also be that there is too much. Both deviations disregard the crucial distinction between the rules for political decision-making and the political decisions themselves, each in its own way. In the first case, the tension is dissolved in favour of politics. The constitution will fail to fulfill its function of guiding and limiting government efficiently. Such a constitution will hardly be able to legitimate the exercise of public power. In the second case, the tension is dissolved in favour of the law. The democratic process is fettered. Politics is reduced to an execution of constitutional prescriptions. The administration and the judiciary marginalize the legislature.

There are no universally applicable principles for determining what belongs in a constitution and what not. New constitutions react to past experiences and seek to provide for a better future. Every country must decide for itself what it deems so important for a better future that it should be exempted from the wavering will of simple majorities. These questions are not uncontroversial. Agreements between different forces in a convention or a constituent assembly require compromises. Some can only be reached by leaving gaps where one would expect a rule, some others may only be reached by accommodating many interests, and thereby inflate the constitution.

However, even if it is difficult to formulate substantive rules for constitution-making, the function of constitutions allows some generalizations that transcend the particular design of political systems, which differs from country to country: federal or unitary, presidential or parliamentary, pluralist voting system or proportional representation, bicameral or unicameral parliament, with or without judicial review, with or without social and economic rights, etc. The function of constitutions is to legitimate and to limit political power, but not to replace it. Constitutions are a framework for politics, not the blueprint for all political decisions.

Where the distinction between a constitution and ordinary law, or dualist democracy in Ackerman's terms, is lost one will not enjoy the benefits of constitutionalism. The constitution furnishes the basic structure and the lasting principles for politics. Politics concretizes them and fills the space they leave according to changing preferences and circumstances. Constitutions thus provide a durable structure for change. They combine principles that enjoy a broad consensus with flexibility to meet new challenges or changing majorities and thereby enable a peaceful transition of power.

However, the text of the constitution is one thing, its interpretation and application to individual cases is quite another. Even if the text avoids the risks of radicalism, courts may interpret it in a way that increasingly narrows the space for political decisions. To the same extent the power of courts will increase. Constitutionalization of ordinary law by way of interpretation may have the same cementing effect. The more ordinary law is regarded as constitutionally mandated, the less politics can change it if this is required by the circumstances or by a shift of political preferences.

This danger exists especially where courts have the last word on the meaning of constitutional provisions. It is true that constitutions are of little value without judicial enforcement. To be sure, courts should have the power to adapt constitutional law to new challenges. But even though it may be difficult to define, there is a distinction between interpreting law and making law under the disguise of interpretation. When courts overstep this line, the only remedy for politics is to re-programme the judiciary by amending the constitution, which is easy in some countries, but extremely difficult in others. The more difficult constitutional amendments are, the less space remains for democratic re-direction of courts.

## II. EUROPE: CONSTITUTIONALIZATION OF THE TREATIES

### 1. *The Cause: Supremacy of EU Law*

It is generally accepted that the European Union (EU) suffers from a democratic deficit that affects its legitimacy. But it is rarely noticed that this deficit has a source in the state of European constitutionalism. How can this be true, even though the EU does not have a constitution? After all, the legal foundation of the EU are treaties under international law, originally concluded by six member states in Rome in 1957, several times amended, and now in force in the form of the Lisbon Treaty of 2010, ratified by twenty-eight member states after the so-called Treaty on a Constitution for Europe of 2003 had failed in two referenda.

Nevertheless, the treaty fulfills many functions of a constitution. It specifies the purposes of the EU, establishes its organs, determines their powers and procedures, regulates the relationship with the member states, and contains a charter of fundamental rights just as constitutions do. It differs from a constitution because it does not have its source in an autonomous act of a European constituent power. It is instead given to the EU by the member states and continues to depend on their agreement. Only they have the power of amendment. They are the 'Masters of the Treaties'.

Although suggested from time to time, the transformation of the treaties into a constitution in the full sense of the concept has not been undertaken up to now. Even the Constitutional Treaty of 2003, the most far-reaching endeavour to form a closer union, did not attempt to change the nature of the Union's legal foundation. If adopted by all member states, it would still have remained a treaty under international law since the constituent power was not handed over to the EU itself. Rather the member states reserved this power for themselves so that no transition from hetero-determination to auto-determination has taken place.[9]

Applied to the EU, the word 'constitutionalization' must therefore have a meaning different from the usual one. It neither denotes a process of making a constitution nor the permeation of ordinary law by constitutional law through interpretation, which is characteristic for a number of states with a strong constitutional court. In Europe, the expression is used rather to characterize the result of two groundbreaking judgments of the European Court of Justice (ECJ) that endowed the treaties with effects typical of constitutional law. It was an American observer, Joseph Weiler, who first described this effect as 'constitutionalization'.[10]

In 1963, the ECJ initially confronted the relationship between European and national law. The traditional answer to that question was clear: since European law is international law, it binds the member states, but produces legal effects for the individual citizens only after having been incorporated into or concretized by national law. This was the position of several member states when they argued the case in court, and it was equally the position of the Court's Advocate General. In contrast, the ECJ declared European law to be directly applicable in the member states, to the effect that individuals could derive rights from it and claim them before the national courts without waiting for further concretization by the national legislature.[11]

However, the initial decision did not answer the question of what would happen if European and national law conflicted. The answer followed a year later in a second decisive ruling.[12] The Court declared that the treaties, and European law in general, enjoyed primacy over national law, even over national constitutions. National law that contradicted European law lost its applicability. No national court or other agency was permitted to apply it. In case of doubt, national courts had to refer the question of compatibility to the ECJ, whose decision was binding on them.

The ECJ had opened the door to these judgments by a methodological turn.[13] In its view, European law was neither a part of international law nor dependent

---

[9] This distinction separates a treaty from a constitution, see Dieter Grimm, 'Treaty or Constitution?' in Erik Oddvar Erikson et al. (eds), *Developing a Constitution for Europe* (London: Routledge, 2004), p. 69; Dieter Grimm, 'Verfassung—Verfassungsvertrag—Vertrag über eine Verfassung' in Olivier Beaud et al. (eds), *L'Europe en voie de constitution* (Brussels: Bruyant, 2004), p. 279.

[10] Joseph H. H. Weiler, 'The Transformation of Europe' (1991) 100 *Yale Law Journal* 2403.

[11] *Van Gend & Loos v. Netherlands* (1963), ECR 1.      [12] *Costa v. ENEL* (1964), ECR 585.

[13] Stephan Grundmann, *Die Auslegung des Gemeinschaftsrechts durch den Europäischen Gerichtshof: Zugleich eine rechtsvergleichende Studie zur Auslegung im Völkerrecht und im Gemeinschaftsrecht* (Konstanz: Hartung-Gorre, 1997); Jochen Anweiler, *Die Auslegungsmethoden des Gerichtshofs der Europäischen Gemeinschaften* (Frankfurt am

on a national order to apply it, but was an autonomous legal order that had emancipated itself from the national sources. This is why the Court did not find it necessary to interpret European law in the cautious manner of international law, emphasizing the will of the contracting parties and limiting the adverse impacts on national sovereignty. Instead, the ECJ began to interpret the European treaties in a constitutional mode, namely as more or less detached from the member states' will and oriented instead by an objectivized purpose.

Part of this methodological programme was the so-called *effet utile*, which 'rounds out' the direct effect and the supremacy of European law. According to this maxim, European law has to be interpreted in a way that gives the utmost effect to its provisions. If there are several possible interpretations, judges should choose the one that favours the effectiveness of European law and consequently restricts the application of national law. The ECJ understands this maxim not only as a guideline for itself but above all as one for the national courts when they decide cases that involve European law.

In hindsight these judgments were perceived as revolutionary. When they were handed down, they remained largely below the threshold of public attention. They appeared as decisions in singular and non-conspicuous cases, rendered by a court that went more or less unnoticed. Revolutionary they were because neither direct effect nor primacy of European law were explicitly mentioned in the treaties. Rather, they resulted from a purposive interpretation that was by no means without alternative. They were revolutionary also because, without them, the EU would not have become what it is today, namely an unprecedented political entity somewhere between an international organization and a federal state, but because of the amount of its powers and the density of its organizational structure closer to the latter than to the former.

Yet, those judgments deserve the characterization as revolutionary for still another reason: they radically changed the position of the ECJ itself. Although remaining completely within the framework of its procedural limits, the Court enlarged its own power by the extensive interpretation of substantive law. By re-defining the legal nature of the treaties, the Court gained a position that by far exceeded the powers of an international court and resembled more that of constitutional courts. Its judgments participated in the direct effect and primacy of European law, not only regarding the organs of the EU but also those of the member states. It was no longer the exclusive power of the member states to adjust their laws to European requirements. The ECJ could do this itself by declaring national law inapplicable that it regarded as incompatible with European law.

However, the purpose of this chapter is not to discuss the question of whether these judgments were 'right' or 'wrong' from a legal point of view. They were accepted by the member states and in principle also by the national courts on whose cooperation the ECJ depends. They are now the law of the EU. The only

Main: Lang, 1997); Carsten Buck, *Über die Auslegungsmethoden des Gerichtshofs der Europäischen Gemeinschaft* (Frankfurt am Main: Lang, 1998).

issue that is contested is the question of whether the identity of national constitutions imposes an outer limit to the supremacy of European law and who is authorized to determine whether the EU acted *ultra vires*, the ECJ alone or the national constitutional courts as well, as many constitutional courts of the member states assume. What is of interest here are rather the consequences of these judgments.

### 2. *The Effect: De-politicization*

As an immediate consequence of the two revolutionary judgments member states were no longer needed in order to establish the single market. Direct effect and supremacy of European law allowed the Commission (as the organ charged with enforcing the treaties vis-à-vis the member states) and the ECJ (as the organ charged with determining the meaning of the treaties in concrete cases) to take the task of implementing economic integration in their own hands. If they declared that national law impeded the common market, the national law became inapplicable without the member states having a realistic chance to defend their own law in an effective way.

A precondition was, however, that the ECJ had the opportunity to use its expanded power. This depended in particular on the willingness of the national courts to refer to Luxemburg questions regarding the compatibility of domestic law with European law. Lower courts may do this, last instance courts have to do it. In general the national courts cooperated with the ECJ. Only a few judgments of the ECJ, which were difficult to swallow for the national courts, temporarily reduced their willingness to refer further questions to Luxemburg. Once again we owe the explanation of this—by no means evident—behaviour of the national courts to an American observer, Karen Alter.[14]

Everything depended now on how the ECJ would interpret the treaties, favouring uniformity or diversity of the law, market-friendly or regulation-friendly, liberal or social. As it turned out, the ECJ pursued the goal of market integration with considerable zeal, subordinating other concerns to this goal. It was a court with an agenda, as Rainer Wahl has put it.[15] Powers transferred to the EU were interpreted broadly, powers retained by the member states narrowly. The same can be observed regarding the principle of proportionality. When applied to national laws, the ECJ submitted them to strict scrutiny; when applied to European laws, it used a lenient standard of review.

The main beneficiaries were the four fundamental freedoms, all economic in nature (free movement of goods, persons, services, and capital) and their concretization in the treaties. These freedoms were transformed from objective principles for legislation into subjective rights of the market participants who could claim them against the member states before the national courts. Their

---

[14] Karen Alter, *Establishing the Supremacy of European Law* (Oxford: Oxford University Press, 2001). See also Alec Stone Sweet, *The Judicial Construction of Europe* (Oxford: Oxford University Press, 2004).

[15] Rainer Wahl, 'Das Recht der Integrationsgemeinschaft Europäische Union' in *Beharren—Bewegen, Festschrift für Michael Kloepfer* (Berlin: Duncker & Humblot, 2013), p. 233, at p. 248.

implementation thus became a matter of jurisdiction rather than legislation. There is not enough space to describe this in detail.[16] Three examples of the impact of the Court's jurisprudence must suffice to illustrate this.

First, the ECJ not only prevented the member states from upholding protectionist measures in favour of the national economy, as was explicitly mandated by the treaties. The anti-protectionist provisions of the treaties were also interpreted as anti-regulation provisions. Any national law that, in the Court's view, impeded the four economic freedoms as concretized in the treaties became a target for review under the treaty prohibition of customs duties and quantitative restrictions on imports and exports as well as measures having an 'equivalent effect', irrespective of whether the law had a protectionist purpose or even an economic motive and irrespective of whether the market was able to provide the goods or services in the same way. The rule thereby lost its contours since almost every law can be understood as an impediment on the economic freedoms.

The decisive step was an ECJ judgment that insisted that any good lawfully produced in one member state was marketable in every other member state, notwithstanding the laws of this state.[17] The same is true for those subsidies granted by the member states that distort or threaten to distort free competition. The ECJ did not limit this prohibition to private enterprises but extended it to public services, again regardless of whether the motive behind the subsidies was influencing the competition or pursuing other purposes. In contrast, exceptions for certain impediments or subsidies, which the treaties allowed in the interest of public morals, public policy, public security, etc., were usually interpreted narrowly.

Secondly, the ECJ's position on European directives reveals the same activist approach. In contrast with EU regulations, directives are binding for the member states only insofar as they stipulate goals, while it is for the member states to determine the ways and means of reaching them. However, the space for member states' decisions has been constantly narrowed. The ECJ ruled that, in the case of non-compliance or insufficient compliance, the directive applies directly within the member states, provided it is clear and precise enough. As could be expected, this encouraged the EU to make directives more and more detailed.

The Court also required national courts to interpret national law in conformity with directives, regardless of whether the specific law implements a directive or was caused by a directive. Directives are declared applicable even before the deadline for implementation ends. If a directive is not implemented on time or in a deficient way the member state may have to pay damages to those who can prove damage by virtue of this non-compliance. This non-contractual liability

---

[16] For a comprehensive account, see Anna Katharina Mangold, *Gemeinschaftsrecht und deutsches Recht* (Tübingen: Mohr Siebeck, 2011).

[17] See the decisions *Dassonville* (1974), ECR 837, and *Cassis de Dijon* (1978), ECR 649. Generally Martin Höppner and Armin Schäfer (eds), *Die Politische Ökonomie der europäischen Integration* (Frankfurt am Main: Campus Verlag, 2008).

even extends to so-called judicial injustice, that is, a 'wrong' interpretation of European law by national courts.

Thirdly, the ECJ's most recent step concerns the scope of the European Charter of Fundamental Rights that became legally binding with the Lisbon Treaty. According to its Art. 51, the Charter binds all institutions of the EU, whereas the member states are bound 'only when implementing Union law'. However, for the ECJ implementing Union law includes the implementation of national law, provided that it has some connection with European law.[18] Due to the degree of entanglement between European and national law, the ECJ has little difficulty finding such a connection wherever it wants.

Furthermore, the scope of the European Charter is limited insofar that, according to Art. 53, its interpretation may not lead to a decrease of the national standard of fundamental rights protection in their field of application. Since this field is defined in Art. 51, the value of the limit depends on the Court's understanding of this provision. The problem is aggravated in constellations where two fundamental rights conflict so that the courts have to accommodate them by a process of balancing. Every objection against the result of the national courts' balancing will inevitably lead to a decrease of the fundamental right that enjoyed priority on the national level.

The jurisprudence of the ECJ leaves deep marks on national law and politics.[19] The broad interpretation of the impediments to trade deprives the member states of the possibility to uphold national standards of consumer protection, workers protection, health protection, etc. The extension of prohibited state subsidies to public services deprives the member states of the power to determine the borderline between the public and the private sector. The privatization of many public services finds its origin here. The jurisprudence on directives narrows the space for national legislation. The expanded scope of Charter rights and the salience of the four fundamental freedoms impose the ECJ's preference for economic freedoms on the member states, whose constitutional courts tend to prioritize personal, communicative, cultural, and social rights over economic liberties.

## III. DEMOCRATIC COSTS

### 1. The problem: Over-constitutionalization

The integration-friendly jurisprudence of the ECJ is usually told as a success story. And a success story it is, at least insofar as the economic integration of Europe is concerned. But the economic perspective is not the only possible one. The economic success has a legitimacy drawback whose deeper reasons are

---

[18] See the decision *Åkerberg Fransson* (2013), EC-617/10. Other decisions show, however, that there is not yet a stable jurisprudence on this matter, see e.g. Gabriele Britz, 'Grundrechtsschutz durch das Bundesverfassungsgericht und den Europäischen Gerichtshof' (2015) 42 *Europäische Grundrechte-Zeitschrift* 275; Claudio Franzius, 'Strategien der Grundrechtsoptimierung in Europa' (2015) 42 *Europäische Grundrechte-Zeitschrift* 139.

[19] See Mangold (n. 16).

still not sufficiently noticed. The drawback manifested itself when the public became aware of the fact that the object of integration was no longer the economy alone but also the political, yet without the people or their representatives having a chance to influence it.

Due to the jurisprudence of the ECJ, there are now two paths towards integration instead of one. The original path, provided by the treaties, consists of creating European primary law and of enacting European secondary law. This path can be taken by the member states only—regarding the treaties, by a unanimous decision in the conference of the heads of state and government, followed by ratification in each member state; and regarding secondary law, by a decision of the Council of Ministers that also required unanimity until the Single European Act of 1987 and has been difficult to achieve to the present day. The new path consists of applying the treaties as understood by the ECJ. This path is open to the executive and judicial powers of the EU.

The two paths towards integration differ considerably. On the basis of the first, powers are transferred by the member states to the EU. This path is political and involves the democratically legitimated and accountable governments of the member states and, to varying degrees, the parliaments of the member states as well as—more recently—the European Parliament. On the basis of the second path, the EU restricts the competences of member states by a broad interpretation of the treaties. This path is administrative and adjudicative in nature. The democratically legitimated and controlled governments of the member states, their parliaments as well as the European Parliament, have no share in it. It is integration by stealth.[20]

However, the non-political mode of decision-making in the second path does not deprive the decisions themselves of their political character. It only shifts the power to decide questions of high political impact from the political organs of the EU to non-political institutions. To the same extent, the political means to secure democratic legitimacy and accountability fail to work. In the field of treaty application, the administrative and judicial organs of the EU are uncoupled from the democratic process in the member states and the EU and enjoy far-reaching independence. This has a number of consequences.

The difference between the political and non-political mode of integration is responsible for the asymmetry between negative and positive integration that was first identified by Fritz Scharpf.[21] Negative integration means deregulation on the national level; positive integration means re-regulation on the European level. As a consequence of the constitutionalization of the treaties, negative integration occurs in a non-political mode by a stroke of pen by the Commission or the ECJ, whereas positive integration requires a political decision where the member states, the European Parliament, and the Commission

[20]  See Domenico Majone, *Dilemmas of European Integration* (Oxford: Oxford University Press, 2005).

[21]  Fritz Scharpf, *Governing in Europe: Effective and Democratic?* (Oxford: Oxford University Press, 1999), p. 43. See also Majone (n. 20), p. 143.

must find an agreement. This has worked in some fields, such as protection of the environment, whereas it fails in other areas.

The asymmetry also accounts for the liberalizing tendency of the ECJ's juris-prudence.[22] This is not to say that the ECJ pursues an agenda of economic lib-eralism. It rather pursues the treaty goal to establish and maintain the single market. Yet, since the vast majority of requests for a preliminary ruling, which reach the ECJ, has its origin in actions by economic actors who see their inter-ests threatened by national legislation, and since the ECJ can contribute to the establishment of the single market only negatively, the result is a structural bias in favour of liberalization. This, in turn, affects social policy. Although reserved for member states, social policy gets under pressure because of the liberalizing effects of the ECJ's jurisprudence, combined with the effects of globalization, the national social policy gets under pressure because upholding a high standard of social security tends to weaken the competitiveness of national economy.[23]

Why is all this a reason for concern? Aren't member states the 'Masters of the Treaties'? Aren't they in a position to stop these judicially created tendencies if they are not happy with them? After all, they decide in the European Council on the direction, extent, and pace of integration and they are the main actors of European legislation in the Council of Ministers. This should give them the opportunity to re-program the jurisprudence of the ECJ by explicit legislation if they do not recognize their intentions in the Court's interpretation of the trea-ties or observe detrimental effects caused by that interpretation.

At this point the special character of the European quasi-constitution comes to the fore. Unlike national constitutions, the treaties are not confined to those provisions that reflect the functions of a constitution. They are full of provi-sions that would be ordinary law in the member states. This is why they are so voluminous. As long as the treaties were treated as international law this was not a problem. As soon as they were constitutionalized their volume became problematic: in the EU the crucial difference between the rules for political deci-sions and the decisions themselves is to a large extent levelled. *The EU is over-constitutionalized.* This has two important consequences.

First, the over-constitutionalization severely limits the member states' role as 'Masters of the Treaties'. It exists with regards to formal amendments, but it is undermined at the level of treaty application. The principle of conferral that limits the power of the EU to those competences that have been explic-itly transferred by the member states is undermined. The *Kompetenz-Kompetenz*, which guarantees that only the member states have the power to determine the allocation of competences, is also undermined. There is a creeping power shift

---

[22]  See Vivien Schmidt and Mark Thatcher (eds), *Resilient Liberalism in Europe's Economy* (Cambridge: Cambridge University Press, 2013).

[23]  See Fritz Scharpf, *Community and Autonomy* (Frankfurt am Main: Campus, 2010), pp. 221, 353; Fritz Scharpf and Vivien A. Schmidt (eds), *Welfare and Work in the Open Economy*, 2 vols, (Oxford: Oxford University Press, 2000); Christian Joerges and Florian Rödl, 'Informal Politics, Formalised Law and the "Social Deficit" of European Integration: Reflections after the Judgments of the ECJ in Viking and Laval' (2009) 15 *European Law Journal* 1.

from member states towards the EU that blurs the borderline between treaty amendment and treaty interpretation and particularly bothers the German Constitutional Court.[24]

Second, the lack of differentiation between the constitutional law level and the ordinary law level, combined with the constitutionalization of the treaties, immunizes the Commission and particularly the ECJ against any attempt by the democratically responsible institutions of the EU to react to the Court's jurisprudence by changing the law. Likewise they immunize the executive and judicial institutions of the EU against public pressure. As far as the treaty extends elections do not matter. The political actors who have to take public opinion into account cannot change anything. The administrative and judicial actors who could change things don't have to pay attention to public opinion.

To be sure, the member states are not without any means to defend themselves against the creeping power shift towards the EU. They can bring an action for annulment of decisions by the Commission if, in their view, they transgress the competences of the EU. And they can amend the treaties. But the practical use of these instruments is limited. Given the pro-integration attitude of an ECJ that does not understand itself as an umpire between the EU and the member states, there is little chance of success of an annulment action. Amendments to the treaties are practically unavailable because of the extremely high hurdles they face. It seems almost impossible to mobilize this instrument in order to reach a seemingly minor goal such as the correction of a line of jurisprudence.

Thus, the example of the EU confirms the assertion that more constitutional law means less democracy. The confusion of elements of constitutional law with elements of ordinary law in the treaties favours the unelected and non-accountable institutions of the EU over the democratically legitimized and accountable organs. Decisions of great political impact are taken in a non-political mode. The result is a state of integration that the citizens were never asked to agree to, but cannot change either, even if they do not support it.

### 2. The Remedy: Re-politicization

Over-constitutionalization is not the only cause of the legitimacy problem the EU faces, but it is the most neglected one. The blindness towards the de-legitimizing effects of over-constitutionalization misguides the search for remedies. The reason for the democratic deficit of the EU is mostly sought in the European Parliament's lack of adequate powers. It does not possess all the competences that national parliaments used to have. Therefore, many believe that the democratic deficit would be repaired if only the European Parliament were endowed with the competences that parliaments in a parliamentary democracy enjoy.

---

[24] See *BVerfGE* 123, 267 (2009); Dieter Grimm, 'Defending Sovereign Statehood against Transforming the European Union into a State' (2009) 5 *European Constitutional Law Review* 353.

The call for increased powers of the Parliament is by no means unsound. The European Parliament is needed as a counterweight against the dominance of national interests in the Council and the technocratic tendencies in the Commission. But it seems doubtful whether full parliamentarization could solve the deeper problems of European democracy. The reasons are manifold. In general, parliaments are the losers in the growing internationalization of politics. This plays into the hands of the executive. It would be surprising if only the European Parliament was exempted from this secular trend.

But there are also specific European reasons that contribute to this effect. The European Parliament is much less representative than the national parliaments.[25] The main reason for this is that European elections are not truly Europeanized. The European Parliament is elected according to twenty-eight national election laws. The seats are allocated according to national quotas that do not reflect the size of the national population. The voters can vote only for national parties, which campaign with national programs. The result of the election is usually evaluated under a national perspective: did the national ruling parties or the national opposition parties win?

Yet, after the elections have taken place, the national political parties (presently 200) do not play a decisive role in the European Parliament. There, European factions, loose associations of ideologically related parties, are decisive, but these factions are neither rooted in society nor do they maintain contact with the voters. This affects the salience of European elections. The parties for which one may vote are not the actors in the European Parliament. The factions that are the actors on the European level do not stand for elections. The legitimacy chain running from the voters to the parliament is thus interrupted.

Finally and most important, the European public sphere and European public discourse is weak compared to the national situation (which, itself, is not always satisfactory). The institutions that mediate between the people and the political organs of the EU are either missing or underdeveloped. There are no European parties. Interest groups, popular movements, non-governmental organizations are quite weak on the European level and, most importantly, there are no European media. The absence of a sufficient societal substructure that is needed for a vibrant democracy makes it unlikely that full parliamentarization would reach its goal, namely to close the gap between the citizenry and the institutions.

Furthermore, the power of the European Parliament cannot be enhanced without decreasing the power of the Council. As a matter of fact, many reform plans want to reduce the Council to a second chamber of the European Parliament. In turn, the Commission would be upgraded to a genuine European government dependent on parliamentary support. For many, a directly elected European President is the apex of the reform. Yet, the strengthening of the Parliament on the institutional level would add little to European democracy

---

[25] See Richard Rose, *Representing Europeans* (Oxford: Oxford University Press, 2013).

as long as the socio-political substructure of parliamentarianism is missing or underdeveloped.

On the contrary, one must fear that the legitimacy structure of the EU would be weakened rather than strengthened. Originally the democratic legitimacy of European politics emanated exclusively from the member states. The Council, in which their governments are represented, was the central organ of the EU and its exclusive legislator. A decision of the Council required unanimity. This meant that no member state was subject to laws to which its democratically legitimated organs had not consented. If the citizens disagreed with their governments, they could voice this in the national election.

The unanimity requirement was given up after a long period of stagnation with the Single European Act of 1987. In certain matters, the Council now decided by a majority. As a consequence it could happen that member states were subject to laws and legal acts to which their democratically and accountable representatives had not agreed. To the same extent the legitimation chain which ran from national elections over the national parliament and government to the European organs was broken, at least for states that were outvoted in the Council.

This legitimation gap could no longer be bridged by national democracies. As compensation, the European Parliament got a share in European legislation which increased with every treaty amendment. The monistic legitimation of the EU has since been replaced by a dualistic one. The reform project would return to a monistic legitimation, yet one that would not consist in hetero-legitimation but in auto-legitimation. Therefore, the question is whether the EU has sufficient legitimation resources to support itself. This is more than doubtful, given the weak societal substructure of the European democracy. Rather it is likely that a full parliamentarization of the EU would minimize the external legitimation without being able to increase the internal legitimation.

Finally, and most importantly in this context, the parliamentarization of the EU would leave the effects of the over-constitutionalization completely unaffected. In the area that is determined by constitutional law, elections do not matter and parliaments have no say. This source of the democratic deficit can only be repaired by a politicization of the decision-making processes in the EU. If one wants to enhance the legitimacy of the EU the power to decide questions of high political salience must be shifted from the executive and judicial branches to the political organs, the Council and the European Parliament. The only way to achieve this goal is to scale back the treaties to their truly constitutional elements and downgrade all treaty provisions of a non-constitutional nature to the status of secondary law.

This should not be misunderstood as a reversal of the constitutionalization of the treaties and a rollback of the present state of integration. Rather it draws out the consequences of precisely that constitutionalization by giving the constitutionalized treaties the outlook of a constitution. Not a single norm of the treaties would be sacrificed. Neither would the function of the ECJ as guardian of the treaties be undermined. This solution would merely open the door for a re-direction of the Court's jurisprudence by the politically legitimated and accountable organs of the EU, if they find it necessary. Legally speaking, this is easy. Politically, it is difficult as long as the democratic costs of over-constitutionalization escape public attention.

# PART VIII

# INTERNATIONALIZATION

# ∽ 15 ∽

# The Constitution in the Process
# of De-nationalization

## I. THE CLAIM OF THE CONSTITUTION

In 1973 Niklas Luhmann could still assert that a radical change of the state of the constitution and the institutional and operational understanding of constitutional arrangements comparable to the establishment of the constitutional state in the late eighteenth century has never occured again.[1] In the meantime, such change is looming. Its cause is the process of the decline of statehood (*Entstaatlichung*), which could not then be foreseen. In essence, this consists of the transfer of public power to non-state actors and its exercise in non-state procedures. This has consequences for the constitution because it originally referred to the state. Its historical significance lay in the juridification (*Verrechtlichung*) of public power, and public power was identical to the state power. Owing to the advantages associated with this, the constitution was regarded as a civilizing achievement up to the present day.[2] Pre-state forms of political rule not only had no constitution, they could not have had one. The question is whether this achievement can survive in the 'postnational constellation'.[3]

By constitution I mean here the law produced through a political decision that regulates the establishment and exercise of political rule. The constitution in this sense is a novelty of the eighteenth century that of course did not arise out of nothing, but had not previously existed in this form.[4] The normative constitution came into being in 1776 on the periphery of what was then the western world, in North America. Thirteen years later, in 1789, it reached Europe. In Europe and the other parts of the world it influenced, the whole nineteenth century was permeated and determined by the struggle around the spread of the constitution. But the victory the idea of constitutionalism seemed to win at the end of the First World War turned out to be short-lived. Only towards the end of the twentieth century, after numerous detours and reversals,

---

[1] Niklas Luhmann, 'Politische Verfassungen im Kontext des Gesellschaftssystems' (1973) 12 *Der Staat* 4.

[2] Niklas Luhmann, 'Verfassung als evolutionäre Errungenschaft' (1990) 9 *Rechtshistorisches Journal* 176.

[3] Jürgen Habermas, *The Postnational Constellation* (Cambridge: MIT Press, 2001).

[4] See Ch. 2 of this volume. See further Dieter Grimm, *Deutsche Verfassungsgeschichte* (Frankfurt am Main: Suhrkamp, 3rd edn, 1995), p. 10.

did constitutionalism prevail universally. Today constitutionless states are the exception, which, of course, is not to say that the constitution is intended to be or is taken seriously everywhere.

Concerning its novelty, we should not let ourselves be deceived by the fact that the notion of 'constitution' is older than the United States and French constitutions. Before their appearance it was not a normative concept but an empirical one.[5] Brought into political language from the description of nature, it designated the condition of a country, as shaped by the character of its territory and inhabitants, its historical development and prevailing power relations, its legal norms and political institutions. With social philosophy's increasing effort to restrict state power in favour of the freedom of subjects, the notion 'constitution' was narrowed; its non-normative elements were gradually cast off until the constitution finally appeared to be the condition determined by public law. It was nevertheless not the kernel of constitutional norms but rather the condition they determined that was designated by the word 'constitution'.

Only with the late-eighteenth-century revolutions in North America and France, which violently overthrew ancestral rule and established a new order on the basis of rational planning and legal codification, was there a transition from a descriptive to a prescriptive concept. Since then the constitution has ordinarily been identified with the complex of norms that fundamentally and comprehensively regulate the establishment and exercise of state power. The empirical constitution did not disappear, but returned in the shape of the 'constitutional reality' that influences the law. But when we speak of constitutionalization, we always speak of the legal and not the factual constitution. The legal constitution does not reproduce social reality but addresses expectations to it, the fulfillment of which does not go without saying and for just this reason requires legal support. The constitution thus takes its distance from political reality and only thereby acquires the ability to serve as standard for political behaviour and judgement.

If the legal constitution did not arise earlier, this is because it depends on preconditions that did not exist in the past. For a long time the constitution in the sense of a law that specializes in norming political rule lacked an object.[6] Before the functional differentiation of society there was no social system that, by its delimitation from other systems, specialized in the exercise of political rule. Rather, the tasks of ruling were divided up by location, subject matter, and function among numerous independent bearers. There was no comprehensive political body to which the particular rights of rule could have been ascribed. Rights referred less to territories than to people. Their bearers exercised them

---

[5] See Heinz Mohnhaupt and Dieter Grimm, *Verfassung* (Berlin: Duncker & Humblot, 2nd edn, 2002).

[6] See Helmut Quaritsch, *Staat und Souveränität* (Frankfurt am Main: Athenäum, 1970), p. 182. On the older order of domination, see ibid., p. 196; Otto Brunner, *Land und Herrschaft* (Darmstadt: Wissenschaftliche Buchgesellschaft, 6th edn, 1970). On the significance of the transition to functional differentiation, see Niklas Luhmann, *Die Gesellschaft der Gesellschaft* (Frankfurt am Main: Suhrkamp, 1997), p. 595, and *Die Politik der Gesellschaft* (Frankfurt am Main: Suhrkamp, 2000), p. 69.

not as independent functions but as an adjunct of a certain social status, namely, as landholders. What are now held apart as private and public were still mixed together.

This is not to say that rule was exercised without any legal bounds. To the contrary, there was a dense mesh of legal bonds that were traced back to a divine foundation or held traditionally. For this reason they had priority over the enacted law and could not be altered by it. But these legal bonds did not represent a constitution in the sense of a particular law specializing in the exercise of political rule. Just as the authority to rule was only a dependent adjunct of other legal positions, it was governed by the corresponding law. From this we see that not every juridification of authority results in a constitution. The many works devoted to the ancient or medieval constitution do not thereby lose their value. But one must not confuse these constitutions with the normative text, implemented on the basis of a political decision, that claims to regulate rule.

From the perspective that interests us here, the decline of statehood, however, it is more significant that only with the modern state does an object emerge capable of having a constitution. Like the normative constitution, the state too was a historical novelty, but temporally it preceded the constitution. State-building arose when religious divisions removed the basis for the medieval order based on divine revelation and a new form of political domination developed in continental Europe in reaction to the confessional civil wars of the sixteenth and seventeenth centuries.[7] It was based on the conviction, prepared by Bodin and other French theorists, that civil wars can only be settled by a superior power that raises itself above the warring parties and possesses sufficient power resources to establish and enforce a new order independent of contested religious truths, and thus to reestablish domestic peace.

In this effort, the princes of various territories, starting with France, undertook to unite the numerous, scattered prerogatives and consolidate comprehensive public power over the territory. Because of the need to build a new order, public power also included the right to make laws, which was no longer limited by a higher law derived from God. In fact, rulers continued to regard themselves as divinely legitimated, and did not disavow the bindingness of divine command. But this command no longer had legal effect. Instead, law was made by a worldly authority and in this sense positivized. As positive, it no longer drew its validity from its accordance with God's plan for salvation, but from the ruler's will; divine or natural law, its name notwithstanding, lost its legal quality and was now only morally binding.

The previously unknown notion of the 'state' soon became current for this new kind of polity. If it was later also applied by historians to earlier periods, this was a matter of the reassignation of an object of another kind. The state

---

[7] See Roman Schnur, *Die französischen Juristen im konfessionellen Bürgerkrieg des 16. Jahrhunderts* (Berlin: Duncker & Humblot, 1962); Charles Tilly (ed.), *The Formation of the National States in Western Europe* (Princeton: Princeton University Press, 1975); Perry Anderson, *The Rise of the Absolutist State* (London: Verso, 1979); Kenneth Dyson, *The State Tradition in Western Europe* (Oxford: Oxford University Press, 1980).

possessed sovereignty, defined as the highest power, subordinate to no other external or internal power. Like the thing it designated, this concept too was new.[8] At its core, sovereignty signified the ruler's right to make the law for all his subjects without himself being legally bound. Externally, this designated the right to determine domestic conditions free from the interference of other states. The means for enforcing this claim was the monopoly on the use of force in Max Weber's sense,[9] the flipside of which was the elimination of all intermediary powers. The establishment of the sovereign state thus went along with the privatization of society. The mixture of private and public was dissolved.

Of course, the establishment of the state was not an event but a process that did not reach its conclusion anywhere on the continent before the French Revolution and had scarcely begun in England when it was limited by the Glorious Revolution of 1688.[10] Different from the French and American Revolutions that followed a century later, England saw a revolution in defence of the old order, namely the rights of parliament, against the crown's transformative designs. For this reason it did not lead to a constitution in the modern sense.[11] On the continent, however, there was now an object capable of having a constitution in the form of a state that did not hold a number of prerogatives but public power, and specialized in its exercise. If nevertheless no constitution in the modern sense emerged, this was because the state developed under these conditions as an absolutist princely state, defined precisely by not being bound by law.

This is not to assert the complete absence of legal restrictions on the ruler. There were restrictions of this kind even under absolute monarchy. But insofar as they were not simply the vestiges of earlier historical layers, they could only be conceived as self-restrictions on princely power. Normally they were wrested from the ruler by particular groups of well-placed subjects and fixed in so-called charters (*Herrschaftsverträgen*), whose validity was based on the unanimous wills of the participants.[12] As contractually binding, however, these restrictions always presupposed the authority of the monarch to rule. They restricted his authority to rule, which was in principle comprehensive, only punctually. They did not benefit all the subjects; rather, their effects were reserved for the privileged

---

[8] See Quaritsch (n. 6); Helmut Quaritsch, *Souveränität* (Berlin: Duncker & Humblot, 1986); Hans Boldt et al., 'Staat und Souveränität' in Otto Brunner, Werner Conze, and Reinhart Koselleck (eds), *Geschichtliche Grundbegriffe*, vol. 6 (Stuttgart: Klett, 1990), p. 1; Paul Ludwig Weinacht, *Staat* (Berlin: Gesamtverein der deutschen Geschichts- und Altertumsvereine, 1968).

[9] Max Weber, *Economy and Society*, 1921, pt. I, ch. 1 §17; pt. II, ch. 8 §2; ch. 9 §2. See Andreas Anter, *Max Webers Theorie des modernen Staates* (Berlin: Duncker & Humblot, 1995).

[10] See Hans-Christoph Schröder, *Die Revolutionen Englands im 17. Jahrhundert* (Frankfurt am Main: Suhrkamp, 1986).

[11] But see the short-lived 'Instrument of Government' imposed after the abolition of the monarchy under Cromwell: Samuel Gardiner (ed.), *The Constitutional Documents of the Puritan Revolution* (Oxford: Oxford University Press, 1968), p. 405.

[12] See Rudolf Vierhaus (ed.), *Herrschaftsverträge, Wahlkapitulationen, Fundamentalgesetze* (Göttingen: Vandenhoek und Ruprecht, 1977).

contractual partners. As far as they extended, they juridified political rule, but nowhere did they appear with the comprehensive claim to legitimation and regulation that distinguishes the modern constitution.

Nor did the social philosophy of the time, which saw at once that the new concentration of power confronted it with the question of a non-transcendental legitimation of rule, extend its efforts as far as the idea of a constitution.[13] For social philosophy, any rule that—assuming rational behaviour—could be *thought of* as emerging from the free agreement of all was legitimate. In this way, the consensus of the subjects of rule was elevated to the central category grounding legitimacy. In social-contract theory, however, it was neither traced back to an actual contract nor fixed in a written agreement, but rather used as a hypothetical test of whether one could consent to rule. The theory of the social contract thus did not fundamentally place in question existing rule that was independent of consensus as long as it corresponded to the particular rational imperatives for which the contract was only a theoretical bridge.

Nevertheless, the conditions under which philosophy assumed the readiness of rational beings to leave the state of nature and to submit themselves to government changed in the course of time.[14] In response to civil war, it even arrived at a justification of absolute rule: only when the individual ceded all his natural rights to the state and completely submitted to it would the state be in the position to guarantee his physical safety, which, in the face of the existential threat of civil war, had the highest priority. Once the absolutist state had successfully concluded the civil war and re-established domestic peace, the complete surrender of natural rights no longer appeared plausible. Now it sufficed for the individual to give up the right to use force in pursuit of his own interests. Otherwise he retained his natural freedoms, and the state drew its justification precisely from protecting those freedoms from encroachments.

These ideas were put into action when in North America and France ancestral rule was toppled by revolution and the resulting power vacuum had to be filled. In this situation, it was decisive for the emergence of the constitution that in both cases the revolutionaries were not satisfied with replacing the overthrown rulers with other ones. Acting as representatives of the people they first designed a model of legitimate rule and only on the basis of this model were individuals called upon to exercise the rights of rule. Central here were two basic principles that had been developed in theory as mere regulative ideas and were now reformulated as real conditions: first, that legitimate power arose from the consensus of those subject to it; and second, that the latter had innate and inalienable rights, the securing of which was the legitimizing aim of political rule.

[13] The sole exception was Emer de Vattel, *Le droit des gens ou principe de la loi naturelle* (Leiden, 1758); see Mohnhaupt and Grimm (n 5), pp. 91, 105.

[14] See Otto von Gierke, *Johannes Althusius und die Entwicklung der naturrechtlichen Staatstheorien* (Aalen: Scientia, 5th edn, 1958); Wolfgang Kersting, *Die politische Philosophie des Gesellschaftsvertrages* (Darmstadt: Wissenschaftliche Buchgesellschaft, 1994); Diethelm Klippel, *Politische Freiheit und Freiheitsrechte im deutschen Naturrecht des 18. Jahrhunderts* (Paderborn: Schöningh, 1976).

The task of securing equal freedom, which according to the conviction of the time would lead to prosperity and justice without intervention of the state, also required power. The French Revolution therefore touched neither the state nor its attribute of sovereignty. It rather completed the state-building that had begun under absolutism by dissolving the intermediary powers that had survived under the absolutist regime, thus making public and state power identical. By the same stroke, however, the bearer of state power was replaced. The nation took the place of the monarch. Rule could therefore not be legitimated by one's own but only be a derived right. Article 3 of the 1789 *Déclaration des droits de l'homme et du citoyen* formulated the basic principle of the democratic constitutional state: 'The principle of all sovereignty resides essentially in the nation. No body or individual may exercise any authority which does not proceed directly from the nation.'

Unlike in France, in America the revolution was not preceded by state-building in the continental sense. In the motherland of the American colonists, religious disunity had not led to the rise of absolutist monarchy but, on the contrary, to the strengthening of parliament and an essentially liberal legal order. The American revolutionaries therefore were not in a position to take over a state in the continental sense in order to supply it with a new basis of legitimacy and adjust it to the principle of individual freedom. Nonetheless, they too constituted a political unity they understood as government, which possessed the qualities of states. Although the American state lagged behind continental states in its tasks, instruments, and bureaucratic apparatus, it too was the focal point of all public power, which it took from the people so that there could no longer be any claim to rule that could not be traced back to its will.

The possession and the exercise of public power were thus separated. The political system therefore had to be organized in a way that established a relation of legitimation and responsibility between those who possessed the ruling powers and those who exercised them, as much as possible preventing their misuse. It was these constructive tasks of state organization and limitation that well-nigh compelled legal regulation. Only law had the ability to elevate the consensus concerning the project of legitimate rule above the fleetingness of the moment, to make it last, and to give it binding force. It helped the Americans, who were the first to take this step, that they already had a familiar model for the legally binding organization of public power in the English declarations of rights and colonial charters bestowed on them by the mother country,[15] while in its revolution thirteen years later France could look to the American model.

First, however, it was necessary to clear another hurdle: since its positivization, the law that was now to bind the state was a product of precisely this state. Under these circumstances, the state could only be bound successfully if

---

[15] See Alfred H. Kelly and Winfried A. Harbison, *The American Constitution* (New York: Macmillan, 4th edn, 1963), chs. 1 and 2; Willi Paul Adams, *Republikanische Verfassung und bürgerliche Freiheit* (Darmstadt: Luchterhand, 1973), p. 30; Donald Lutz, *The Origins of American Constitutionalism* (Baton Rouge: Louisiana State University Press, 1988), p. 13; Gerald Stourzh, *Wege zur Grundrechtsdemokratie* (Vienna: Böhlau, 1989), p. 1.

one resorted to the idea of a hierarchy of norms, but cut it off from its transcendental roots. This led to a splitting of the positivized legal order into two complexes: a traditional one that was produced by the state and bound the individual; and a new one that proceeded from or was ascribed to the sovereign and bound the state. The latter is the constitution as distinct from the laws and taking precedent over them. This was the very step by which the Americans surpassed the English 'constitution'.[16] While the English 'constitution' did not constitute government but only partially restricted it, American and then French constitutional law was to precede all governmental powers. In the constitution the law accordingly became reflexive: the process of legislation and implementation were for their part juridified.

Primacy therefore is an indispensable element of constitutionalism. Where it is missing, the constitution cannot carry out the task for which it was invented.[17] In America and France this was clear from the beginning. In the *Federalist Papers* it was compared to the relationship of principal to deputy, servant to master.[18] Sieyès summed it up in the distinction between the *pouvoir constituant* and the *pouvoir constitué*.[19] The *pouvoir constituant* generates the *pouvoir constitué*; its decision is thus not itself legally bound. But it does not go beyond creating and regulating legitimate rule. Ruling itself is a matter for the *pouvoir constitué*. However, the latter may act only on the basis of and within the framework of the constitution. In a constitutional state there can be no extra- or supraconstitutional powers beneath the *pouvoir constituant*. Only thus can the goal of constitutionalization of public power be ensured—a 'government of laws and not of men'.[20]

As against older legal restrictions on rule, the constitution was not only rule-modifying but rule-constituting, limiting state power not only for the benefit of a privileged group but generally, and deploying its state-limiting effect not only in certain respects but comprehensively.[21] This is not to assert the total juridification of the state. That would render politics impossible and ultimately dissolve it into a mere implementation of the constitution. The constitution is not to make politics superfluous but only to channel it, commit it to certain principles, and contain it within certain limits. It prescribes certain principles and procedures, not outcomes. But it is comprehensive insofar as no one who lacks constitutional legitimation is entitled to exercise public power, and no act of rule can claim validity that is not consistent with constitutional requirements.

This tacitly presupposes the concentration of all ruling authority in the state. Only on this presupposition could the claim to comprehensively juridify political rule through a special set of legal norms addressed to the state be redeemed.

---

[16] See Ch. 2 of this volume.

[17] See Rainer Wahl, 'Der Vorrang der Verfassung' (1981) 20 *Der Staat* 485.      [18] *The Federalist*, No.78.

[19] Emmanuel Sieyès, 'Was ist der Dritte Stand?' in Eberhard Schmitt and Rolf Reichardt (eds), *Emmanuel Sieyès, Politische Schriften* (Berlin: Akademie, 1975), pp. 117–96; Pasquale Pasquino, *Sieyès et l'invention de la constitution en France* (Paris: Odile-Jacob, 1998).

[20] *Marbury v. Madison*, 5 US (1 Cranch) 137, at 163.      [21] See further Ch. 1 of this volume.

This presupposition implies the clear distinction between private and public. Only when society is privatized in the sense that it does not possess the instruments of rule, while, conversely, all authorities to rule are concentrated in the state, can the principle of freedom, which is fundamental for the private, and the principle of bindingness, which is fundamental for the state, hold. Here we have not one conceivable form of constitution among others, but a constitutive feature of constitutionalism in general. The constitution would be undermined if the state enjoyed the freedom of the private, just as if the private possessed the coercive means of the state. To this extent, the border between private and public is essential to constitutionalism.

But the constitution was also bound to the state constitution in the sense that its comprehensive validity claim was territorially limited from the beginning. Although the idea of constitutionalism claimed universal validity, it was realized in different states and different ways from the start. These were separated by borders, beyond which state power did not extend. The borders might shift, for example as a result of wars. But that did not alter the fact that only one state power existed on the territory of a state, and that it did not share its entitlement to rule with anyone. To this extent, the constitution also presupposed a clear separation of inside and outside. Had its borders been permeable to external claims to rule, 'it could not have fulfilled its own. Above the state was not a lawless space, but rather international law. However, it regulated only relations between states and lacked a supranational power that could hold sway irrespective of state power.

Of course, a constitution could fail to fulfill its function of comprehensively juridifying public power, for instance because it was porous and contradictary from the start, was unable to adjust to later social change, or lost acceptance. There are many examples of this in constitutional history. But such a failure discredits constitutionalism as little as the existence of numerous semi- and pseudo-constitutions that sprang up shortly after the founding of the constitutional state in the American and French Revolutions, and continue to appear today. The constitution's character as an achievement is rather demonstrated by the fact that in such cases its function can only be taken over by another constitution, not sustained without one. No functional equivalent can stand in for a failed or ineffective constitution.[22]

## II. THE CONSEQUENCESS OF DE-NATIONALIZATION

The decline of statehood places not individual constitutions but constitutionalism as such in question. The reason for this lies in the constitution's reference to the state. The rise of the state awoke the need to tame it legally and at the same time allowed it to be satisfied in the form of the constitution. From a historical perspective, the constitution presupposes the state as a form of political

[22] See Luhmann (n. 1), p. 168.

community. It is distinguished from older forms of the political community by the bundling of the various scattered powers and their concentration in a uniform public power, including the authority to use physical force within a delimited territory. De-nationalization thus means that ruling authority is detached from the state and transferred to non-state bearers. This transition need not necessarily lead to the end of the state. It is entirely possible that it will remain as a basic unit of a new political order; however, just as it had initially *not yet* arrogated all powers, in the future it will *no longer* possess all powers.

The constitution is of course not only affected when the state disappears. Its claim to comprehensively regulate political rule is already impaired when the identity of state power and public power dissolves, so that acts of public authority can be taken on the territory of the state by, or with the participation of, non-state institutions. The understanding of de-nationalization allows to grasp two processes that started in the second half of the twentieth century, without their consequences for constitutionalism initially being noticed. They concern precisely the two borders that are presupposed by and constitutive of the constitution: that between inside and outside, and that between private and public. In the domestic realm it has to do with the participation of private actors in the exercise of public power. Outside the state it has to do with the rise of supranational entities or institutions that can make decisions that claim validity within state territory.

Regarding the border between private and public,[23] it is striking that sovereign measures often no longer come about through one-sided state decisions in legally regulated procedures, but are rather the result of bilateral agreements between state bodies and private interests that come out of informal negotiations. We encounter such negotiations in the fields of administration and adjudication, but also in legislation. Either the state enters into negotiations over the content of a law with its private addressees or the latter offer talks with the prospects of avoiding or mitigating regulation. The result can be a negotiated bill that must then go through the constitutionally prescribed procedures in order to become generally binding. But the legislative power can also serve merely as a threat in order to reach an agreement in which a private party that creates a problem agrees to commit itself to 'good behaviour' while the state responds by forgoing regulation.

While agreements that result in a bill only reach their goal when they subsequently achieve legal form through the designated state procedures, in the case of agreements that replace law, not only the negotiation but also its result, the solution of the problem, remain in the informal realm. All the same, the desired effect only sets in when both sides feel bound by it. For this reason, such negotiations cannot be equated with the long-customary influence of pressure groups on legislation. The attempt to influence legislation is limited to a prelimary

---

[23] On the early developments, see Ernst-Wolfgang Böckenförde, 'Die politische Funktion wirtschaftlich-sozialer Verbände und Interessenträger in der sozialstaatlichen Demokratie' (1976) 15 *Der Staat* 457. For more recent developments see Ch. 12 of this volume.

stage that is not governed by constitutional law, whereas the final decision is solely a matter for the state. Where informal agreements replace the law, however, the results of negotiations and the content of regulation are identical. It therefore does not do justice to the negotiations to describe them in terms of influence. They can only be adequately grasped in terms of participation.

With regards to de-nationalization, this means, on the one hand, that there are now private parties who are no longer restricted to their general civic status as voters, participants in public discourse, and representatives of interests; beyond this they participate in political decision making without being subject to the principles of legitimation and accountability to which the constitution submits the bearers of public power. On the other hand, to the extent that the state commits itself at the negotiating table, the constitutionally prescribed decision-making authorities and procedures are downgraded. This affects the legislature in particular. The negotiations are conducted not by it, but by the government. If a bill emerges, it can only attain legal validity through a parliamentary decision. The majority parties, however, are under practically irresistable pressure to ratify. If there is an agreement to forego regulation, parliament remains outside the game altogether.

Without parliament, the advantages of parliamentary procedures are lost. These are above all transparency, participation, and control. They have no place in negotiations. Negotiations are not public, include only those who possess veto power rather than all those affected, and give the opposition no chance to intervene. But the weakening of parliament also affects the content of the law or its informal substitute. Since the government only negotiates with those in a position to veto, their interests have a better chance of being considered. Under these circumstances the law risks falling short of general acceptance on which its legitimacy is based. The reason for privileging particular private parties lies not in their pre-political strength, which to a certain extent can be shrugged off, but in the procedures created by the state that reward precisely the positions of social power the constitution sought to neutralize.

The losses affect not only the constitution's democratic claim, but also the rule of law. The linchpin of all constitutional functions is the law.[24] Without the law's inherent formality, its effect would not be achieved. The agreements, however, evade this formalization. As a rule they are set into writing, but not necessary publicized. Rather, the parties to the negotiation have discretion over whether and how they are announced. Compliance is not institutionally guaranteed. Sometimes reporting duties and control mechanisms are included, sometimes not. Above all, however, affected third parties have no legal protection against informal agreements. Often even the necessary knowledge of the agreement's content is lacking. If one knows nothing about it, one can neither bring a claim against it nor have it reviewed. In the absence of a law there is

---

[24] For more detail, see Dieter Grimm, *Die Zukunft der Verfassung* (Frankfurt am Main: Suhrkamp, 1991), p. 159.

neither a legal standard for controlling compliance nor an object for constitutional review.

Despite these losses to democracy and the rule of law, the practice cannot simply be eliminated because it has its own logic. This results from the fact that many state tasks can no longer be adequately fulfilled with the specific state tool of imperative law. Sometimes the tasks are such that the use of imperative tools is in fact impossible because they elude regulation. Research results or economic upturns cannot be commanded. Sometimes the use of imperative tools is not legally permissible because basic rights ensure private actors' freedom of choice. Ordering them to invest or obliging them to create jobs would be unconstitutional. Sometimes imperative tools are in fact possible and permissible, but ineffective or inopportune, be it because the addressees of regulation could evade it, because the state lacks the information for effective steering, or because the implementation costs are too high.

Negotiation owes its emergence to this situation. To this extent, it has structural causes and is thus largely immune to constitutional prohibition. The claim of the constitution can therefore only be re-established by constitutionalizing the practice of negotiation. This would of course be essentially to approve it, including its basic characteristic, its informality. A thoroughgoing formalization would deprive it of its distinctiveness and therefore has little chance of success. On the other hand, if informality is retained, constitutional regulation cannot penetrate to the core of the phenomenon but only alter its parameters, for instance by requiring publicity, making it obligatory to inform parliament, and opening possibilities for constitutional review.[25] That does not change the fact, however, that the constitution cannot cope satisfactorily with phenomena that cross the border between private and public. It can fulfill its claim of comprehensive regulation only to a diminished extent.

Like the border between public and private, the border between inside and outside has not disappeared.[26] In relations among states it retains its traditional significance. The authority of the state and the applicability of domestic law ends at the border. Above the states, however, entities and organization have developed that, while owing their existence to international treaties between states, differ from traditional international organizations since their activity is not limited to the international realm but penetrates states. This is because they are authorized to take acts of public authority that claim domestic validity without being transformed by the state into national law. On the other hand, the pooling of sovereignty has not gone so far that various states have been fused into a new superstate which would displace rather than relativize the borders between inside and outside.

This development is not expressly directed against the constitution. More recent constitutions often open themselves to international law by stipulating

---

[25] See Winfried Brohm, 'Rechtsgrundsätze für normersetzende Absprachen' *DÖV* 1992, 1025.

[26] On the significance of the state's borders, see Udo di Fabio, *Der Verfassungsstaat in der Weltgesellschaft* (Tübingen: Mohr Siebeck, 2001), 51.

that it be applied domestically or allowing sovereign rights to be transferred.[27] All the same, the constitution does not remain untouched. It determines the conditions under which states may transfer sovereign rights to supranational entities. Once transferred, however, their use by these entities is no longer subject to the rules of the national constitution.[28] It then regulates domestic laws and their application only partially—namely, to the extent that they stem from a national source of law. These are, however, confronted with a growing number of legal measures that make the same validity claim as national law, but without having to satisfy the same constitutional requirements. The most advanced example of this is the European Union (EU), with its numerous sovereign rights replacing the regulative power of the nation state.

So far there has been no supranational arrangement of the same density either outside Europe or on a global scale. But other international organizations also contribute to the relativization of borders. The most prominent of these is the World Trade Organization (WTO).[29] To be sure, it does not itself make law, but rather provides a forum for the treaty agreements of its member states. But since 1995 its dispute-settlement mechanism has made the treaty-based law independent of the contracting parties and submitted them to the decisions of WTO authority. The World Bank and the International Monetary Fund lack such powers.[30] They may not interfere in the politics of states. However, law and justice are not considered politics in this sense. As a result, they often make their financial assistance conditional on domestic legal changes that the affected countries usually cannot avoid. To this extent, the requirements of their own constitutions concerning political decisions are supplanted.

Alongside these institutions created by states, meanwhile, are global actors like multinational firms and non-government organizations, which, by virtue of the range of their activities, can largely follow their own systemic logic without having to respect the standards and obligations that prevail within states. All the same, they too cannot live without legal regulation. The globalized sector of the economy

---

[27] See Udo di Fabio, *Das Recht offener Staaten* (Berlin: Erich Schmidt, 1998); Stefan Hobe, *Der offene Verfassungsstaat zwischen Souveränität und Inderdependenz* (Berlin: Duncker & Humblot, 1998); Rainer Wahl, 'Internationalisierung des Staates' in Joachim Bohnert (ed.), *Verfassung – Philosophie – Kirche, Festschrift für Alexander Hollerbach* (Berlin: Duncker & Humblot, 2001), p. 193; Rainer Wahl, 'Der einzelne in der Welt jenseits des Staates' in Wahl and Joachim Wieland (eds), *Das Recht des Menschen in der Welt* (Berlin: Duncker & Humblot, 2002), p. 59; Jan Hecker, 'Grundgesetz und horizontale Öffnung des Staates' (2002) 127 *Archiv des öffentlichen Rechts* 291.

[28] This is recognized in principle, although the particulars are still contested. See the ruling of the Bundesverfassungsgericht on the review of European legislation, BVerfGE 37, 271 (1974); 73, 339 (1986); 89, 155 (1993). See Dieter Grimm, 'The European Court of Justice and National Courts' (1997) 3 *Columbia Journal of European Law* 229; Anne-Marie Slaughter, Alec Stone Sweet, and Joseph H. H. Weiler (eds), *The European Court and National Courts* (Oxford: Hart, 1998).

[29] See Armin von Bogdandy, 'Verfassungsrechtliche Dimensionen der Welthandelsorganisation' (2001) 264 *Kritische Justiz* 264, 425; Markus Krajewski, *Verfassungsperspektiven und Legitimation des Rechts der Welthandelsorganisation* (Berlin: Duncker & Humblot, 2001).

[30] See Jerzy Kranz, *Entre l'influence et l'intervention* (Frankfurt am Main: Peter Lang, 1994); Ibrahim Shihata, *The World Bank in a Changing World*, 2 vols. (Washington DC: World Bank, 1995).

depends on a transnational law no national legislator can provide. But even the international organizations developed by states can only satisfy this need in part. Global actors therefore take up law-making themselves. Beyond nation states and the international organizations they have established forms of law-making that are no longer under the control of politics, be it domestic or international, but are driven mainly by large global law firms and international arbitration panels.[31]

In addition, international courts relativize the constitution to the extent that they do not stay within the traditional framework of international law and may only administer justice if parties submit themselves to judgment in a concrete case in advance. The European Court of Human Rights is an early example of this. In the meantime, however, international criminal courts have emerged to try war crimes and crimes against humanity even when it concerns members of states that have not submitted themselves to their jurisdiction or have refused to hand over the accused.[32] Here again, the jurisdiction of the EU has an exceptional position. It was the European Court that secured the immediate validity of Community law and its precedence over national law, including national constitutions. In this way, it considerably narrowed the latter's field of application, and for its part took up functions that constitutional courts possess on the national level.[33]

This development is nevertheless still far from the end of stateness. States are ceding functions to supranational units and organizations. But they are doing so in the interests of increasing problem-solving capacity without thereby making themselves superfluous. Rather, in the end supranational organizations and even global economic actors depend on states. The reason is that as yet no supranational political unit or international organization possesses the means of physical coercion, which belongs specifically to states. As soon as the coercive enforcement or implementation of international law is required, national authorities must step in. This is true even of the EU. The norms whose implementation is in question may be made externally; their implementation is a national matter and falls under national law. But this does not change the fact that the scope of validity of the national constitution constricts as that of law made externally expands.

The question this raises is whether and how the achievement of constitutionalism can be preserved in view of this development. Here we must distinguish

---

[31] See Gunther Teubner, *Global Law without a State* (Aldershot: Dartmouth, 1997); Boaventura de Sousa Santos, *Toward a New Common Sense* (New York: Routledge, 1995); Klaus Günther, 'Rechtspluralismus und universaler Code der Legalität' in *Festschrift für Habermas* (Frankfurt am Main: Suhrkamp, 2001), p. 539.

[32] See Antonio Cassese, 'On the Current Trends towards Criminal Prosecution and Punishment of Breaches of International Humanitarian Law' (1998) 9 *European Journal of International Law* 2; Theodor Meron, *War Crimes Law Comes of Age* (Oxford: Oxford University Press, 1998); Symposium: 'Genocide, War Crimes, and Crimes Against Humanity' (1999) 23 *Fordham International Law Journal* 275 ss.

[33] See Joseph H. H. Weiler, 'The Transformation of Europe' in his *The Constitution of Europe* (Cambridge: Cambridge University Press, 1999), p. 10; Carlos Rodriguez Iglesias, 'Der Gerichtshof der Europäischen Gemeinschaften als Verfassungsgericht' (1992) 27 *Europarecht* 225; Franz C. Mayer, 'Europäische Verfassungsgerichtsbarkeit' in Armin von Bogdandy (ed.), *Europäisches Verfassungsrecht* (Berlin: Springer, 2003), p. 229.

between the national and the international level. On the national level the possibilities appear limited. National constitutions can provide for the state's opening to supranational arrangements and establish the conditions for the transfer of sovereign rights. Beyond this, they can safeguard constitutional requirements in the determination of national negotiating positions for supranational decision-making processes, such as parliamentary participation. This is not unimportant, since supranational legislation is consistently executive legislation, following a model of bargaining rather than deliberation.[34] This does not, however, guarantee that these positions will prevail. Other possibilities on the national level are not visible. The national constitution has neither formal nor material influence on laws that penetrate the state from the outside.

The more important question is thus whether the constitution can be transferred to the international level. There has been much discussion of this of late. Scholars see constitutionalization at work everywhere. A constitutionalization of the EU was ascertained very early on. But in the meantime a constitutionalization of international organizations like the WTO and the UN has been perceived as well. Even international law as a whole is supposed to be on the way to a constitution.[35] This observation is correct insofar as a strong push towards juridification has been occuring at the international level. But not all juridification merits the name of constitutionalization.[36] Rather, constitutionalization has shown itself to be a special form of the juridification of rule that presupposes the concentration of all ruling authority within a territory, and is

---

[34] See Armin von Bogdandy (ed.), *Gubernative Rechtsetzung* (Tübingen: Mohr Siebeck, 1999).

[35] On the EU, see Weiler (n. 33); Ingolf Pernice, 'Multilevel Constitutionalism' (1999) 36 *Common Market Law Review* 427; Christoph Möllers, 'Verfassungsgebende Gewalt – Verfassung – Konstitutionalisierung' in von Bogdandy (ed.), *Europäisches Verfassungsrecht* (Berlin: Springer, 2003), p. 1; Peter Badura, 'Die föderative Verfassung der Europäischen Union' in *Festschrift für Martin Heckel* (Tübingen: Mohr Siebeck, 1999), p. 695; Stefan Oeter, 'Europäische Integration als Konstitutionalisierungsprozess' (1999) 59 *ZaöRV* 901; Anne Peters, *Elemente einer Theorie der Verfassung Europas* (Berlin: Duncker & Humblot, 2001). On the ECHR, see Christan Walter, 'Die EMRK als Konstitutionalisierungsprozess' (1999) 59 *ZaöRV* 961. On the WTO see Ernst-Ulrich Petersmann, *Constitutional Functions and Constitutional Problems of International Economic Law* (Fribourg: University Press, 1991); Stefan Langer, *Grundlagen einer internationalen Wirtschaftsverfassung* (München: Beck, 1995); von Bogdandy (n. 29); Markus Krajweski, *Verfassungsperspektiven und Legitimation des Rechts der Welthandelsorganisation* (Berlin: Duncker & Humblot, 2001); Peter-Tobias Stoll, 'Freihandel und Verfassung' (1997) 57 *ZaöRV* 83; Martin Nettesheim, 'Von der Verhandlungsdiplomatie zur internationalen Verfassungsordnung' in Claus-Dieter Classen (ed.), 'In einem vereinten Europa dem Frieden der Welt zu dienen ...', *Liber amicorum Thomas Oppermann* (Berlin: Duncker & Humblot, 2001), p. 381. On the UN, see Bardo Faßbender, 'The United Nations Charter as Constitution of the International Community' (1998) 36 *Columbia Journal of Transnational Law* 529. On international law, see Jochen A. Frowein, 'Konstitutionalisierung des Völkerrechts' (1999) 39 *BDGVR* 427.

[36] On constitutionalization and 'international' constitutional law, see Giovanni Biaggini, 'Die Idee der Verfassung – Neuausrichtung im Zeitalter der Globalisierung?' (2000) 119 *ZSR* 445; Robert Uerpmann, 'Internationales Verfassungsrecht,' (2001) *JZ* 565; Christian Walter, 'Die Folgen der Globalisierung für die europäische Verfassungsdiskussion' (2000) *DVBl.* 1; Ingolf Pernice, Peter M. Huber, Gertrude Lübbe-Wolff, and Christoph Grabenwarter, 'Europäisches und nationales Verfassungsrecht' (2001) 60 *VVDStRL* 148–349 (esp. 155ff, 199ff); Rainer Wahl, 'Konstitutionalisierung – Leitbegriff oder Allerweltsbegriff?' in *Der Wandel des Staates vor den Herausforderungen der Gegenwart, Festschrift für Winfried Brohm* (Munich: Beck, 2002), p. 191; Ulrich Haltern, 'Internationales Verfassungsrecht?' (2003) 128 *Archiv des öffentlichen Rechts* 128.

distinguished by a certain standard of juridification. This standard includes a democratic origin, supremacy, and comprehensiveness.[37]

The need for juridification develops where political rule is exercised. Whether it can be satisfied in the form of a constitution depends on certain preconditions and standards being met. More strongly put, the question is whether the constitution, as a form of juridification that originally referred to the state, can be detached from it and transferred to non-state political entities that exercise public power. If not, it will remain a matter of mere juridification, which is by no means worthless, but should not be passed off as equivalent to a constitution. Of course, the question cannot be answered in the same way for all political entities that are ascertained to exercise sovereign powers or make decisions whose effect is tantamount to such powers. There are important differences between them in the degree of consolidation and plenitude of powers that are relevant to the possibility of constitutionalization.

If we ask this question first of all concerning the EU, we find a structure that has grown far beyond traditional international organizations but has still not become a state. It unites a considerable number of sovereign rights in different political fields that can be exercised with immediate validity in the member states. Even without a monopoly on the use of force, which its members so far retain, it is closely interwoven with the member states and their legal orders in a way similar to the national and the member states in a federal state. The resulting need for a juridification of the public power has surely long since been satisfied. Primary Community law, which spread step by step, has overlain the EU with a tightly woven net of provisions that have preeminence over the secondary Community law produced by the EU and fulfills most of the functions of constitutions in the member states.

Measured by the demanding concept of the constitution that has become the standard since the American and French Revolutions, they lack only one element which, however, is surely essential. They are, not only in their development but also according to their legal nature, international treaties that have been contracted by the member states and can only be altered by them in the intergovernmental Conference, which is not an EU organ, with subsequent ratification within each member state. The public power the EU exercises accordingly emanates not from the people, but from the member states. Responsibility for the basic order that sets its goals, establishes its organs, and regulates its authorities and procedures cannot be ascribed to the constituent power of the people. Nor is any EU organ that represents the people responsible for it. As distinct from the constitution as the basic legal order of states, it is heteronomously, not autonomously, determined.[38] Not being attributed to the people it lacks democratic origin, which is an element of a somewhat meaningful notion of constitution.

---

[37] See further Ch. 1 of this volume.

[38] See Dieter Grimm, 'Does Europe need a Constitution?' (1995) 1 *European Law Journal* 282.

Admittedly, there can be no doubt that the EU, by virtue of its consolidation and range of powers, is capable of being constitutionalized. Nothing prevents the member states from giving up their control over the basic legal order of the EU in a final international treaty, placing the Union on a democratic basis, and thereby bestowing upon it self-determination over the form and content of its political community. They could then still reserve the right to paricipate in amendments of the constitution—not, however, as the bearers of federal power, but rather as parts of its organs. With this, the treaties, without requiring any other substantive change, would carry over into a constitution in the full sense of the word. Yet, by such an act, the EU would quietly transform itself from a federation of states into a federal state. For the line separating the two is heteronomy or self-determination of its basic order.

A constitutionalized EU would nevertheless be no more immune to a relativization of its borders than the nation states are.[39] Its constitution could not, any more than the national constitutions, fulfill the claim to comprehensively regulate all acts of rule on its territory. The constitutional question is therefore posed again at the global level. Here too the process of juridification is proceeding apace. Its main fields of application are, although unconnected, economic relations and human rights. The share of compulsory international law that therefore takes primacy over the treaty-making power of the states is increasing. It is also increasingly judicially enforceable. That the internal constitutionalization (of states) is now being followed by external constitutionalization (of the community of states), as is asserted,[40] however, does not prove true upon closer examination. If we maintain the distinction between juridification and constitutionalization, it emerges that already the basic precondition for the latter is lacking: an object that could be constitutionalized.

Just as public power at the international level breaks down into numerous unconnected institutions with sharply limited jurisdictions, so its legal regulation breaks down into numerous unconnected partial orders. A bundling that could make them appear as the expression of unified intention and would also allow a unified interpretation of them is not to be expected even in the long term. Furthermore, democratic legitimation and responsibility is far off. The aspiration contained in the concept of constitutionalsim can therefore not even be approximately realized on the global level. This is no reason to attach little value to the progress connected to the increasing juridification of the world order. To equate it with the constitution, however, is to paper over the fundamental difference and create the impression that the declining significance of national constitutions can be made good at the international level. There is no prospect of that for the time being.

---

[39] See Walter (n. 36).    [40] See Di Fabio (n. 26), p. 68.

# ༜ 16 ༜

## *Societal Constitutionalism: Compensation for the Decline in the Importance of the State Constitution?*

### I. A NEW TREND: CONSTITUTIONALIZATION

A new word is rapidly gaining currency in legal–political discourse: constitutionalization. Unlike traditional constitution-making, constitutionalizaton does not denote an act that puts a constitution into force, but a process that ends in a constitution. This process does not operate on states; constitutions have become virtually universal at the state level. Rather, constitutionalization refers to the supra-state, international level. The term first emerged within the context of the primary law of the European Community, which in the view of multiple authors has acquired a constitutional quality through the jurisprudence of the European Court of Justice.[1] Today, it is being increasingly applied on the global level. There too, many observers note that a process of constitutionalizaton is under way that comprises a variety of international organizations, most of all the United Nations (UN) and the World Trade Organization (WTO), but also international legal documents such as the European Convention on Human Rights and even the entire body of international law.[2] The concept of societal constitutionalism even transcends the level of international organization and legal instruments: it also regards self-organizing processes by which the power of global private actors is restricted as forms of constitutionalization.[3] The focus is thus entirely on objects which in the past were not usually associated with the concept of constitutions.

---

[1] See e.g. J. Weiler, *The Constitution of Europe* (Cambridge: Cambridge University Press, 1999), p. 10.

[2] See e.g. B. Fassbender, 'The United Nations Charter as Constitution of the International Community' (1998) 36 *Columbia Journal of Transnational Law* 529; D. Cass, *The Constitutionalization of the World Trade Organization* (Oxford: Oxford University Press, 2005).

[3] See n. 16 later in the chapter.

Constitutionalism: Past, Present, and Future. First Edition. Dieter Grimm. © Dieter Grimm 2016. Published 2016 by Oxford University Press.

## II. THE LOSS OF SIGNIFICANCE OF
## THE STATE CONSTITUTION

### 1. *The Erosion of Statehood*

Conceptual changes of this type generally do not occur by happenstance, but rather originate in a change in the conditions to which the term refers. Such a change also seems to be the main reason for the extension of the constitutional concept to the international level. The modern constitution, as it has existed for two hundred years, related to the state. But in recent years, the state has been showing signs of erosion, originating from the fact that, due to changing conditions, states increasingly find themselves confronted with challenges that they cannot master without cooperating with private actors and supra-state institutions. This blurs the boundaries between internal and external, as well as between private and public, which are constitutive for the state.[4] States are no longer the sole holders of public power, but are encountering supranational and private holders of public authority in the sphere of their sovereign activities.

This is new. For several centuries, the state claimed the monopoly of public power and could continue to assert this until very recently. Public power was state power. Indeed, it was essentially the concentration of the public authority in one office, which as late as the Middle Ages rested with numerous mutually independent holders and pertained to individuals and not territories, that transformed a polity into a state. The state claimed the undivided and irresistible power within its territory and recognized no other power above itself. The term 'sovereignty' was adopted to describe these characteristics, and became inseparably associated with the state. Internally, sovereignty meant the exclusive and highest authority to rule, while its converse was the privatization of society; externally, sovereignty stood for the legal independence from other states, which secured self-determination to every state. The prerequisite of both was the mastery of the territorial boundaries.

The area above the states was not a lawless zone. It was governed by international law. However, international law differed fundamentally from domestic law precisely on account of sovereignty. State sovereignty was reconcilable with neither a supra-state legislature nor a supra-state enforcement power. International law was thus based on the voluntary consent of states in the form of treaty or customary law, which depended on transformation for its internal application. The sole principles that applied independently of treaties, because they were systemic prerequisites, were the doctrine of *pacta sunt servanda* and the prohibition of intervention. Even so, there was no supra-state instance that could compel compliance with these principles, so that international law did not preclude the use of force for the assertion of rights, something illegitimate within the state, in relationships between states. Peaceful conflict resolution, for instance by courts, depended on voluntary recognition.

---

[4] See Ch. 15 of this volume.

All this changed after the Second World War, starting with the founding of the UN and proceeding rapidly since the end of the east-west confrontation. To secure peace and improve their problem-solving capabilities, states have established international organizations which, unlike traditional alliances, have gained competencies to make and enforce international law to which states cannot oppose their right to self-determination. The European Union (EU) is the most advanced product of this development. Consequently, the state controls its own borders only with reference to other states, and no longer with reference to international organizations to which it has assigned sovereign authority. This is accompanied by norm-forming processes of transnational private actors taking place outside the political sphere which are based on de facto recognition, which the individual states cannot effectively oppose. The possibilities of transcending state boundaries virtually with the aid of modern information technology has increased porosity even further.

## 2. *The Achievement of the Constitution*

The constitution, which traditionally refers to the state, cannot remain unaffected by the erosion of statehood. However, the nature of this effect cannot be recognized until the essence of a constitution has been determined. It is not enough to say that the purpose of the constitution is the juridification of politics, as is often assumed. This type of juridification has always existed. Even in absolute states, rule was not unbounded by law. Rather, the aim of the constitution was a specific form of regulation of rule, which can best be comprehended by reconstructing the conditions under which it emerged.[5] It was a product of two successful revolutions at the end of the eighteenth century in North America and France that differed from history's numerous revolts and shifts of power in that it did not simply replace one rule with another, but rather restructured the *system* of rule before appointing individuals to rule on this basis.

The principles of the new order had already been developed theoretically and found social support groups that adopted them and transformed them into political demands prior to the revolution. The revolutionary break gave them the opportunity to realize these principles. They became the guiding tenets of the revolution. They derive from four fundamental assumptions: all persons are born free and equal; the right of some individuals to rule over the rest can thus derive neither from a transcendental legitimation nor from a hereditary right, but only from the consensus of all individuals; this, rationally, is only granted when the freedom and equality of individuals is maintained and secured by the power of the state; this is not possible without restrictions on freedom, and to this end the state requires power, but its power is limited to the purpose of rule and, to prevent the abuse of power, is divided among multiple branches that monitor each other.

---

[5] See Ch. 2 of this volume.

This comprises everything that characterizes the later constitution, without the theorists who developed these principles having arrived at the idea of a legal constitution. Before the revolution, these principles functioned as regulatory ideas that described the conditions of legitimate rule and served as a test for the legitimacy of existing rule. But they did not lead to the demand for a law that prescribed how rule was to be established and organized and according to which standards it had to be exercised. It was the revolutions that transformed philosophy into law. Law released the principles from their dependency on momentary circumstances and the participants in the consensus and placed them on a long-term, multi-generational perspective. It endowed them with normative, and not merely argumentative force and imposed sanctions on their violation.

There was, however, one difficulty. Since its positivization, law had become a product of state decision-making. The question thus became: how could the state be subjected to law that it could make at will? The answer was to split positive law into two bodies: one attributable to the authorhood of the people or the nation and binding on those who govern, and one imposed by those who govern and binding on the people. Constitutional law formed the first body, and statute law the other. The two were linked in such a way that the creation of the second body is regulated by the first. The prerequisite for this was that the first body of law took precedence over the second—as a higher law. This dualism is constitutive for the modern constitution. In constitutions, law becomes reflexive. Law can be applied to law and thus enhance its potential. This was theoretically implied in Sieyes' distinction between *pouvoir constituant* and *pouvoir constitué*.

The constitution in the modern sense is thus characterized by five elements:

1. It is an epitome of legal norms, not a compendium of philosophic principles nor a description of the actual power relationships in a body politic.

2. The object of these legal norms is the establishment and exercise of political rule or public power.

3. The constitution regulates this in a systematic, comprehensive manner. The constitution tolerates neither extraconstitutional powers nor extraconstitutional ways and means of rule.

4. As rule is only legitimate when constituted and limited by the constitution, constitutional law takes precedence over all other acts of rule. These are valid only when they comply with the constitutional framework.

5. Constitutional norms originate with the people, since every other principle for the legitimation of rule would undermine all the other elements and prevail over the constitution in the event of a conflict.

The modern constitution therefore differs from the pre-constitutional legal bonds of rule in that it constitutes and not merely modifies rule, applies universally and not selectively, and restricts rule to the benefit of all, and not to the benefit of just a few privileged individuals. The prerequisite for the possibility of a constitution understood in this sense was the concentration of all rights of rule into a uniform public power—in other words, the modern state. The Middle Ages did not have constitutions in this sense; it could not have had them because the object that permitted such a systematic and comprehensive act of regulation was lacking. But international law also lacked the characteristics of a constitution. It did not form the dualism characteristic of constitutions: it was not superior to states but was agreed on between them, it pertained only to selective rights and obligations, and, like any contract, it applied only to the parties and not generally.

A constitution that demonstrates all five elements is one of the great achievements of civilization: it tames political power in the interest of the autonomy of the individual, provides individuals with dependable behaviour in their dealings with power holders and enables peaceful changes in power. Naturally, not everything that has been called a constitution over the course of history possesses these properties. The invention of the constitution also made possible semi- and pseudo-constitutions. However, it is important to note that the constitution in the full meaning of the term is not merely an ideal that serves as an ultimately unattainable goal for reality. Constitutions that possess all five elements exist. They remain today the focus of innumerable hopes. Constitutions that do not fulfil these conditions entirely—such as the German constitutions of the nineteenth century, which all only modified, and did not constitute, rule—can still fulfil key functions of a constitution. But they fall short of the *achievement* of the constitution to the extent that essential elements of constitutions are lacking.[6]

## 3. The Effects of Internationalization

In this context, it is now possible to determine more precisely how internationalization impacts on the constitution and whether it can be reconstructed on the international level. As regards the UN, member states have pledged in the Charter to renounce violence except in cases of self-defence. If this were the full extent of the significance of the UN Charter, of course, this voluntary commitment on the part of the states would not exceed the scope of classical international law. But the UN goes further. Unlike the League of Nations, the UN is also authorized to enforce the renunciation of violence and is provided with the necessary means. Moreover, it has not stood still. Its authority has expanded. Today, humanitarian intervention in states that systematically violate human rights, especially the commission of genocide, is a recognized principle. Only discussion of the prerequisites and limits remains controversial.

There is also a UN jurisdiction. Whereas older courts, specifically the International Court of Justice, may only become active with the consent of the disputing states, the International Criminal Tribunals for the former Yugoslavia and for Rwanda go much further. Unlike the International Court of Justice, they were not created by treaty but established by the Security Council, and

---

[6] Cf. N. Luhmann, 'Die Verfassung als evolutionäre Errungenschaft' (1990) 9 *Rechtshistorisches Journal* 176.

may become active without the consent of affected states. Ultimately, an international *ius cogens* has developed under the umbrella of the UN that is not based on treaties between states but which binds them when treaties are concluded. Consequently, since the UN was founded, no member state is any longer sovereign in the same sense as it was in the Westphalian Age. However, this is not acutely palpable for the majority of states, either because they are permanent members of the Security Council and can thus block actions against themselves, or because they provide no grounds for intervention.

The situation is different with respect to the EU. The member states have assigned a significant portion of their sovereign rights to the EU in all areas—legislative, administrative, and judicial. The EU exercises these with immediate effect on the member states. In the process, it takes precedence over national law, including national constitutional law. This occurs not only in isolated cases and with respect to specific member states that are not meeting their obligations, but daily towards all member states. Certainly, the member states have retained their right of self-determination insofar as they decide which powers they assign to the EU. However, once these powers have been assigned, their exercise is perceived by the member states as an act of heteronomy, at least insofar as they do not require a unanimous resolution of the representatives of the states.[7] In addition, other existing international organizations, such as the WTO, exceed the scope of traditional international law and can take decisions with binding effect on the member states.

The identity of public power and state power has thus been severed. This has a differential impact on the five constitutive elements of the state constitution:

1. Its characteristic as the epitome of legal norms remains unaffected.

2. Likewise, its object remains the establishment and exercise of the public power of the state it constitutes.

3. However, as state power and public power are no longer identical, they lose their comprehensive regulatory character. Actors now exist who exercise public power upon the territory of the states without being subject to the legitimation and responsibility framework prescribed by the national constitutions, and there are acts of rule that are valid in the states without having to fulfil the requirements which the constitutions stipulate for such acts.

4. Consequently, the precedence of the constitution is no longer unconditional. It applies only to domestic law and legal acts of the state, and not universally.

5. National constitutions still originate with the people, but they can no longer ensure that all public power exercised and applied within the state originates and is democratically legitimated by the sovereign people.

Ultimately, the emergence of international public power has not made national constitutions irrelevant or meaningless. However, their importance has

---

[7] See Ch. 13 of this volume.

declined. They can no longer assert their claim to comprehensive legitimation and regulation of public power acting in the territorial area they govern.

### III. SUPPLEMENTARY QUESTION: OUTLOOK FOR INTERNATIONAL CONSTITUTIONALISM?

As public power must be legally tamed, regardless of whether it is exercised by a state or by international organizations, the question arises as to how the loss of significance of national constitutions can be compensated, and it is reasonable to seek an answer in a constitutionalization of public power beyond the state level. However, constitutionalization is not only being asserted as a demand, but also considered an event that is already taking place or even completed. In this view, the Charter of the UN becomes a world constitution, the primary law of the EU a European constitution, the statute of the WTO its own constitution.[8] This is correct insofar as internationally exercised rule is subject to increasing juridification. However, juridification is not the same thing as constitutionalization. Rather, constitutionalization is a particularly ambitious and successful sub-case of the juridification of politics. The question is thus whether the juridification of the international level deserves the name 'constitutionalization'.

In consideration of the conditions that had to be fulfilled before constitutions in the modern sense could emerge, the first question arises as to whether objects exist on the international level that are suitable for constitutionalization. This question can be answered affirmatively for the EU. Although it is not a state, it possesses such extensive powers and organizational density that it is not greatly different from the federal level of a federal state. The public power it exercises is susceptible to comprehensive and systematic regulation. And such a regulation already exists in the form of the European treaties that differ from a constitution only in that they did not emerge through an act of self-determination of a European society but were bestowed on the EU externally through treaties concluded by independent states, which can only be amended in this way and not through an act of the EU itself. However, this would not prevent the member states from relinquishing their power over the basic legal framework of the EU to the EU itself. This would transform the treaties into a constitution, and the EU would be recast as a federal state. To this extent, the question is solely whether this step is desirable, not whether it is possible.

On the global level, however, no organization exists with a range of powers and an organizational density similar to the EU, but only isolated institutions with specific functions and singular powers related to them, which are not interconnected and sometimes even act in opposition to each other—islands in a sea of traditional international relations. This is also true of the UN. Although

---

[8] See n. 1 earlier in the chapter; further R. Wahl, 'Konstitutionalisierung—Leitbegriff oder Allerweltsbegriff?' in C.-E. Eberle et al. (eds), *Der Wandel des Staates vor den Herausforderungen der Gegenwart: Festschrift für Winfried Brohm* (Munich: Beck, 2002), p. 191; U. Haltern, 'Internationales Verfassungsrecht?' (2003) 128 *Archiv des öffentlichen Rechts* 511.

its mission of maintaining the peace puts it far above all other globally active international organizations holding sovereign rights, its sovereign powers do not extend further, and in no way does it bundle all international ruling authority. Its legal basis is thus far removed from a global constitution. This is even more the case for the other international organizations, such as the WTO, the International Monetary Fund, the International Labour Organization, etc. It is true that their statutes regulate the powers of these organizations and determine the legal acts they perform, but the parallels end there. With their selective powers and their completely undemocratic organization, they are not suitable for the specific act of regulation by a constitution. Those who still speak of constitutions here are employing a largely hollow concept of the constitution that eliminates the difference between juridification and constitutionalization.

## IV. SOCIETAL CONSTITUTIONALISM AS A SOLUTION?

### 1. *Sciulli's Societal Constitutionalism*

This is where the theory of societal constitutionalism takes hold. Its advocates do not expect international law or the statutes of international organizations ever to assume the function on the supra-state level that the constitution fulfils in the state. In their view, international institutions could at best 'constitutionalize' themselves, that is, develop an internal dualism of higher and derived law, but not develop a fundamental order that democratically binds state and society the way a constitution does.[9] Rather, they assume that this gap could only be filled if the concept of the constitution were severed from its traditional ties to the state and political sphere and expanded into the social sphere. A third autonomous legal order—transnational law—would then emerge and take its place alongside national and international law. This would emerge from civil-society processes and not political processes, and have the potential for developing into a new form of constitutionalism appropriate to the post-national constellation.[10]

The term 'societal constitutionalism' was introduced by the American sociologist, David Sciulli.[11] Sciulli is responding to the criticism that western democracies are falling short of their promise to restrain partial interests, and that all attempts at improvement undertaken over the course of history have failed. However, he does not resort to a Marxist critique of capitalism, which expects improvement only under a different system. Rather, he counters the conclusion of 'exhausted possibilities' by pointing to societal constitutionalism, in which he sees an untapped potential for bringing western democracies closer to fulfilling

---

[9] Cf. G. Teubner, 'Globale Zivilverfassungen: Alternativen zur staatszentrierten Verfassungstheorie' (2003) 63 *ZaöRV* 5, at 13.

[10] Cf. A. Fischer-Lescano and G. Teubner, *Regime-Kollisionen: Zur Fragmentierung des globalen Rechts* (Frankfurt am Main: Suhrkamp, 2006), pp. 43, 57.

[11] D. Sciulli, *Theory of Societal Constitutionalism* (Cambridge: Cambridge University Press, 1992).

their promise. What Sciulli has in mind is best illustrated by the example with which his essay begins and to which he refers repeatedly to explain his theory:

> A young chemist, William, is employed in one of a dozen or so large research divisions of a major pharmaceutical company. He presents his supervisor, Scott, with the most recent results of his laboratory analyses. Taking one look, Scott hands them back, saying: 'Look, William, I gave you one set of compounds to test drawn from a much larger project. Hundreds of man-hours have been invested in this project already. Your results are not anywhere near the results that we need for your set of compounds. This could delay the entire project. Worse, it could reduce next year's budget for our division. Keep in mind that once this project comes on-line, no one is ever going to take it apart and retest its various sets of compounds in isolation. Not anyone in government, at the Federal Drug Administration. Not anyone in this firm. Not anyone in any competitor's firm. And, certainly, not any of your professors at the Chemistry Department of your Ivy League college. So, be a professional, William. Be a team player and bring me results we can use. There might even be a bonus in this for both of us.'[12]

This example is taken from an area in which, on account of the private legal form and the hierarchic organization, the interests of the supervisor and the company prevail over the interests of research, or in other words: the specific rationality of the economic system prevails over the rationality of the scientific system, and the state is unable to curb this behaviour because it lacks the necessary information. With Sciulli however, we are not operating in a sphere beyond the state. Nor is this a sphere that is fundamentally removed from the influence of the state and the laws it enacts. What happens in the example, and most likely results in William caving in to Scott's instructions, is not merely a violation of scientific standards, but quite probably a violation of law as well. If it goes unpunished, we would not describe that as a failure of law, but at most a weakness in implementation.

However, Sciulli doubts that the state and its regulative law would limit and monitor social power. Rather, basing his approach on a synthesis of Parsons, Fuller, and Habermas,[13] he sees a role for those opposing social forces that are dedicated to a logic other than economic rationality. In particular, these include the organizational forms of those professions that do not specialize in economic 'reason' (in the example above the scientific profession within the enterprise). These are expected to develop norms and standards for adequate behaviour and thus set limits to the economic rationality and its agents that can no longer be expected of state law. This is what Sciulli means by 'societal constitutionalism'. It is the task of the state to legally guarantee the necessary autonomy spaces within the private institutions, which no western state has done to date.[14]

The parallel to traditional state constitutionalism is not immediately apparent.[15] Nowhere does Sciulli define what he understands by 'constitutionalism'.

---

[12] Ibid., p. 11.    [13] Ibid., pp. 85 ff.    [14] Ibid., pp. 205 ff.

[15] Some aspects are reminiscent of 'regulated self-regulation' as discussed in Germany, which is less about constitutional law than about legislation that conforms to the constitution. See 'Regulierte Selbstregulierung als Steuerungskonzept des Gewährleistungsstaates' (2001) 4 *Die Verwaltung*, Supplement.

However, he implies that this is to be sought in the limitation of power positions that exist both in the business and political sectors and which can be exploited to instrumentalize the less powerful social systems for their own systemic ends. With respect to political power, the constitution functions as a safeguard against the abuse of power, for example in the form of fundamental rights. In the example above, it is private power relationships that are limited by professional standards, which then appear as 'societal constitutionalism'. This does not necessarily relate to the transfer of public power to the international level. Sciulli takes no notice of the signs of erosion in the state, but instead fills spaces in which the state is not effective even when the common good is at stake. Traditional constitutionalism is unaffected by this.

## 2. Transferring to the International Level

With respect to the international level, Gunther Teubner in particular has taken up the idea of societal constitutionalism.[16] Unlike Sciulli, Teubner is a jurist trained in systems theory. His starting point is the fundamental phenomenon of the modern era, the functional differentiation of society, in which there is neither a centre nor an apex, but only self-referencing, self-sufficient subsystems that obey their own rationality and cannot be externally controlled. According to Teubner, this differentiation is now spreading to the international level and occurring globally. This is true not only for the economy; many other functional systems are also transcending national boundaries and operating worldwide. Only the political system is unable to keep pace. The state is unable to do so because it explicitly has no international range of action. But international organizations created by states are also unable to keep pace with the global actors, as unlike the state they possess only selective competencies and cannot act broadly or universally.

As a consequence of this 'asymmetry of fully globalized subsystems of society and simply internationalized politics',[17] the functions performed by the political system in the national framework, namely keeping the systemic egoisms of the other functional systems within the boundaries of what is mutually tolerable, are performed extremely ineffectively on the international level. Functional systems expanding into the global dimension thus attain 'degrees of freedom for radically increasing their respective internal rationality, which they exploit without regard to other social systems, and without regard to their natural and human environments.'[18] Still, they cannot entirely do without specific services that the political system performs in the national context. They depend

---

[16] Teubner (n. 9); Fischer-Lescano and Teubner (n. 10), pp. 53 ff. In the following I will focus on these interpretations. For further publications touching on societal constitutionalism, see H. Schepel, *The Constitution of Private Governance* (Oxford: Hart, 2005); L. C. Backer, 'Economic Globalization and the Rise of Efficient Systems of Global Private Lawmaking' (2007) 39 *Connecticut Law Report* 1739; Ladeur and Viellechner, 'The Constitution of Private Governance' (2008) 46 *AVR* 42; A. Fischer-Lescano, 'Globalverfassung: Verfassung der Weltgesellschaft' (2002) 88 *ARSP* 349.

[17] Teubner (n. 9), p. 12.   [18] Fischer-Lescano and Teubner (n. 10), p. 27.

on rules and on the observance of rules. Consequently, they develop a need for law structuring their global transactions that is no longer territorially bound. This cannot be met by states, nor by the international community which has not formed any such capacity for collective action, but only by a few globally operating international organizations with narrowly defined competencies and powers. The global functional systems are thus forced to cover their need for law themselves through autonomous, function-related norm-formation processes: 'Global law without a state'.[19]

Teubner's prime example is the *lex mercatoria* of the Middle Ages, originally a law for travelling traders, which was generally adhered to out of considerations of long-term benefit; it is today a self-created law of globally active conglomerates that agree to it for their transnational transactions and entrust international boards of arbitration, and not a national jurisdiction, with its application in the event of conflicts. The agreed law and the decision-making practice of the arbitration bodies are utilized in subsequent contracts, so that by and by a body of laws develops, which today is being recorded by some private institutions in constantly updated lists. Another example is the internet regime of the Internet Corporation for Assigned Names and Numbers (ICANN), which governs the issuing of domains and for Teubner represents a 'digital constitution' or a 'lex electronica'. A further example is the sport law with sport jurisdiction created by the international sport associations.[20]

Teubner's goals are legal bonds of these globally active subsystems, which, on the one hand, recognize the internal rationality of their subssystems, but prevent, on the other hand, the instrumentalization of other subsystems or self-destructive excesses. Due to the limited intervention opportunities of the political sphere and in the absence of a global political system, these bonds cannot be imposed from outside, but must occur through a process of self-constitutionalization. Unlike most proponents of the constitutionalization thesis, however, Teubner avoids seeing a constitution in every juridification of internationally exercised power. Rather, he adheres to the differentiation between juridification and constitution. His constitutional concept is thus not the diluted form of supranational constitutionalism, but an ambitious form that expressly orients itself towards the achievement of the state constitution. Civil constitutions should achieve for globally exercised private power what state constitutions achieve for territorially bound political power.

To make the concept of the constitution fit for international use, he must 'generalize' it. In other words, he must disconnect it from the state, and 'respecify' it, that is, adapt it to the global parameters. In doing so, several fundamental differences emerge: societal constitutionalism is not the product of a legislator. Societal constitutions do not take force by means of an authoritative act, but instead form in 'long-term, subliminal, evolutionary processes',[21] though these can be encouraged or supported by political powers. They are neither merely

---

[19]  G. Teubner (ed.), *Global Law without a State* (Aldershot: Dartmouth, 1997).

[20]  Further examples are to be found in Fischer-Lescano and Teubner (n. 10).   [21]  Teubner (n. 9), p. 15.

legal texts nor purely de facto social orders. Above all, they do not relate to the totality of internationally exercised private power. Unlike the comprehensive but territorially limited state constitutions, they break down into a multitude of globally effective but sectorially limited civil constitutions. The principle of territorial differentiation of national legal orders is superimposed by the principle of sectoral differentiation of globally applicable law. Beyond that, however, some structural characteristics of state constitutions must reoccur in societal constitutionalism before this can deserve the name 'constitution'.

Teubner provides four criteria for this:[22]

1. Like state constitutions, civil constitutions are higher law that regulates the creation of lower law.
2. The higher law must define the structure of system-internal decision-making processes just like the organizational and procedural provisions of state constitutions do.
3. It must also establish the limits of the system, comparable to the fundamental rights of state constitutions.
4. Finally, like judicial review in state constitutional law, it must provide possibilities for review that enable an examination of compliance with rules in the private establishment of norms.

Teubner admits that to date these elements are present only in rudimentary form ('creeping constitutionalism'),[23] but argues that they have the potential to develop fully.

### 3. Outlook for Success

Teubner's model is much more ambitious than the majority of political constitutionalization theories. But it is also more demanding in its prerequisites. The assessment depends mainly on the state of these prerequisites. Essentially, the aim is, as Teubner himself says, 'to secure the assertion opportunities of so-called non-rational logics of action against the dominant trend of rationalization by winning autonomy spaces for societal reflection over long struggles and guaranteeing them institutionally'.[24] In the constitutional state, this is the task of protection of fundamental rights. Fundamental rights secure not only individual freedom of action, but also the autonomy of functional social systems that can fulfil their function only on the basis of their own specific rationality. This expressly includes those in which 'non-rational logics of action' have an articulation opportunity: science, art, religion, education, the media. But this autonomy depends on the guarantee provided by the state. It cannot be built solely on the individuals acting within the system.

---

[22] Ibid., p. 16 ff.   [23] Ibid., p. 13.

[24] Ibid., p. 11 (for an explanation of the ambiguous term 'non-rational' see p. 9).

The question thus arises as to how the model is to succeed when the state does not exist on the international level and no one else takes its place. Civil constitutions cannot escape their originating conditions. They are private complexes of norms, they apply only within sectors, and they are self-created. Each of these characteristics has consequences. The private character of the complexes of norms means that they reflect partial interests. The sector-related validity means that they obey the specific rationality of the respective sector. The consequence of self-creation is that external interests, such as those of affected persons, other functional systems of society as a whole, are taken into account only to the extent that this accords with self-interest. Self-interest and external or overall interest may coincide to a certain extent, but not entirely. Self-interest can be interpreted as either short term or long term, but not exceeded within the system. It is difficult to understand how, under these conditions, civil constitutions can perform the functions of a political constitution.

Additionally, here, as in international constitutionalism, the participation of those affected, the perception of problems beyond self-interest, and the democratic-representative element that focuses on reconciliation of interests are all lacking, and without these self-restraint that exceeds self-interest can scarcely occur. Teubner does not ignore this point. He relies on an evolutionary concurrence between transnational law that controls institutions of the various social systems and arbitration tribunals with the law enacted by international organizations and states and their courts. The result could be novel collision rules which, unlike traditional collision law, do not determine which national law is to apply in the event of cases with foreign influence. Rather, the focus is on a law 'that restricts itself to creating a loose relationship between fragmented partial legal orders'.[25] But can law that does this also be self-created law of the fragmented civil society if there is nothing higher than the functional systems in the global arena? And who is to assert it when it opposes the interests of the system?

As a matter of fact, international institutions and, even more so, state institutions are by no means completely absent in transnational relations. To date, internationalization of the political sphere has stopped short of the state monopoly of legitimate power. Private persons per se do not have means of compulsion at their disposal. Nor have any of the international organizations to date been granted the use of means of compulsion, not to mention the monopoly of force, not even the highly integrated EU. In the fragmented global civil society, there is no compulsory execution per se. If the self-created law of the global actors or the decisions of the arbitration instances appointed by them are not complied with voluntarily, they must depend for the assertion of legal claims on state courts or international courts established by states and, if their decisions are not obeyed, on state bailiffs and police officers.

[25] Fischer-Lescano and Teubner (n. 10), p. 57.

Thus, for the time being, the state appears to remain the only place where the compliance with system boundaries and autonomy protected by fundamental rights can be asserted with consequences, and for the state, these derive from the national constitutions and international legal documents. However, this would not be sufficient to close the gap created by the process of denationalization. In view of the far-reaching self-limitation to which the global actors would have to agree, it is unlikely that transnational law could develop the four characteristics that, according to Teubner, would elevate it to the rank of 'societal constitutionalism'. Without this anchor 'societal constitutionalism' is far away from providing a compensation for the loss suffered by the national constitution which deserves the name 'constitutionalism'.

## V. A PRELIMINARY EVALUATION

We reach the following preliminary conclusions:

1. When the constitution reached its zenith at the end of the twentieth century, its inner erosion had already commenced. This did not render it meaningless, but it meant that it can no longer completely fulfil its promise.

2. In return, the juridification of international relations intensified. However, it will only deserve the name of constitutionalism if one is prepared to apply the term to anything which even vaguely resembles it.

3. It is unlikely that societal constitutionalism can replace the performance of politically related constitutions. Only in the shadow of public power does it have a limited chance of effectiveness.

4. The erosion of statehood is irreversible. Consequently, it is not possible to maintain the aspiration level of successful constitutional states. What a compensation for this might look like is at present unclear.

5. Under these circumstances, one should not be too ready to sacrifice the state. In spite of the signs of erosion, the achievements that made up the constitution still rest most securely within it.

# ∞ 17 ∞

# Levels of the Rule of Law: On the Possibility of Exporting a Western Achievement

## I. ADHERENCE OF GOVERNMENTAL ACTION TO THE LAW

At the core of the idea of the rule of law is the requirement that the state exercises its power in the form of law.[1] This means that the state governs by law and according to law. Governing by legal rules means that what the state demands from the people is articulated through, and based in, law. Governing according to legal rules means that the state not only prescribes rules for its people but also submits to rules itself. It is in the nature of legal rules that they are not designed to address a particular case but rather that they apply to a wide range of future cases; that law will not be changed as a particular case is being decided; that the law treats everyone equally; and that it decides like cases alike. Governing under the rule of law is the antithesis of arbitrary rule.

The exercise of public power in the form of law prevents the state from too easily converting power into orders or measures. In a rule of law regime, the use of power depends on competences and procedures. Only the compliance to them establishes the binding character of acts of power. A traffic officer may not divorce a couple; a registrar cannot control vehicles. In parliamentary proceedings, no one can be punished; in criminal proceedings the parliament cannot be dissolved. When the state lacks jurisdiction or violates its procedural requirements, the state is in the wrong if it still commands, and not the citizen who refuses to comply. In sum, the core of the rule of law is that governmental action is bound by law. The state does not have the right to flout the law in a state governed by the rule of law.

The state is, however, the source of the law. The great bulk of laws owe their validity to acts of government. That means that the state can revoke or amend these laws anytime. Yet, the power to amend does not include the power to ignore the law. It must be followed even if its compliance is inconvenient to the rulers or has implications that they find detrimental. It is not only lower authorities that have to comply with the law. The highest branches of government must also comply with the law—that is the essence of the rule of law. To put

---

[1] The literature on the rule of law is vast: see Katharina Sobota, *Das Prinzip Rechtsstaat* (Tübingen: Mohr Siebeck, 1997).

Constitutionalism: Past, Present, and Future. First Edition. Dieter Grimm. © Dieter Grimm 2016. Published 2016 by Oxford University Press.

it more concretely, the primary concern is that the executive power complies with the laws the legislature has enacted. In this context, lawyers speak of the concept of legality of the administration.[2]

The regularity of government action, which is designed to reduce arbitrariness, is a value in itself, independent of the content of the law that comes into force. It is a value in itself because it makes government action predictable for those who are affected by it. The stability of laws allows citizens to organize their behaviour in such a way that they do not come into conflict with the law and it provides economic actors with the degree of legal certainty that they need in order to plan rationally. Hence, an important part of any rule of law regime is the prohibition against retroactive laws,[3] because retroactivity means that private behaviour entails legal consequences that were not part of the law at the time of the action so that it was impossible to foresee them and to organize one's behaviour accordingly. The benefits of the rule of law are absent in a system with retroactive laws.

## II. LEGAL CERTAINTY AS AN INTRINSIC VALUE

As plausible as the postulate of the law's bindingness on the state may be, achieving it is just as precarious. Compliance to the law can hinder politicians from pursuing certain goals or taking certain actions which are important to them. Compliance with legal norms by the authorities may have undesirable consequences. Criminal suspects may be set free because the evidence against them is not sufficient. On other occasions, evidence may not be used because it was obtained illegally. In such situations, obedience to the law can appear to be empty formalism which thwarts the achievement of substantive justice. A state which then overrides these legal requirements frequently even has public opinion on its side. But it would not be a rule of law state (*Rechtsstaat*) if it did not possess a willingness to comply with the law even when it is unpopular, inconvenient, or annoying.

If the state wants to remedy an unsatisfactory arrangement, it has to change the law for the future, but it cannot disregard it now. Once it becomes accepted that under certain circumstances there may be reasons to ignore the law, it is only a small step away from disregarding the law for all kinds of illegitimate purposes: because it does not correspond to one's subjective sense of justice; because the outcome in this particular case does not appear desirable; because there are benefits in disregarding the law; to avoid trouble with those in power; because political opponents may be harmed by doing so, etc. If a rule of law state wants to succeed, it needs to appreciate legal certainty as an intrinsic value regardless of whether one believes that the outcome of legal protection is good, bad, useful, or harmful.[4]

---

[2] See Dietrich Jesch, *Gesetz und Verwaltung* (Tübingen: Mohr Siebeck, 2nd edn, 1968).

[3] See Bodo Pieroth, *Rückwirkung und Übergangsrecht* (Berlin: Duncker & Humblot, 1981).

[4] See Andreas von Arnauld, *Rechtssicherheit* (Tübingen: Mohr Siebeck, 2006).

However, the requirements for this are not equally favourable everywhere. The reason lies in a fundamental difference whose importance will come up more than once. There are states that see themselves in the service of a predetermined absolute truth. This might be a religious or secular truth. In this case, political authority derives its legitimacy from that truth. It is legitimate insofar as it helps to enforce the truth. But there are also states that do not identify themselves with a particular truth and acknowledge a plurality of truth claims. They do not derive their legitimacy to rule from one sole truth that is binding for all, but from the consensus of its citizens as to the conditions of peaceful coexistence despite disagreement about the good and just.

For the rule of law state this difference is significant, because states that see themselves in the service of an absolute truth have greater difficulties adhering to rule of law principles than pluralistic ones. They do not view the law as autonomous and develop a purely instrumental relationship to positive law. When truth claims conflict with legal duties, they usually give preference to the truth without much second thought. Pluralistic societies, with competing ideas of the common good and justice, are more prone to accept the rule of law because the law is the product of a political decision that followed established rules, enabled participation, and can be changed at any time.

## III. RESERVATION AND BINDING FORCE OF LAWS

Making the law obligatory on state power as a core value of the rule of law assumes another aspect. The binding character which the rule of law demands is derived from legislation. Consequently it extends only as far as legislation exists. Where there is no law there can also be no legal constraints. Since the state is also the legislator, it therefore holds the extent of the binding character of its law in its own hands. Insofar as the state refrains from establishing laws, it does not submit itself to rules. Under these circumstances, the rule of law reveals gaps. The state can exploit these legal gaps for all kinds of purposes. Therefore, the rule of law is only achieved if the state can pursue certain goals only on the basis of a statutory authorization to do so, the so-called reservation of the law.[5]

Traditionally, the area in which the state may not act without statutory authorization is demarcated by fundamental rights. The state may not infringe upon one's fundamental rights without statutory authorization. Obviously, these statutory authorizations must also have a regulatory content capable of binding state authorities in order to function effectively. This is particularly important in areas where the individual is intensely affected by state actions, such as in criminal or police law. Giving blank cheques to government power cannot result in binding force. Neither do laws consisting of vague and open-ended phrases

---

[5] See Jesch (n. 2), p. 30; Wolfgang Hoffman-Riem, 'Gesetz und Gesetzesvorbehalt im Umbruch' (2005) 130 *Archiv des öffentlichen Rechts* 5.

produce sufficient binding effects. It should not be inferred from this, however, that the binding force of the law increases the more detailed a law gets. The more casuistically a legislature tries to regulate an issue, the more loopholes it will leave behind.

Yet, the degree to which a law is binding is not only dependent on the willingness of the politicians to formulate binding norms. It is also influenced by the subject matter the law seeks to regulate. As long as the task of the state was largely confined to maintaining an existing social order regarded as just, an effective regulation of government activity was rather easy. Maintaining order is a retroactive, narrowly defined, and predictable activity. It can be captured in legal norms that follow the 'if–then' pattern, clearly define what counts as a violation of the order, and indicate what legal consequences the relevant authorities may take to prevent disorder or to restore order.

By contrast, the tasks of the modern regulatory and welfare state are prospective, comprehensive, and less predictable. The norm type tailored towards maintaining a given order does not apply here. Therefore, in these areas a norm type prevails which, in contrast to the traditional conditional programmes, is identified as a purposive programme. The legislature in the modern regulatory and welfare state can only set certain policy goals and name a number of factors which have to be considered in the pursuit of the goals by the administration. But *how* agencies achieve these goals in practice is largely left up to them in the process of implementing these norms. This situation is encapsulated in the book entitled *Wachsende Staatsaufgaben – sinkende Steuerungsfähigkeit des Rechts* [Growing state tasks—diminishing regulatory capacity of law].[6] This is a problem of the rule of law in developed countries with a commitment to rule of law principles.

### IV. MATERIAL RULE OF LAW THROUGH BINDING FUNDAMENTAL RIGHTS

When it was said in a previous statement that the submission of the state to law is a value in itself it must now be added that it is only a limited value. A rule of law state that would exhaust itself in submitting the executive to laws remains purely formal. The binding character would only extend to the form of the law, while the content of the law would be unimportant. Rule of law in a purely formal sense is compatible with oppressive, exploitative, and discriminatory legislation. Such a formal view of the rule of law developed in Germany in the second half of the nineteenth century.[7] Yet, at that time the underlying foundation

---

[6] Dieter Grimm (ed.), *Wachsende Staatsaufgaben – sinkende Steuerungsfähigkeit des Rechts* (Baden-Baden: Nomos, 1990); Dieter Grimm, *Die Zukunft der Verfassung* (Frankfurt am Main: Suhrkamp, 3rd edn, 2002), p. 159; Helge Rossen, *Vollzug und Verhandlung* (Tübingen: Mohr-Siebeck, 1999).

[7] See Olivier Jouanjan (ed.), *Figures de l'Etat de droit. Le Rechtsstaat dans l'histoire intellectuelle et constitutionnelle de l'Allemagne* (Strasbourg: Presses universitaires de Strasbourg, 2001).

of a liberal legal culture was always tacitly assumed. The consequences of this narrowed conception of the rule of law only came to light through the decay of the legal culture during the Nazi regime. Experiencing first hand that the law can also become a tool for injustice led to a return to the original, material understanding of the rule of law.

A state devoted to the rule of law in a substantive sense is therefore not only one in which the state is submitted to the law, whatever its content may be, but one in which law reflects certain notions of justice. Obviously everything then depends on the question of what notions of justice are decisive in the legislative process. If it concerns a notion of justice based in an absolute truth from which no one can be exempt then it will be difficult to achieve the rule of law. As mentioned earlier, when truth claims and legal duties conflict, the latter generally yields to the former. The rule of law state, in contrast, rests on ideas of justice which recognize the intrinsic value of every individual and ensuing from that his or her freedom and equality.

The attempt to achieve the justice of a social order through a structure of fundamental rights is not without its demands. Fundamental rights are primarily designed to limit government power in the interest of individual self-determination. As the experience of the nineteenth century shows, this goal can only be attained if the state is not blind to the actual conditions for the enjoyment of freedom. Otherwise, freedom is either useless for those without the necessary means or coercive, because it drives people into conditions of dependence. It is because of this experience that the rule of law state gradually evolved into a welfare state in which the government is committed to provide for the basic needs of the citizens, to care for the sick, the unemployed and elderly, and to eliminate the exploitation of its weakest members.

Furthermore, the rule of law state as understood in a substantive sense would also be incomplete if it did not address the dangers for fundamental rights that emanate, not from the government, but from third parties and other social forces. These dangers have increased considerably with the unparalleled progress in science and technology and the commercial use of its results. It is true that the state possesses means to mitigate these risks. But as they grow out of activities that are themselves protected by fundamental rights, laws are needed to address the risks. If the legislature were permitted to remain passive in this conflict of constitutional rights, the most assertive interests would tend to prevail over the interests of those in need of protection. It therefore is an essential element of a substantive rule of law concept today that fundamental rights not merely serve as checks on government power but also incorporate a duty to protect its citizens against the dangers that result from the constitutionally protected activities of third parties.[8]

---

[8] See Ch. 8 of this volume.

## V. LEGAL PROTECTIONS AGAINST STATE ACTIONS AND JUDICIAL REVIEW

These remarks suggest that the idea of the rule of law cannot be expected to sell itself. This holds true not only for autocratic or theocratic regimes but also for pluralistic societies and democratic states. Therefore, it is of paramount importance to ask what a state has to expect when it chooses to ignore its submission to the law. If individuals act illegally the state may intervene with its police powers. But if the state itself breaks the law, there is no higher authority to enforce the law. The rule of law state is therefore dependent on the existence of devices within its own structure which monitor the lawfulness of state action. In common law countries, these devices have always existed. The executive could be sued in court. In countries with an absolutist past, the state was able to evade this kind of judicial scrutiny.

Generally, it took enormous efforts before the judiciary was able to regain the power to review the legality of governmental acts. In Germany, the legal protection against the state became the most important demand after the attempt to democratize it had failed in 1849. The result of these efforts was the establishment of special administrative courts, rather than expansion of the competence of ordinary courts as in the common law model.[9] There are, however, still many countries in which citizens cannot hold public authorities accountable, whether at the highest or the lowest level. In states which derive their legitimacy from an absolute truth rather than from consensus, the lack of judicial review tends to be the rule. As all experience teaches us, the rule of law is on shaky ground without the possibility of judicial control.

If the rule of law is not only defined in formal but material terms, then it does not exhaust itself in the legality of the administration. The legislature is also subject to legal constraints laid down in the constitution. However, the adherence of the legislature to the constitution cannot be determined by administrative courts. If the legislature should not be allowed to ignore the constitution with impunity, then its actions must also be subject to judicial review. This is the conclusion to which the United States was already drawn at the time its Constitution was adopted. In the rest of the world, this insight has only found gradual acceptance after bitter experiences with blatantly unjust regimes. The second half of the twentieth century saw the triumph of constitutional adjudication, with judicial review of legislation at its core.[10] Today, judicial review is widely regarded as an integral component of the rule of law.

The existence of judicial review alone means very little, however, if courts are not independent, but remain bound by the political chain of command. It is an essential part of the rule of law that laws, once enacted, emancipate

---

[9] See Regina Ogorek, 'Individueller Rechtsschutz gegenüber der Staatsgewalt. Zur Entwicklung der Verwaltungsgerichtsbarkeit im 19. Jahrhundert' in Jürgen Kocka (ed.), *Bürgertum im 19. Jahrhundert*, vol. 1 (Göttingen: Vandenhoeck & Ruprecht, 1988), p. 372.

[10] See C. Neal Tate and Torbjörn Vallinder, *The Global Expansion of Judicial Power* (New York: New York University Press, 1995).

themselves from political control and obtain an autonomous status, that is, that they will be interpreted and applied according to legal rather than political criteria. This is the only way to guarantee that the political branches are bound by law. The guarantee for this is the separation of powers.[11] This is why the rule of law is weak not only where there is no judicial review but also where there is no separation of powers. Separation of powers is more than the exercise of public functions by various departments; it also entails the independence of powers within their functional areas. This is difficult for countries that are committed to an absolute truth to accept. Absolute truths demand hierarchy; separation of powers prevents hierarchy.

## VI. CONDITIONS OF THE RULE OF LAW

In sum, the rule of law proves to be full of conditions. This also answers the question of whether it is a cure-all for the entire world. It is not because the conditions for its realization are lacking in many parts of the world. They also cannot be brought about that easily. Only at first glance does the rule of law seem to be a merely technical legal device which could be established anywhere if only the political will was there. In truth, it is a cultural achievement which does not necessarily take roots in other cultural contexts. In the Western world it has helped to bridge the tension between political power and individual self-development by imposing legal boundaries on governance in the interest of individual liberties. The rule of law does not find favourable ground in cultures in which self-development has no worth and law is not associated with the protection of freedom.

However, this does not mean that the spread of the rule of law outside of the cultural context from which the concept emerged presents an insurmountable obstacle. Rather, in order to export the idea of the rule of law it is of crucial importance to realize that there are different levels of the rule of law. The rule of law is not a matter of all or nothing, but of more or less. In fact, rule of law is not a process, as it is often claimed; it is a state of affairs. But its realization can take the form of a process, level by level. Even in the Western world, not all levels were achieved at the outset. Many were won only after bitter setbacks and hard struggles. Still today these levels differ from country to country.

Each new step means a step forward compared to the previous level. Even the minimum concept of making the law binding on the administration, irrespective of the content of the law, is progress compared to arbitrary rule. The more elementary the level embarked upon, the greater the demand for it. This demand to be subjected to a rule-based rather than arbitrary government can be expected to meet universal approval. For the fulfilment of such a demand,

---

[11] See Christoph Möllers, *The Three Branches: A Comparative Model of Separation of Powers* (Oxford: Oxford University Press, 2013). For judicial independence, see Karl August Bettermann, *Die Unabhängigkeit des Richters* (Cologne: Carl Heymanns Verlag, 1969); Kurt Eichenberger, *Die richterliche Unabhängigkeit als staatsrechtliches Problem* (Berne: Stämpfli und Cie, 1960).

one can easily mobilize popular support. Other levels of the rule of law may be in the interest of the political leaders themselves, albeit the interest will often be a pragmatic and not necessarily a principled interest in the rule of law. A state that relies on economic growth, for example, will accept those rule of law elements which are conducive to attract investors.

However, the realization of the rule of law becomes more demanding with each additional level. This not only affects the prospects of success but even the mere willingness to try it out. Not every progress in the realization of the rule of law can count on popular support. Anyone who is convinced of the existence of a God-given order over which human beings are not allowed to dispose will have a hard time seeing the benefits that religious freedom and freedom of expression bring. Without acceptance of freedom as a human right, there can be no rule of law in the substantive sense described above. Where all public power is in the service of an absolute truth, it would appear contradictory if the supreme power could be prevented from enforcement of such truth by an independent body of judicial review.

## VII. RULE OF LAW AND DEMOCRACY

That brings us finally to the relationship between the rule of law and democracy. Does one necessarily go with the other? This question is obviously of great significance for the global spread of the rule of law. From a historical perspective, the question can be answered in the negative. Before it became a democracy, Germany had been a rule of law state for more than one hundred years. As early as the era of enlightened absolutism of the eighteenth century, the rule of law became increasingly accepted. This was the time when the great codifications began. Rulers gave up using their prerogative to repeal court judgments and replace them with mere authoritative decisions. In the constitutional monarchies of the nineteenth century, princes bound themselves in the exercise of public power by constitutions, which granted fundamental rights to its citizens and allowed elected representatives to participate in the legislative process.

However, these pre-democratic states did not reach all the levels which we would associate with the rule of law idea today. Even if the enlightened monarchs were willing to treat their subjects in accordance with the laws, which they had unilaterally enacted, they were not prepared to subordinate their power to law. They were bound by the law only to the extent that they were willing to comply with it. They could depart from it at any time and subjects lacked the means to enforce the law against the ruler. Although constitutional monarchs did not derive their power from the constitution—they had granted constitutions voluntarily by way of self-binding—they were no longer free to unilaterally take them back. But the binding force of the constitution did not extend further than as granted by the monarch, and judicial review was considered incompatible with monarchical principles.

By today's standards, then, the rule of law is not fully realized in non-democratic states. On the other hand, it is not the case that democracies are always accompanied by a fully developed rule of law regime. Just as there are many different political regimes that could be called 'non-democratic', so too are there countless forms of governance that could be called 'democratic'. Where democracy is identified with majority rule and protection of minorities and a guarantee for free political competition and communication is lacking, democracy can easily turn into a tyranny of the majority. This notion of a dictatorship of the majority alone should suffice to demonstrate that a democracy without rule of law seems contradictory and tends towards self-destruction.

Democracy without rule of law is not immune to the disfranchisement of minorities; but similarly, the rule of law without democracy is not immune to particularism. When those who are affected by a law cannot participate in the law's making, it is unlikely that a reasonable balance of interests between all sectors of the population will be achieved. Those who are not involved in the formation of the state's will can easily, and without consequences, be neglected in the political decision-making process. They will become mere objects of governmental power, no matter how well meaning this power may be. For these reasons, both the rule of law and democracy treated independently are in danger of failing the common good. Only in conjunction do they constitute the achievement that ultimately secures the common interest.[12]

---

[12] See Jürgen Habermas, *Between Facts and Norms* (Cambridge: Polity Press, 1996); Jürgen Habermas, *The Inclusion of the Other* (Cambridge, Mass: MIT, 2000).

# PART IX

# CONCLUSION

## ᗞ 18 ᗞ

# *The Achievement of Constitutionalism and its Prospects in a Changed World*

## I. EXTERNAL CULMINATION—INTERNAL EROSION

Constitutionalism is a relatively recent innovation in the history of political institutions. It emerged in the last quarter of the eighteenth century from two successful revolutions against the hereditary rulers, first in the British colonies of North-America, then in France. Immediately understood as an important achievement, it appealed to many people outside the countries of origin, and attempts to introduce modern constitutions started all over Europe and soon also in other parts of the world. The nineteenth century was a period of struggle for constitutionalism in a lot of countries. But after many detours and setbacks constitutionalism had finally gained universal recognition by the end of the twentieth century. Today, only a handful of the nearly 200 states in the world is still without a constitution.

This is not to say that these constitutions are everywhere taken seriously, or that constitutional norms always prevail in cases of conflict with political intentions. But the universal recognition of constitutionalism as a model for the organization and legitimation of political power is shown by the fact that even rulers who are not inclined to submit themselves to legal norms feel compelled at least to pretend to be exercising their power within the constitutional framework. Further, the general willingness of rulers to govern in accordance with the provisions of the constitution has recently increased considerably, as is indicated by the great number of constitutional courts or courts with constitutional jurisdiction that were established during the last quarter of the twentieth century. After 225 years, constitutionalism seems now to have reached the peak of its development.

This external success of constitutionalism, however, should not mislead the observer. It is accompanied by an internal erosion that started almost unnoticed in the wake of a transformation of statehood, domestically as well as internationally, and eventually cost the state the monopoly of public power over its territory.[1] Today, the state shares its power with a number of non-state actors,

---

[1] For the domestic causes and effects, which are not the central concern of this chapter, see Dieter Grimm, *Die Zukunft der Verfassung* (Frankfurt am Main: Suhrkamp, 1991, 3rd edn, 2002), p. 399. See further Ch. 1 of this volume.

Constitutionalism: Past, Present, and Future. First Edition. Dieter Grimm. © Dieter Grimm 2016. Published 2016 by Oxford University Press.

most of them international organizations to whom sovereign rights have been transferred and whose exercise escapes the arrangements of national constitutions. This differs from the fact that constitutional norms may be violated or have little impact on political action; such a gap between norm and fact has always existed, but does not of itself undermine the potential of constitutionalism. The internal erosion, by contrast, endangers the capacity of the constitution to fulfil its claim of establishing and regulating all public power that has an impact on the territory where the constitution is in force. This is why the erosion affects not only this or that constitution, but the achievement of constitutionalism altogether.

One response to this development has been the attempt to elevate constitutionalism to the international level. The recent boom of the term 'constitutionalization' is an indicator of this tendency. Different from traditional constitution-making, it describes not an act by which a constitution takes legal force, but a process which eventually ends up in a constitution. Such processes are already underway, certainly in Europe where the European Convention of Human Rights (ECHR) and the primary law of the European Union (EU) are analysed in terms of constitutional law, but also globally. For many authors, public international law is acquiring constitutional status. The Charter of the United Nations (UN) as well as the statutes of other international organizations such as the World Trade Organization (WTO) are interpreted as constitutions. Even global public policy networks and self-organization processes of private global actors are discussed in terms of constitutionalism—all objects not regarded as constitutions just a few years ago.[2]

---

[2] The literature is increasing rapidly. See in general R. St.J. Macdonald and D. M. Johnston (eds), *Towards World Constitutionalism* (Leiden: Brill, 2005); A. Peters, 'Compensatory Constitutionalism: The Function and Potential of Fundamental International Norms and Structures' (2006) 19 *Leiden Journal of International Law* 579; E. de Wet, 'The International Legal Order' (2006) 55 *International & Comparative Law Quarterly* 51; R. Uerpmann, 'Internationales Verfassungsrecht' (2001) *Juristenzeitung* 565; M. Knauff, 'Konstitutionalisierung im inner- und überstaatlichen Recht' (2008) 68 *Zeitschrift für ausländisches öffentliches Recht und Völkerrecht* 453; 'Constitutionalism in an Era of Globalization and Privatization' (2008) 6 *International Journal of Constitutional Law* issues 3 and 4; C. Walter, 'Constitutionalizing International Governance' (2001) 44 *German Yearbook of International Law* 170; R. Kreide and A. Niederberger (eds), *Transnationale Verrechtlichung* (Frankfurt am Main: Campus, 2008). For public international law, see: J. A. Frowein, 'Konstitutionalisierung des Völkerrechts' (1999) 39 *Berichte der Deutschen Gesellschaft für Völkerrecht* 427. For the UN, see B. Fassbender, 'The United Nations Charter as Constitution of the International Community' (1998) 36 *Columbia Journal of Transnational Law* 529. For the WTO, see D. Cass, *The Constitutionalization of the World Trade Organisation* (Oxford: Oxford University Press, 2005); J. P. Trachtman, 'The Constitution of the WTO' (2006) 17 *European Journal of International Law* 623. For the ECHR, see C. Walter, 'Die EMRK als Konstitutionalisierungsprozess' (1999) 59 *Zeitschrift für ausländisches öffentliches Recht und Völkerrecht* 961. For the EU, the literature is immense: see e.g. J. Weiler, *The Constitution of Europe* (Cambridge: Cambridge University Press, 1999); I. Pernice, 'Multilevel Constitutionalism and the Treaty of Amsterdam' (1999) 36 *Common Market Law Review* 703; A. Peters, *Elemente einer Theorie der Verfassung Europas* (Berlin: Duncker & Humblot, 2001). For societal constitutionalism, see G. Teubner, 'Globale Zivilverfassungen: Alternativen zur staatszentrierten Verfassungstheorie' (2003) 63 *Zeitschrift für ausländisches öffentliches Recht und Völkerrecht* 1; A. Fischer-Lescano and G. Teubner, *Regimekollisionen* (Frankfurt am Main: Suhrkamp, 2006); H. Schepel, *The Constitution of Private Governance* (Oxford: Hart, 2005). For some critical voices, see R. Wahl, 'Konstitutionalisierung – Leitbegriff oder Allerweltsbegriff?' in C.-E. Eberle (ed.), *Der Wandel des Staates vor den Herausforderung der Gegenwart. Festschrift für W. Brohm* (Munich: Beck, 2002), p. 191; U. Haltern, 'Internationales Verfassungsrecht?' (2003) 128 *Archiv des öffentlichen Rechts* 511; P. Dobner,

In order to realize the extent to which the development affects the constitution on the national level one needs a clear notion of what constitutionalism entails. This is not always present in discussions over the process of constitutionalization and the future of constitutionalism. Many authors tend to identify constitutionalism as involving a submission of politics to law. This is not wrong, but it is not the whole story. Legalization of politics is nothing new; it existed long before the constitution emerged. A clear notion of constitutionalism can therefore be best obtained if one tries to determine what was new about the constitution when it emerged from the two revolutions, and which conditions had to be present before it was able to emerge.[3] This, in turn, will allow a comparison of constitutionalism in the traditional sense with new developments on the international level and permit an assessment to be made of the possibility of its reconstruction at the global level.

## II. THE ACHIEVEMENT AND ITS PRECONDITIONS

The emergence of the modern constitution from revolution is not accidental. The American and the French Revolutions differed from the many upheavals and revolts in history in that they did not content themselves with replacing one ruler by another. They aimed at establishing a new political *system* that differed fundamentally from the one they had accused of being unjust and oppressive. In order to achieve this, they devised a plan of legitimate rule, with persons being called to govern on the basis and in accordance with these pre-established conditions. The historic novelty of this step is often obscured by the fact that the legalization of politics did not start with the first constitutions. Neither was the term 'constitution' new. It had been in use long before constitutionalism emerged. But the earlier legal bonds of politics were of a different kind and the term 'constitution' had a different meaning before and after the revolutionary break.[4]

In its traditional meaning, the term referred to the state of a country as determined by various factors, such as the geographical conditions, the nature of its population, the division of power. Also among these factors were the fundamental legal rules that determined the social and political structure of a country. Later in the eighteenth century the notion was used in a narrower sense, referring to the country's state as formed by the fundamental rules. But still the term 'constitution' did not designate these rules. It was an empirical rather than a normative notion. Understood in a descriptive sense, every

---

*Konstitutionalismus als Politikform* (Baden-Baden: Nomos 2002); see also Ch. 15 of this volume. D. Grimm, 'The Constitution in the Process of Denationalization' (2005) 12 *Constellations* 447.

[3] See Grimm (n. 1), p. 31; D. Grimm, *Deutsche Verfassungsgeschichte* (Frankfurt am Main: Suhrkamp, 3rd edn, 1995), p. 10 et seq.

[4] See H. Mohnhaupt and D. Grimm, *Verfassung. Zur Geschichte des Begriffs von der Antike bis zur Gegenwart* (Berlin: Duncker & Humblot, 2nd edn, 2002); C. H. McIlwain, *Constitutionalism, Ancient and Modern* (Ithaca: Cornell University Press, 1940).

country had a—or more precisely was in a—constitution. If used in a normative sense, constitution designated some specific laws, such as laws enacted
by the Emperor in the Holy Roman Empire (*Constitutio Criminalis Carolina*).
On the other hand, there existed laws regulating the exercise of public power,
though these were not called 'constitutions', but forms of government, *leges
fundamentales* etc.

In the medieval era, these fundamental laws were regarded as of divine origin. They were by definition higher law and the political powers could not
dispose of them. The function of politics consisted in enforcing God's will.
Legislation, if it occurred, was not understood as law-creation, but as concretization of eternal law, adapting it to exigencies of time and space. This
understanding lost its ground with the Reformation of the early sixteenth century. The devastating civil wars that followed the schism made the restoration
of social peace the ruler's primary function. This required a concentration of
all powers and prerogatives, which in the medieval order had been dispersed
among many independent bearers who exercised them not as a separate function but as an adjunct of a certain status, for example that of a landowner. In
addition, this power did not extend to a territory; it referred to persons so that
various authorities coexisted on the same territory, each of them exercising
different prerogatives.

Restoration of internal peace seemed possible only if all holders of prerogatives were deprived of their power in favour of one single ruler, historically the
prince, who combined them in his person and condensed them to the public
power in the singular. This power was no longer limited to law enforcement. It
included the right to create a legal order that was independent of the competing faiths and secular in nature. Eternal law thereby lost its legal validity and
retreated to a moral obligation. In order to enforce the law against resisting
groups in society the prince claimed the monopoly of legitimate use of force,
which entailed on the other side a privatization of civil society. A new notion for
this completely new type of political rule soon came into use: the *state*, whose
most important attribute was sovereignty, understood since Bodin's seminal
work as the ruler's right to dictate law for everybody without being bound by
law himself.[5] The state originated as an absolute state.

Absolutism nevertheless remained an aspiration of the rulers that was
nowhere completely fulfilled before the French Revolution ended this period.
Sovereignty, although defined as highest and indivisible authority over all subjects, was but relative in practice. Old bonds dating from the medieval period
survived, new ones were established. But they did not form an integral whole.
Most of these laws had a contractual basis. They took the form of agreements
between the ruler and the privileged estates of a territory on whose support
the ruler depended. They were regarded as mutually binding and could sometimes even be enforced by courts. Yet none of these legal norms questioned

---

[5]  J. Bodin, *Les six livres de la République* (Paris: Du Puys, 1576).

the ruler's right to rule. Based on transcendental or hereditary legitimation this right preceded the legal bonds. They merely limited the right in this or that respect, not comprehensively, and in favour of the parties to the agreement, not universally.

The existence of such legal bonds, first eternal and then secular, indicates that it would not be sufficient to characterize constitutionalism as a submission of politics to law. Different from the older legal bonds of political power, the new constitutions did not modify a pre-existing right to rule: they preceded the rulers right to rule. They created this right, determined the procedure in which individuals were called into office, and laid down the conditions under which they were entitled to exercise the power given to them. In contrast to the older legal bonds, the constitution regulated public power coherently and comprehensively. This is not to say that political power was again reduced to law enforcement, as with the medieval order. It means, rather, that constitutionalism recognized neither any extraconstitutional bearer of public power, nor any extra constitutional ways and means to exercise this power vis-à-vis citizens. Finally, the legal regulation of public power not only favoured certain privileged groups in society who possessed sufficient bargaining power, but society as a whole.

These differences had some consequences that further characterize the constitution. As an act that constituted legitimate public power in the first place, the constitution could not emanate from the ruler himself. It presupposed a different source. This source was found in the people that had decided to form a polity. The legitimating principle of the modern constitution was popular rather than monarchical sovereignty. This was by no means an original idea of the American and the French revolutionaries. It had older roots and gained widespread recognition when religion no longer served as basis of the social order after the Reformation. In the absence of a divine legitimation the philosophers of the time turned to reason as a common endowment of mankind, independent of religious creeds. In order to find out how political rule could be legitimized, they placed themselves in a fictitious state of nature where everybody was by definition equally free. The question, then, was why and under which conditions reasonable people would be willing to leave the state of nature and submit themselves to a government.

The reason for this was the fundamental insecurity of life and limb in the state of nature. Leaving the state of nature became a dictate of reason. Given the equal freedom of all individuals, the step from the state of nature to government called for a general agreement. Legitimacy could be acquired only by a government based on the consent of the governed. It was also up to the governed to determine the conditions under which political power could be exercised. These conditions varied over time. For those philosophers who elaborated their theory against the backcloth of the religious wars of the sixteenth and seventeenth centuries, ending civil war and enabling peaceful coexistence of believers in different faiths, enjoyed absolute priority. For them, this goal could be achieved only if individuals handed over all their natural rights to the ruler in exchange of the overarching good of security. Here, the theory of the social contract justified absolutism.

The better the absolute ruler fulfilled his historical function of pacifying society, the less plausible seemed the claim that peaceful coexistence in one society required a total relinquishment of all natural rights. The ruler's task was now seen to be the protection of individual freedom, which required no more from the individuals than handing over the right to self-justice. From the mid-eighteenth century, the treatises of natural law contained growing catalogues of fundamental rights that the state was obliged to respect and protect. This coincided with the economic theory that freedom of contract and property would be a better way of achieving justice and welfare in society than feudalism and state regulation of the economy. The idea that individual freedom remained endangered vis-à-vis a concentrated governmental power also gained ground. To guarantee that the state respected individual rights, some separation of powers and certain checks and balances were regarded as indispensable.

Although these theories contained all the ingredients that later appeared in the constitutions, they were not pushed forward to the postulate of a constitution by the philosophers. For them, they functioned as a test of the legitimacy of a political system: a political system was deemed legitimate if it could be considered *as if* established by a consensus of the governed. Like the state of nature, the social contract was fictitious. With the sole exception of Emer de Vattel,[6] neither a document nor a popular decision was required. The social contract served as a regulative idea. It was not considered to be the result of a real process of consensus-building. Its authority was based on argumentation, not on enactment. No ruler before the revolution had been willing to adopt it, and most rulers had explicitly rejected it. Natural law and positive law contradicted each other.

Only after the revolutionary break with traditional rule were these ideas able to become a blue-print for the establishment of the new order needed to fill the vacuum of legitimate public power. By their very nature they worked in favour of a constitution. Popular sovereignty was the legitimating principle of the new order. But unlike the sovereign monarch, the people were incapable of ruling themselves. They needed representatives who governed in their name. Democratic government is government by mandate and as such stands in need of being organized. In addition, the mandate was not conferred upon the representatives unconditionally. In contrast to the unlimited power of the British Parliament and the French monarch, the revolutionaries wanted to establish a limited government. The limits in scope and time as well as the division of power among various branches of government also required a determination in the form of rules.

Hence, the contribution of the American and French revolutionaries was to turn the idea from philosophy into law. Only law had the capacity

---

[6] E. de Vattel, *Le droit des gens ou principe de la loi naturelle* (Leiden: 1758), I, 3 § 27.

to dissolve the consensus as to the purpose and form of government from the historical moment and transfer it into a binding rule for the future, so that it no longer rested on the power of persuasion but on the power of a commitment. There was, however, the problem that, after the collapse of the divinely inspired medieval legal order, all law had become the product of political decision. Law was irreducibly positive law. Nothing else could be true for the law whose function it was to regulate the establishment and exercise of political power. The question that emerged from this positivization of law was how a law that emanated from the political process could at the same time bind this process.

This problem was solved by taking up the old idea of a hierarchy of norms (divine and secular) and re-introducing it into positive law. This was done by a division of positive law into two different bodies: one that emanated from or was attributed to the people and bound the government, and one that emanated from government and bound the people. The first one regulated the production and application of the second. Law became reflexive. This presupposed, however, that the first took primacy over the second. The revolutionary theoreticians had a clear notion of this consequence of constitution-making. The Americans expressed it as 'paramount law' and deployed the distinction between master and servant or principal and agent, while Sieyes conceptualized it in the dichotomy of *pouvoir constituant* and *pouvoir constitué*.[7] Without this distinction and the ensuing distinction between constitutional law and ordinary law and of the subordination of the latter to the former, constitutionalism would have been unable to fulfil its function.

Constitutionalism is therefore not identical to legalization of public power. It is a special and particularly ambitious form of legalization. Its characteristics can now be summarized:

1. The constitution in the modern sense is a set of legal norms, not a philosophical construct. The norms emanate from a political decision rather than some pre-established truth.

2. The purpose of these norms is to regulate the establishment and exercise of public power as opposed to a mere modification of a pre-existing public power.

3. The regulation is comprehensive in the sense that no extraconstitutional bearers of public power and no extraconstitutional ways and means to exercise this power are recognized.

4. Constitutional law finds its origin with the people as the only legitimate source of power. The distinction between *pouvoir constituant* and *pouvoir constitué* is essential to the constitution.

---

[7] J. Madison, A. Hamilton, and J. Jay, *The Federalist Papers* (1788), No. 78; E. Sieyes, *Qu'est-ce le Tiers Etat?* (Paris: 1789).

5. Constitutional law is higher law. It enjoys primacy over all other laws and legal acts emanating from government. Acts incompatible with the constitution do not acquire legal force.

These five characteristics refer to the function of the constitution. As such they differ from the many attempts to describe the modern constitution in substantive terms: democracy, rule of law, separation of powers, fundamental rights. The reason is that constitutionalism leaves room for many ways of establishing and organizing political power: monarchical or republican, unitarian or federal, parliamentarian or presidential, unicameral or bicameral, with or without a bill of rights, with or without judicial review, etc. All this is left to the decision of the *pouvoir constituant*. But this is not to say that the constitution in the modern sense is compatible with any content. The reason is supplied by the function of the constitution, namely to establish legitimate rule and to regulate its exercise by the rulers comprehensively. A system that rejects the democratic origin of public power and is not interested in limited government does not meet the standards of the modern constitution.

The two elements of constitutionalism, the democratic element and the rule of law element, cannot be separated from each other without diminishing the achievement of constitutionalism. It is widely accepted that a document which does not attempt to submit politics to law is not worth being called 'constitution'. But it is not as clear with regards to democracy as a necessary principle to legitimize public power. Yet, every principle of legitimacy other than democracy would undermine the function of the constitution. If political power is based on some absolute truth, be it religious or secular, the truth will always prevail in cases of conflict with positive law. This will also happen if an elite claims superior insight in the common good and derives from this insight the right to rule independently of popular consent. For this reason, it would be wrong to recognize two types of constitutions as equally representing the achievement of constitutionalism: a democratic type and a rule of law type.[8] In terms of achievement only a constitution that comprises both elements is capable of fulfilling the expectations of constitutionalism fully.

Constitutionalism in this sense deserves to be called an achievement,[9] because it rules out any absolute or arbitrary power of men over men. By submitting all government action to rules, it makes the use of public power predictable and enables the governed to anticipate governmental behaviour vis-à-vis themselves and to face public agents without fear. It provides a consensual basis for persons and groups with different ideas and interests to resolve their disputes in a civilized manner. And it enables a peaceful transition of power to be made. Under favourable conditions it can even contribute to the integration of a society.[10]

---

[8] For this attempt, see C. Möllers, 'Verfassunggebende Gewalt – Verfassung – Konstitutionalisierung' in A. von Bogdandy (ed.), *Europäisches Verfassungsrecht* (Baden-Baden: Nomos, 2003), p. 1.

[9] See N. Luhmann, 'Die Verfassung als evolutionäre Errungenschaft' (1990) 9 *Rechtshistorisches Journal* 176.

[10] See Ch. 6 of this volume; H. Vorländer (ed.), *Integration durch Verfassung* (Wiesbaden: Westdeutscher Verlag, 2002).

Although there is no achievement without shortcomings, constitutionalism as characterized by the five features is not an ideal type in the Weberian sense that allows only an approximation, but can never be completely reached. It is a historical reality that was in principle already fully developed by the first constitutions in North America and France and fulfilled its promise in a number of countries that had adopted constitutions in this sense.

Yet, the five characteristics do *not* describe everything that in constitutional history or in present times presents itself under the name 'constitution'. There are many more legal documents labelled 'constitution' or considered as constitutions than constitutions in the full sense of the achievement. The reason is that once the constitution was invented and inspired many hopes, it became possible to use the form without adopting all of the features that characterize the achievement. There were constitutions that left a pre-constitutional right to rule untouched. There were constitutions without a serious intention to limit the ruler's power. There were constitutions whose rules did not enjoy full primacy over the acts of government, but could legally be superseded by political decisions. But to the extent that these constitutions lacked some of the essential features of constitutionalism they failed to meet the achievement and were regarded as deficient.

The fact that the achievement was reached rather late in history nourishes the presumption that additional preconditions had to exist before a constitution in the sense described here, that is, different from a mere legalization of public power, could arrive. Although the first constitutions were a product of revolutions, a revolutionary break is not an indispensable precondition of the constitution. For the invention of the constitution the break with the traditional rule, combined with a new imagination of legitimate government, may have been necessary. But once invented the constitution no longer depends on a revolutionary origin. It can be adopted in an evolutionary way. It is sufficient that questions of legitimacy and organization of political power are open to political decision. If the political order is pre-determined independently of a consensus of the people, there is no room for a constitution. A document that bears this name is unlikely to enjoy primacy, but will be subordinated to an ultimate truth.

However, understood as a coherent and comprehensive regulation of the establishment and exercise of public power, the constitution could not emerge unless two further preconditions were in place. First, there has to be an object capable of being regulated in the specific form of a constitution. Such an object did not exist before the emergence of the modern state in the sixteenth and seventeenth centuries. Unlike the medieval order, the state was characterized by a concentration of all prerogatives on a certain territory in one hand. Only after public power had become identical with state power could it be comprehensively regulated in one specific law. The medieval world did not have a constitution, and it could not have had one.[11] All talk about the constitution of the

---

[11] See H. Quaritsch, *Staat und Souveränität* (Frankfurt am Main: Athenäum, 1970), p. 184; E. W. Böckenförde, 'Geschichtliche Entwicklung und Bedeutungswandel der Verfassung' in *Festschrift für R. Gmür* (Bielefeld: Gieseking, 1983), p. 9; Grimm (n. 1), p. 37 et seq.

ancient Roman Empire, or of medieval kingdoms, or of the British constitution refers to a different object.

Although being a necessary condition for the realization of the constitution, the state was not a sufficient condition. For historical reasons, the state emerged on the European continent as the absolute state. This meant that it did not depend on the consent of its citizens; it claimed unlimited power over them. Unlike political power that is exercised in the form of a mandate, power that a ruler claims as his own right requires no regulation of the relationship between principal and agent. Omnipotence is then the only rule of constitutional rank. But even if the ruler has a mandate but it is unconditional, no regulation is necessary. Unlimited government stands opposed to constitutional government. Only when the idea had taken roots that the power of the state should be limited in the interest of individual freedom and autonomy of various social functions was a constitution needed.

The concentration of all public power in the hands of the state has a corollary: the privatization of society. The constitution did not change this. It only changed the order between the two. Individual freedom takes primacy while the state's task is to protect it against aggressors and criminals. In order to fulfil this limited function the state continued to claim the entire public power and the monopoly of legitimate force. Only the purpose for which and the conditions under which it might be used were limited. The border between public and private is thus constitutive for the constitution.[12] A system where the state enjoys the freedom of individuals would have as little a constitution as a system in which individuals may exercise public power. If the citizens gain a share in public power, the constitution can no longer fulfil its claim to regulate the establishment and exercise of public power comprehensively unless the private actors submit to constitutional rules whereby they would lose their status as free members of society.

The fact that an object capable of being constitutionalized emerged in the form of the territorial state had the consequence that a plurality of states existed side by side. A second precondition for the constitution's claim to comprehensive validity was therefore that the public power of the state was without an external competitor within the territory. Consequently its legal force ended at the border of the territory. No constitution submitted domestic power to a foreign power or granted acts of a foreign power binding force within the domestic sphere. Just as the boundary between public and private is of constitutive importance for the constitution, so too is the boundary between external and internal.[13] A state that was unable to shield its borders from acts of a foreign public power could not secure the comprehensive functioning of its constitution.

Above the states there was no lawless zone. Rather the rules of public international law applied. But public international law rested on the basic assumption

---

[12] See Ch. 1 of this volume; S. Sassen, *Territory, Authority, Rights* (Princeton: Princeton University Press, 2008).

[13] Ch. 1 of this volume; R. Walker, *Inside/Outside* (Cambridge: Cambridge University Press, 1993).

of the sovereignty and integrity of the states. It regulated their relationship based on the prohibition of intervention in the internal affairs of states. Legal bonds among states were therefore recognized only if they emanated from a voluntary agreement that was limited to the external relations of states. Only the precondition of this order, the rule *pacta sunt servanda,* was valid independently of consent. But the international order lacked the means to enforce contractual obligations. This is why war could not be ruled out. But there were no legal means for states or the international community to interfere with the internal affairs of a state. The two bodies of law—constitutional law as internal law and international law as external law—could thus exist independently of one another.

## III. PROSPECTS UNDER CHANGED CONDITIONS

If the modern constitution could only come into existence because of the prior development of certain conditions, it cannot be denied that these conditions may disappear, just as they once arrived. This does not necessarily mean that the constitution will cease to exist. The disappearance of such conditions is unlikely to be a sudden event. If it occurred it would most probably be a long process with remote rather than immediate consequences. But should the constitution survive, it is almost certain that it would acquire a new meaning and produce different effects. It is therefore of crucial importance for the future of constitutionalism to inquire whether, or to what extent, the situation that brought forth the constitution has changed, and to gauge how this affects the achievement of constitutionalism. The question of the prospects of the constitution is a question concerning the continued existence of its preconditions.

For two of these preconditions the answer seems straightforward. They do not pose a problem, at least in most parts of the world. Questions of political order continue to be open to political decision. They are not regarded as pre-determined by some transcendental will and removed from political influence. Furthermore, the idea of limited government is still the leading concept in countries in the Western tradition. The problem rather arises in relation to the state and its two constitutive borders: the boundary between internal and external and between public and private. It is generally observed that we are living in a period of erosion of statehood,[14] although it is not always precisely determined in what that consists. If the feature that distinguished the state from previous political entities was the concentration of public power in a given territory and the fact that this power was not submitted to any external will, it seems likely that here the source of the erosion has to be sought.

---

[14] See e.g. S. Leibfried and M. Zürn (eds), *Transformationen des Staates?* (Frankfurt am Main: Suhrkamp, 2006); M. Beisheim et al. (eds), *Im Zeitalter der Globalisierung? Thesen und Daten zur gesellschaftlichen und politischen Denationalisierung* (Baden-Baden: Nomos, 1999); D. Held et al. (eds), *Global Transformations* (Stanford: Stanford University Press, 1999); S. Sassen, *Losing Control? Sovereignty in an Age of Globalization* (New York: Columbia University Press, 1996); Sassen (n. 12); Ch. 15 of this volume.

In fact, both boundaries become blurred. The boundary between public and private has become porous as a consequence of the expansion of state tasks. No longer only a guardian of individual freedom and market economy the state regulates the economy, engages in social development and welfare politics, and tries to protect society against all sorts of potential risks. Many of these tasks cannot be carried out with the traditional instruments of order and enforcement. In a growing number of cases the state relies on negotiations with private actors rather than legal orders addressed to them. Agreements replace laws. This means that private actors gain a share in public power, yet without being integrated into the framework of legitimation and accountability that the constitution establishes for public actors. In addition, there are modes of decision-making that are not submitted to the requirements prescribed by the constitution for acts of public authority. Since there are structural reasons for this development, it can neither be simply prohibited nor fully constitutionalized.[15]

The same is true for the boundary between inside and outside. After having been unchallenged for almost 300 years, the border became permeable when, in order to enhance their problem-solving capacity, the states began to establish international organizations to whom they transferred sovereign rights which these organizations exercise within the states and unimpeded by their right to self-determination. The first step in this direction was the foundation of the UN in 1945 whose task it was not only to coordinate state activities but also to fulfil a peacekeeping mission of its own. To reach this end, member states not only gave up the right to solve their conflicts by means of violence, except in cases of self-defence. As a self-limitation this would have remained within the framework of traditional international law and left their sovereignty intact. They also empowered the UN to enforce the prohibition, if necessary by military intervention. As a consequence, the right to self-determination is limited to the relationship among states, but cannot be invoked against the public power exercised by the international organization.

This development has meanwhile progressed further. It is no longer doubtful that, if a state completely disregards the human rights of its population or of minorities within the population, the UN has in principle the power of humanitarian intervention. Moreover, international courts have been established that can prosecute war crimes and crimes against humanity. Some of these courts, the criminal courts for the former Yugoslavia and for Rwanda were established not by way of treaties, but by a decision of the Security Council and may act on the territory of the states independently of their permission. Beyond that, under the umbrella of the UN, a *jus cogens* has developed that claims validity independently of the state's consent, but which, in turn, limits them in their treaty-making power. Similar effects went along with the foundation of the WTO, basically a forum for negotiations and agreements of states, but independent from these states through its court-like treaty enforcement mechanism.

---

[15] See Ch. 12 of this volume.

As a consequence, no state remains sovereign to the extent states used to be before 1945. But nowhere has this development progressed as far as in Europe. It is true that UN interventions, if they occur, can be much more massive than acts of European institutions. But they do not occur frequently, in part because the great majority of member states provide no reason for an intervention, in part because some states are permanent members of the Security Council and thereby enjoy a veto-right that they can use to prevent interventions. Unlike the sovereign power of states, the UN power actualizes itself very rarely and only vis-à-vis states that disregard their treaty obligations and provoke UN actions. The majority of states have never been subjected to measures of the UN. For them, the change that occurred with the founding of the UN is less visible, the loss of sovereignty not obvious.

This is different on the European level. Although no European organization has yet acquired the power to use physical force vis-à-vis its members, the states are constantly subject to European legal acts which they have to observe. Only the degree varies. So far as the Council of Europe is concerned, these are judicial acts. The Council of Europe exercises public power solely through the European Court of Human Rights (ECtHR). Its judgments are binding for the forty-six member states, but they do not take direct effect within them. The ECtHR is not an appellate court with the power to reverse judgments of national courts. It can only state a violation of the European Convention, but has to leave the redress to the states themselves. Still, the effects on member states' legal systems are far-reaching. They may even include an obligation to change the national constitution.

The power of the EU is broader in scope and deeper in effect on the member states' sovereignty. It includes legislative, administrative, and judicial acts. It is true that the EU has only those powers that the member states have transferred to it. As far as the transfer of sovereign rights is concerned they retain their power of self-determination. They remain the 'masters of the treaties'. Once transferred, however, the powers are exercised by organs of the EU and claim not only direct effect within the member states but also primacy over domestic law, including national constitutions. Although this lacks an explicit basis in the treaties, it has been accepted in principle as a necessary precondition of the functioning of the EU. Only the outer limits remain controversial, as both the European Court of Justice and some constitutional courts of the member states each claim the last word concerning *ultra vires* acts of the EU.[16]

Hence, the state is no longer the exclusive source of law within its territory. Laws and acts of law enforcement claim validity within the state that emanate from external sources and prevail over domestic law. The identity of public power and state power that was implied in the notion of sovereignty and had been the basis of the national as well as the international order is thus

---

[16] See F. C. Mayer, *Kompetenzüberschreitung und Letztentscheidung* (München: Beck 2000); M. Claes, *The National Courts' Mandate in the European Constitution* (Oxford: Oxford University Press, 2006); A. M. Slaughter et al. (eds), *The European Court and National Courts* (Oxford: Oxford University Press, 1998).

dissolving. This development cannot leave the constitution unaffected.[17] Since the constitution presupposed the state and referred to its power, the fragmentation of public power inevitably entails a diminution of the constitution's impact. Of course, the loss did not occur contrary to the will of the states. Sovereign rights were given up voluntarily because they expected something in return: an increase in problem-solving capacity in matters that could no longer be effectively handled on the national level. In addition, the states usually retain a share in the decision-making processes of the international institutions that now exercises these rights. But this cannot compensate for the decrease in constitutional legitimation and limitation of public power.

With respect to the five criteria that were found to be constitutive for the modern constitution consequences are the following:

1. The constitution remains a set of legal norms which owe their validity to a political decision.
2. Their object continues to be the establishment and exercise of the public power, but only insofar as it is state power.
3. Since public power and state power are no longer congruent, the constitution ceases to regulate public power coherently and comprehensively.
4. Consequently, the primacy of constitutional law is no longer exclusive. It prevails over ordinary domestic law and acts applying domestic law, not in general.
5. The constitution still emanates from or is attributed to the people. But it can no longer secure that any public power taking effect within the state finds its source with the people and is democratically legitimized by the people.

In sum, the emergence of an international public power does not render the constitution obsolete or ineffective. But to the extent that statehood is eroding, the constitution is in decline. It shrinks in importance since it can no longer fulfil its claim to legitimize and regulate all public authority that is effective within its realm. Acts of public authority that do not emanate from the state are not submitted to the requirements of the state's constitution, and their validity on the state's territory does not depend on their being in harmony with the domestic constitution. The constitution shrinks to a partial order. Only when national constitutional law and international law are seen together is one able to obtain a complete picture of the legal conditions for political rule in a country. The fact that many constitutions permit the transfer of sovereign rights prevents the situation from being unconstitutional. But it does not close the gap between the range of public power on the one hand and that of constitutional norms on the other.

---

[17] See Ch. 13 of this volume; M. Ruffert, *Die Globalisierung als Herausforderung des Öffentlichen Rechts* (Stuttgart: Boorberg, 2004); R. Wahl, *Herausforderungen und Antworten. Das Öffentliche Recht der letzten fünf Jahrzehnte* (Berlin: De Gruyter, 2006).

This gives rise to the question of whether the loss of importance that the constitution suffers at the national level can be compensated for at the international level. Public power stands in need of legitimation and limitation regardless of the power-holder. The constitution has successfully solved this problem vis-à-vis the state. It therefore comes as no surprise that the question is posed as to whether the achievement of constitutionalism can be elevated to the international level.[18] This, in fact, is the reason why the new term 'constitutionalization' has acquired its current popularity in academic writing and public discourse. 'Constitutionalization' means a constitution-building process beyond the state.[19] It applies to international political entities and international legal documents and is even extended to rule-making of public–private partnerships on the international level and of globally active private actors.

In view of the preconditions that had to be fulfilled before national constitutions became possible, the question is whether an object capable of being constitutionalized exists at the international level. The answer cannot be the same for all international organizations, the differences between them being too big. This is even more true if societal institutions are included into the consideration. The easiest case seems to be the EU. The EU is certainly not a state, but neither is it an international organization within the usual meaning. It differs from other international organizations first in its range of competencies which are not limited to a single issue but cover an increasing variety of objects. It differs secondly in the density of its organizational structure, comprising all the branches of government possessed by a state. And it differs finally in the intensity of the effects that its operations have on the member states and their citizens. Given all these features, the EU comes quite close to comparison with the central unit of a federal state.

The power of the EU is by no means unregulated. It is, on the contrary, embedded in a closely meshed net of legal norms. Although these legal norms are not contained in a constitution but in international treaties concluded by the member states, the treaties fulfil within the EU most of the functions that constitutions fulfil in states. The European treaties established what is today the EU. They created the organs of the EU, determine their powers and procedures, regulate the relationship between the EU and the member states as well as the citizens—all rules that in the state one would find in the constitution. The treaties are also higher law: all legal acts of the EU must comply with the provisions of the treaties. This is why many authors do not hesitate to call the treaties the constitution of the EU, and neither does the European Court of Justice.

However, this mode of speaking neglects one of the elements that characterize a constitution in the full sense of the notion.[20] Different from constitutions,

---

[18] See the indications suggested in n. 2 earlier in the chapter.

[19] Cf. M. Loughlin, ‚What is constitutionalisation?' in P. Dobner and M. Loughlin (eds), *The Twilight of Constitutionalism?* (Oxford: Oxford University Press, 2010), ch. 3.

[20] See D. Grimm, 'Does Europe need a Constitution?' (1995) 1 *European Law Journal* 278; D. Grimm, 'Entwicklung und Funktion des Verfassungsbegriffs' in T. Cottier and W. Kälin (eds), *Die Öffnung des*

the treaties are not an expression of the self-determination of a people or a society about the form and substance of their political union. The EU does not decide upon its own legal foundation. It receives this foundation from the member states which create it by an agreement concluded according to international law. Consequently, the treaties lack a democratic origin. This does not make them illegitimate. But they do not enjoy the democratic legitimacy that characterizes a constitution. The citizens of the EU have no share in making the basic document. They do not give a mandate to a constitutional assembly. They do not adopt the text. Ratification within the member states, even if it happens by a referendum, is not a European but a national act deciding whether a state approves of the treaty. The document is not even attributed to the citizens as the source of all public power.

Nevertheless, there are examples in history in which a constitution in the full sense originates in the form of a treaty concluded by states which unite into a greater state. But in these cases the founding treaty is only the mode to establish a constitution. As soon as the treaty is adopted as the legal foundation of the new political entity, the founding states give up the power to determine the future fate of the text and hand this power over to the new entity which thereby gains the full authority to maintain, change, or abolish it. It is a treaty by origin, but a constitution by legal nature. The test is the provision for amendments. If the amendment power remains in the hands of the member states and is exercised by way of treaties, the transition from treaty to constitution has not taken place. If the newly created state has gained the power of self-determination (even if the member states retain a share in the decision of the new entity) the legal foundation has turned into a constitution.

Such a transfer has not taken place in the EU. It was not even provided for by the failed Constitutional Treaty. Even if ratified in all member states, it would not have acquired the quality of a constitution. However, this does not deprive the EU of its capacity to be a potential object of constitutionalization. Its status as an entity comparable to the central unit of a federation qualifies the EU to a legal foundation in form of a constitution. The member states would simply have to give up their power to determine themselves the legal foundation of the EU. The question is not one of possibility but of desirability. However, by doing so they would inevitably transform the EU into a federal state. It is here that doubts arise. Would the formal democratization of the EU be accompanied by a gain in substantive democracy, or does it serve the democratic principle better if the decision about the legal foundation of the EU remains in the hands of the states where the democratic mechanisms work better than in the EU? Would it deprive the EU of its innovative character as a genuine entity between an international organization and a federal state?

The issue is different at the global level. Here, no organization exists whose range of powers and organizational density is comparable to that of the EU.

*Verfassungsstaats, Recht-Sonderheft* 2005; D. Grimm, Verfassung – Verfassungsvertrag – Vertrag über eine Verfassung, in O. Beaud et al. (eds), *L'Europe en voie de constitution* (Bruxelles: Bruylant, 2004), p. 279.

There are some isolated institutions with limited tasks, most of them single-issue organizations, and with correspondingly limited powers. They are not only unconnected, but sometimes even pursue goals that are not in harmony with each other, such as economic interests on the one hand and humanitarian interests on the other. Rather than forming a global system of international public power they are islands within an ocean of traditional international relations. In this respect, the international order currently resembles the pre-state medieval order with its many independent bearers of dispersed powers.[21] Like medieval ordering, the international level is not susceptible to the type of coherent and comprehensive regulation that characterizes the constitution.

The UN is no exception. It stands out among international organizations because of its all-encompassing nature, its peacekeeping purpose, and its corresponding powers. But it is far from aggregating all public power exercised on the global level and even farther from the concentrated and all embracing public power of the state. Its charter therefore does not come close to a world constitution. It marks an important step in legalizing international relations but does not go beyond. This is doubly so with respect to institutions like the WTO, the International Monetary Fund, the International Labour Organisation, and such like. Their statutes regulate the powers of these institutions and guide them in the exercise of their functions. But their limited competencies and their non-democratic structure do not qualify them for the specific form of regulation that is characteristic of the constitution.

It has nonetheless become quite common to see constitutionalizing processes at work on this level as well, and to call the statutes or charters of international organizations or the *jus cogens* within public international law a constitution. The term is, of course, not reserved to one single meaning. As could be seen, the notion 'constitution' has covered a number of phenomena in the past.[22] But if it is applied to international institutions and their legal foundation one should not forget that it does not have much in common with the *achievement* of constitutionalism. Without doubt, international law is undergoing important changes, covering new ground and becoming more effective.[23] But calling it a constitution empties the notion and reflects a very thin idea of constitutionalism. Basically, it identifies constitutionalization with legalization of public power, a phenomenon that existed long before the constitution emerged and from which the constitution differed considerably. This difference is levelled by the new use of the term which does not contribute to a clarification of the current state of affairs.

This argument applies with even greater force to so-called societal constitutionalism.[24] This type of constitutionalism is not only disconnected from the state but also from international organizations created by states. The proponents of societal constitutionalism realize on the one hand that the state is

---

[21] See Sassen (n. 12).     [22] See Mohnhaupt and Grimm (n. 4).

[23] See B. Zangl and M. Zürn (eds), *Verrechtlichung – Bausteine für Global Governance?* (Bonn: Dietz, 2004); B. Zangl, *Die Internationalisierung der Rechtstaatlichkeit* (Frankfurt am Main: Campus, 2006).

[24] See Ch. 16 of this volume.

unable to regulate the transactions of global actors. On the other hand they do not believe either that international organizations have sufficient regulatory power to provide a legal framework for the operations of global actors that would prevent them from pursuing their own interests in an unihibited way. At best, international organizations could 'constitutionalize' themselves, that is, submit their actions to self-created standards. The gap between international rule-making and transnational operations of private actors could only be closed if the idea of constitutionalism is disconnected from its traditional link with politics and adapted to the societal sphere. In this case a body of transnational law would emerge alongside national and international law.

This law is seen as being capable of fulfilling the function of constitutions vis-à-vis private global actors. However, this requires an adaptation of the notion 'constitutionalism' to its object, the global private actors. In contrast to state constitutions, societal constitutions do not take legal force by an authoritative act of a constitution-maker. They emerge from a long-lasting evolutionary process, even though this process may be stimulated by political incentives or supported by formal legal requirements. Societal constitutions are neither mere legal texts, nor simply reflections of the factual situation. And, more importantly, they do not encompass the internationally exercised private power in its totality. In contrast to traditional state constitutions that cover public power comprehensively but are territorially limited, societal constitutions claim global validity but are limited to certain sectors of society. The territorial differentiation of national law is relativized by the sectoral limitation of global law.

In order to deserve the name 'constitution', societal law must show in addition some of the structural elements of state constitutions. First, societal constitutions must function as higher law that regulates the making of ordinary law. Secondly, this higher law must contain provisions that regulate the organization and the procedures of the global actors. Thirdly, it must limit the scope of action of the private global actors, just as fundamental rights limit the scope of action of state actors in domestic law. Finally, it must provide control mechanisms similar to constitutional adjudication that guarantee an effective review of the acts of global organizations with respect to their compliance with higher law. The proponents of this idea concede that up to now societal constitutionalism exists only in rudimentary form. But they believe in its potential for institutionalizing within these global sectors respect for the autonomy of other social sectors and their needs as well as recognition of areas where the behaviour of global actors can be observed independently and criticized freely.

However, this potential, if it exists, depends on some preconditions which cannot be taken for granted. In the absence of a global legislator, the limitation by societal constitutions will always be self-limitation guided by the actor's interest, not the common interest. Both interests may partly coincide, but not completely. Hence, self-limitation capable of harmonizing actors' own interests with the interests of those affected by their actions and the communal interests is unlikely if not imposed by a public authority whose task it is to keep the self-interest of the various sectors of society within the limits of the common best. On the national level, government fulfils this function. But how can the same result be reached on the international level in the absence of an equivalent of the state or of other institutions with sufficiently broad regulatory power? And even if existing international institutions possessed this power, how effectively would they use it without the democratic and representative element that guarantees participation of those affected by the decisions and thus enables a perception of problems beyond the institutional interests of the actors? No so-called constitution on the international and transnational level is yet able of fulfilling only minimal democratic demands.

## IV. WHICH CONCLUSION?

This analysis suggests that the gap between public power and its constitutional legitimation and limitation, which is opening up as a result of the erosion of statehood and transfer of public power to the international level cannot for the time being be closed. On the one hand, it seems neither possible nor desirable to return to the Westphalian system. On the other, the achievement of constitutionalism cannot be reconstructed on the international or transnational level. National constitutions will not regain their capacity to legitimize and regulate comprehensively the public power that takes effect within the territory of the state. The regulation of internationally exercised public power is expanding, but remains a legalization unable to live up to the standard of constitutionalism. Whoever invokes constitutionalism in this connection uses a thin notion of constitutionalism with its democratic element almost always left out.

If a full preservation of constitutionalism is not available, the second best solution would be to preserve as much of the achievement as possible under given conditions. In principle, this can occur in two directions: by striving for a greater accumulation of public power on the international level,[25] or by limiting the erosion of statehood on the national level. Strengthening the international level would be a solution only if the international order could develop into an object capable of being constitutionalized in the sense of the achievement, that is, as different from mere legalization. This is neither likely in a medium-term perspective, nor are there convincing models for democratic governance on the global level.[26] A democracy that is not deprived of its participatory element but maintains a substantive rather than a purely formal outlook including the societal preconditions of democratic government such as a lively public discourse is already difficult to realize within the EU. On the global level even a democracy reduced to the formal element of free elections seems unlikely.

---

[25] See M. Lutz-Bachmann and J. Bohman (eds), *Weltstaat oder Staatenwelt?* (Frankfurt am Main: Suhrkamp, 2002); M. Albert and R. Stichweh (eds), *Weltstaat und Weltstaatlichkeit* (Wiesbaden: Westdeutscher Verlag, 2007).

[26] See A. Kuper, *Democracy Beyond Borders* (Oxford: Oxford University Press, 2004); J. Anderson (ed.), *Transnational Democracy: Political Spaces and Border Crossings* (London: Routledge, 2002); A. Niederberger, 'Wie demokratisch ist die transnationale Demokratie?' in Albert and Stichweh (n. 25), p. 109; G. de Burca, 'Developing Democracy Beyond the State' (2008) 46 *Columbia Journal of Transnational Law* 221.

The consequence would be to put the emphasis on states where constitutionalism still finds more favourable conditions and where the potential for democratic legitimization and accountability of public power remains greater than on the international level. This should not be misunderstood as a call to restore the traditional nation state. To the contrary, the international turn of politics is in need of further development. An approximation of the scope of politics to the scope of action of private global actors seems an urgent postulate. But it is likewise important that democratic states remain the most important source of legitimation, including the legitimation of international organizations. They must be prevented from becoming self-supporting entities distant from the citizenry and largely uncontrollable in their activities and unaccountable for the results.

In fact, states are by no means out of the international and transnational game. Up to now the process of internationalization has not touched the monopoly of the legitimate use of force. No international organization possesses its own means of physical force, let alone a monopoly. The fragmented global society has no enforcement mechanisms per se. International courts and even more so private arbitration bodies depend on states when it comes to enforcing judgments against reluctant parties. In addition the states retain a share in the direction and control over the international organizations they have formed. This is as important in the EU as it is on the global level. In all these matters they are subservient to the requirements of their national constitutions. These bonds should neither be prematurely relinquished, nor severely weakened.

Regarding the supranational level, it seems preferable to leave the constitutional path and drop the notions of constitutionalism and constitutionalization altogether. They are misleading insofar as they nourish the hope that the loss national constitutions suffer from internationalization and globalization could be compensated for on the supranational level. This would, however, be an illusion. The submission of internationally exercised public power to law will always lag behind the achievement of constitutionalism on the national level. The conditions that would allow a reconstruction of the achievement beyond the nation state are not given. The internationalization of public power is a new phenomenon that poses new challenges. The illusion that these challenges could be met by using a model that was invented for a different object tends to obstruct the search for solutions that are oriented towards the new situation and will suit it better.

# References

1. 'Ursprung und Wandel der Verfassung' in J. Isensee and P. Kirchhof (eds), *Handbuch des Staatsrechts*, vol. 1 (Heidelberg, C. F. Müller, 3rd edn, 2003), pp. 3–43. (Also in Japanese and Chinese.)

2. 'Entstehungs- und Wirkungsbedingungen des modernen Konstitutionalismus' in D. Simon (ed.), *Akten des 26. Deutschen Rechtshistorikertages*, vol. 1 (Frankfurt: Klostermann, 1987), pp. 45–76. (Also in Spanish and Chinese.)

3. 'Die Grundrechte im Entstehungszusammenhang der bürgerlichen Gesellschaft' in J. Kocka (ed.), *Bürgertum im 19. Jahrhundert*, vol. I (München: dtv, 1988), pp. 340–71. (Also in Spanish.)

4. 'Verfassung II' in O. Brunner, W. Conze, and R. Koselleck (eds), *Geschichtliche Grundbegriffe*, vol. 6 (Stuttgart: Klett, 1990), pp. 863–99. In book form: Heinz Mohnhaupt and Dieter Grimm, *Verfassung. Zur Geschichte des Begriffs von der Antike bis zur Gegenwart* (Berlin: Duncker & Humblot, 1995, 2nd edn, 2002), pp. 100–44. (Translations into Italian and Portuguese.)

5. 'Verfassungsfunktion und Grundgesetzreform, part 1' in (1972) 97 *Archiv des öffentlichen Rechts* 489–508.

6. 'Integration by Constitution' in (2005) 3 *International Journal of Constitutional Law* 193–208. In German: 'Integration durch Verfassung' (2004) 32 *Leviathan* 448–63. (Also in Spanish, Polish, and Croatian.)

7. 'The Role of Fundamental Rights after Sixty-Five Years of Constitutional Jurisprudence in Germany' in (2015) 13 *International Journal of Constitutional Law* 2–21. In German: 'Die Bedeutung der Grundrechte nach 60 Jahren Verfassungsrechtsprechung in Deutschland' in *Viva Vox Iuris Civilis* (Budapest: Szent István Társulat, 2012), pp. 134–56.

8. 'Rückkehr zum liberalen Grundrechtsverständnis?' in (1998) *Recht. Zeitschrift für Ausbildung und Praxis* 41–50. (Also in Spanish.)

9. 'Constitutional Courts and Constitutional Interpretation at the Interface of Law and Politics' in B. Iancu (ed.), *The Law/Politics Distinction in Contemporary Public Law Adjudication* (Utrecht: Eleven, 2009), pp. 311–24.

10. 'Constitutional Adjudication and Democracy' in M. Andenas (ed.), *Judicial Review in International Perspective. Liber amicorum Gordon Slynn*, vol. 2 (The Hague: Kluwer, 2000), pp. 103–20. (Also in Chinese.)

11. 'Die Zukunft der Verfassung' in (1990) 1 *Staatswissenschaften und Staatspraxis* 5–53. (Also in Italian, Spanish, and Chinese.)

12. 'Lässt sich die Verhandlungsdemokratie konstitutionalisieren?' in C. Offe (ed.), *Demokratisierung der Demokratie* (Frankfurt: Campus, 2003), p. 193–210.

13. 'Zur Bedeutung nationaler Verfassungen in einem vereinten Europa' in D. Merten and H.-J. Papier (eds), *Handbuch der Grundrechte*, vol. VI/2 (Heidelberg: C. F. Müller, 2009), pp. 3–32.

14. 'The Democratic Costs of Constitutionalization: the European Case' in (2015) 21 *European Law Journal* 460–73. Revised and enlarged for this volume.

15. 'The Constitution in the Process of Denationalization' in (2005) 12 *Constellations* 447–63. In German: 'Die Verfassung im Prozess der Entstaatlichung' in P. M. Huber, M. Brenner, and M. Möstl (eds), *Der Staat des Grundgesetzes – Kontinuität und Wandel, Festschrift für Peter Badura* (Tübingen: Mohr Siebeck, 2004), pp. 145–67.

16. 'Gesellschaftlicher Konstitutionalismus – eine Kompensation für den Bedeutungsschwund der Staatsverfassung?' in M. Herdegen, H. H. Klein, H.-J. Papier, and R. Scholz (eds), *Staatsrecht und Politik. Festschrift für Roman Herzog* (München: C.H. Beck, 2009), pp. 67–81.

17. 'Levels of the Rule of Law – On the Possibility of Exporting a Western Achievement' in (2011) 1 *European-Asian Journal of Law and Governance* 5–12. In German: 'Stufen der Rechtsstaatlichkeit. Zur Exportfähigkeit einer westlichen Errungenschaft' in (2009) 64 *Juristenzeitung* 596–600.

18. 'The Achievement of Constitutionalism and its Prospects in a Changed World' in P. Dobner and M. Loughlin (eds), *The Twilight of Constitutionalism?* (Oxford: Oxford University Press, 2010), pp. 3–22.

Some of the articles have also appeared in: Dieter Grimm, *Die Zukunft der Verfassung* (Frankfurt am Main: Suhrkamp, 1991, 3rd edn, 2002), and Dieter Grimm, *Die Zukunft der Verfassung II* (Berlin: Suhrkamp, 2012).

# Index

The manufacturer's authorised representative in the EU for product safety is Oxford
University Press España S.A. of El Parque Empresarial San Fernando de Henares,
Avenida de Castilla, 2 – 28830 Madrid (www.oup.es/en or product.safety@oup.com).
OUP España S.A. also acts as importer into Spain of products made by the manufacturer.

Printed in the USA/Agawam, MA
October 24, 2025

895041.043